GOD SENT HIS SON

CHRISTOPH CARDINAL SCHÖNBORN

God Sent His Son
A Contemporary Christology

With the assistance of
Michael Konrad and Hubert Philipp Weber

TRANSLATED BY HENRY TAYLOR

IGNATIUS PRESS   SAN FRANCISCO

First published in English in Europe by
LIT Verlag under the title *Christology*
© 2004 by LIT Verlag, Berlin, Münster, Vienna, Zurich
This edition has been published under license from LIT Verlag

Original German edition:
Gott sandte seinen Sohn: Christologie
Volume 7, AMATECA: Lehbücher zur katolischen Theologie
© 2002 by Bonifatius GmbH Druck, Paderborn

Cover art:
The Death of Christ
Sano di Pietro (1406–1481)
Gemaeldegalerie Alte Meister, Staatliche
Kunstsammlungen, Dresden, Germany
© Bildarchiv Preussischer Kulturbesitz /
Art Resource, New York

Cover design by Roxanne Mei Lum

Contents

 2. *The Arian Crisis and the First Council of Nicaea (325)* 78

 a. The Concerns and Teaching of Arius 79

 b. The First Council of Nicaea—Interpreting the
    Profession of Faith in Christ 81

 THE ONLY-BEGOTTEN GENERATED FROM THE FATHER 83

 BEGOTTEN, NOT MADE 84

 CONSUBSTANTIAL WITH THE FATHER 86

 c. Beginning or End? The Hellenization Theory 89

 THE HELLENIZATION OR THE DE-HELLENIZATION OF
    CHRISTIANITY? 89

 ORTHODOXY AND HERESY AS A PROCESS OF DIFFERENTIATION . . 91

 THE IMAGE OF CHRIST AND IMPERIAL POLITICS AFTER NICAEA . . 94

 THE CRITERIA AND LIMITATIONS OF UNITY IN MULTIPLICITY . . . 97

 SUMMARY 99

 3. *The Implications of the Nicene Creed* 100

 a. Christ as the Perfect Image of the Father 100

 b. The Incarnation of the Logos and the Divinization of Man   104

II. The Incarnation of the Son of God 110

 1. *Approaches to the Incarnation of God in the Old Testament
    and Judaism* 110

 a. God's Self-Abasement in Jewish Theology 111

 b. The Prophet as the Representative of God 116

 2. *"Conceived by the Holy Spirit—Born of the Virgin Mary"* . . . 120

 a. A Historical Question but Not Only That 121

 b. The Symbolic Language in the Bible 127

 c. Life Wrought by the Spirit: The Root of the New Man . . . 129

 3. *The Council of Chalcedon: "True God—True Man"* 131

 a. Two "Wrong Tracks": Christologies of Separation and of
    Intermixture 132

 THE LOGOS-SARX SCHEMA IN APOLLINARIS OF LAODICAEA 133

 ANTIOCH, THE LOGOS-MAN SCHEMA, AND NESTORIUS 136

 THE DEVELOPMENT OF THE CHRISTIAN UNDERSTANDING OF
    PERSON 142

 THE PERPETUATION OF THE SCHISM 147

Approach: An Account

"But when the time had fully come, God sent forth his Son, born of woman, born under the law, to redeem those who were under the law, so that we might receive adoption as sons" (Gal 4:4-5). This key sentence, which sums up the heart of what the Apostle Paul was preaching, is the theme of the Christology presented here. Resulting from sixteen years of lecturing on Christology and more than thirty years of dealing with christological subjects, it is founded on the simple conviction—which has been confirmed again and again by the study of many particular themes and, above all, by spiritual and pastoral experience—that the starting point for all Christology is the certainty of faith that Jesus of Nazareth is the Messiah of Israel, the Son of the living God (cf. Mt 16:16). This certainty is not something that comes at the end of an extended process of reflection; it is not a theological conclusion drawn from various converging factors; rather, it is the "original illumination" in whose light all the reasoning, clarification, and formulation of Christology takes place. Reduced to a single sentence, that is the approach of this Christology that I am now presenting for theological discussion.

This light illuminated Paul on the road to Damascus—indeed, it blinded him. It was in this light that the whole of his thinking and preaching developed, and above all the certainty that we have been made righteous, not by the law, but by Jesus the Messiah, the Son of God. The first, and most basic, obvious fact that was presented to Paul outside Damascus was that Jesus is "the Son of God". Thus it is that, according to witness of the Acts of the Apostles, the first thing that Paul preached in Damascus, right after his baptism, was: "He is the Son of God" (Acts 9:20). And so he himself describes his conversion as a revelation of Jesus as the Son: "But when he who had set me apart before I was born, and had called me through his grace, was pleased to reveal his Son to me, in order that I might preach him among the Gentiles, I did not confer with flesh and blood" (Gal 1:15-16). It was no different for Peter, to whom "flesh and blood has not revealed" that Jesus is the Messiah, the Son of the living God, "but my Father who

is in heaven" (Mt 16:17). It was, and is to this very day, no different
when the "Father, Lord of heaven and earth" hid the mystery of Jesus
"from the wise and understanding" and yet "revealed [it] to infants"
(Mt 11:25).

Now, it may be objected that this may well have been according to
validity at the beginning but not according to genesis. Faith in Christ,
it will be said, developed gradually: looking back from the viewpoint
of the fully developed form of faith, the beginning would also have
been "christologically illuminated". The approach to Christology offered here does not, of course, dispute the fact of the development of
doctrine. Rather, it traces the paths of such developments by trying to
identify the central themes of the most important stages of development, because in them the most prominent positions with regard to
content also come up for discussion. Thus for instance the systematic
questions about the "constitution" of the God-man are covered within
the framework of the development of doctrine in the councils of the
early Church, while the central themes of the basic questions of soteriology are brought out with the help of the three writers who represent especially formative positions, Anselm of Canterbury (d. 1109),
Thomas Aquinas (d. 1274), and Martin Luther (d. 1546); and thus
questions about the self-awareness of Jesus are addressed, above all,
by way of the more recent interpretations attempted by Jacques Maritain (d. 1973), Karl Rahner (d. 1985), and Hans Urs von Balthasar
(d. 1988). The genetic method is not rejected, then, but it is applied in
the sense of an unfolding of the light vouchsafed as a gift in faith right
from the beginning. The way I see the development of Christology,
it is always the one "original light" granted by the Father in making
manifest his Son, which splits, as if in a prism, into the brightly colored
spectrum of christological themes. Christology, in every phase of its
development, follows its path in this light: "In your light do we see
light" (Ps 36:9). It is always *fides quaerens intellectum,* faith that seeks to
understand what, in faith, it already affirms with certainty.

It is in this sense that the attempt will be made, in what follows,
to trace the stages of my own path in Christology, in the sense of a
confessio, of a grateful confession of him who "has revealed his Son"
also to me, from my youth onward—without my having deserved it
—so that I may know him and confess him, just as I, too, am known
by him (cf. Phil 3:12; Gal 4:9; 1 Cor 8:2; 13:12).

In my first year as a student, 1964, a year that was in many respects a turning point,[1] in the Council itself, in theology, in the life of the Church (though this first became clear in 1968), we were confronted with the demythologization program of Rudolf Bultmann (d. 1976). I can remember how, full of my new "knowledge", I tried to explain to my mother that the "title of Son of God" as applied to Jesus was to be understood on the basis of the contemporary Hellenistic environment, which was pregnant with myth, and that, when it was "demythologized", it simply meant Jesus' significance for us. In response to my youthful erudition, my mother uttered just a single astonished sentence: "But if Jesus is not the Son of God, then our faith is meaningless." To this day, I thank her and the Lord for this shortest and most important lecture in Christology.

I recall with gratitude in this *confessio* a second turning in the path: my meeting in 1967 with the Orthodox monk and philosopher, who died just recently, André Scrima (d. 2000), who in unforgettable evening conversations opened up for a small group of Dominican students the fascination and the intellectual timeliness of the Church Fathers, especially of Saint Maximus the Confessor (d. 662), whom he made come alive to us in a dialogue with contemporary philosophy. The result of this encounter was my turning to the Greek Church Fathers, but also to Nicholas of Cusa (d. 1464), someone about whom André Scrima loved to talk. In the *Docta ignorantia* I found something like a christological key, not only to the whole of the Cusan theologian's work, but also to the great philosophical questions of the relation of finitude to infinity, of time to eternity, of freedom and contingency, of God and world. Christ is that *"maximum concretum"* in which the relationship between God and the world becomes "tangible" as the independent existence of what is finite, in what is entirely derived from the infinite. There proved to be no limits here to the fruitfulness of the christological formula of the Council of Chalcedon (451).[2] I have since then encountered its capacity to support the thought of many authors, and this has strengthened my conviction of its unsurpassable effectualness as a positive inspiration for thought, but also as a critical corrective against reductive versions of Christology. Fidelity to the

---

[1] See P. Chaunu, *La Femme et Dieu: Réflexions d'un chrétien sur la transmission de la vie* (Paris, 2001), p. 211.

[2] See C. Schönborn, "De docta ignorantia" als christozentrischer Entwurf", in *Nikolaus von Kues*, ed. K. Jacobi, pp. 138–56 (Freiburg, 1979).

Chalcedonian teaching of "true God and true man" in "undivided and unconfused unity" remains the reliable compass along all the paths of Christology.

There followed a time of intensive engagement with the Church Fathers, especially with Cyril of Alexandria (d. 444), with his exegetical works and with his christological dialogues. I owe to the spiritual father of the Council of Ephesus—along with an acquaintance with the often unjustly disdained Alexandrian allegorical exegesis—above all the belief, which has shaped this textbook, that Christology must always take its starting point from the identity of Jesus Christ as the eternal Son: he has always been the incarnate Son of the Father. In every manifestation of Jesus' human life, it is really the Son of God we are encountering. The Council of Chalcedon simply made this even more clear by emphasizing that Jesus' being God and being man are preserved without confusion in the unity of the person. This clear orientation to the "Christology of descent" of someone like Cyril of Alexandria was further enriched in the course of the years in many ways, a selection of which may be mentioned here.

Mention should be made in the first place of Maximus the Confessor and his environment. I turned to his spiritual father, Saint Sophronius of Jerusalem (d. 639), while my confrères Father Alain Riou and Father Jean-Miguel Garrigues took Maximus himself as their central theme. A kind of Maximus-trilogy[3] grew out of this shared work, which contributed to the fact that today Maximus the Confessor more clearly occupies the place befitting him. It is to him, before all others, that we owe the whole Chalcedon-based development of Christology in the difficult questions of the divine and human action and will of Christ. All those who too easily speak of the "aporia of the doctrine of the two natures" are advised to study Maximus. Sophronius, Maximus, and the great monastic tradition to which they belong make it clear, besides, to how great an extent the Christology of Chalcedon corresponds with the experience of Christian life, which has probed in spiritual terms the free interrelation and correlation of the divine and human wills.

After this preparatory work I was able to venture upon a first synthesis (which seems to me today like a "leap in the dark"): an overall

---

[3] J. M. Garrigues, *Maxime le Confesseur: La Charité, avenir divin de l'homme*, ThH 38 (Paris, 1976); A. Riou, *Le Monde et l'Église selon Maxime le Confesseur*, ThH 22 (Paris, 1973); C. Schönborn, *Sophrone de Jérusalem: Vie monastique et confession dogmatique*, ThH 20 (Paris, 1972); see also F. Heinzer and C. Schönborn, eds., *Maximus Confessor: Actes du Symposion sur Maxime le Confesseur, Fribourg 2–5 septembre 1980*, Par. 27 (Freiburg, 1982).

view of the great christological councils and Fathers from the point of
view of their image of Christ, starting from Athanasius (d. 373) and
the First Nicene Council (325), running up to the Iconoclast controversy and its theological resolution by the later Fathers, John Damascene (d. before 754), Nicephoros (d. 828/829) and Theodore the
Studite (d. 826), and by the Seventh Ecumenical Council, the Second
Nicene (787). To my joy, this book, *Die Christusikone: Eine theologische
Hinführung*,[4] has found a warm welcome, especially on the part of Orthodoxy. A good many individual studies of the theology of icons and
of questions concerning Christian art have since added to this book.

It should also be mentioned with gratitude that for many years Irenaeus of Lyons (d. ca. 202), the early and incomparable master of the
Christian overview, time and again accompanied me on the way. I
have several times worked through the whole of Irenaeus with students, plunging joyfully into this symphony of faith, so fresh, alive,
and close to the Bible.

Thomas Aquinas cannot be left out of this *confessio*. Removed in 1968
from the official theology curriculum of our house of study, he was
passed on to us "clandestinely", so to speak, by Father Martin Hubert,
O.P., *sine glossa*, simply taking us into the school of the master, arous-
ing our taste for reading him directly. Later, as a professor, I followed
the example of the man who taught me Thomas and always tried to
encourage the students to read the great master for themselves and
to restrict their consumption of secondary literature to the necessary
minimum.

It was good to read Thomas coming from the Church Fathers and
not so much from the later commentators and Scholastic theology
(though these in fact are often unjustly treated today). Father Yves
Congar (d. 1995) pointed out to us how unique Thomas' knowledge of the Christian East was, for his period. Unlike anyone else,
Thomas took his knowledge of the christological councils of the early
Church from primary sources, included Cyril of Alexandria and Maximus the Confessor (as transmitted by John Damascene) in his Christology,[5] especially in the concept—so determinative for the whole *Summa*

---

[4] C. Schönborn, *L'Icône du Christ: Fondements théologiques élaborés entre le 1er et le 2e Concile
de Nicée, 325–787* (Freiburg, 1976; 4th ed.: Paris, 2003); trans. by Lothar Krauth as *God's
Human Face: The Christ-Icon* (San Francisco: Ignatius Press, 1994); and into German, Span-
ish, Italian, Magyar, Romanian, Russian, and Polish.

[5] See I. Backes, *Die Christologie des heiligen Thomas von Aquin und die griechischen Kirchen-
väter*, FChLDG 17, 3/4 (Paderborn, 1931).

wow
Aquinas

theologica—of the humanity of Christ as his divinity's instrument of salvation.[6] Yet it was also Thomas more than anyone else who took up the Antiochene tradition of exegesis, above all by way of John Chrysostom (d. 407). This finds expression especially in the *Summa's* long tractate on the life of Jesus. Following the biblical witness closely and faithfully, Thomas created in the thirty-three (!) *quaestiones* of this tractate a model of a theological reading of the *acta, dicta, et passa* of Jesus Christ, which have been far too neglected by the theology of the schools.[7] The theological and meditative approach of Saint Thomas to the life and work of the Lord has gained a new relevance in the present century through the work done toward a "theology of the mysteries of the life of Jesus".[8] Following the *Catechism of the Catholic Church* in this, we have tried to make this point of view the structural principle of Christology as a whole by following the earthly path of the Son of God as Thomas does (and as the Creed itself already does) and have tried to see each stage of this way as a mystery, as a theandric, divine-and-human event, in its concrete human historicity and without division, but without confusion in its true divinity.

Yet we also learn from Thomas something exemplary for theological method that has a particular effect in Christology. If Anselm of Canterbury (d. 1109), in the enthusiasm of early Scholastic learning, had still been looking in his Christology and his teaching on redemption, in his *Cur Deus homo*, as we shall see, for "necessary reasons" (*rationes necessariae*) for the Incarnation of the Son of God and for his work of redemption, Thomas, from the start, approaches Christology —the entire history of salvation, indeed—with a different theological method. Everything that God, in his sovereign freedom, has disposed, all that he sets to work in accordance with his plan for creation and salvation, transcends our rational powers and does not allow itself to be deduced as "rationally necessary": neither the creation, nor the elec-

---

[6] See T. Tschipke, *Die Menschheit Christi als Heilsorgan der Gottheit: Unter besonderer Berücksichtigung der Lehre des heiligen Thomas von Aquin*, FThSt 55 (Freiburg im Breisgau, 1940); E. Schillebeeckx, *Christus: Sakrament der Gottbegegnung* (Mainz, 1960).

[7] We refer to two recent works that make up for long neglect: I. Biffi, *I Misteri di Cristo in Tommaso d'Aquino*, vol. 1 (Milan, 1994); and J.-P. Torrell, *Le Christ en ses mystères: La Vie et l'oeuvre de Jésus selon saint Thomas d'Aquin*, 2 vols., Jésus et Jésus Christ 78–79 (Paris, 1999).

[8] The extent to which Karl Rahner, at least in his younger days, pursued this perspective, particularly on the basis of Ignatius Loyola, has recently been shown by the work of A. R. Batlogg, *Die Mysterien des Lebens Jesu bei Karl Rahner: Zugang zum Christusglauben*, ITS 58 (Innsbruck, 2001).

tion of Israel, the Son's saving mission, the work of redemption on the Cross or the mission of the Church may be deduced as necessary on rational grounds. They are not, however, on that account irrational and arbitrary, as Nominalism thought. All these works of the goodness and wisdom of God make sense, have their coherence, have indeed— as Anselm himself says—their own beauty. In the words of Irenaeus of Lyons, they are symphonic, they "are in harmony",[9] or (as Thomas says) they are "fitting". The *argument from fitness* plays a central role in the Christology of Saint Thomas. In response to the question of why God should become man, Thomas offers no demonstration of "rational necessity", but he does suggest ten "grounds of fitness" that show this act of God to be extremely appropriate, coherent, consistent with God's other actions.[10]

The question of what this method has to say to us today in the context of the post-Enlightenment complex of problems about reason and history, especially with regard to historical-critical exegesis, is one that has long occupied my attention. The efforts repeatedly renewed in biblical studies, despite all the historical-analytical fragmentation, to attain something like a clear and historically credible figure of Jesus has without doubt enormously enriched our approach to the historical reality of Jesus, has made it stand out in more concrete fashion.[11] And yet an overall view, in which exegesis and dogma, historical consideration and the religious-scientific (= theological) view do not diverge, has often been lacking.

Now, the very strength of the Thomistic argument of fitness is that it does not attempt to derive what is concrete and historical from some general concept but, on the contrary, seeks to arrive at a view of the whole through the most precise examination possible of the concrete historical events and likewise, therefore, through an exact comprehension of the literal sense of texts. The search for "fitness" thus keeps

---

[9] See Torrell, *Christ en ses mystères* 1:36: it is a matter of "connecting with one another those truths that we receive from the faith and of showing that there is no doubt that they stand above reason yet are not therefore without rationality. In this connection, theology is not rationally demonstrative but shows indicatively (is *ostensive*, from the Latin *ostendere* = to show)."

[10] See below, main section, chap. 4:2, "Died for Us on the Cross: The Doctrine of Redemption".

[11] See on this point F. Mussner, *Jesus von Nazareth im Umfeld Israels und der Urkirche: Gesammelte Aufsätze*, ed. M. Theobald, WUNT 111 (Tübingen, 1999), and especially the introduction by M. Theobald, pp. 1–10.

a balance between strict attention to textual and historical facts and a sense of the interconnections in the larger whole.

For a long time I concerned myself with the question of whether Hans Urs von Balthasar's theological aesthetic does not represent a further development, in the current context, of Saint Thomas' method of fitness. In the meantime, my confrère Gilbert Narcisse, O.P., has devoted an excellent study to this very subject.[12] What von Balthasar calls "seeing the form", taking up Goethe's concept of a form, does in fact seem to me to be very close to what results from the argument from fitness in Thomas' work. Common to both is the careful attention to the concrete reality of the history of salvation. Both have an outstanding knowledge of Holy Scripture, which they served all their lives as faithful commentators. Yet both have a keen sense that the overall view of the many details is not produced by the efforts of their own reason but results from a point of view granted by grace, from the "eye of faith", which shares in the light of the divine wisdom and which views the interrelationships in this light, even if only "as in a mirror" (1 Cor 13:12), that is, in faith and not yet by full vision.

Here we are coming to the difficult question of the relation between exegesis and dogmatics, which I cannot leave unaddressed in this account of my own path. Yet I turn first to another important stage, to which I owe considerable encouragement on my path: the discussion with the book *Grundzüge der Christologie*, by Wolfhart Pannenberg.[13]

This work, which is surely among the best of recent Christologies, has the advantage that it formulates with great clarity the conflict surrounding Chalcedon, around the teaching about the two natures, about the classic ecclesiastical Christology. At the heart of the discussion lies the question of how Jesus Christ can be at the same time "true God and true man", without this resulting in a "top-heavy" dominance of the divine nature over the human, whereby "Jesus' concrete living unity would be ruptured".[14] It is therefore a matter of making enough

---

[12] G. Narcisse, *Les Raisons de Dieu: Argument de convenance et esthétique théologique selon saint Thomas d'Aquin et Hans Urs von Balthasar*, SF NS 83 (Freiburg, 1997).

[13] W. Pannenberg, *Jesus, God and Man*, trans. Lewis L. Wilkins and Duane A. Priebe (London: S.C.M. Press, 1968). See also C. Schönborn, " 'Aporie der Zweinaturenlehre': Überlegungen zur Christologie von Wolfhart Pannenberg", *Freiburger Zeitschrift für Philosophie und Theologie* 24 (1977): 428–45, and W. Pannenberg, "Zur 'Aporie der Zweinaturenlehre': Brief an Christoph von Schönborn", *Freiburger Zeitschrift für Philosophie und Theologie* 25 (1978): 100–103.

[14] Pannenberg, *Jesus, God and Man*, p. 287.

"room" for the true human existence of Jesus, which seems somehow not to be sufficiently provided by the Chalcedonian view of Jesus' divine humanity.

Pannenberg rightly rejects the approach of the nineteenth-century "kenotic" theologians, who tried to ensure Jesus' full humanity by assuming that God, in becoming man, so divested himself of his divinity, "withdrew" it to such an extent, that room enough remained for the man Jesus. With his "eschatological ontology", Pannenberg takes another path: it is only from the end, from the Paschal eschaton, that Jesus' divine humanity is "constituted", he says, brought "retrospectively" to the fore. The point is not to repeat here the discussion with this impressive approach that we have undertaken elsewhere.[15] Here I am simply recording the fact that I was able to deepen my conviction that Chalcedon does not lead to an aporia, to a contradiction; quite the contrary, all attempts to distinguish or even to separate the earthly life of Jesus from his existence as Son of God end in an impasse. Jesus is the Son of God from the beginning; his truly human path is at every moment the human path of the Son of God. That has nothing to do with mythology, nor does it lead to inconceivable concepts, provided that the contemplation of and reflection upon this human life of Jesus takes place in the "primitive light" of faith that God sent his Son. In the course of the discussion with Pannenberg it became increasingly clear to me that Christology does not take the Easter event as its starting point and that it is legitimate to begin with the mystery of the Incarnation, in the very same order that is followed by the Creed and that corresponds to the "*ordo rerum*", the order in which things did in fact happen.

A consistent assent to Chalcedon would, however, now have to lead to a discussion with exegesis. Time and again, I found myself exposed to the accusation that I was not taking modern biblical interpretation seriously, and especially not historical-critical exegesis, which (it was said) had not really been given any place in my writings. Thus an attempt should be made to render an account in this question, too, as this concerns the "heart of theology", as Vatican II wished Holy Scripture to be (*Dei Verbum*, no. 24).

I had the good fortune to have as a teacher of New Testament exegesis, in Le Saulchoir, the House of Studies of the Dominicans' Paris

---

[15] See above, n. 13.

Province, Father François Paul Dreyfus, O.P. (d. 1999). This son of Israel who, as a French soldier, had come to recognize Jesus of Nazareth
as the Messiah of Israel, as the Son of God, managed to undertake
exegesis with the eyes of Paul, so to speak. I still remember him with
gratitude.[16] Over the years, I became ever more clearly conscious of
the Jewish soil that nourished Jesus and the New Testament. The book
Jesus,[17] by David Flusser (d. 2000)—God bless this "true Israelite" (cf.
Jn 1:47), who investigated the figure of Jesus with such integrity—
may be mentioned as an example of the things I read that influenced
my path. Among these were also the books of the Viennese authority on Judaism Kurt Schubert (d. 2007), especially his book *Jesus im
Lichte der Religionsgeschichte des Judentums*,[18] which I value greatly. This
Catholic specialist on Qumran, with an all-round knowledge of Jewish
studies, to whom I have been indebted for thirty years, has been able
to make helpful suggestions in many exegetical discussions, on the basis of his knowledge of Judaism. As have Joachim Jeremias (d. 1982),
for instance, and Martin Hengel, to name but two classic authorities
among the exegetes who have always been especially attracted by and
very conversant with this native Jewish soil. That is why I can wholeheartedly subscribe to Franz Mussner's statement: "The Council of
Chalcedon's christological statement of belief: Jesus Christ, '*vere deus
—vere homo*', needs to be expanded with regard to Jesus the Jew and
his Jewishness thus: Jesus Christ, '*vere deus—vere homo iudaeus*'!"[19]

My interest in questions about the history of tradition and redaction
history was consequently not very great. And the hypotheses to be
found in this area have often put me off to such an extent that simple historical common sense made me skeptical of them. This same
common sense has always strengthened my reliance on the historical
trustworthiness of the Gospels. There is no person in the ancient world
about whom we are so fully and so reliably informed as we are about
Jesus of Nazareth. If, besides this, according to *Dei Verbum*, no. 12, 3,
Scripture "must be read and interpreted in the sacred spirit in which
it was written", then the "analogy of faith" also permits the life of
Jesus to be read in "the living tradition of the whole Church" (ibid.).

---

[16] See below, main part, chap. 1, "Jesus Christ as Preexistent Son of God".

[17] D. Flusser, *Jesus: In Selbstzeugnissen und Bilddokumenten* (Reinbek, 1968; 21st rev. ed.,
1999).

[18] K. Schubert, *Jesus im Licht der Religionsgeschichte des Judentums* (Vienna, 1973).

[19] Mussner, *Jesus von Nazareth*, pp. 2 and 97.

I have never understood why the historicity of Jesus' miracles can be doubted, when for each of them there are countless analogies, excellently attested, from the lives of saints; or how Jesus' prophecies can be so easily reinterpreted as *vaticinia ex eventu*, as "prophesying after the fact", when there are ample analogies from Christian history.

I am pained by the calling into question, on allegedly scholarly grounds, of the two mysteries from the life of Jesus that particularly concern and attest to his divine humanity: his conception by the Holy Spirit from the Virgin Mary and his bodily Resurrection, with the empty tomb as its necessary indication. If, in dealing with these questions, this Christology occasionally has an apologetic character, then that springs from the conviction that in these truly central points of belief it is the task of theology (and not just of the Magisterium) to defend and to strengthen the "faith of the simple".

For some years I was able to be a part of the small audience who attended Emmanuel Lévinas' (d. 1995) biweekly lectures on rabbinic exegesis. Every two weeks he came from Paris to Fribourg as a visiting lecturer and always gave four hours of lectures in one afternoon. Three were on philosophy, and the last on the rabbinic interpretation of Scripture. I once asked Professor Lévinas what his attitude was to historical-critical exegesis. Quite in the tradition of rabbinic exegesis, he gave no direct reply to this. He said more or less that there were three crises a young man goes through if he gets involved with the word of God. The first could be called the scientific one, when the young man notices that the Bible is not consistent with the findings of natural science, for instance when it pictures the earth as being like a flat plate. This crisis is overcome by astonishment at the riddles of creation and an inkling of the greatness of God. The second crisis, rather later, strikes the young person when he realizes that there are instances of historical incoherence in the Bible, that for instance the story of Jonah could not have happened like that. This "historical crisis" is overcome through a growing sense of God's action in history. The third, the existential crisis, goes deeper, when the content of God's instructions —indeed, the very existence of God—is questioned. Overcoming this is the object of a faith in a still greater God. There was of course a fourth crisis, added Lévinas, and this one had no answer: Auschwitz.

These thoughts of Lévinas, reproduced as best I can from memory, have prompted me to write this "preamble" to Christology. They have strengthened my belief that God's Word has power of its own to build

up (cf. Acts 20:32), that it carries within it the light of its own evidence, and that it brings this into all the darkness of our questioning. In a certain sense, Jesus Christ goes through all these crises and
temptations, just as at Nazareth he went through the hostile crowd
(cf. Lk 4:30); he penetrates all the barriers of questioning, anxiety, and
doubts, just as on the evening of Easter Day he passed through the
disciples' barred doors (cf. Jn 20:19); but not so as to push aside all
our questions as irrelevant or even lacking in respect, but in order to
give the answer that takes all questions by surprise and transcends all
expectations: "Did not our hearts burn within us while he talked to
us on the road, while he opened to us the Scriptures?" (Lk 24:32).

In this account it is necessary in closing also to point out themes that
receive too little attention in the present Christology. Among these,
there is above all the broad range of topics relating to "Christ and the
world religions". There is hardly any subject that has so much occupied theology worldwide in recent years, especially in the controversial shape of "pluralistic theology of religion". The Declaration of the
Congregation for the Doctrine of the Faith on the Unicity and Salvific
Universality of Jesus Christ and the Church *Dominus Iesus*, of August
6, 2000, has this controversy above all in view. Even if the particular
question of "pluralistic theology of religion" is not itself broached as
an issue in our Christology, it seems to me that there are approaches
to a resolution available that perhaps receive insufficient notice in the
current discussion.[20]

The uniqueness of Jesus Christ, his universal significance, does not
emerge more strongly through minimizing his concrete origin and his
roots in Judaism, "dejudaizing him and wresting him from his people".[21] It is most surprising that (unfortunately, even in *Dominus Iesus*)
the uniqueness of Jesus is hardly ever explicitly linked with the uniqueness of the election of Israel. How, for instance in theological discussion (which *Dominus Iesus* joins in a particular way) is the status of
Jesus Christ as sole mediator of salvation to be credibly advocated if
it is not at the same time clearly emphasized that Jesus Christ is first
of all the Messiah of Israel, in whom the promises made to Abraham

---

[20] See K.-H. Menke, *Die Einzigkeit Jesu Christi im Horizont der Sinnfrage* (Freiburg im
Breisgau, 1995); The International Theological Commission, *Das Christentum und die Religionen: 30. September 1996*, ed. Sekretariat der Deutschen Bischofskonferenz, Arbeitshilfen
136 (Bonn, 1997); G.L. Müller and M. Serretti, eds., *Einzigkeit und Universalität Jesu Christi:
Im Dialog mit den Religionen* (Einsiedeln, 2001).

[21] Theobald, introduction to Mussner, *Jesus von Nazareth*, p. 1.

and his descendents—which through this one particular "chosen one" are made applicable to all peoples (cf. Gen 12:3)—have been realized? A commentary on the mystery of the Epiphany in the *Catechism of the Catholic Church* expresses what ought to be the guiding principle of a Christian theology of religions:

> The magi's coming to Jerusalem in order to pay homage to the king of the Jews shows that they seek in Israel, in the messianic light of the star of David, the one who will be king of the nations [cf. Mt 2:2; Num 24:17–19; Rev 22:16]. Their coming means that pagans can discover Jesus and worship him as Son of God and Savior of the world only by turning toward the Jews and receiving from them the messianic promise as contained in the Old Testament [cf. Jn 4:22; Mt 2:4–6]. The Epiphany shows that "the full number of the nations" now takes its "place in the family of the patriarchs," and acquires *Israelitica dignitas* (are made "worthy of the heritage of Israel").[22]

We shall not succeed in giving the uniqueness of Christ a credible basis by using abstract concepts such as "absolute mediator of salvation" or "absolute significance". Only by keeping in view the fact that one people was chosen, from among all the nations upon earth, to be the vehicle and the mediator of the revelation and the promise of salvation made to all peoples will it be possible to withstand the immense pressure of the relativism of the philosophy of religion. Without the concrete and graphic connection to the election of Israel, the uniqueness of the Church of Jesus Christ cannot, by the way, be effectively argued (this connection, too, is unfortunately lacking from *Dominus Iesus*, while it is constitutive for the view of the Church in *Lumen Gentium*).[23] This overall view, which will doubtless prove decisive for the future of theology, is excellently presented in *Gerhard Lohfink's* great work *Braucht Gott die Kirche?*[24] The christologically precise view of religions is, for me, determined by the christological view of the mystery of Israel. A great deal on this subject can be found in the Christology presented here, yet on the whole it is certainly insufficient. So

---

[22] CCC 528; cf. Cardinal Ratzinger's profound commentary *Many Religions—One Covenant: Israel, the Church and the World*, trans. Graham Harrison (San Francisco: Ignatius Press, 1999), pp. 25–28.

[23] See C. Schönborn, *Loving the Church: Spiritual Exercises Preached in the Presence of Pope John Paul II*, trans. John Saward (San Francisco: Ignatius Press, 1998), esp. the meditations for the second day.

[24] G. Lohfink, *Braucht Gott die Kirche? Zur Theologie des Volkes Gottes* (Freiburg im Breisgau, 1998).

we must at least refer to the relevant works of Jacques Maritain[25] and Charles Journet[26] (d. 1975), that of Jean Miguel Garrigues,[27] and also to the most significant essay by Hans Urs von Balthasar (d. 1988),[28] who looks at the question of the absolute claims of Christianity, so often posed in the abstract, precisely in view of this election of Israel.

The question of the uniqueness of Christ and his Church needs graphic description so as not to remain an empty concept. A part of this, along with its being made concrete by the mystery of Israel, is also the rich history of Christian life experience, which Hans Urs von Balthasar has appropriately referred to as "experimental dogmatics". That also receives rather too little attention in this Christology, although the interrelationship between dogma and spirituality has interested me since my early days as a student. I will make grateful mention here especially of my work together for some years with Father François-Marie Léthel, O.C.D., whose great interest in the "theology of the saints" I wholly share. He is right in seeing in the saints the real theologians, whose lives and words only rarely present academic theology, yet who are theologically relevant in their lives as a whole.[29] Even if this relation to experience is perhaps too little brought forward as a central theme, the closing chapter on little Saint Thérèse, the most recent doctor of the Church, should offer a taste of such "experimental dogmatics" and be a stimulus for pursuing this path farther.[30]

At the end of this report it remains only for me to thank, in the first place, my teachers, some of whom I have mentioned in this account; my students, whose critical inquiries have often helped me to go on and whose committed sharing of my way has often lent me wings; my fellow pilgrims, friends, and colleagues, especially the "Symmaximites", our circle of friends who gathered together under the patronage of Saint Maximus the Confessor; those friends who at the suggestion of

---

[25] J. Maritain, *Le Mystère d'Israël, et autres essais* (Paris, 1965), and in *Oeuvres complètes* 12:429–660.

[26] C. Journet, *Destinées d'Israël: À propos du Salut pour les Juifs* (Paris, 1945).

[27] J.-M. Garrigues, ed., *L'Unique Israël de Dieu: Approches chrétiennes du mystère d'Israël* (Limoges, 1987).

[28] H. U. von Balthasar, "Die Absolutheit des Christentums und die Katholizität der Kirche", in *Absolutheit des Christentums*, ed. W. Kasper, pp. 131–56, QD 79 (Freiburg im Breisgau, 1977).

[29] F.-M. Léthel, *Connaître l'amour du Christ qui surpasse toute connaissance: La Théologie des saints*, Centre Notre-Dame de Vie, Théologie 2 (Venasque, 1989).

[30] See John Paul II, apostolic letter *Novo Millennio Ineunte*, January 6, 2001, no. 27.

Bishop Eugenio Correco (d. 1995), and at first under his leadership, got together on the project of the AMATECA series and without whose patient and expectant urging this textbook would never have seen the light of day; I would especially thank the Viennese dogmatic theologian Josef Weismayer; and finally my two young colleagues Michael Konrad and Hubert Philipp Weber, who have set things in order, revised, researched, and in parts written or amplified the material that, despite my lack of time, has thus gradually grown into a whole as a textbook. Any imperfections that remain are not their responsibility but my own. And yet, after all the years of work on Christology, I can wholeheartedly say what Nicholas of Cusa (d. 1464) describes as the path he followed with the *Docta ignorantia:*

> And through my growth in faith, the Lord Jesus Christ has constantly become greater for me in spirit and mind. For no one who believes in Christ can deny that along this path he becomes more fired with longing, so that after long contemplation and exaltation he perceives that Jesus alone should be loved. With joy he abandons all else and embraces him as the true life and the everlasting joy. Everything else gives way before anyone who thus enters into Christ, and neither anything written nor this world can offer any difficulties to him, for he is transformed into Jesus on account of the Spirit of Christ that dwells within him and that is the goal of spiritual desire. May you, most reverend Father, pray to him without ceasing and with a humble heart for me, a poor sinner, that we may both be found worthy to enjoy him eternally.[31]

My most wonderful reward would be for the reader of this Christology to be able to say the same of himself at the end.

+ Christoph Cardinal Schönborn
Vienna, on the Feast of
Saint Maximus the Confessor,
August 13, 2001

---

[31] Nicholas of Cusa, *De docta ignorantia*, Philosophisch-theologische Schriften 1:517.

INTRODUCTION

PRAEAMBULA CHRISTOLOGIAE

Can we preach Jesus Christ today at all? Are we able to know him? Preaching in some sense presupposes knowledge. Can we follow him —him, and not some illusion or other, a chimera, a projection of our own desires or of the concepts of other people today or of earlier generations? Do we know Jesus?[1] This question is important, if what we seek, do, and live is supposed to be "being Christ". We do indeed talk about following Christ; we try to live it, but: Whom are we really following? Has the man we are following not become, in the meantime, a quite different person from the one who lived two thousand years ago in Galilee?

Paul writes, time and again, that he is preaching Jesus Christ (2 Cor 1:19: "Jesus Christ, whom we preached among you"; 2 Cor 4:5: "For what we preach is not ourselves, but Jesus Christ") To the "foolish Galatians", he says, "Before [your] eyes Jesus Christ was publicly portrayed [literally, προεγραφη, painted forth] as crucified" (Gal 3:1). So Paul "knows" Jesus—but from where and how?[2] Is not the picture of Jesus that Paul draws already distorted? Many maintain that it is. Paul's Christ, they say, is a theologically retouched version of the real, "historical" Jesus.

If such doubts are raised already about Paul's portrait of Christ, how much more dubious is our talk about Jesus today, then. Is the Jesus who is preached in Africa today, for instance, a projection of an African model of culture and worship? And is not our European picture of Jesus hopelessly imprisoned in the shackles of a bourgeois, late-capitalist mentality? Are we running around in circles? Are the many ways that Jesus is depicted in our time the *fata morgana*, the deceptive reflections, of our own desires? Sigmund Freud (d. 1939) subjected Christian faith to the suspicion of being merely that kind of projection.[3] Historical criticism has, on its part, sharpened the suspicion. Can we grasp anything other than miscellaneous, quite varied reactions to a historical personality whose actual figure blurs in the mist?

Do we know Jesus? Everything seems to dissolve into uncertainty as

---

[1] H. U. von Balthasar, *Does Jesus Know Us—Do We Know Him?* trans. Graham Harrison (San Francisco: Ignatius Press, 1983).

[2] On the relationship between Paul and Jesus, see J. Klausner, *Von Jesus zu Paulus* (Jerusalem, 1950); H. Merklein, *Studien zu Jesus und Paulus*, WUNT 105 (Tübingen, 1998).

[3] S. Freud, *Group Psychology and the Analysis of the Ego* (London: Hogarth Press, 1922); *The Future of an Illusion* (London: Hogarth Press, 1928); both reprinted in: *A General Selection from the Works of Sigmund Freud* (London: Hogarth Press, 1937).

soon as we pursue the question critically. We can certainly set something quite different against this uncertainty. Somehow, in a still more
definitive way, we very well have a certainty about Jesus. It is typical,
for instance, that we quite spontaneously sense that certain things do
not correspond to "the spirit of Jesus", or that certain people are seen
as particularly clear "images" of Jesus (Francis of Assisi, John XXIII,
and others). There are many people for whom Jesus is an entirely living
reality with whom they have a relationship (in prayer, in the liturgy, in a
commitment to loving their neighbor), who answer the question "Do
you know Jesus?" with a positive response, in a particular, distinctive
sense. The whole of Christology is set within this tension. On the one
hand, there is the fact that there is a living faith, for which Jesus is the
center, the basis, and the goal. On the other hand, there remains the
penetrating question of whether this basis is sound, whether the goal
is not an illusion.

Wolfhart Pannenberg says that "The doctrine about Jesus Christ
forms the core of every Christian theology."[4] With the question about
the soundness of the doctrine about Jesus Christ, the soundness of
theology as a whole is at stake. It is not surprising that, from the beginning, the arguments about Christology have been especially passionate. Even the women in the market at Constantinople used to argue about the iota.[5] This is comprehensible if we bear in mind that it
concerns not merely the basis of theology, but also that of Christian
life. The doctrine about Jesus Christ has never been a neutral matter,
because it is not concerned with some field of knowledge that can be
examined objectively from a distance. In the realm of natural science,
for instance, one's personal interest in the progress of research is not
ultimately decisive. In the arguments concerning the correct doctrine
about Jesus Christ, on the other hand, the passion and the personal
commitment are perceptible already in Paul: "If Christ has not been
raised, then your faith is futile and you are still in your sins. Then
those also who have fallen asleep in Christ have perished" (1 Cor
15:17–18; cf. also 15:12–16). Here a direct connection is being seen
between doctrine and living. Anyone who distorts the doctrine about

---

[4] W. Pannenberg, *Jesus, God and Man*, trans. Lewis L. Wilkins and Duane A. Priebe (London: S.C.M. Press, 1968), p. 19.
[5] Cf. E. Gibbon, *The Decline and Fall of the Roman Empire*, chap. 27, 2.

Jesus Christ deprives Christians of the basis of their life, and their life becomes pointless.

Only thus can we understand why the arguments about Christology have been so passionately conducted, not only in the ancient world, but now again since the Enlightenment.[6] It is always a matter of the identity of Jesus: Who is he? What did he want? What did he teach? Where can we find the answer to these questions? A Protestant, well-versed in the Bible, would no doubt answer: In the Bible; a traditional Catholic: In the teaching of the Church; a politically committed Christian, in Latin America for instance: We find the identity of Christ in the experience of the people. All three are right in their way, but not in isolation, apart on their own. Each corresponds to one christological site of knowledge.

---

[6] For the history of German Christology in the nineteenth century, the following are still worth consulting: R. Slenczka, *Geschichtlichkeit und Personsein Jesu Christi: Studien zur christologischen Problematik der historischen Jesusfrage* (Göttingen, 1967); F. Courth, *Christologie: Von der Reformation bis ins 19. Jahrhundert*, HDG 3/1d (Freiburg im Breisgau, 2000).

1. The Three Pillars of Christology (Scripture—Tradition—Experience)

Three pillars together support Christology: Scripture, tradition, and experience. The soundness of these three determines the soundness of Christology. Our first chapter is devoted to this trio and to their reliability.

1. The Three Pillars

The first pillar is *Scripture*. What we know (historically) about Jesus of Nazareth derives almost exclusively (apart from a few mentions in Pliny, Tacitus, or Jewish writings) from the New Testament, above all from the Gospels. These, in turn, are traditions about Jesus, about what he did and said. The entire canon of the New Testament is reviewed, assembled, and filtered tradition. Scripture and tradition are indivisible from the very beginning; Scripture is unthinkable without tradition; it is itself a "product" of tradition.

Because almost everything we know about Christ derives from the Holy Scripture, the question of the trustworthiness of the Gospels is thus of fundamental importance. For hundreds of years, no one questioned it. People were convinced that the Gospels reliably transmitted the experiences of the first witnesses of Jesus, of his disciples, his companions, those people who were eyewitnesses and who heard for themselves. Scripture is thus itself tradition, tradition for which there is written testimony, and it transmits concrete experiences of the people who were with Jesus.

And yet this *tradition* continues, as *traditio apostolica*,[1] as the handing on of the *depositum fidei*. It finds its particular expression in the great councils of the early Church, which unfolded and safeguarded the Christian confession of faith. The doctrinal tradition cannot of course be separated from the tradition of Christian living. Athanasius of

---

[1] This concept is used by Vatican II in the Constitution on Divine Revelation, *Die Verbum*, no. 8.

Alexandria (d. 373) not only defended the divinity of Christ, he also wrote the life of Saint Anthony, in whom the whole power of the mystery of Christ shines forth.

The saints are "lived Christology". Not only Christology as taught, but Christology as celebrated is part of the tradition: the liturgy is a living wellspring of the tradition of the mystery of Christ. Not only is the story of Jesus read ever anew in the liturgy, it is also celebrated and, thus, present. Tradition is thus fidelity to this testimony about Jesus by the original witnesses (Scripture) at the same time as it is brought to life by the experience of discipleship, of Christian living. Tradition thus contains within it both Scripture and experience.

Finally, the living *experience* of the Lord as present and active is one of the foundations of Christology. Anthony heard the Gospel story of the wealthy young man one Sunday in Church, and he heard it as something that Jesus was saying to him right now: "Follow me!" (Jn 21:22).[2] In the encounter with Scripture, in hearing and entering into what the New Testament witnesses are saying, its meaning, its beneficial value, its importance for salvation may be opened up. The experience of individuals, but also the shared experience of a whole people are part of the history of faith and, thus, part of Christology. Such experiences never take place in isolation but are always related to others—not just contemporary experiences, but also the experiences of generations before us. Liberation theology was an attempt to make the particular experience of the people productive for Christology. Christian experience can never be separated from Scripture and tradition.

Scripture, tradition, and experience are the pillars of Christology, by which we can be sure that even today we can talk about Christ, that we can truly preach him, the same person that the apostles knew, the man who was their teacher, whose words and actions they experienced directly and transmitted.

2. The Pillars Give Way

For hundreds of years this unity was seen and lived out without any problem. The current difficulties are all the more explosive. When one of these three pillars gives way, the whole of Christology—indeed,

---

[2] Athanasius of Alexandria, *Vita Antonii* (SC 400). The story of the conversion of Anthony was also a decisive milestone on the path leading Saint Augustine to faith. Augustine, *Confessions* 8, 6, 14–15 (CC Ser. Lat. 27:121–23).

theology altogether—starts to totter. Today Christology must face the fact that in recent centuries—to be more precise, since the Reformation—one pillar after another has given way. We will now briefly outline this process, which characterizes modern Christology. In doing so, we will also be able to show, however, that in the struggle with the foundations of Christology, the living figure of the Lord also emerges with new clarity.

The first crack is the *Reformation*. It calls tradition into question and from there proceeds to the supposition that the original pure teaching, the "pure Gospel", has been adulterated, that "Rome", the papacy, the Catholic Church, has no longer preserved it in its pure form. It is therefore a matter of getting back to the original—this is the approach of Martin Luther (d. 1546)—bypassing tradition to go directly to the Bible. Scripture alone is valid; it is the only criterion—*sola scriptura!* Yet how shall we attain certainty about Scripture if the interpretations of it contradict each other? Hitherto tradition, understood as the transmission of living interpretation of Scripture, has been the hermeneutical means to this end. Luther puts an end to that. Yet who was to tell him what was consonant with Scriptures, "what", in his own words, "promotes Christ" ("Was Christum treibet")? As Gerhard Ebeling has shown, in Luther, *sola experientia* complements *sola scriptura*. Experience thus becomes the criterion of what promotes Christ. Scripture and experience enable Luther to attack the *magistri* and *doctores*, tradition and Scholastic theology. That is how the Reformation solves the hermeneutic problem, by reducing the three pillars of Christology to two. For Luther, "Scripture and experience" are "the two unanimous witnesses that may be trusted unconditionally".[3] His own experience is the sure starting point: "*Sola . . . experientia facit theologum*",[4] he says. It is established as equally certain that this experience of his agrees with Scripture, or is at least suitable for understanding Scripture in the correct sense. Scripture and experience safeguard the access to Christ. The third element, tradition, has become suspect.

The *Enlightenment* breaks the next pillar. The *sola scriptura* also becomes questionable. From Hermann Samuel Reimarus (d. 1768) onward, radical historical biblical criticism puts Scripture on the side of

---

[3] G. Ebeling, "Die Klage über das Erfahrungsdefizit in der Theologie als Frage nach ihrer Sache", in *Wort und Glaube*, vol. 3: *Beiträge zur Fundamentaltheologie, Soteriologie und Ekklesiologie* (Tübingen, 1975), p. 12.

[4] WATR 1; 16, 13 (no. 46, of 1531). For further references, see Ebeling, "Die Klage über das Erfahrungsdefizit", p. 10.

tradition, which falsifies and retouches.[5] Scripture, too, conceals, falsifies, and covers up the original, which it is now necessary to ascertain
by historical criticism: the Bible is subjected to merciless criticism.
Little of the certainty that Luther believed he found in Scripture now
remains. With Friedrich Schleiermacher (d. 1834) and Rudolf Bultmann (d. 1976), theology withdraws to the final sure pillar, that of experience, and abandons Scripture to historical criticism. For Bultmann
it is not historical certainty concerning Jesus that is important but the
existential effect.

With psychology, especially with Sigmund Freud, but even as early
as Ludwig Feuerbach (d. 1872), religious *experience* likewise becomes
problematical. It is exposed as a projection of human needs and, thus, as
illusion, which basically is concealing something else that can now be
laid bare: man's secret desires, which can be discovered as the real content behind these projections. Behind the religious projections stand,
in reality, other needs, sublimations, and projections.

What can Christology build upon, then? If tradition can no longer
be trusted, because it is seen to be merely a retouching with the tints
of dogma that obscures the original simple figure of Jesus; if Scripture
itself comes under the suspicion of already being tradition, which distorts the original Jesus; if, finally, personal experience is subject to the
suspicion of creating the figure of a savior and redeemer from the projection of the person's own desires—what foundation is still sound?
Upon what can Christology still be built?

---

[5] A. Schweitzer, *Die Geschichte der Leben-Jesu Forschung*, 5th ed. (Tübingen, 1933); trans.
by W. Montgomery as *The Quest of the Historical Jesus* (Mineola, N.Y.: Dover, 2005).

II. The Three Crises of Modern Times

In order for Scripture, tradition, and experience to be able to serve as foundations for Christology, they must next be subjected to analysis. In examining the crises Christology has undergone, it will become clear whether the pillars are sound and what constitutes their soundness. We will distinguish three crises, the natural scientific, the historical, and the existential crisis.

1. The Crisis of Natural Science

"The eternal silence of these infinite spaces frightens me",[1] said Blaise Pascal (d. 1662). The beginning of modern times is characterized by the discovery of "infinite spaces": discoverers leave Europe and find the "New World" of America, the expanses of Africa and Asia. With the multiplicity of religions, the variety of cultures, the question of the unity and multiplicity of the human race arises in a new dramatic form. Then follows the discovery of the heliocentricity of the universe, of the great expanses of outer space; the earth becomes one among many planets; it loses its central place. Is it henceforth still possible to speak of this world as the center, of man as the crown of creation? Does it still make sense, then, to believe that God became man for us men (*propter nos homines*)? In light of the way natural science sees the world, is "anthropocentrism", as still advocated by the Second Vatican Council—"according to the almost unanimous opinion of believers and unbelievers alike, all things on earth should be related to man as their center and crown" (*Gaudium et Spes*, no. 12)—a responsible position?

Attacks upon Christian anthropocentrism are not new: deriving from the world view of antiquity, they existed from the beginning of Christianity. Celsus (second/third century) the philosopher, who wrote a work against Christianity around 178, holds it absurd to maintain that

---

[1] B. Pascal, *Pensées*, no. 201 (elsewhere, 206; 91), ed. L. Lafuma (Paris: Le Seuil, 1962), p. 122; English from *Pascal's Pensées*, Everyman's Library 874 (London and New York, 1931), p. 61.

God created everything for the sake of man, as Jews and Christians say. Man is rather a part of the whole, of all nature, incorporated into it, he can contribute his little mite toward it.[2] In the case of Galilei (d. 1642), the representatives of the ecclesiastical hierarchy feared that a heliocentric world view might endanger the central position of man in the cosmos, thus threatening his dignity as the highest of the creatures and also Christology, that is, the teaching that, for the sake of this man, God became man.[3] In the face of modern cosmology, the question has become far more radical. It is that same dilemma which as early as the nineteenth century led to an existentially tragic situation for many people. They saw themselves faced with the choice of either opting for faith against reason or for reason against faith. Can we today, when people have become incomparably more aware of the cosmic insignificance of the planet earth, really still maintain that God produced the entire work of creation for man and for the sake of man?

"Hundreds of billions of galaxies of the size of our Milky Way— and nevertheless the conviction that the fate of the cosmos depends on the course of events on this one planet, our earth",[4] says an indignant contemporary scientific journalist (Hoimar von Ditfurth, d. 1989). There is no lack of voices today reproaching the Church for this "anthropological misconception". Many would like to "take man back" into nature, to see him as a small and rather bothersome part of nature as a whole, who has no place of particular importance. Such emphases may be heard especially in the environment of a new "creation spirituality". Is man just a brief "snapshot" in the vast flood of evolution, a transitional stage that will soon be past? In this perspective, does not Christology lose its basis?

God is supposed to have become man on *this* earth? Is *this* earth—as the place of the Incarnation, of the saving event—not being thereby unduly privileged? At first sight, this is an urgent question. How small man is, how tiny our earth is, in comparison with the infinite spaces of the universe. Yet Blaise Pascal had already found the answer to his

---

[2] Origen, *Contra Celsum* 4, 74–81 (GCS 16:342–52).

[3] A first introduction to this is offered by S. Drake, *Galilei* (Freiburg im Breisgau, 1999); see also F. Beretta, "Le Procès de Galilée et les Archives du Saint-Office: Aspects judiciaires et théologiques d'une condamnation célèbre", *Revue de sciences philosophiques et théologiques* 83 (1999): 441–90.

[4] H. von Ditfurth, *Wir sind nicht nur von dieser Welt: Naturwissenschaft, Religion und die Zukunft des Menschen* (Hamburg, 1981), p. 140.

own fear of this vastness in his teaching about the *three orders of being*. In *Pensées* no. 308 (793, 829) it is said, about "three orders differing in kind":

> All bodies, the firmament, the stars, the earth and its kingdoms, are not equal to the lowest mind; for mind knows all these and itself; and these bodies nothing.
>
> All bodies together, and all minds together, and all their products, are not equal to the least feeling of charity. This is of an order infinitely more exalted.
>
> From all bodies together, we cannot obtain one little thought; this is impossible, and of another order. From all bodies and minds, we cannot produce a feeling of true charity; this is impossible, and of another and supernatural order.[5]

Anyone who sees only the material greatness of the cosmos, and not the orders of mind and of love, will also find it difficult to have any understanding for the mystery of the Incarnation. Without the order of love, it is incomprehensible that God should have chosen, on this planet, the small, unimpressive existence of a man, of a child, in order to redeem us.

2. The Historical Crisis

Historical events are "accidental truths of history", they just happen to turn out as they do; they might have happened differently. How can such accidental truths of history represent necessary truths of reason? How can individual points in the stream of history have an absolute and unconditional meaning? Can the history of one people—and a small and insignificant people at that—be the obligatory history of God's dealing with men? Gotthold Ephraim Lessing (d. 1781), the master of the Enlightenment, expressed this crisis in a nutshell: "Accidental truths of history can never become the proof of necessary truths of reason."[6]

---

[5] B. Pascal, *Pensées*, no. 308 (no. 829), ed. Lafuma, p. 157; English from *Pascal's Pensées*, no. 792, p. 235.

[6] G. E. Lessing, *Über den Beweis des Geistes und der Kraft* (1777), in *Gesammelte Werke*, vol. 8: *Philosophische und theologische Schriften II* ([East] Berlin, 1956), p. 12 (TzT F 5/1, no. 101, p. 65). Cf. J. Moltmann, *Was ist heute Theologie?* QD 114 (Freiburg im Breisgau, 1988), p. 64 n. 6.

That is what the Enlightenment maintains: historical events are always relative; they have a limited, never an absolute, meaning. Even the figure of Jesus is not exempt from this claim: even he must put up with the fact that *all* historical events are fundamentally capable of being relativized. So it is with someone associated with Lessing (Reimarus) that the dramatic history of the relativizing of Jesus has its explicit beginning. Protestant biblical criticism starts to strip off from Jesus the "ceremonial robes" of dogma, to bring him down from the heights of the dogma taught by the Church, so that he can once more become the simple Galilean that—so it is maintained—he actually was. The "original" Jesus has to be freed from the shrouds of ecclesiastical dogma and return once more as a simple man among the men of his own time. In one of his late writings, David Friedrich Strauss (d. 1874) drew the obvious conclusion: "We are no longer Christians."[7] His mockery of all those who believe they can get by with half-measures is biting. He castigates "the half-measures of a theology that can no longer believe in the Ascension yet will not admit that Jesus might simply have died".[8] Bultmann's program of demythologizing was the long-term consequence of this Enlightenment program.

The result of this path is sobering: People wanted to strip Jesus of his "dogmatic" robes, to remove the "ecclesiastical retouching", to free him from the "shackles" of dogma. What resulted from that was not the "original" Jesus of Nazareth, but pictures of Jesus that corresponded to whatever was the current fashion or the spirit of the age. You could find anything in the "life of Jesus" literature of the nineteenth and twentieth centuries: a Jesus who was a kind of freemason belonging to secret societies, a model of virtue, a simple but noble man, a prophet uttering apocalyptic threats, a revolutionary, and so on.

Yet it was a curious thing about the "life-of-Jesus research": the many portraits of Jesus followed one after another, but they could not pin *him* down. Jesus turned out to be "stronger". His own picture, his own words, his own figure could not be reduced to preconceived ideas and notions.[9] The intensive historical research into the figure, the acts, and the words of Jesus had a surprising effect: The more honestly, the more

---

[7] D. F. Strauss, *Der alte und der neue Glaube*, 15th ed. (Leipzig, 1903), p. 61.

[8] D. F. Strauss, *Das Leben Jesu: Für das Deutsche Volk bearbeitet* (Leipzig, 1864), p. 29.

[9] A. Schweitzer, *Die Geschichte der Leben-Jesu Forschung*, 6th ed. (Tübingen, 1951), pp. 631–32.

precisely the figure of Jesus was viewed historically, the more clearly his distinctiveness, his uniqueness emerged; the more clear it became that the "historical Jesus" was not "undogmatic", not "predogmatic", but that all subsequent christological dogmas are merely an attempt to express in words and formulas what is apparent in the figure of Jesus himself.

Thus the research into the historical Jesus is ever more clearly faced with the question of what Jesus' most characteristic claim means, of how it is possible for a man from a certain historical epoch to speak and act with regard to himself, both directly and indirectly, in such a way that God himself comes fully and entirely into play in this person.

That, of course, calls into question a fundamental principle of the Enlightenment, which to this day often finds its way, unnoticed, into "historical-critical exegesis", the principle of the complete "immanence" of all historical events. If, in nature and in history, there are only strictly immanent processes, then any belief that Jesus Christ is both God and man is untenable from the outset. But in that case, Jesus' claim to be one with the Father and to act with his authority must also be reckoned unacceptable.

Today a diffuse kind of "neo-Arianism" seems to be widespread, which sees Jesus as, certainly, a man accredited by God, but not as the true Son of God. Only rarely is the Incarnation so explicitly denied as in the book *The Metaphor of God Incarnate*,[10] yet an implicit denial of the divinity of Jesus, of his preexistence, and thereby of the true Incarnation of the Son of God seems to me to be widespread. Through this presupposition of radical immanence, the figure of Jesus is reduced to one historical phenomenon among others.

The historical crisis also has positive effects. It demands a deepening of faith and more thorough historical work. We have to give the sources a chance to speak for themselves. Yet that can happen only if we have a certain positive prejudice. If it is assumed from the outset that this or that could never ever happen in history, then that amounts to an immunization against the sources and their message. Yet for the present, it is essential to take a look at the third and most radical crisis,

---

[10] J. Hick, *The Metaphor of God Incarnate* (London, 1993). See also H. Küng, *Christsein* (Munich, 1974); K.-H. Ohlig, *Ein Gott in drei Personen? Vom Vater Jesu zum "Mysterium" der Trinität* (Mainz, 1999); a discussion of this in the review by M. Kunzler, in *Theologie und Glaube* 89 (1999): 592–95.

the existential crisis. If we manage to catch sight of the figure of Jesus undisguised and in its own right, then the much more serious question arises—more radical than the objections of natural science and those of historical relativism—the question of whether the figure of Jesus himself is "right", of whether it is not contradicted by the drama of living.

3. The Existential Crisis

This challenge takes us farthest into the question of Christology: it touches its core. The problem must first be located in a historical place and then described on that basis.

In the year 1263 in Barcelona, a public disputation took place between a Jew who had converted to Christianity, Pablo Christiano, and a great Jewish scholar, Moses Nachmanides (d. 1270). It concerned the question of whether or not Jesus was the Messiah. Nachmanides advanced against Pablo Christiano and the Christians an argument that shook them severely: Jesus cannot be the Messiah, because universal peace is promised to us when the Messiah comes (cf. Is 2:4). "Yet from the days of Jesus until now, the whole world is full of violence and devastation, and the Christians spill far more blood than all the other peoples."[11] This is indeed a strong argument; Nachmanides demonstrates by referring to the contemporary scene why he cannot see Jesus as the Messiah who has come. In his novel *Der letzte der Gerechten* [The last of the righteous], André Schwartz-Bart relates a similar scene. According to Jewish legend, a disputation was held in Paris in the year 1240 in the presence of the king, Saint Louis, between the great theologians of the Sorbonne and the most distinguished Talmudic scholars of the kingdom. Once more, it concerned the question of whether Jesus of Nazareth is the Messiah and the Son of God. Concerning the question of Jesus' divinity, after a long silence on the part of the Jewish scholars —life or death could depend upon a single wrong word—a shy rabbi named Solomon Levi answered; "coughing slightly from fear and in a thin, threadlike voice", he put forward the following: "If it is true that the Messiah, about whom our ancient prophets speak, has already come, then how do you explain the present state of the world . . . ?

---

[11] Based on Nachmanides' account in Hebrew, §49; H.-G. Mutius, *Die christlich-jüdische Zwangsdisputation zu Barcelona: Nach dem hebräischen Protokoll des Moses Nachmanides*, Judentum und Umwelt 5 (Frankfurt am Main, 1982), p. 160; see also K. Schubert, "Das christlich-jüdische Religionsgespräch im 12. und 13. Jahrhundert", *Kairos* 19 (1977): 161–86.

Noble lords, the prophets said that when the Messiah comes, moaning and weeping would disappear from the world—did they not . . . ? And also, that all peoples would break their swords, yes, indeed, in order to cast them into ploughshares . . . did they not?" When, finally, he asked the king, "Ah, what would people say, Sire, if you forgot how to wage war?" He was then, on account of this answer, burned in the name of Jesus Christ.[12] Christians, apparently unchallenged by the current state of the world, insist that in Christ the Kingdom of God has appeared. That is the weak point. If the Kingdom of God has definitively come in Christ, then "this definitive Christ" threatens to become "totalitarian".[13] The result is a more than arrogant attitude of the new people of God toward the old. The long story of ecclesiastical and Christian anti-Judaism speaks quite clearly.

This is a radical argument, and anyone who is not, as a Christian, disturbed by this question is probably not taking it seriously enough. How could Christians maintain that this Jesus of Nazareth is the one who matters, when it is obvious that with him no peace has come, the world has not taken a turn for the better, nor have tears been wiped away? Does not everything therefore argue against his being the Messiah, being that turning point through whom everything is made new?

The Christians of the second and third generations were already troubled by this question. Everything seems to argue that things remain "as they were from the beginning of creation" (2 Pet 3:4). Where is the new element, the thing that changes the world? How can it be perceived that Jesus is the Christ and the Kyrios? The rabbi's question gives rise only to an embarrassed silence. This third crisis is certainly the most profound, because it leads directly to the central question of Christology: Who actually is he, himself? The point is no longer merely: Does dogma obstruct Scripture? or: Does Scripture (as a form of dogmatizing) displace Jesus, the historical person? Much more radically: Is the figure of Jesus right? Here he himself becomes the great question. Jesus puts this question to his disciples, then, in Caesarea Philippi, just as today: "But who do you say that I am?" (Mk 8:29).

---

[12] A. Schwartz-Bart, *Der letzte der Gerechten* (Frankfurt am Main, 1960), pp. 12–13, as quoted by Dorothee Sölle, *Stellvertretung*, new ed. (Stuttgart, 1982), p. 123.

[13] Sölle, *Stellvertretung*, p. 124.

III. The Resistance of the Figure of Jesus

Despite the results of historical criticism in the writings of Hermann Samuel Reimarus, David Friedrich Strauss, and others, at first sight so destructive, despite the radical verdict of critical reason, time and again the figure of Jesus has proved to be the greatest of challenges. When we look more closely, it turns out that in the nineteenth century it was not so much the struggle for the faith of the Church, for dogma, that was at the center, or the credibility of Scripture, as important as these matters were. The decisive question concerned the figure of Jesus himself, the claim he makes, the question he himself poses and that cannot be withdrawn. If historical criticism had truly relativized the figure of Jesus, had simply put it back within the boundaries of its own time, and had finally demonstrated that he was just one historical phenomenon among others, then it would be incomprehensible why such great minds as Fyodor M. Dostoyevsky (d. 1881) or Friedrich Nietzsche (d. 1900) were still wrestling with him. Nietzsche's struggle with Christ, his *"Ecce homo!"* and the "Antichrist", show what this is about. The questions posed by the figure of Jesus himself are too great, too essential, to be handled simply by historical criticism. Nietzsche, too, had read Strauss. In the "Antichrist" of 1889, he says:

> The time is long past when I, like every young scholar, savored the work of the incomparable Strauss with the knowing laboriousness of a sophisticated philologist. I was then twenty years of age: now, I am too serious for that. . . . What I am interested in is the psychological type of the redeemer. This could be contained in the Gospels in spite of those Gospels, however distorted or overloaded with extraneous features: just as the figure of Francis of Assisi is contained in his legends, despite those legends. Not the truth about what he did, what he said, and how he actually died: but the question of whether his type is still conceivable at all, if it has been "handed down"?[1]

Following the trail indicated by Nietzsche, the following pages are not primarily going to continue depicting the history of scientific, his-

---

[1] F. Nietzsche, *Der Antichrist*, §§ 28–29, in *Werke*, ed. Colli and Montinari, 6/3:197.

torical, and existential criticism; on the contrary, they are concerned instead with the question of what momentum emanates from the figure of Jesus himself. The astonishing thing, the marvelous thing about two hundred years of biblical criticism is that the figure of Jesus has not merely not been shattered, but has even gained in clarity. This fact, that the figure of Jesus is "resistant" to all crises, that against all analyses and fragmentation, it stands again and again as the great question, may be called the "impressiveness" of Jesus. This figure comes through again and again; it has such motive power that even in overloaded distortions it cannot be entirely hidden. Along this trail, perhaps an answer may also be found to the question of what a Christology in a "postcritical" age can build upon. This discrepancy between the results of criticism and the collapse of the pillars of Christology, on one hand, and, on the other, the fact that the figure of Jesus remains as impressive and effective as ever seems to be a decisive clue in the search for a sound basis for Christology.

The starting point of our observations is the obvious "resistance" of the figure of Jesus against the crises. To this day, people continue to say to Jesus, as Peter did then: "Lord, to whom shall we go? *You* have the words of eternal life" (Jn 6:68). Nowhere is this contrast, between the denial arising from the existential crisis and the believing assent to Jesus, clearer than in the figure of Saul of Tarsus. How did this passionate opponent of Jesus and his followers come suddenly to recognize Jesus as the Messiah? How did the "turnaround" in Paul's vision—as a result of which he saw Jesus of Nazareth, not as the profane blasphemer, but as the Son of God—come about? How did it come about that everything that had seemed to Saul a mass of contradictions now suddenly seemed to Paul as the revelation of the mysteries of God that had been hidden from the very beginning (cf. Rom 16:25–26)? What happened then at Paul's conversion is still happening to this day, in ever differing ways: it is clear that Jesus Christ "turns people around" by encountering them and by "illuminating" them, by "ascending".

1. The Impression Made by the Figure: Recognizing Jesus as Christ

How did the first Christians understand Jesus Christ? The question of the impression Jesus made on the first Christians should be pursued with the help of one of the oldest passages in the New Testament. We have in mind the hymn that Paul uses to make Jesus come alive as Christ for the congregation in Philippi:

> Though he was in the form of God,
> [he] did not count equality with God a thing to be grasped,
> but emptied himself,
> taking the form of a servant,
> being born in the likeness of men.
> And being found in human form
> he humbled himself
> and became obedient unto death,
> even death on a cross.
> Therefore God has highly exalted him
> and bestowed on him the name
> which is above every name,
> that at the name of Jesus every knee should bow,
> in heaven and on earth and under the earth,
> and every tongue confess
> that Jesus Christ is Lord,
> to the glory of God the Father. (Phil 2:6–11)

The hymn from Philippians is generally recognized today as being pre-Pauline.[2] It must have originated in around the forties, that is to say, a mere ten years after Easter. This passage contains perhaps the most far-reaching christological statements of the entire New Testament. Its implications become clear when we look at it against its Old Testament background. In the Book of Isaiah 45:23–24, it says: "By myself I have sworn, from my mouth has gone forth in righteousness a word that shall not return: 'To me every knee shall bow, every tongue shall swear.' Only in the LORD, it shall be said of me, are righteousness and strength" (Is 45:23–24). With an amazing matter-of-factness, the first Christians, after Jesus' death, without hesitation applied to him what the Old Testament says about God.[3] He, Jesus, the Galilean carpenter, had received from God the "name above all names", the

---

[2] See J. Gnilka, *Der Philipperbrief*, HThK 10/3 (Freiburg im Breisgau, 1968), pp. 131–33; R. Schnackenburg, "Christologische Entwicklungen im Neuen Testament", in *Mysterium Salutis* 3/1 (Einsiedeln, 1970), pp. 227–388, here p. 322; W. Egger, *Galaterbrief—Philipperbrief—Philemonbrief*, NEB NT 9, 11, 15 (Würzburg, 1985), p. 60.

[3] O. Cullmann, *Die Christologie des Neuen Testaments*, 5th ed. (Tübingen, 1975), p. 242.

name that is nothing less than the name of God himself. In the "name of Jesus", every knee shall bow and all confess: "Jesus Christ is the Lord", the κύριος (which, again, in the Septuagint stands for the name of God). Martin Hengel's verdict is: "Basically, the later developments are given *in nuce* in the Philippian hymn."[4] Neither the Pauline nor the Johannine Christology will say more. We are faced with the puzzling fact that Christians of the first generation worship Christ as divine and attribute divinity to him in a manner that is unbearable to Jewish sensitivities. Hengel is therefore right in saying "that in the space of not even two decades, more happened in Christology than in the whole of the next seven centuries, up to the completion of the dogma of the early Church".[5]

I can see only two ways of explaining this development: The first generation themselves achieved in an unbelievably short time this process of the "divinization" of Jesus. In that case, of course, the question arises of where this idea came from. Since the emergence of historical criticism, external influences have been asserted time and again to explain this process. Perhaps the Greek myth of Heracles or the oriental anthropos myth of the first man/redeemer, from the realm of Gnosticism, might have served as models. The pattern of humiliation and exaltation, on which the hymn is constructed, is also found in Gnosticism. Since the infiltration of the concept of preexistence could also be explained in this way, this notion is at first sight tempting. Yet there is a whole series of reasons that argue against this hypothesis, the most important of which is that the hymn clearly stands within the biblical tradition, more specifically, in that of the Wisdom literature and of Deutero-Isaiah. The possibility of some points of contact in terminology is conceivable, but even the existence of a uniform Gnostic redeemer myth that early Christianity might have encountered is extremely doubtful.[6]

Or, alternatively, the reason for this belief was, "the potency of Jesus, whose enormous effect on the disciples and, beyond them, on the broad circle of people both in Galilee and in Judaea is something we can hardly

[4] M. Hengel, "Christologische Hoheitstitel im Urchristentum: Der gekreuzigte Gottessohn", in *Der Name Gottes*, ed. H. von Stietencron, pp. 90–111, here p. 107 (Düsseldorf, 1975).

[5] M. Hengel, *Der Sohn Gottes* (Tübingen, 1977).

[6] See Schnackenburg, *Christologische Entwicklungen*, p. 321; Gnilka, *Philipperbrief*, pp. 138–44.

conceive today".[7] The reason for what the first Christian community thought and accepted about Jesus right after Easter had to be found in Jesus himself. A text like the hymn from Philippians is conceivable only if Jesus himself, in what he did and said, offered some basis and premise for this. Assuming that between the earthly Jesus and the Christology of the early Church there is a deep, "horrible" divide is a misunderstanding that has serious consequences. This misunderstanding can exist, of course, only if (as Hengel says) we are willing "to recognize the modern dogma of a completely unmessianic Jesus".[8] The question of how the experience of Jesus, the knowledge about the historical figure, was so quickly "changed" into a belief in the heavenly Son of God, is left unanswered. This entire process is inconceivable without the central event in Jerusalem in the year 30: Jesus' death on the Cross and the radical turn of events through experience of the Risen One in his appearances. However we understand these as having been, their effect is to make the disciples certain that Jesus' death on the Cross had a meaning and, furthermore, that both his death and his previous activity were supported by God and were what God willed, that his teaching has been shown to be true, his claims justified: This is God himself at work.

2. A Reversal of View: The Case of Paul

Paul had the same experience as the primitive Church. The all-surpassing "knowledge" of Jesus Christ was allotted to him and completely reversed the way he saw Jesus. He already, before his conversion, knew who Jesus was: a dangerous, blasphemous rabble-rouser from Galilee, whose disciples had departed from the tradition of the Fathers and had to be persecuted (Phil 3:5–6; Gal 1:13–14). And yet after his conversion, Paul would judge this knowledge of Jesus to be knowledge according to "human standards", literally "according to the flesh" (2 Cor 5:16). What happened to Paul on the road to Damascus was something he later understood as an event whose importance was comparable to the first day of creation: Through his encounter with Jesus ("Have I

---

[7] M. Hengel, "Christologie und neutestamentliche Chronologie: Zu einer Aporie in der Geschichte des Urchristentums", in *Neues Testament und Geschichte*, Festschrift O. Cullmann, ed. H. Baltensweiler, pp. 43–67, here p. 64 (Tübingen, 1972).

[8] Hengel, "Christologie und neutestamentliche Chronologie", p. 48.

not seen Jesus our Lord?" 1 Cor 9:1), he himself became a new person
and fundamentally changed his view of Jesus of Nazareth. "For it is
the God who said, 'Let light shine out of darkness' [Gen 1:3], who has
shone in our hearts to give the light of the knowledge of the glory of
God in the face of Christ" (2 Cor 4:6).

Here Paul is drawing a parallel between conversion to Christ and
the first day of creation: It is the creation of light that first makes it
possible to see anything. It is just such a creative act of God when he
"shines in our hearts". New creation is happening here. Only after
"the eyes of our hearts" (cf. Eph 1:18) have been enlightened thus—
to be more precise, after they have been created anew, beyond their
natural capacity for perception—only then can the "glory of God"
(that is, his splendor, in which he appears in the Old Testament) shine
on us in Jesus, so that we recognize him as Son of God. Paul's conversion, his perception of Jesus as Son of God, is a new creation of
man (2 Cor 5:17). This "shining" did not distort Paul's view of the
"real historical Jesus"; it indeed blinded his earthly eyes, but it made
Jesus' true identity clear to him. All at once the ἐπίγνωσις, the true
and profound perception of Jesus, was given to him.

Paul quite clearly ascribes the initiative for this to God: "But when
[God] . . . was pleased to reveal his Son to me" (Gal 1:15–16; cf.
2 Cor 4:6). Here, knowing God and knowing Christ merge, one into
the other, just as Christ's making himself available to be known, his
self-revelation, and God's self-revelation merge into each other. That is
particularly important for Pauline Christology, because the complete
unity of action of God and Jesus is thus made clear, a unity that will
prove to be a unity of being. Thus it can also be said that the "conversion" of Paul can be traced back to the fact that Christ revealed himself to him (1 Cor 15:8; 9:1). Christ made him his own (Phil 3:12),
became known by him (Gal 4:8–9; 1 Cor 13:12b). In the story of his
conversion in the Acts of the Apostles, it is the appearance of Christ
in a flash of light, with the words, "Why do you persecute me?", that
brings about the conversion (Acts 9:4). The whole of Pauline Christology exists only because the revelation of Christ was given him, God
"opening himself up". Yet if all knowledge of Christ is grace, then we
have to ask: How is it that many people have this, but others do not?
Is theological discourse not then superfluous? It becomes clear that
knowing Jesus as the Christ is not brought about by greater knowledge. And this is one of the scandalous points, that there is no other

access to knowledge of Christ for anyone except the free, unmerited revelation of God. The true knowledge of Christ is "hidden . . . from the wise and understanding and revealed . . . to infants" (Mt 11:25). This living knowledge is possible only if it is given: "No one can come to me unless the Father who sent me draws him" (Jn 6:44, literally).

This process of making the figure of Christ evident to Paul, however, was not isolated or individualistic, without any relation to society; it was not a purely subjective, private experience that could not be communicated. The experience that Jesus is the Christ also affected Paul's attitude toward those who also held Jesus to be the Messiah and, beyond them, toward all men. The congregations in Judaea "only heard it said, 'He who once persecuted us is now preaching the faith he once tried to destroy' " (Gal 1:23). For Paul, conversion meant, not just breaking off old relationships, but also opening new ones, a new fellowship. Belief in Jesus as the Christ and fellowship with those who believe in Jesus as the Christ are indivisible. And Paul took this seriously. Although he had been called by God, and not by men, although he had seen Jesus, after fourteen years he went up to Jerusalem and laid his gospel before "those who were of repute", in order to go on with the assurance that he was not "running nor had run in vain" (cf. Gal 2:1–2).

For him, the "knowledge of Jesus Christ" was not separated from *tradition*, the memory of the Church. That is shown time and again in his letters, whether he is explicitly appealing to the community's tradition (in 1 Cor 15:1–11, Paul talks precisely about this in the Resurrection kerygma); or whether it is where Paul is picking up liturgical traditions of the churches (the hymn in Philippians, Phil 2:6–11). At the starting point of his Christology stands the *experience* that was imparted to him. But so as not just to be floating in the void, this experience needs to be integrated into the mind, the memory of the Church. And the experience of Jesus Christ can only be interpreted and proclaimed through constant reference to *Scripture*, that is, to the Old Testament. That is part of the common basis for proclamation, that the figure of Jesus, his significance and path, is "in accordance with the Scriptures" (1 Cor 15:3). The knowledge of Jesus Christ goes hand-in-hand with a far-reaching rereading of Scripture, starting from him as the center and pivotal point of perception.

Something does of course have to be added here so as to avoid misunderstandings: Jesus bears these divine traits as the one who was cru-cified. That in particular is the offense that pagans, just like Jews—and even the Christians themselves—resent. The hymn in Philippians shows that clearly: the exaltation happens to the one who has been humiliated. Paul was quite well aware of the danger of forgetting the Cross; he adamantly reminds people time and again to preach Jesus as the one who was crucified. And yet precisely this central point of Christian faith, in the oldest pagan witnesses to Christ and the Chris-tians, met with lack of understanding, rejection, and mockery.

Some of those accused of being Christians between A.D. 110 and 112 described their misconduct to the Governor, Pliny the Younger (d. 113), thus: "Our whole offense or mistake lay in this, that regularly on a certain day we met together before sunrise; and then we sang in alternation a hymn *to Christ as our God*."[9] Pliny, who recounts this incident in a letter to the emperor Trajan (d. 117), then obliged them to renounce Christ. Nothing is said here about this Christ himself. A little later, Tacitus (first/second century), in his well-known account of the persecution under Nero, tells us that "Christ, the founder of the sect of Christians, was executed by the procurator Pontius Pilate under Tiberius."[10] A simple and uneducated carpenter from the de-spised Jewish people, who was condemned to a shameful death as a political criminal, is supposed to be the one who reveals the truth of God, the future judge of the world, and God himself? On the Palatine Hill is found a caricature of the crucified man, with the head of an ass and the text beneath: "Alexander worships his God".

What we have talked about under the heading of "the existential crisis" is already put into words quite clearly by the pagan philosopher Celsus (second/third century):

How were we supposed to regard as a god someone who . . . demon-strated none of the marvels he proclaimed, and when we had convicted him and condemned him and intended to punish him, he hid himself and tried to flee, and was apprehended in the most ignominious fashion and was betrayed by those very ones he called his disciples? And yet if he had been a god, he could neither have fled nor be led away bound, and least of all could he be deserted and delivered by his associates, who had

---

[9] Pliny, *Letters* 10, 96; TzT F 5/1, no. 17, 32–33.
[10] Tacitus, *Annals* 15, 44; TzT F 5/1, no. 19, 33–34.

shared all things with him and whose teacher he had been and who had regarded him as the Savior and the Son and messenger of the most high God.[11]

Celsus deliberately puts this accusation into the mouth of a Jew. Jews and pagans were agreed about this, and that is why Paul so decidedly emphasizes: "But we preach Christ crucified" (1 Cor 1:23; cf. 2:1–2). A crucified Son of God, Kyrios, Messiah, σωτήρ (savior)—that is an unparalleled offense. There is therefore no credible "explanation" for the development of this grossly offensive doctrine, except for the assumption that it is Jesus himself who was the basis for this doctrine. Neither Jews nor pagans could "invent" the figure of a crucified Messiah, of a Son of God who died on the Cross. There is only one reasonable explanation for it: that Jesus himself, through his ministry and his word, through his life and his suffering, through his death and his Resurrection, is coherent. He himself is the basis of Christology; he is the light that makes his figure evident. It is not the case that christological dogma "retouches" or "disguises" him. Rather, it is he from whom the light issues forth: "In your light do we see light" (Ps 36:9). This light dazzled Paul and threw him to the ground; it blinded him and thus "enlightened the eyes of his heart" (cf. Eph 1:18), so that he could recognize Christ.[12]

Christology will therefore always be a renewed attempt to see the figure of Jesus in its own light, to fathom and portray its "coherence", and thus to try to understand why it was "necessary that the Christ should suffer these things and enter into his glory" (Lk 24:26). Christology is concerned with this "necessity", which cannot be derived from any human logic or reason and yet at the same time is the most profound answer to all human questioning, failure, and longing: Jesus is God's answer to the restlessness in the human heart—an answer that is astonishing, unexpected, offensive, and yet brings a happiness that surpasses all hopes.[13]

---

[11] Origen, *Contra Celsum* 2, 9 (SC 132:300–303).

[12] On all of this, see Hengel, "Die christologischen Hoheitstitel im Urchristentum", pp. 90–92; cf. A. Grillmeier, *Christ in Christian Tradition*, vol. 1: *From the Apostolic Age to Chalcedon (451)*, trans. John Bowden, 2nd ed. (Atlanta: John Knox Press, 1975), pp. 11–13.

[13] "Inquietum est cor nostrum, donec requiescat in te" (Our hearts are restless until they rest in Thee): Augustine, *Confessions* 1, 1, 1 (CChr.SL 27:1).

3. Authority and Lowliness

Yet how did Jesus' contemporaries, his fellow countrymen, experience his earthly activity? If we look more closely at the witness of the Gospels, the strange tension between Cross and glory is striking even on the earthly path of Jesus. On the one hand, Jesus' claim to be acting on God's behalf is astonishing. On the other hand, he goes to the poorest, he attends to the little and the weak. Both things scandalize his Jewish contemporaries.

a. The Dispute about Authority—A Day in Capernaum

Anyone who reads the opening of Mark's Gospel as an "exposition of the drama" of the Passion will realize that the first impression made by Jesus in his public appearance was one of astonishing authority. Mark describes there the beginning of his ministry in Capernaum and the first signs of conflict (Mk 2:1–3:6).

After the first climax of his ministry in Galilee, Jesus returns to Capernaum. Here, according to Mark's account, a dispute develops about Jesus' authority. Mark depicts a day in Capernaum that begins with the healing of the paralytic (Mk 2:1–12), which leads to an argument between Jesus and the Pharisees that makes clear the whole dimension of the approaching conflict. "Child, your sins are forgiven!" (Mk 2:5). The scandal is ignited by these words. "It is blasphemy! Who can forgive sins but God alone?" (Mk 2:7). The dispute of Jesus' opponents is a dispute on behalf of God, for the holiness of God alone. According to the Jewish conception, the Messiah himself cannot forgive sins (cf. Ex 34:7; Is 43:25; 44:22). Even Jesus does not question the fact that God alone forgives sins, but he claims that this action of God is taking place in his words and action. To provide proof of his authority, Jesus says: "Which is easier, to say to the paralytic, 'Your sins are forgiven,' or to say, 'Rise, take up your pallet and walk'?" (Mk 2:9). His healings are not merely the actions of a charismatic healer; they go farther than that; they have a theological meaning: Jesus is the Son of man, who has authority on earth to forgive sins (cf. Mk 2:10). At stake from the beginning is the question of God. Jesus' business is God's business. Those in Israel who reject Jesus intend to do it for the sake of God, in order to "give God the praise" (cf. Jn 9:24). For those who follow Jesus, a new and unexpected view of God opens up.[14]

In Jesus' dinner with the sinner (Mk 2:13–17), in his own house (Mk 2:15), it becomes clear what is meant by the cry, "The kingdom of God is at hand!" (Mk 1:15). Here forgiveness and fellowship with God are being opened to sinners. On account of his table fellowship with those who were impure according to the law, Jesus was soon mocked as "a glutton and a drunkard" (Mt 11:19). This was prompted not only by Jesus' fellowship with sinners, but by the fact that he did not exclude anyone and, thus, went beyond the distinction between the righteous and sinners. In this action, however, the heart of what he is proclaiming is realized: he is announcing the good news that God forgives sins. The parable Jesus tells on the occasion of his encounter with the woman sinner who anoints his feet presupposes that it is he who forgives sins (cf. Lk 7:36–50). Jesus' action shows that his words mean what they say: "I came not to call the righteous, but sinners" (Mk 2:17).

With the coming of Jesus, something new is happening. Jesus' disciples do not fast, and the justification for this is even more offensive than their behavior itself: "Can the wedding guests fast while the bridegroom is with them?" (Mk 2:19). Jesus is talking about his meals —and what he says is also true of his feasts with sinners—in the image of the wedding feast. The wedding, however, is an Old Testament image for the messianic age of salvation.[15] The actual bone of contention exists now, not in the fact that here the talk is about a time of universal salvation, but that Jesus is referring to himself as the bridegroom. He is the one who is bringing the time of salvation. The disciples do not need to fast because he has come to call sinners (Mk 2:17c). The radical nature of Jesus' claim is expressed with increasing clarity in Jesus' saying, in justification of the disciples' not fasting: "New wine is for fresh skins!" (Mk 2:22). Here, for the first time, Jesus' claim to be above the law is obvious. We have to bear in mind what an impossibility was being presented to those who were faithful to the law. The most holy thing there is, the Torah, is being interpreted by Jesus with sovereign authority.[16]

---

[14] See below, main part, chap. 3:3c, "The Signs of the Coming Kingdom of God".

[15] J. Gnilka, *Das Evangelium nach Markus* 1, EKK 2/1:114.

[16] See J. Neusner, *A Rabbi Talks with Jesus* (Montreal, 2000); Jacqueline Genot-Bismuth,

With the first dispute about the Sabbath, the conflict between Jesus and the scribes reached a new height. The disciples plucked heads of grain on the Sabbath (Mk 2:23–28). Thereupon the Pharisees addressed Jesus, as the one responsible, and warned him, since the sentence of death was due for deliberate desecration of the Sabbath. The Sabbath law is the most holy among the laws of Israel, what distinguishes them among all other peoples. Through his reply, Jesus set himself above the Sabbath. He regarded himself as the authentic interpreter of the order of creation, who stands above the law, which for Jews is the ultimate statement of God himself about the meaning of creation. In the concluding christological sentence, this is explicitly said: "So the Son of man is lord even of the sabbath" (Mk 2:28).

The climax of this conflict is reached in the story of the healing on the Sabbath (Mk 3:1–6). Relentlessly, Jesus asks: "Is it lawful on the sabbath to do good or to do harm, to save life or to kill?" (Mk 3:4). Doing good is God's will. The law cannot intend anything different from God's will. Doing good, saving life, healing, making someone healthy, that is God's will. Is it, for instance, permissible to do evil on the Sabbath by destroying life? Two things characteristic of Jesus' ministry become apparent in this line of argument: first, Jesus stands in the tradition of Torah interpretation. He argues within that framework and seeks to win the assent of his hearers. On the other hand, he combines with this his entirely personal claim to relate directly to God in an unheard-of way, which could only give offense. He lays claim to unlimited authority to interpret the Torah authentically in accord with God's will.[17]

A consideration of the first pericopes in Mark shows the first impression of Jesus appeared from the outset in a theological light. The conduct of Jesus is experienced as something amazing that elicits praise to God (Mk 2:12) or else is perceived to be blasphemous (Mk 2:6–7). The phenomenon of "Jesus" is not unambiguous; it can be understood in ways that are contradictory, even on the basis of the same facts. We could assemble all the historically certain data, yet of themselves they do not produce any unambiguous portrait of Jesus. It becomes

---

Un Homme nommé Salut: Genèse d'une hérésie à Jérusalem, 2nd ed. (Paris, 1995); Hans Urs von Balthasar, *Glory*, vol. 7: *Theology: The New Covenant*, trans. Brian McNeil, C.R.V. (San Francisco: Ignatius Press, 1989), pp. 115–28.

[17] On all of this, see main part, chap. 4:1a, "The Law".

clear, from the growing rejection of Jesus, that everything Jesus says
and does provides ever new evidence for his opponents that he is blas-
pheming God, that he is "beside himself" (Mk 3:21), indeed, that he
is possessed (Mk 3:22; 3:30). This attitude goes so far as a hardening
of the heart, as shown in the murderous thoughts of his opponents
(Mk 3:6). For Jesus' disciples, on the contrary, the same facts become
ever clearer signs that Jesus comes from God. How Jesus is perceived
depends on the attitude toward him, on the readiness to follow him
or not. That is the key to understanding Jesus: in faith. Jesus demands
conversion; proclaims that the Kingdom of God is at hand. He does
this with the claim that faith in his own person is indissolubly linked
with acceptance or rejection of the Kingdom of God.

b. "Evangelizare Pauperibus" as
the Basic Shape of Jesus' Proclamation

It is striking that in the New Testament it is particularly the little people
who understand Jesus. That has something to do with Jesus himself.
He identifies himself not only with God, but also with the poorest
people, and the two cannot be separated. To get a clear view of the
figure of Jesus, let us now turn to this complementary aspect. Vis-à-vis
the amazingly exalted claim of Jesus stands a no less astonishing lowliness, which before as well as after Easter remains just as offensive as
Jesus' claim to sovereignty.

Jesus did not merely live in poverty himself, he also identified himself with the poor in an unmistakable way. This is expressed in Jesus'
parable of the "final judgment" (Mt 25:31–46). There, the "King" (v.
40), the "Son of man" (v. 31), says to the astonished people on his
right: "As you did it to one of the least of these my brethren, you did it
to me" (v. 40). Jesus identifies himself with the lowliest. He is in them.
Whoever sees them, sees him. Yet at the same time Jesus' self-awareness
becomes apparent precisely here: He is the eschatological Son of man,
who is announcing God's judgment over all peoples.[18] Jesus links the
salvation of Jews and pagans to his own person. A comparison with a
midrash makes it clear that Jesus is claiming to take the place of God:

[18] See the interpretation of Matthew 25 by G. Lohfink, "Universalismus und Exklusivität
des Heils im Neuen Testament", in *Absolutheit des Christentums*, ed. W. Kasper, pp. 63–82,
here, pp. 74–79, QD 79 (Freiburg im Breisgau, 1977).

"God speaks to Israel, 'My children, when you have given the poor something to eat, I set it to your account as if you had given me something to eat.' "[19]

This brief look at the parable shows to what extent precisely Jesus' identification with the poor reveals his identity. Jesus knows he has been sent to the poor, and it is precisely in this that he shows the Father to be the one who saves the poor. Jesus' "I and the Father are one" (Jn 10:30) and his being one with the least of people (Mt 25:40) are the two sides of his person. When Jesus blesses the poor and awards them the Kingdom of God, it is obviously a matter of something central in Jesus' proclamation. His gospel is directed to three groups of people closely connected with each other: the poor, sinners, the littlest ones.[20] Who are they, and why is Jesus' mission particularly for them?

The *poor* are, first of all, the poor in a literal sense. Lazarus is really poor, "full of sores", and hungry (Lk 16:19–31). Along with the poor, those who mourn and those who are hungry are blessed (Mt 5:3–6). The "least" among the brethren of Jesus are those who are hungry, thirsty, who are strangers, naked, sick, or prisoners (Mt 25:31–46). They are those who labor hard and are heavily laden (Mt 11:28). The good news is preached to the poor. The sign of this is that the blind see, the lame walk, lepers are cleansed, the deaf hear, and the dead are raised up (Mt 11:5). The "poor and maimed and blind and lame" are brought in to the wedding feast (Lk 14:21). Those concerned here are the least, who have no security, are helpless and unprotected. A healthy poor person is not one of the poorest; he still has the fortune of good health. The poorest among the poor are poor who are ill. The option for the poor must always also be an option for the poorest of the poor.[21]

Yet Jesus' poor are not simply a social category. There are also really wealthy people among them, people who are often substantially wealthier than the orthodox scribes. Jesus' opponents reproach him for being "a friend of tax collectors and sinners" (Mt 11:19). *Sinners*—those are people who notoriously disobey God: robbers, swindlers, adulterers,

---

[19] Midrash Tann. 15:9, quoted in J. Jeremias, *Die Gleichnisse Jesu*, 6th ed. (Göttingen, 1962), p. 205.

[20] On what follows, see especially J. Dupont, *Les Béatitudes*, vol. 2 (Paris, 1969), pp. 13–278.

[21] In Qumran, in contrast, everyone afflicted with any kind of blemish or impurity was explicitly excluded. See 1QM7:3–6; 4QDb; quoted in Dupont, *Béatitudes* 2:147–48.

and especially people who do work that is despised, in which they are
either tempted to transgress the law or are obliged to do so by their
job: "tax collectors and harlots" (Mt 21:32; Lk 11:18). It is with such
people that Jesus keeps company and makes friends (Lk 7:34). What
gives further offense is that Jesus does not expose "women who are
sinners", but accepts them (Lk 7:36–40). That is felt to be in contradiction with the mission he claims to have. "If this man were a prophet,
he would have known who and what sort of woman this is who is
touching him" (Lk 7:39).

A third group is characteristic of what Jesus means by the promise
of the Kingdom of God to the poor. "Whoever does not receive the
kingdom of God like a child shall not enter it" (Mk 10:15). It is not
the wise and understanding who have access to the mystery of the
Kingdom of God (Mt 11:25). Rather, it has pleased God to reveal this
to the little ones, to *children*. This is one of the offensive traits in Jesus'
behavior and proclamation. Contrary to our notions nowadays, in the
ancient world and in the world of the Bible "being a child" was a
contemptible or at least regrettable situation. In Jesus' preaching, these
little ones are always mentioned in a context concerned with the poor
and despised, with "fools", or with becoming like them. The disciples
must become like children (Mk 9:33–37), which in concrete terms
means humbling themselves. They must become poor in spirit. Children and fools, simpletons, are considered to be incapable of wisdom
—and what can be worse than to be without wisdom! This attitude of
Jesus, in particular, struck the scribes on perhaps their most sensitive
spot, for surely ignorance of the law is the worst poverty they could
conceive.[22]

But what is meant by this attention of Christ to the poor? In the
view of the Old Testament, the poor are under God's special protection. The Magnificat sums up this notion in praise: "He has put down
the mighty from their thrones, and exalted those of low degree; he has
filled the hungry with good things, and the rich he has sent empty
away" (Lk 1:52–53). The prophetic preaching depicts the time of sal-

---

[22] H. L. Strack and P. Billerbeck, *Kommentar zum Neuen Testament aus Talmud und Midrasch*,
vol. 1 (Munich, 1922), pp. 190–91. On this point, see also H. U. von Balthasar, *Wenn ihr nicht
werdet wie dieses Kind* (Einsiedeln, 1998); F. Ulrich, *Der Mensch als Anfang: Zur philosophischen
Anthropologie der Kindheit* (Einsiedeln, 1970); H. Spaemann, *Orientierung am Kinde: Medita-
tionsskizzen zu Mt 18,3*, 8th ed. (Einsiedeln, 1989).

vation as God's judgment in favor of the poor. He will do justice for them. Now, the poor are still oppressed in many ways, but "on his day" God will prove himself to be the Lord by finally intervening on their behalf.[23] The endtime will begin with the message of good news for the poor (the *anawim*), which will be brought by the eschatological messenger from God (cf. Is 61:1–3; Lk 4:18–19).

There can be no doubt that Jesus understood himself to be this eschatological messenger of good news. Thus, to the Baptist's question: "Are you he who is to come?" he does not reply directly, but only says, "The blind receive their sight, the lame walk, . . . the poor have good news preached to them. And blessed is he who takes no offense at me" (Lk 7:19, 22–23). Jesus points to the fact that through his ministry the signs of the great divine intervention promised by Isaiah are being fulfilled. That is why Jesus invites the Baptist and his audience to rejoice.

They are to rejoice above all that now, at the beginning of the time of salvation, God's mercy is on its way to sinners. This is where Jesus' consciousness of his mission becomes most pointedly clear. Jesus knows he has been sent to bring the good news to sinners. This is happening quite concretely. His meals with sinners are "anticipatory celebrations of the feast in the end time".[24] Jesus urges even his opponents to keep table fellowship with sinners; they should overcome their too narrow understanding of the law. "A Pharisee does not dwell with them (the *'ammē hā-āres*) as a guest, nor does he entertain one of them at home in his garments."[25] How dramatic this reorientation of thinking was, even for Jesus' disciples, is shown in Peter's vision at Joppa (Acts 10:9–23).

For the Pharisees, the commandment to love one's enemies is not the greatest difficulty. In Qumran it does indeed say: "I (the person praying) will not have mercy on all of those who have abandoned the way, I will not comfort the contrite until their change is complete."[26] Jesus, however, goes farther than even the Pharisee advocates of love

---

[23] Numerous texts in Dupont, *Béatitudes* 2:65–88.

[24] J. Jeremias, *New Testament Theology* (New York, 1971), p. 116.

[25] Damascus Doc. 2:3; quoted in ibid., p. 118.

[26] 1 QS 10:20f. To get a balanced picture, one should read the texts quoted by David Flusser, which show that at that time many thought the same as Jesus; D. Flusser, *Jesus*, 21st ed. (Reinbek, 1999), pp. 79–83.

of the school of Hillel (d. ca. 10). "Rabbi Hanina said that one should love the righteous and one should not hate the sinner; but Jesus said, 'But I say to you, Love your enemies and pray for those who persecute you' (Mt 5:44)."[27] The unacceptable point, for Jesus' opponents, seems to have been the inseparable combination of God's mercy and Jesus' own acts, the "implicitly christological situation". After the appearance of Jesus, people can no longer hold to God's mercy without accepting Jesus himself. This is not verbalized anywhere and yet is presumed everywhere. Jesus knows he is so at one with God's will that he can base his behavior directly on it. This conformity with God's will is also shown in his life: "Which of you convicts me of sin?" (Jn 8:46). The accusation that he is a sinner is in fact not made anywhere against Jesus. The accusations are always directed at the whole; they are general: "He is beside himself" (Mk 3:21). "It is blasphemy" (Mk 2:7). "He has an unclean spirit" (Mk 3:30). On the other hand, Jesus, too, demands a total decision: "He who is not with me is against me" (Mt 12:30).

Jesus' attention to the poor, to sinners, and to children corroborates his claim, which we came across in the pericopes in Mark, to be acting in God's place and with divine authority. It proves that he himself is God. This claim, if we follow the Gospel of Mark, becomes ever clearer through the whole story of Jesus' life on earth. It comes to a climax on the Cross. Everything is working up to the confession of the pagan centurion: "Truly this man was the Son of God" (Mk 15:39).

From the hymn in Philippians up to the Letter to the Hebrews, it can be observed that Jesus' divine stature, his divine Sonship, is always seen together with the scandal of the Cross. The Christians worship a crucified God. That is the impression the pagans have of them and one that does in fact correspond to the belief of Christians. The assertions of Jesus' sovereignty become that much more offensive in that they refer to the one who was crucified. All this argues that this combination could not have been invented, either by Jews or by pagans. Indeed, even for the disciples of Christ it was so awkward that time and again they were tempted, and are still tempted, to this day, to find a way to avoid it. It could be mitigated only by reducing either Jesus' divinity or his Cross. The experience of the Emmaus disciples shows how great

---

[27] Flusser, *Jesus*, p. 74.

the tension is. The Cross seems to foil all the messianic hopes centered on Jesus. Only gradually do they begin to grasp that it had to be like that, exactly like that: "Was it not necessary that the Christ should suffer these things and enter into his glory?" (Lk 24:26).

Main Part

"God Sent His Son"

Preliminary Remarks

The Mission of the Son as the Heart of Christology
The Creed as the Framework of Christology

Most recent Christologies prefer to start with the Easter event in order then to develop the Christology in two directions: on one hand, backward, so as to illuminate Jesus' earthly path on the basis of Easter; and on the other, forward, so as to follow the development after Easter. The main argument in favor of this approach has always been the theory that in terms of knowability the experience of Easter was the starting point for Christology. From this point of view, statements about the Incarnation appear somehow to be secondary, the conclusion of a retrospective deduction that the Risen One had always been at one with God. Behind this question of the point of departure for Christology, there is however a far more all-embracing question: Is Easter or Christmas the center of our faith? The Incarnation or the mysterious Paschal event? Since the nineteenth century an opposition has consistently been seen here. If, on the one hand, we start from the Incarnation, when God became man, then it seems to follow that Christmas is the central saving event: God became man! With that, everything has already been fulfilled. Yet is Easter then any more than an appendix? Have redemption and salvation not come to us already, before Easter? On the other hand, Christ's Paschal Mystery does nonetheless seem to be central: Easter is the turning point of salvation, the new thing that makes everything new. Is Easter the noun, then, and Christmas merely the preposition? We have to pay attention to this opposition if we take Easter as our starting point and not, as in tradition, the Incarnation. Neoscholastic theology neglected the Paschal Mystery and restricted itself to the Incarnation (the tractate on the Word which became flesh, *De verbo incarnato*). In modern theology we may rather notice the opposite tendency, that of regarding the Incarnation as just a secondary statement. Yet in fact the two belong together, each unthinkable without the other. Both are central for Christology, as for theology in general, like the two focal points of an ellipse. The starting point for Christology has to be the New Testament view, which Paul sums up in one phrase: "God [sent] his own Son" (Rom 8:3; cf. Gal 4:4).

In what follows it will be shown that in the profession of faith in Christ there is from the beginning an inner unity. It has always been understood as a whole, as including the mission, the Incarnation, the earthly life, the Passion, the Cross, the Resurrection, and the glorification of Jesus. None of these elements on its own is the central point of Christology—rather, they are closely interconnected. Jesus' whole pathway appears as a unity, because it is all seen together under the title "Son of God" and in the comprehensive assertion of salvation: "God sent his Son." This confession of faith serves as the framework for our Christology.[1]

In all the tripartite forms of the Creed we find the same structure in the second, christological article. Thus for instance in the Apostles' Creed it says:

> . . . and in Jesus Christ, his only Son, our Lord, who was conceived by the Holy Spirit, born of the Virgin Mary, suffered under Pontius Pilate, was crucified, died and was buried; he descended into hell; on the third day he rose again from the dead; he ascended into heaven, and is seated at the right hand of God the Father almighty; from there he will come to judge the living and the dead.

In the Niceno-Constantinopolitan Creed, the structure is the same in principle but is simply expanded. Both proceed from the Christmas to the Paschal Mystery, not the other way around. This structure forms the basis for the whole of Christian catechetics and proclamation. Even the course of the liturgical year corresponds to this.

We find the same structure in the proclamation of the early Church, for instance that of Melito of Sardis (second century) in his Paschal homily (160–170). It says there: "For the sake of suffering humanity he came down from heaven to earth, [and] clothed himself in that humanity" (no. 66), and in the following: "It is he who was made man of the Virgin, he who was hung on the tree; it is he who was buried in

---

[1] See J. Ratzinger, "Taking Bearings in Christology", in *Behold the Pierced One: An Approach to a Spiritual Christology*, trans. Graham Harrison (San Francisco: Ignatius Press, 1986), pp. 13–46; cf. J. N. D. Kelly, *Early Christian Creeds*, 3rd ed. (London: Continuum, 2006), pp. 1–29.

the earth, raised from the dead, and taken up to the heights of heaven"
(no. 70).[2]

This pattern is maintained already in the New Testament. From the
oldest texts down to the latest, the same structure predominates. We
have already talked about the hymn in Philippians.[3] It clearly shows
the composition: preexistence—Incarnation—Passion—exaltation. In
late texts, also, this form is noticeable, for instance, in the Prologue
to John: "In the beginning was the Word", and "the Word became
flesh" (Jn 1:1, 14). Between these two poles lies an impressive wealth
of textual witnesses, which all exhibit this structure.

Romans 8:31–32 shows that Incarnation and Cross, becoming man
and dying, should not be played off one against the other: "If God is
for us, who is against us? He who did not spare his own Son but gave
him up for us all, will he not also give us all things with him?" Here, all
dimensions are included, which are also mentioned in the hymn from
Philippians: becoming man and offering up his life. Everything that
God brought about for us in Jesus Christ is included in this summa-
tion of Paul's preaching: "But when the time had fully come, God sent
forth his Son, born of woman, born under the law, to redeem those
who were under the law, so that we might receive adoption as sons"
(Gal 4:4–5). Another of Paul's central texts shows to what degree this
is the essence of the message of salvation: "For God has done what
the law, weakened by the flesh, could not do: sending his own Son in
the likeness of sinful flesh, and for sin" (Rom 8:3). God's response to
the hopelessness of the servitude to the flesh is this: God sent his Son
(literally) "in the flesh of sin". The sending of the Son is the response
to the helpless situation of sin.

At the close of the New Testament period, in John, it will say: "For
God so loved the world that he gave his only-begotten Son, that whoever believes in him should not perish but have eternal life. For God
sent the Son into the world, not to condemn the world, but that the
world might be saved through him" (Jn 3:16–17). Here too, Incarnation and redemption are a single reality.

---

[2] Melito of Sardis, *Easter Homily* 66, 70 (SC 123:96–99), from the Office of Readings for
Thursday of Holy Week, *Liturgy of the Hours*, vol. 2 (New York: Catholic Book Publishing
Co., 1976), pp. 458–59.

[3] See above, introduction, chap. 3:1, "The Impression Made by the Figure: Recognizing
Jesus as Christ".

What is true of Paul and John is also to be found in the Synoptic Gospels, quite clearly in the parable of the wicked tenants (Mk 12:1–12 and par.).[4] When all the owner's efforts to collect his rent have been to no avail, after his servants have been beaten by the tenants, it says: "He had still one other, a beloved son; finally he sent him to them." But the tenants took no notice of him, "They took him and killed him, and cast him out of the vineyard" (Mk 12:6, 8). This text says some important things about the mission of Jesus and about his consciousness of that mission. Here the Incarnation, the coming-into-the-world, is combined with Jesus' understanding of his death, as becomes clear at the Last Supper (Mk 14:22–25).[5] In the parable, Jesus stands in the succession of men sent by God, yet with two essential differences: he is not one of the servants, but the beloved Son; and he is the last one God sends. That is what lends drama and seriousness to the situation. Israel has rejected the previous messengers from God. Will it now reject the last one, too? Jesus himself describes his mission as that of God's final messenger and thereby places himself, in a manner that surpasses all previous prophetic missions, in proximity to God: he is the beloved Son. Is the preexistence of Jesus being presumed with this? This question will have to be clarified in detail.

The prologue of the Letter to the Hebrews may be considered a commentary on this parable: "In many and various ways God spoke of old to our fathers by the prophets; but in these last days he has spoken to us by a Son, whom he appointed the heir of all things, through whom also he created the ages" (Heb 1:1–2). Preexistence, the Son's participation in the creation, Incarnation, and exaltation are enunciated again here. The whole christological viewpoint of the primitive Church is summed up in this passage.

"God sent his Son" can thus be considered the very essence of the good news, and in this sending, he gives us what is everything to him: his Son. All other statements are contained in this and, on its basis, are to be understood as a unified whole. The structure of the main part

---

[4] See on this point M. Hubaut, *La Parabole des vignerons homicides*, Cahiers de la Revue Biblique 16 (Paris, 1976); M. Hengel, "Das Gleichnis von den Weingärtnern Mk 12,1–12 im Lichte der Zenonpapyri und der rabbinischen Gleichnisse", *Zeitschrift für die neutestamentliche Wissenschaft und die Kunde der älteren Kirche* 59 (1968): 1–39; X. Léon-Dufour, "La Parole des homicides", in *Études d'Évangile* (Paris, 1965), pp. 308–30.

[5] See R. Pesch, *Das Markusevangelium*, vol. 2, 4th ed., HThK 2/2 (Freiburg im Breisgau, 1991), p. 222.

of this book follows from that. The five chapters reflect the order of the history of salvation. We will ask about the Son of God and will do so in the order of the articles of the Creed, asking first about his preexistence, secondly about his becoming man, third about his path on earth, fourth about the Passion, and finally, fifth, about the glorifica-tion of the Son of God. In each individual chapter the *biblical* aspect of the particular subject will be developed. Examples will be taken from the wealth of the *tradition* of the Church, from her life, her theology, and her liturgy. Christian *experience*, especially that of the saints, will consistently provide the background as the place of encounter with Christ.

I. Jesus Christ as Preexistent Son of God

In response to the question of how Paul, a believing Jew, could say: "that at the name of Jesus every knee should bow" (Phil 2:10), how he could call for kneeling in worship before Jesus, my much-respected teacher François Dreyfus (d. 1999), a Dominican of Jewish extraction, replied:

> It would be necessary to have experienced for oneself the spiritual journey of a St. Paul in order to measure the enormous difficulty which faith in the mystery of the Incarnation presents for an orthodox Jew. With respect to this, all the other obstacles are ridiculous child's play. This obstacle is so radical that it cannot be surmounted frontally. It must be skirted, like a summit whose northern face is inaccessible and which can only be scaled from the south. It is only afterward, through the light of faith, that one discovers that the Trinity and the Incarnation are not opposed to the monotheistic dogma of Israel: "Hear O Israel, the Lord our God, the Lord is one" (Mk 12:29, citing Dt 6:4). And one discovers that not only is there no contradiction, but on the contrary the Christian dogma is as it were the full blossoming out, the crowning of the faith of Israel. And for someone who has made a similar experience, there is a conviction which comes to bear on the subject: The pious Jew of the first century is in an identical situation to someone of today. Only a very strong certitude can lead him to skirt around this obstacle. Only an indisputable teaching of Jesus fulfills this condition.[1]

1. Biblical Witness to the Idea of Preexistence

Belief in the preexistence of Christ did not just "fall from heaven"; even in Jewish belief there are a variety of concepts of preexistent realities. Thus, for instance, in the time of Jesus the idea was current that the Torah was preexistent, that it was there "before the foundation of the world". The same is true of the Wisdom of God, of his Word, the

---

[1] F. Dreyfus, *Did Jesus Know He Was God?* trans. Michael J. Wrenn (Chicago: Franciscan Herald Press, 1989), pp. 138–39 n. 16.

Logos, and finally, also, of the Messiah himself. His name was being kept hidden beneath the throne of God. The boundaries between a purely "notional" or "ideal" preexistence in the thought of God and a "real" preexistence are fluid.[2] Even in relation to the son of man, we find the notion of his preexistence in apocalyptic literature. "According to a Jewish theologoumenon that was widely handed down, seven (or sometimes, six) things existed 'before the creation of the world' . . . the Torah, Penitence, the Garden of Eden, Gehenna, the Throne of Glory, the Sanctuary, and the Name of the Messiah."[3]

Rabbinic traditions concerning the preexistence of the Messiah are of particular interest here, for instance that in the midrash Pesikta Rabbati: "What is the evidence that the Messiah has existed since the beginning of the world's creation? 'And the Spirit of God hovered.' That is the messiah king! For it is said: 'And the Spirit of the Lord shall rest upon him' (Is 11:2)." Therefore the Messiah is present at the creation of the world.[4] It is equally striking that in Pes. R. 36:1, the original light of creation (Gen 1:4) is identified with the light of the Messiah that God is hiding beneath his throne. Who could fail to think of John 8:12: "I am the light of the world"? The introduction of the idea of preexistence is thus not a startling invention, still less a Hellenistic overgrowth,[5] but "took place from an inner necessity".[6] In what sense?

Jewish sources contribute to the conceptions of preexistence in the New Testament. It is not the idea that a being preexisting alongside God is sent to us in the messianic era that is new. The roles played by Enoch or Elijah in apocalyptic tend toward this and also the idea of the return of Elijah, as it is documented in the New Testament. Even today, Jews at Seder are waiting for Elijah, who was swept up to God and will not come again until the end-time. It is not the concept of preexistence in itself that is new and unusual, but the fact that the preexistent being "was in the form of God". Torah, Wisdom, Logos,

---

[2] See M. Hengel, *Der Sohn Gottes: Die Entstehung der Christologie und die jüdisch-hellenistische Religionsgeschichte*, 2nd ed. (Tübingen, 1977), pp. 108–9.

[3] R. Schnackenburg, *Das Johannesevangelium*, 7th ed., vol. 1, HThK 4/1 (Freiburg im Breisgau, 1992), p. 291.

[4] The passage is taken from Pesikta Rabbati (Pes. R. 33:6, ed. Friedmann 152b), and quoted by Hengel, *Der Sohn Gottes*, pp. 110–11 n. 126. Jesus himself refers this passage from Isaiah to himself, which can probably be interpreted only in a messianic sense (see Lk 4:18).

[5] On the theory of Hellenization, see below in this chapter, sec. 2c: "Beginning or End? The Hellenization Theory".

[6] Hengel, *Der Sohn Gottes*, pp. 111–12.

and Messiah are created entities. Enoch and Elijah are creatures. But in Judaism, as soon as this fundamental dividing line is threatened, voices are raised in warning. In the third Hebrew Book of Enoch, Enoch is taken up to God (cf. Gen 5:24) and obtains the throne next to God, above all angels; he becomes the vizier of God, his fully authorized representative. Indeed, he is even called a "lesser Yahweh". The rabbinic warning against confusing him with God is that much more weighty. We find in the Mishnah that Rabbi Aquiba interprets the two thrones in Daniel 7:9 as being one for God and the other for the Messiah. Rabbi Jose the Galilean indignantly contradicts him: "Aquiba, how long will you continue to profane the Shekinah [dwelling place of God]?"[7]

It was not preexistence that was the problem, or even the sending of a heavenly, preexistent figure, his descent from the heavenly into the earthly realm. All of that was known to Jewish theology in the speculations concerning the Shekinah.[8] The unusual thing about the Christian proclamation is that this preexistent Messiah and Son of man, Logos and Wisdom, Son of God, stands "no longer simply on the side of creatures, but at the same time also on the side of God".[9] Judaism is, to be sure, familiar with heavenly entities who stand alongside God, such as personified characteristics of God like justice and mercy. In the Talmud, God prays that his mercy may get the better of his wrath.[10] But that some personal entity, a preexistent Son of God, should himself be God, that is singular and new.

Hellenistic pagan thought, which knew nothing of the clear biblical teaching about creation, could accept fluid transitions between God and the world, a greater or lesser degree of divinity, a hierarchy. The dangers that were to arise from this possible Hellenization of the message about Christ will become clear later. Yet the very fact that the interpretative model for the figure of Jesus was of Jewish origin makes it that much clearer how offensive it was that Jesus, as a preexistent being, was seen at God's side (cf. Jn 1:1). In Judaism, a greater or lesser degree of divinity was unthinkable. Thus it was inevitable that the question of monotheism arose.

How can the primitive Christian confession of Jesus as the Kyrios be

---

[7] Cf. ibid., pp. 73–75.
[8] See below, chap. 2:1a, "God's Self-Abasement in Jewish Theology".
[9] Hengel, *Der Sohn Gottes*, p. 119.
[10] bBer 1, 1, 7a (Goldschmidt 1:22).

reconciled with the confession of the uniqueness of God, as expressed
in the "Hear, O Israel" (Deut 6:4)? It must have been shocking when
Paul talked about the one God and at the same time set the uniqueness
of the Kyrios side-by-side with that of God, when he joined together
the confession of the one God with the confession of the one Lord: we
have "one God, the Father, from whom are all things and for whom
we exist, and one Lord, Jesus Christ, through whom are all things
and through whom we exist" (1 Cor 8:6; cf. 1 Tim 2:5). Everything
comes from the one God and through the one Lord. One could probably hardly associate the one God more closely with the one Lord.
Yet the difference in the prepositions shows that this is not a matter of
complete identification. God clearly remains the origin; it is he "from
whom everything" (ἐξ) comes; the Kyrios, on the other hand, is clearly
characterized as the intermediary; it is he "through whom everything"
(διά) exists. And yet Paul has certainly not ascribed everything to both
of them, to God and the Kyrios, through rhetorical naïveté. It was inevitable that this should be perceived as a problem for the uniqueness
of God, when God and the Kyrios were spoken of in this way. Even
if Paul had spoken naïvely about the one God and the one Lord as
being side by side, without being aware of what problems this posed
for monotheism, there could not then also fail to be further reflection
upon it. Even if the primitive community in its self-concept had not
felt this to be a problem, yet the Jews, who did not believe in Jesus the
Kyrios, took offense at it and thus obliged the Christians to consider
this question.

   If we look for traces of this conflict in the New Testament, then certainly we will find no explicit comments about it, such as have been
handed down to us from the dispute over Arianism, for instance. And
yet Mark begins: "The beginning of the gospel of Jesus Christ, the Son
of God", and closes his work with the confession of the pagan centurion: "Truly this man was the Son of God" (Mk 1:1; 15:39). It really
is difficult to see this as naïve storytelling; it has rather to be evaluated
as the conscious expression of what was proclaimed. John, who has
been given the appellation of "the Theologian" by the Eastern Church,
speaks on this point in terms impossible to misunderstand. He frames
his Gospel with two decisive passages about the divinity of Jesus. It is
in his book that we find the two places in which the predicate "God"
(Θεός) is indisputably ascribed to Jesus and where at the same time the
question arises of how this predication of divinity is to be reconciled

with the uniqueness of God. We are talking about John 1:1: "and the Word was God" (καὶ Θεὸς ἦν ὁ λόγος); and about the confession of Thomas, in John 20:28: "My Lord and my God!" These two declarations constitute the framework for the Gospel, if one regards John 21 as an addition. The confession of Thomas, like the words of the pagan centurion in Mark, forms the central declaration of the Gospel. Just as, in Mark, the confession of the centurion opens the Gospel to the belief of pagans, so in John the confession of Thomas is opened to the confession of those many later ones who "have not seen and yet believe" (Jn 20:29). This is not placed just anywhere; rather, it is meant to show that the whole Gospel, as a witness to the life of Jesus, is intended to lead to the confession of faith of whoever hears it: "My Lord and my God!" The Gospel's explicit aim is "that you may believe that Jesus is the Christ, the Son of God, and that believing you may have life in his name" (Jn 20:31).

The confession of Thomas makes it clear "that the belief in Jesus as the Son of God (cf 20:31) that was demanded of the congregation implies that Jesus is God".[11] Viewed in close relation with the Prologue of John, this makes it clear that identifying Jesus as Lord and God by no means occurred in a naïve way. This conferral of the title "Kyrios" is found several times in the New Testament, for instance in Acts 2:21, where Joel 3:5 is quoted: "And it shall be that whoever calls on the name of the Lord shall be saved." What is said about God in the book of the prophet Joel is here ascribed to Christ. In a similar way, a saying from Isaiah (Is 40:3, LXX) is transferred to Christ by Mark (Mk 1:3): "Prepare the way of the Lord"—The Lord who is coming is Christ. These passages, in which the Old Testament synonym for the name of God is attributed to Christ, offer a profound insight into the way in which Jesus' divinity means, not just any kind of participation in the sphere of divinity, but Jesus' being fully one with God in his actions and in his being.

We shall talk about the title of "Logos" again in connection with Arius. It is one of the most significant christological titles and refers to the God-Christ relationship, giving definition to its content. Christ is in the first place God's Word, which is with God before all time. Then the Logos is the intermediary for creation; it is through him that God created everything. Finally, he is the one and only mediator of

---

[11] Schnackenburg, *Johannesevangelium* 3:397.

salvation (Jn 1:14). He is mediator in such a way that it can be affirmed that he himself is God. The Prologue of John is a precisely constructed theological text whose central theme is the divinity of the Logos and his role as mediator of salvation.

How does the Gospel of John regard the mutual relationship between the divinity of God and that of the Logos? One can certainly say, along with Oscar Cullmann (d. 1999) and many others, that the Prologue as a whole is primarily concerned with God's action in revelation. Logos, Word, is in fact a title of Christ that refers to his function of revelation: God utters his Word, and thereby he reveals himself. Yet, at the same time, the point is that this Word cannot be separated from God himself. It was with God from the beginning. Here it is not being regarded as a created reality, as in Arius' writings, but is "given along with God himself". "Nor is the Logos subordinate to God, for he simply belongs to him. He is neither subordinate to him nor coordinate with him as a second being."[12] We must of course take care here not to limit the definition of the Logos only to his action in revelation, as if the title of Logos were simply the name for God insofar as he reveals himself: that is, a name for God under the aspect of revelation. The Word as God's mode of being in his revelation would be the interpretation the Church has rejected as "modalism". The Logos is not simply one aspect of God, one way in which he appears. In the Prologue he is clearly described in personal terms: "He 'was with God' as persons are with one another";[13] he was with God even "before the foundation of the world", and thus, we ultimately have to say, independently of the foundation of the world. The Logos was with God, not because God created everything through him, but because he himself was God. He was himself God and eternally with God. That constitutes his nature, and only on the basis of this constitution of his nature can the entire scope of his "function", his action in revelation, be understood. For the function presupposes the nature.

How, then, does the Prologue of John reconcile the divinity of God with that of the Logos? Rudolf Schnackenburg considers that in verse 1c "the Θεός that precedes [Logos] here is a predicate, but does not equate the Logos with the ὁ Θεός already mentioned. Rather, the Logos is just as much 'God' as the one, with whom he stands in the closest

---

[12] O. Cullmann, *Die Christologie des Neuen Testaments*, 5th ed. (Tübingen, 1975), p. 272.

[13] Schnackenburg, *Johannesevangelium* 1:209.

possible community of life and being. Thereby, Θεός does not become a concept of God but, rather, refers to the nature that is common to both the Logos and God."[14] "The Word was with God, and the Word was God" (Jn 1:1). Yet in order to exclude any misunderstanding this to mean that the Logos might be another, second God, John immediately adds: "He was in the beginning with God" (Jn 1:2). The divinity of the Logos is never, in any way, a matter of being God for himself alone. He is God in such a way as to be wholly with God. The fact that God is being talked about, and has to be talked about, in this extraordinary way, does not imply any polytheism, since there is never any question but that God is one. This manner of speaking does, however, also break open the previous conception of monotheism, since God eternally has with him his Word, who is himself God.

It is the business of faith to accept this, and yet faith cannot consist in believing something plainly absurd. Faith can certainly include in it something unexpected, something surprising or unimaginable. But this surprising new thing immediately reveals a new meaning and thereby renders possible a new understanding, a novel view of things. Believing in God as a Christian signifies something different, something new compared with Jewish monotheism: one can no longer talk about God without talking about Christ. God and Christ are one in such a way that Christ can, and must, be referred to as God, without thereby producing a rivalry for the divinity of God. The meaning of this unity, which completely reshapes our understanding of God, is only unlocked, of course, in the concrete life, death, and Resurrection of Jesus. Only through the witness of the earthly life of the incarnated Logos is it understandable for faith in what way the Logos is God. But the Johannine perspective begins at the origin of everything: The Prologue establishes the fact that Christ is the perfect mediator of salvation on the basis of his nature, in his being one with God. Only if the Son really has received from the love of the Father the fullness of divine nature—and thus not sharing in divinity only in a certain sense, but truly and completely—then he also has full power to reveal and to save, then God himself has truly been revealed in him, completely and conclusively.[15] With the Prologue, John roots the whole work of Jesus in this unity. Thus, a correct understanding of function is what

---

[14] Ibid., p. 211.
[15] See here Ibid., p. 211.

leads directly to the conclusions about the nature of Christ's divinity. Because he himself is God, eternal and in union with God, the Logos can freely become man and freely communicate the divine life. Because the Logos, in his eternal being-with-God, is himself God, John is able to say: "From his fulness have we all received" (Jn 1:16). As the last word his Prologue says, as a transition to the body of the Gospel of the life and death of Jesus stands the sentence that condenses this and sums it up once more: "No one has ever seen God; the only-begotten Son, who is in the bosom of the Father, he has made him known" (Jn 1:18). Here the whole dignity of the Only One, his divine nature, is once again expressed as well as the capacity for revelation of the Son of God who appeared upon earth.[16]

This faith, and the reflections upon it, did not unfold harmoniously from what was previously given in Judaism. They were possible only on the basis of God's revelation of himself, in which he went beyond his Old Testament revelation by sending his Son and thus revealed himself as the One who is eternally community.

It would now be possible to show that the Johannine view makes explicit what is implicitly expressed in the other Gospels in the words, deeds, and gestures of Jesus. The Gospel of John reveals how deliberately the claims of the divinity of Jesus were considered, particularly in the face of Jewish questioning. It becomes clear, moreover, that the Gospel's reply is not abstract but, rather, is concrete in the figure of Jesus. He demonstrates his divinity in his complete unity of being with the one he calls "Father". The Christian confession of faith has, then, from the beginning recognized Jesus the Christ as the Son of God in this full sense.

2. The Arian Crisis and the First Council of Nicaea (325)

The confession of the divinity of Christ is inextricably linked with one of the greatest crises in Church history, the conflict about Arius and Arianism. This was concerned with the question of whether Christ was, as Paul says, "the image of the invisible God" (Col 1:15) or just a similar, albeit preeminent, copy, as is every man. The First Ecumenical Council, the Council of Nicaea, responded to this crisis and recognized Christ as being "consubstantial with the Father".

---

[16] See ibid., pp. 255–56; Cullmann, *Christologie des Neuen Testaments*, p. 317.

a. The Concerns and Teaching of Arius

Arius (d. ca. 336) was the "parish priest" of Baukalis in Alexandria, where he had the task of explaining Scripture. His intention was to be, not a philosopher who devised new theories, but an exegete and preacher. Nor was he coming to Christianity from the outside, like for instance the philosopher Celsus; rather, his concern was the correct understanding of Scripture. He belonged to the Church hierarchy, was a pupil of Lucian of Antioch the martyr (d. 312), a famous Antiochene exegete, and was appointed to his position by his bishop, the Patriarch of Alexandria.[17]

In his preaching he sought to counter the various heretical tendencies of his age, Modalism in particular, but also Gnostic conceptions. On one hand, he emphasized the autonomy of Christ in relation to the Father, and, on the other, he tried to safeguard the unity of God.[18] The basic principle and central point of the Alexandrian presbyter's theory is the scriptural text: "Hear, O Israel: the Lord our God is one Lord" (Deut 6:4). In his "creed", Arius declares his belief in "one single God, the only true God, who alone is immortal". Since God is one, everything that threatens his unique status must be rejected. Arius' God is alone, a solitary God, "who alone is wise, alone is good, alone is powerful".[19]

All his other statements follow from this basic principle. That is why nothing can be connatural to him. The Son can be his image only in the brokenness of radical dissimilarity. There remains, between God and everything that is not God, an unbridgeable abyss: the absolute difference between what is uncreated and what is created. On the side of the uncreated there is only God's eternal solitude. To safeguard God's uniqueness, Arius isolates God in a realm beyond all possible expression, beyond any positive definition. The only things that can be said

---

[17] On Arius: T. Böhm, *Die Christologie des Arius: Dogmengeschichtliche Überlegungen unter besonderer Berücksichtigung der Hellenisierungsfrage* (St. Ottilien, 1991); A. Grillmeier, *Christ in Christian Tradition*, vol. 1: *From the Apostolic Age to Chalcedon (451)*, 2nd ed. (Atlanta, 1975), pp. 219–32; F. Courth, *Der Gott der dreifaltigen Liebe*, AMATECA 6 (Paderborn, 1993), pp. 179–83; F. Courth, *Trinität: In der Schrift und Patristik*, HDG 2/1a (Freiburg im Breisgau, 1988), pp. 110–13; H.R. Drobner, *Lehrbuch der Patrologie* (Freiburg im Breisgau, 1994), pp. 197–200; É. Boularand, *L'Hérésie d'Arius et la "Foi" de Nicée*, 2 vols. (Paris, 1972).

[18] See the confession of faith of Arius in his letter to Alexander of Alexandria, in Athanasius, *Werke*, ed. Opitz, 3/1:12–13 (English text in Grillmeier, *Christ in Christian Tradition*, 1:225–26).

[19] Arius, according to Athanasius of Alexandria, *De synodis Arimini in Italia et Seleuciae in Isauria* 15 (ed. Opitz, 2/1:243).

of him are those that can be denied, by finite definition, in the case of creatures. "He alone has neither anyone the same as him nor anyone like him", and, consequentially, that is also true of the Logos. "He himself is invisible (ἀόρατος) to all who exist through the Son, and to the Son himself." Furthermore, "God himself, in so far as he is, is inexpressible for all (ἄρρητος). He is inexpressible (even) for the Son. For he (the Father) is what he is for himself, that is (he is) unutterable (ἄλεκτος), so that the Son cannot express any of the statements which encompass (God's being). For it is impossible for him to search out (ἐξιχνιάσαι) the Father who is in himself."[20] God is a Monas, in the sense in which Platonic philosophy speaks of God. The primary concern of Arian faith is to safeguard the absolute solitude of God.

To explain the role of the Logos, Arius makes use of the categories current in his time. So-called "Middle Platonism" understood the relationship between God and the world as being mediated through intermediary beings. Between the sole and transcendent God, an incommunicable Monad, and the realm of cosmic multiplicity stands the Logos, the principle of all multiplicity, the mediator between the One and the many. This concept, of course, conflicts with any creation-oriented thought.

The Arian explanation of the role of the Logos remains entirely within this Platonic scheme. The Logos was created by God with the creation of the world in view; he is clearly seen as a creature. At the same time, Arius takes up the Platonic notion that God has need of an intermediary being in order to create. The mediator is necessary because the creation can have no part "in the strong hand of the Father". Since creation cannot endure the power of God, there must be a mediator.

That is why he creates "first of all only the sole and only One, and calls this one Son and Logos, so that he may be the mediator; thus the rest could come to be through him."[21] This notion is completely alien to the Judaeo-Christian belief about creation. God the Creator creates everything of his own free will and gives each and every thing its being directly. For Arius, on the contrary, God needs a "buffer" to diminish his almighty power so that the creation can endure it. In the

---

[20] *The Blasphemies of Arius* 2; 12; 32–35, in Athanasius, *De Synodis* 15 (ed. Opitz, 2/1:242–43); partial English trans. in Grillmeier, *Christ in Christian Tradition*, 1:228).
[21] Athanasius, *Orationes contra Arianos* 2, 24 (ed. Tetz, 1:201).

Arian conception of creation, the world is the work of a subordinate servant, and that is also why it does not bear the traces of God; it is not transparent toward the Creator.

b. The First Council of Nicaea— Interpreting the Profession of Faith in Christ

The theories Arius was preaching soon met with opposition from his bishop, Alexander. His expulsion from the Church of Alexandria was followed by a schism in the Church throughout the empire. To clear up the disagreement, Emperor Constantine convened a synod of the bishops of the empire in the year 325 in Nicaea, the first ecumenical council.

Historically, the council took place in the context of the Constantinian "shift" (312). Only through the edict of Milan, convoked by a Christian emperor in a civilization that had become Christian, was an ecumenical council possible. Western Christendom begins with the edict of Milan, and classic Western theology with Nicaea. It seems reasonable to extend the parallel to the present day. As cautious as one must be with slogans such as "post-Constantinian era", it is surely no coincidence that in the present century the age of Western Christendom is drawing to a close and that at the same time the post-Nicaean classic theology is in an upheaval at least as great as during the time of the Nicene upheaval. That is why it is so important to try to define a position. At a time when the Church and Christianity are setting out into a new and unknown situation, into a new civilization that is no longer Constantinian, no longer Western, theology seeks a new articulation of faith that will correspond to this new civilization. That is why the inquiry into and careful scrutiny of what happened then, seems so important, since on the basis of this consideration we may in a meaningful way inquire about the possible restructuring of theology.

Arius places the Logos quite decidedly on the side of creatures. The Nicene Council is convinced that this choice leads away from the core of the Christian gospel. Christ stands on the side of God. Everything said in the New Testament about the origin, ancestry, and nature of Christ the Logos and Kyrios is to be interpreted on the basis of the eternal unity of Father and Son. This decision means that Christian theology has to ask itself definitively about the unity of God—a question that Arius avoids: How can there be a God in three Persons without calling God's unity into question? Just as the Arian variant had far-reaching consequences for faith and for life, so also does Nicene theology.

This is not the place to discuss the Nicene Creed (DH 125) as a whole.[22] Its basic features repeat the early creeds: the belief in the one God, the Father, the almighty, Creator of all things, in Christ and his work of salvation, in the Holy Spirit. The part that is important for Christology reads:

> [I believe] in one Lord Jesus Christ, the Son of God, the Only-Begotten, generated from the Father, that is, from the substance of the Father, God from God, Light from Light, true God from true God, begotten, not made, consubstantial with the Father (ὁμοούσιον τῷ Πατρί), through whom all things were made, those in heaven and those on earth. (DH 125)

For the question of Christology, the three clauses added in elucidation are, above all, significant. Nicaea confesses that Jesus Christ, the Son of God, is first of all "the Only-Begotten generated from the Father, that is, from the substance of the Father", as an explanation of what it means to say that the Son is from the Father (ἐκ τοῦ πατρός). Furthermore he is "begotten, not made" so as to make clear what "begotten" means—or rather, what it does not mean. Finally, it is said that he is "consubstantial with the Father". Here the key word of Nicaea, *homoousios*, is introduced. This concept is so important that it was deemed necessary, in the Latin translation, to add the clause "what is called ὁμοούσιος in Greek" (DH 125).

The early creeds were understood as being simply summaries of the apostolic kerygma, and thus wholly as a matter of course they used the language of the Bible.[23] We believe "in one Lord Jesus Christ, the Son of God, the Only-Begotten generated from the Father". There is only one God and one Lord (κύριος). That is the confession of faith that

[22] See on this subject Courth, *Der Gott der dreifaltigen Liebe*, pp. 186–89; Courth, *Trinität: In der Schrift und Patristik*, HDG 2/1a (Freiburg im Breisgau, 1988), pp. 113–19; J.N.D. Kelly, *Early Christian Creeds*, 3rd ed. (London, 1972), pp. 231–62; Grillmeier, *Christ in Christian Tradition* 1:264–70; Grillmeier, "Bekenntnisse der alten Kirche—das Nicaeno-Constantinopolitanum", in *Fragmente zur Christologie: Studien zum altkirchlichen Christusbild*, ed. Theresia Hainthaler, pp. 112–33 (Freiburg im Breisgau, 1997).
[23] H. de Lubac, *The Christian Faith: An Essay on the Structure of the Apostles' Creed*, trans. Brother Richard Arnandez, F.S.C. (San Francisco: Ignatius Press, 1986), pp. 261–317; T. Schneider, *Was wir glauben: Eine Auslegung des Apostolischen Glaubensbekenntnisses*, 2nd ed. (Düsseldorf, 1986), pp. 11–62.

stands in a monotheistic context already with Paul, "that 'an idol has no real existence' and that 'there is no God but one' " (1 Cor 8:4). And Paul goes on, "yet for us there is one God, the Father, from whom are all things and for whom we exist, and one Lord, Jesus Christ, through whom are all things and through whom we exist" (1 Cor 8:6).[24] This latter is the Son of God, the Only-Begotten generated from the Father. That expression is among the oldest christological profession formulas, and refers to Psalm 2:7: "You are my son, today I have begotten you" (cf. Acts 13:33; Heb 1:5); also of significance here is the reference back to Psalm 110.

A comparison with older creeds shows that these three additions were inserted deliberately. The decision had to be made either simply to repeat the old formulas or to go farther linguistically. These three additions introduce a new and unfamiliar note into the Creed, as these are philosophical terms (substance, οὐσία; consubstantial, ὁμοούσιος). This is consciously moving beyond biblical language. With the decision to admit even nonbiblical expressions, a step was taken that went far beyond the situation of the moment. A strict biblicism would have slammed the door on any theological development, and theology would henceforth not only have been declaring the same things, but also declaring them in the same terms. Instead of safeguarding the essential matter, it would have been holding fast to formulae. If we consider the declarations in detail, then the three additions in their literary characteristics can clearly be recognized as elucidations, as a more specific definition. This observation is important for the hermeneutic of the Council declarations.

THE ONLY–BEGOTTEN GENERATED FROM THE FATHER

The expression μονογενής (see Jn 1:14, 18; 3:16, 18; 1 Jn 4:9) probably corresponds to the Hebrew word *yachid*, which is as much as to say "only", "only-begotten", but can also mean "only-beloved". John 1:18 is especially important here: (literally) "the only-begotten Son, who is in the bosom of the Father". These two expressions articulate Jesus' eternal "being-with-God".[25] Most important is the fact, basic to the New Testament and peculiar to it, that Jesus calls God "Abba", "Father", that he is thus the Son. Yet what does this relationship

---

[24] See above, pp. 73–74.
[25] Schnackenburg, *Johannesevangelium* 1:246–47.

signify? It is an essential element in Jesus' understanding of himself and for his person. The question of his origins is an inner consequence of Jesus' revelation that God is his Father. The first attempts to say something theoretical about this begetting, about how the relationship came about, about how Jesus came to be, were undertaken by Gnostics. Irenaeus of Lyons (d. ca. 202), opposing them, still held that the exact way in which Jesus came into being was, and would remain, a mystery.[26] With Arius, however, this position changed. He said clearly that the Son came from the Father, just as every creature comes from the Father. And he was still more explicit: He came from the Father's will. God creates of his own free will. "Begotten" thus means created from nothing, like any other creature. The Council originally wanted to specify thus: "The Son was not drawn from nothing, but from God; he is the Word and the Wisdom, not a being that has been created or made, but the Father's own offspring."[27] But this biblical formulation was insufficient, since the Arians maintained in reply that this "from God" (ἐκ τοῦ Θεοῦ) was true of all creatures (cf. 1 Cor 8:6). Athanasius explains that the Council therefore decided in favor of the expression, "from the substance (οὐσία) of the Father" in order to express the fact that the way in which creatures come from God is essentially different from the coming forth of the Son. It cannot be said of any creature that it comes from the substance of the Father; rather, God creates it from nothingness in accordance with his will.[28] This explanation by Athanasius is an important aid to understanding. The additional phrase "that is, from the substance of the Father" is not intended as an independent philosophical declaration. It is, rather, meant as a rejection of the Arians' equating the begetting of the Son with the creation of creatures—which is made even clearer when it says, "begotten, not made". The Council wants to draw the dividing line differently from the way in which Arius does it. The Logos is on the same side as God, not on the side of the creatures.

BEGOTTEN, NOT MADE

Yet what does it mean that the Son is begotten? The starting point for Arius' reflections is the language of Scripture, of the New Testament.

---

[26] Irenaeus, *Adversus haereses* 2, 13, 3 (FChr 8/2:94-97); cf. the selection edited by H. U. von Balthasar, *Irenaeus, Gott in Fleisch und Blut: Ein Durchblick in Texten*, Christliche Meister 11 (Einsiedeln, 1981), pp. 24-29.

[27] Athanasius, *De decretis Nicaeni synodi* 19 (ed. Opitz, 2/1:15-16).

[28] Ibid., 19, 25 (ed. Opitz, 2/1:16, 20-21).

Here the following is the case: the γεννητός is begotten (from γεννάω, to beget or to bear); while the γενητός is the one who has become or who has come to be (from γίγνομαι, to become, to come into being). Just as the two terms are practically impossible to distinguish when pronounced, so similarly in human logic. Anything, anyone begotten or born has ultimately come into being, by human reckoning. God, however, has neither come into being nor been begotten. Thus Arius draws the conclusion that when Scripture says of the Son that he is begotten, is the only begotten Son, then he has also come into being and, thus, is not God.

God cannot beget an equally eternal Son of the same nature as himself, so Arius maintains, otherwise we would be asserting that within God there are two similar eternal principles. He is unable to imagine the begetting of the eternal Son as a purely spiritual and immanent process of engendering: "Before he [the Son] was begotten or created . . . he did not exist, since he was not unbegotten."[29] God first became Father when he produced the Son. The name "Father" cannot therefore refer to the substantial and eternal characteristic nature of God, just as the name "Son" does not reveal an eternal relationship but merely denotes the particular quality of a creature that God has adopted as a son. The following text of Arius clearly articulates the perspective of this radical distinction between God and the Word:

> Know that the Monad was; but that the Dyad (duality) was not, until it came into being. So long as the Son does not exist, God is not Father. Before, the Son was not (but he came into being through the will of the Father); he is the only God who has come to be, and each of the two is alien to the other.[30]

Athanasius exposes the weaknesses of Arian speculation with a sure instinct for that existential content of the Christian creed that is relevant to salvation.[31] He shows that behind the views of Arius lies a fundamental misinterpretation of the transcendence of God. If we wish to understand what the word "begotten" means here, then we have to look at the person about whom it is said:

> It is clear that God does not beget as men beget but as God begets. For God does not imitate man; rather, men were themselves called fathers

[29] Arius, *Letter to Eusebius of Nicomedia* (in Athanasius, *Werke*, ed. Opitz, 3/1:5).
[30] *The Blasphemies of Arius* 19–22, in Athanasius, *De Synodis* 15 (ed. Opitz, 2/1:243).
[31] On Athanasius' Christology, see Grillmeier, *Christ in Christian Tradition* 1:308–28.

of their own children on account of God, who is in the real sense, and alone truly, Father of his Son; for "from him every fatherhood in heaven and on earth is named" (Eph 3:15).[32]

Calling God "Father" does not mean attributing something contingent to him, as is the case with man. God *is* Father—he is the only one who is truly Father. Christ *is* Son, from all eternity, that is to say, before all creation, and that is why he is "not created". Athanasius usually argued, against the Arians, that if God had not always had his Wisdom and his Power (as Scripture itself refers to the Word) at his side, then there would have been a time when he was without wisdom and power.[33] "The Father alone is the origin of everything. Yet in this origin there is also the Son, as the Gospel proclaims; of his nature, he is what the origin is. For God is the origin, and the Word that is in the beginning is God"[34]—that is how Gregory of Nyssa (d. 395) paraphrases the opening of the Gospel of John a few decades later, in the spirit of the Nicene Creed. The expression "from the substance of the Father" therefore means that the scriptural designation "only begotten Son of the Father" is appropriately interpreted only if we understand it as meaning that the Son comes "from the substance of the Father" and is therefore "not made", that is, not created.

CONSUBSTANTIAL WITH THE FATHER

The third addition is the most controversial. Christ, the Son, is "consubstantial with the Father". Here, in contrast to early Christian creeds, it is not a matter of statements about the work of Christ, the economy [of salvation], but also about the relation of Christ to the Father in itself. The question is, who the Kyrios and Son of God really is: this concerns the "immanent Trinity". The three parallel formulas that precede this addition—"God from God, Light from Light, true God from true God"—are not new at Nicaea. They are already used in earlier creeds, for instance in the creed that Eusebius of Caesarea (d. 339) submitted to the Council as his baptismal creed.[35] They are not indeed used word for word in Scripture, but are certainly rooted in Johannine terminology. "God from God" and "Light from Light" were equally

---

[32] Athanasius, *Orationes contra Arianos* 1, 23 (ed. Tetz 1:133).

[33] Athanasius, *Contra Gentes* 46 (SC 18bis, pp. 206–8).

[34] Gregory of Nyssa, *Contra Eunomium* 3, 6, 22 (ed. Jaeger 2:193).

[35] DH 40. On the creed of Eusebius, see Kelly, *Early Christian Creeds*, pp. 181–83; Grillmeier, *Christ in Christian Tradition* 1:266.

acceptable for Arians. In the sense used in Middle Platonism, the Logos could be understood as a "second God" (δεύτερος Θεός), as did Numenius of Apamaea (d. ca. 200), as divine through having a share in divinity, and yet nonetheless created.[36] But the third dual assertion clearly turns against it: "true God from true God". The one thing a creature's participation in divinity cannot do is to make it a true God. All these statements have as their content the singular connection, the unique relationship of Jesus with the Father. Just as "from the substance of the Father" is intended to say something about the origin of the Son, so "consubstantial" is meant to say something about the nature of Christ, whereas the emphasis laid upon divinity, upon being consubstantial, is pointedly directed against the idea of participation. Chalcedon would amplify that: Jesus Christ is consubstantial with the Father and consubstantial with us men.[37] Here, however, the *homoousios* is introduced in order to exclude any evasion through a figurative interpretation. "God from God, Light from Light, true God from true God"—all this is to be understood in its full meaning. And thus the two assertions, "begotten, not made", and "consubstantial with the Father" seemed to be dialectically ordered to each other. The first is intended to exclude the view of the Son as a creature; the second, to prevent any gradation, any question of more or less within God. The point of view is always that of biblical exegesis. The statements about the divinity of Christ are not being understood in accordance with the Scriptures if "from the Father" is read as meaning anything other than "consubstantial with the Father".

But what meaning does the concept of "substance" (οὐσία, *substantia*), and consubstantial (ὁμοούσιος, *consubstantialis*) have in the Council's text? This concept already had a particular philosophical meaning before Nicaea. Although in the early fourth century the concept of substance already had a long philosophical tradition behind it, the matter-of-factness with which the Council appropriates it may seem surprising. The concept of being, of substance, originally had a place in everyday language and still has a place there today. "Going to the substance", "substantial", "essential" are synonyms for "important", "of special significance".

When Nicaea speaks of substance, then, that means that a philosophical term is being given a new field of meaning and that its previous

---

[36] See Grillmeier, *Christ in Christian Tradition* 1:225.
[37] See below, chap. 2:3c, "The Creed of Chalcedon".

range of meaning is thereby extended. That is not surprising. Aristotle derives the concept of substance from analytical observation of reality. The fact that there must be something like an ultimate subject, to which other things are attributed, may be concluded from language as well as from observation; and equally the fact that we may meaningfully speak of a highest, supreme, an absolutely final subject (God).

Aristotle only defines the ultimate subject of all statements as being, substance (οὐσία), as distinguished from conditions and qualifications that could be said of it: these he calls accidents (τὰ συμβεβήκοτα). These cannot exist in themselves, but only in and with respect to something that is not separate from them but, rather, is experienced through them and in them; and only concerning this can it ever meaningfully be asked, referring to the thing in itself, what it is. In a further logical definition, Aristotle gives a name to the πρώτη οὐσία, literally "the first being", "the first substance", and by that he means an individual being existing in and for itself: Peter, Paul, this person—insofar as he is the ultimate subject of all the statements that may be made about him. Aristotle distinguishes from this the δεύτερα οὐσία, the secondary beings or substances, insofar as a term expresses a collectivity of being: that is, general terms and terms of classification.[38] Both these meanings are inadequate for trinitarian theology. The "first substance" cannot be meant here, otherwise no distinction could be expressed about the Father and the Son; it would only be possible to speak of the Trinity in a modalist sense. If, on the contrary, we conceived of the being of God in the second sense, then "divinity" would be no more than a term of classification, and Father, Son, and Holy Spirit would be three divine individuals.

A being, an οὐσία that is one and yet has three attributive subjects, is nowhere to be met with in philosophical considerations. Talk about the triune God, which has its basis in revelation, can only be brought into harmony with the concept of being if the concept itself undergoes a specifically Christian change. That is also true for the use of the concept of being by the Council of Nicaea.[39]

Against the background of Arianism, the intention of Nicaea's statement can be clearly perceived. Even the wording of this formulation is directed against the confession of the clever Arius, who had alleged:

---

[38] Aristotle, *Categories* 2a–4b.
[39] See J. Halfwassen, "Substanz; Substanz/Akzidens I", in *Historisches Wörterbuch der Philosophie* 10 (1988), pp. 495–507.

"He [Christ] is not equal [to God] or consubstantial (ὁμοούσιος) with him."[40] According to Nicaea, the Son cannot be understood as a creature of God, nor can he be an intermediate being. He can therefore only be God himself, and that in such a way that God's unique divine existence is not thereby destroyed but receives an entirely different meaning corresponding to his divinity, just as he has revealed himself. The Fathers of Nicaea intend to indicate this sense with the word *homoousios*. Nicaea believed that it could only do justice to the living unity of relationship between Jesus and the Father, which can be observed in the New Testament as constitutive for Jesus' action in revelation and salvation, by defining Jesus' relationship to the Father as that of the Son who is consubstantial with him.

c. Beginning or End? The Hellenization Theory

The Council of Nicaea formulates its Creed in terms taken from the Greek philosophy of its time and, in doing so, elevates these to the status of dogmatic formulas. Arius had also made use of such terms for his teaching. Is it not the case that a form of thought that no longer corresponds to biblical faith has thereby entered into Christianity? Are the councils part of a process that began when Greek philosophy laid its cuckoo's egg in the clean nest of primitive Christianity—that egg which, having meanwhile hatched, has by now thrown out of the nest all that remained of the genuine, "unhellenized" Christianity? This allegation has been raised often in the history of theology, most clearly by Adolf von Harnack, who advanced it in his textbook on the history of dogma under the term "Hellenization of Christianity". The way back to true faith could then only be found by a process of de-Hellenizing.[41]

THE HELLENIZATION OR THE
DE-HELLENIZATION OF CHRISTIANITY?

Formulas like this are too simplistic to be right. They are, however, sufficiently plausible to be repeatedly and effectively promoted. Alois Grillmeier (d. 1998), among others, devoted several studies to this

---

[40] *The Blasphemies of Arius* 9, in Athanasius, *De Synodis* 15 (ed. Opitz, 2/1:242); see also TzT D4, 1, text 90, p. 132.

[41] On the presentation of the theory of Hellenization in the various editions of this textbook, see K.-H. Neufeld, *Adolf von Harnack: Theologie als Suche nach der Kirche: "Tertium genus Ecclesia"*, KKTS (Paderborn, 1977); T. Böhm, *Christologie des Arius*, pp. 16–23.

question that have become classic.[42] His principal work, *Jesus der Christus*,[43] consists of a protracted quarrel with this theory. Thanks to the many detailed analyses undertaken in the course of his long life of research, Grillmeier is able to draw a clearly differentiated picture of this problem, from which only the most important results will be cited here.

The Hellenization theory assumes that talk about the triune God, and likewise about the Incarnation of God, first originated from the encounter of the gospel of Jesus Christ with the philosophy of the Graeco-Roman world and was distorted by it. In fact, it is said, this was only an attempt to express the significance of Jesus Christ in the language of the time, in a philosophical, metaphorical, or poetic way. In plain language, uttered in "direct" speech, that means that "Jesus was not, on this view, the second person of a divine Trinity, . . . but a man responding totally to divine grace and doing the will of God."[44]. It is imperative, therefore, to return to a stage before this process began, in which the "genuine kerygma" was not yet hidden beneath Hellenism.

The debate about Hellenization is concerned not merely with historical questions, but above all with the interpretation of history; not only with "genesis" but above all "validity". The historical question

---

[42] Above all, A. Grillmeier, "Hellenisierung-Judaisierung des Christentums als Deuteprinzipien der Geschichte des kirchlichen Dogmas", in *Mit ihm und in ihm: Christologische Forschungen und Perspektiven* (Freiburg im Breisgau, 1975), pp. 423–88; Grillmeier, "Christus licet vobis invitis deus: Ein Beitrag zur Diskussion über die Hellenisierung der christlichen Botschaft", in *Kerygma und Logos*, Festschrift for Andresen, ed. A.M. Ritter, pp. 227–57 (Göttingen, 1979), republished in A. Grillmeier, *Fragmente zur Christologie: Studien zum altkirchlichen Christusbild*, ed. Theresia Hainthaler, pp. 81–111 (Freiburg im Breisgau, 1997).

[43] A. Grillmeier, *Jesus der Christus im Glauben der Kirche*, vol. 1: *Von der Apostolischen Zeit bis zum Konzil von Chalcedon (451)*, 2nd ed. (Freiburg im Breisgau, 1986) [trans. by John Bowden as *Christ in Christian Tradition*, vol. 1: *From the Apostolic Age to Chalcedon*, 2nd rev. ed. (Atlanta: John Knox Press, 1975)]; vol. 2/1: *Das Konzil von Chalcedon (451): Rezeption und Widerspruch (451–518)* (Freiburg im Breisgau, 1986) [trans. by Pauline Allen and John Cawte as vol. 2: *From the Council of Chalcedon (451) to Gregory the Great (590–604)*, pt. 1: *Reception and Contradiction* (Atlanta: John Knox Press, 1987); vol. 2/2:*Die Kirche von Konstantinopel im 6. Jahrhundert* (Freiburg im Breisgau, 1989) [trans. by John Cawte and Pauline Allen as vol. 2/2: *The Church of Constantinople in the Sixth Century* (Louisville, Ky.: John Knox Press, 1995); vol. 2/3: *Die Kirchen von Jerusalem und Antiochien nach 451 bis 600* (Freiburg im Breisgau, 2002); vol. 2/4: *Die Kirche von Alexandrien mit Nubien und Äthiopien nach 451* (Freiburg im Breisgau, 1990) [trans. by O.C. Dean as vol. 2/4: *The Church of Alexandria with Nubia and Ethiopia after 451* (Louisville, Ky.: John Knox Press, 1996)]; in preparation: vol. 2/5: *Die Kirche des lateinischen Westens im 6. Jahrhundert*; vol. 2/6: *Die Kirchen in Persien, Armenien und Georgien*; now ed. by Theresia Hainthaler.

[44] J. Hick, *The Metaphor of God Incarnate* (London, 1993); quotation p. 108; see esp. pp. 27–46 and 99–111.

leads to the question of truth. The Hellenization theory sees in the trend toward "Hellenization of the Christian message" the common denominator of the many Christologies in the early Church. Against that, we must ask: How can it be maintained that "the belief in Jesus of Nazareth as God, Son of God, and Kyrios first *arose* at all only in the interest of adapting the Christian message to the Greek understanding when, on the other hand, it is a fact that Hellenistic philosophers experienced real difficulty vis-à-vis the Christians precisely because the latter held the crucified Nazarene to be God and Kyrios or the true Basileus and emperor of the world"?[45] Why was it in particular that the philosophers of Middle Platonism, whose system would lead one to expect them to be especially open to the Christian teaching about the Incarnation of the Logos, had such "difficulties in accepting the Incarnation of the Logos in Jesus of Nazareth"?[46] The philosophical criticism of Christianity shows that for most philosophers "to describe and worship a man as God or Son of God was an unacceptable contradiction—especially one who had been crucified."[47] On this point one should read with what caustic sarcasm the philosopher *Celsus* pursued the worship of the Crucified by Christians.[48] That does not, of course, mean that there was no "process of Hellenization" at all, in Christianity. Grillmeier shows that the reality is far more subtle. Both tendencies, that of "Hellenizing" and that of "de-Hellenizing", exist within Christian theology itself. The two main questions of Christian theology, the problem of monotheism and the doctrine of the Incarnation, demanded philosophical reflection. That could happen only if Christian theologians became involved with the realm of Greek thought and brought about an encounter between the Christian message and Greek thought.

ORTHODOXY AND HERESY AS
A PROCESS OF DIFFERENTIATION

The phenomenon of heresy and its separation from orthodoxy played a decisive role in this long process of clarification. The Council of Nicaea is repeatedly cited by Grillmeier as a turning point that exemplifies this. He demonstrates in detail that the rejection of Arius' teaching was imperative because the Christian message had been "acutely"

---

[45] Grillmeier, "Christus licet vobis invitis deus", p. 227.

[46] Ibid., p. 232.

[47] Ibid., p. 234.

[48] See Origen, *Contra Celsum* 6, 74 (SC 147:364–66).

Hellenized in it: "With Arius, the process of Hellenization reached an unmistakable climax. The Greek view of God and the world was being consciously adopted, and this in terms of a reshaping that changed the baptismal creed".[49] The denial of the divinity of Christ, reducing him to a kind of angelic being, separated from the solitary and unapproachable God by an unbridgeable abyss—that all takes place in Arius through the unambiguous dominance exercised over the Christian creed by a particular philosophical conception.

"Arius had set a mark. He forced the Church to think about her own kerygma in a more fundamental way and to reappraise the process of engagement that had been underway since her message had encountered the Greek *logos*. . . . Reflection about her own message demanded a de-Hellenizing wherever the Hellenization had gone too far."[50] The Council of Nicaea was a significant milestone in this process. The *homoousios*, the profession of faith in the consubstantial divinity of Christ, in the "God from God . . . , true God from true God", meant something new, something that pointed the way beyond all of Greek philosophy's categories of thought. Athanasius calls Christ "the consubstantial image" of the Father. That God should have an image of himself that exhibits no differences, no diminishment in comparison with its original, is inconceivable within the existing categories of Greek philosophy.[51] Seen in this light, the theology of the Trinity developed in the fourth century is in fact an acute case of de-Hellenizing.

In his interpretation of the encyclical *Fides et Ratio*, Joseph Cardinal Ratzinger has pointed out another important point on this subject. Christianity's encounter with a culture occurs not only in such a way that the culture opens up for religion a way to reach people. At the same time, the culture itself is taken into the dynamic of what is Christian and is changed from within. That is already the case in the Old Testament. "The faith of Israel signifies a continual transcending of the limits of its own culture into the wide-open spaces of truth that is common to all."[52] Faith also militates against "what belongs to us"

---

[49] Grillmeier, "Christus licet vobis invitis deus", p. 250.

[50] Ibid., p. 251.

[51] See C. Schönborn, *God's Human Face: The Christ-Icon*, trans. Lothar Krauth (San Francisco: Ignatius Press, 1994), pp. 8–14.

[52] J. Ratzinger, *Truth and Tolerance: Christian Belief and World Religions*, pt. 2, chap. 2, sec. 3: "Faith, Truth, and Culture: Reflections Prompted by the Encyclical *Fides et Ratio*", trans. Henry Taylor (San Francisco: Ignatius Press, 2004), pp. 183–209; this quotation p. 199. This

and, thus, leads the believer away from himself toward a more profound truth, to God. This model applies even more to the encounter of Christianity with Greek culture and philosophy. Here, too, something new arose from the encounter; faith burst open philosophy and led it toward the truth in such a way that it transcended itself.

> The Fathers did not just mix into the gospel a static and self-contained Greek culture. They could take up a dialogue with Greek philosophy and could make it an instrument of the gospel, wherever in the Hellenistic world the search for God had brought into being a self-criticism of that world's own culture and its own thought.[53]

Yet Pope John Paul II also formulates a supplementary criterion: "In engaging great cultures for the first time, the Church cannot abandon what she has gained from her inculturation in the world of Greco-Latin thought." This event, the inculturation that took place at that time, forms part of God's plan of salvation for man. On that account, however, it also remains significant for the continuing history of the Church, in particular wherever this process starts over again, thus, wherever Christianity encounters other cultures. "To reject this heritage would be to deny the providential plan of God who guides his Church down the paths of time and history."[54] The Graeco-Latin element can no longer be imagined away from the form into which the Church has grown.[55]

The situation of Christians in their own time is never a dualistic one: truth here, error there. The attempts made by the theologians of the early Church speak quite clearly. It is not simply a matter of rejecting everything else in order to put Christianity in its place; rather, it is a matter of attempting to discern the voice of the Logos in the

---

section originally published as: "Culture and Truth: Reflections on the Encyclical", *Origins*, vol. 28, no. 36 (1999): 625–631; also in *Sacerdos*, no. 26 (March–April 2000): 19–28; in German, "Die Einheit des Glaubens und die Vielfalt der Kulturen: Reflexionen im Anschluß an die Enzyklika 'Fides et ratio'", *Theologie und Glaube* 89 (1999): 141–52; in *Wahrheit, die uns trägt* (Paderborn, 1999), pp. 24–40; and in *Communio* 28 (1999): 289–305 (November 17, 1998); see also: Ratzinger, *Principles of Catholic Theology: Building Stones for a Fundamental Theology*, trans. Sister Mary Frances McCarthy, S.N.D. (San Francisco: Ignatius Press, 1987), pp. 355–64.

[53] Ratzinger, *Truth and Tolerance*, p. 200.

[54] These two quotations from Pope John Paul II, encyclical *Fides et Ratio*, no. 72.

[55] On this whole subject, see the exchange of letters from 1928 between Erik Peterson and Adolf von Harnack, and also Peterson's epilogue, published in: E. Peterson, *Ausgewählte Schriften*, vol. 1: *Theologische Traktate*, ed. Barbara Nichtweiss (Würzburg, 1994), pp. 177–94.

Greeks' search for truth. This openness is inherent in the catholicity of the Christ-event itself: If all the treasures of wisdom and knowledge are hidden in Christ (cf. Col 2:3), then everything the Greeks accumulated by way of knowledge and wisdom must also be able to be rediscovered in Christ, must be "kept safe" in him. Only on the basis of this openness can we understand why Christianity did not remain a sect, like the Qumran community. At the same time it shows that those who spurn philosophy are sometimes close in substance to the Qumran group.

At the same time, however, the encounter of Greek thought with Christianity is a crisis, a judgment. Paul says of this crisis that with the weapons of God we have "power to destroy strongholds. We destroy arguments and every proud obstacle to the knowledge of God and take every thought captive to obey Christ" (2 Cor 10:4–5). The Arian crisis is also such a crisis between Greek wisdom and the wisdom of Christ, and it made a deep impression on all ecclesiastical, theological, and liturgical development.

The history of Christology in the early Church is one of a confrontation, often painful and not always conducted in a civilized way, between the claims of the kerygma and the pressures exerted by the various ancient philosophical systems. The "Hellenization", which (pace Harnack) should be seen as the fruitful encounter of Christianity with Greek philosophy, is only one side of this. At the same time there is always a new dawn occurring, progress in philosophy and in culture itself, another step on the path toward truth.

THE IMAGE OF CHRIST AND
IMPERIAL POLITICS AFTER NICAEA

In 312, five years before the outbreak of the Arian conflict, the Edict of Milan had brought the "Constantinian shift". This event is often interpreted, in a rather undifferentiated and oversimplified way, as meaning that the Church sold herself to the imperial power. The Church became an imperial church, and the era of Constantine was the beginning of this process, which was to determine the fate of the Church for centuries. But how far did the influence of the emperor upon the Church actually extend? In *Das Christusdogma*, Erich Fromm sees a parallel between the Constantinian shift and the dogma of Nicaea.[56] The divinized Christ

---

[56] E. Fromm, *Das Christusdogma und andere Essays*, 3rd ed. (Munich, 1990).

appears as an instrument of power for a Church sold to the divinized emperor and his interests of state. Out of the revolutionary Jesus of the primitive Church comes the enthroned Christ who demands obedient submission, a symbol of domination. This criticism is justified, insofar as the Arian conflict transformed the image of Christ. And there is no doubt that imperial art exercised a strong influence on Christian iconography. Indeed, the development of Christian art is comprehensible only on the basis of the Nicene Creed,[57] for if the Son were only a creature, albeit the first among creatures, then venerating the image of Christ would be idolatry, since worship is due only to God.

A more nuanced view of the historical events, however, allows these to appear in an essentially different light. If the emperor had at first hoped, after the condemnation of Arius at the Council of Nicaea in 325, that the dispute had been settled, as early as the Synod of Antioch in 330 a clear alliance had developed between imperial politics and Arianism. It is also worth bearing in mind, in this connection, that the two "court bishops", Eusebius of Caesarea and Eusebius of Nicomedia (d. 341), were convinced supporters of Arius. Constantine, indeed, probably scarcely understood what the theological issue was in this dispute, but he could see that the Arian picture of God corresponded better to his conception of the role of the emperor and of his role vis-à-vis the Church than did Athanasius' trinitarian image of God. His cult of the *summus deus*, God most High, whose servant and instrument Constantine believed himself to be in the task of extending his providence over all peoples, was more in line with the Arian picture of God as an absolute sovereign who remained invisible behind the veil, like an oriental ruler, at once unapproachably distant and all-powerfully present. He has his sacrosanct will proclaimed by his herald. The Arian Logos is just such a herald, a servant of the invisible emperor, who can and may do no more himself than communicate the will, impenetrable even to him, of the sovereign. The picture of God behind the Nicene Creed, on the other hand, recognized God as being, not someone who conceals himself in unapproachable majesty behind his almighty power, but someone whose power consists precisely in being able to reveal himself, to impart himself. If God has an eternal Son, then God's divinity is such that it does not exclude the divinity

---

[57] A. Grabar, *Die Kunst des frühen Christentums: Von den ersten Zeugnissen christlicher Kunst bis zur Zeit Theodosius I* (Munich, 1967).

of Christ, but facilitates it, reveals it, connotes it. But in that case, the role of the emperor can no longer be understood exclusively as reflecting an unapproachable, incomprehensible, absolute most High God. Constantine's struggle, and that of his son Constantius, with the "orthodox" bishops is concerned with something more than just politics; it also concerns the freedom of the Church, particularly in an empire that was officially Christian.[58]

If one would like to see more clearly what the Arian variant of Christianity would have looked like if Arianism had been victorious, one should study Eusebius of Caesarea,[59] the Church historian, the biographer and panegyrist of Emperor Constantine. Eusebius' merit is based on his historical works, above all on his *Historia ecclesiastica*.[60] His theology proves to be a Christianity completely adapted to the thought of the time.[61] Jesus Christ is the herald of a God who resembles the emperor, a pale reflection of the unapproachable brilliance of his glory. The Incarnation takes place when the herald, the Logos of God, clothes himself with mortal flesh so as to speak to what is earthly through this instrument. This earthly raiment, however, is itself but a distant reflection of the beauty of the Logos. It was this earthly garment that suffered on the Cross, not the Logos itself, who is no more nor less perturbed by the suffering of his flesh than is a harpist when the strings of his instrument break. This Christianity has truly been Hellenized.

---

[58] H. Rahner, "Die Konstantinische Wende", in *Abendland: Reden und Aufsätze* (Freiburg im Breisgau, 1966), pp. 189–98; see H. Rahner, *Kirche und Staat im frühen Christentum: Dokumente aus acht Jahrhunderten und ihre Deutung* (Munich, 1961), pp. 73–201.

[59] Cf. V. Twoomey, *Apostolikos Thronos: The Primacy of Rome as Reflected in the Church History of Eusebius and the Historico-Apologetic Writings of Saint Athanasius the Great*, MBTh 49 (Münster, 1982), pp. 346–476.

[60] Eusebius of Caesarea, *Ecclesiastical History*, vol. 1, ed. Loeb, trans. Kirsopp Lake (Cambridge, Mass. and London, 1926); vol. 2, ed. Loeb, trans. J. E. L. Oulton (Cambridge, Mass., and London, 1932).

[61] See A. Weber, 'ARXH: *Ein Beitrag zur Christologie des Eusebius von Caesarea* (Rome, 1965); E. Peterson, *Der Monotheismus als politisches Problem: Ein Beitrag zur Geschichte der politischen Theologie im Imperium Romanum* (Leipzig, 1935) = *Ausgewählte Schriften*, vol. 1: *Theologische Traktate*, ed. Barbara Nichtweiss (Würzburg, 1994), pp. 23–81; see on this: Barbara Nichtweiss, *Erik Peterson: Neue Sicht auf Leben und Werk* (Freiburg im Breisgau, 1992).

THE CRITERIA AND LIMITATIONS
OF UNITY IN MULTIPLICITY

What were the criteria by which the early Church designated certain Christologies as heretical? What constitutes the unity of the orthodox Christologies—which are still quite diverse among themselves? The various references to this question are among the most important things to be gained by reading Cardinal Grillmeier's great work. His basic idea is that all Christologies are ultimately measured by one yardstick: their fidelity to the kerygma. In the great crises during the development of Christian doctrine, it was always by reference back to the kerygma, the simple formula of tradition, that orthodoxy was demonstrated.

Is that not just deferring the question? Who can say what a correct reference back to the kerygma looks like? Does not everyone, even heretics, refer to the kerygma as the basis of his Christology? Who would ever say that he wanted to teach something different from the original proclamation? Grillmeier says:

> that the church grasped the totality of the picture of Christ more in a kind of spiritual intuition than in words and formulas. For this reason expressions could vary even to the point of formulas which apparently contradicted each other. The church measured newly emerging doctrines as much by her intuition as by her formula and made from them new fixed forms for her proclamation.[62]

This "intuition", this intuitive comprehension, precedes all speculative interpretation and is the ultimate yardstick for any possible correction of it. The *intuitus fidei* is shared both by the "simple believer" and by the learned theologian. On the basis of this intuition, both proclamation and theology attain that certitude which alone makes understandable an undeviating adherence to faith in the one Lord Jesus Christ. How does Grillmeier understand this "intuition"? To start with, it is above all the unique dynamic-creative impulse of experience of and with Jesus Christ. This experience is itself the basis on which the Word becomes Scripture. In addition, it is "condensed" in those simple forms of professions of faith which form the basis of the believing community from the New Testament onward. And finally this intuition is kept

---

[62] Grillmeier, *Christ in Christian Tradition* 1:36.

alive by the living relationship with *Christus praesens* in the liturgy, in prayer, in service.[63]

Irenaeus of Lyons referred to this basis, simple and complex at the same time, which is prior to all reflective theology, as the "rule of truth". Tertullian talks about the "rule of faith". Is there not a danger, concerning such a basis, of its being misused? How can intuition be tested? Do not orthodoxy and heresy become arbitrary categories applied according to political or other such requirements? This suspicion is repeatedly voiced, especially when it is a matter of drawing the boundaries of orthodoxy. Against that, it may of course be argued that there can only be unity of belief in Jesus Christ through all the differences of periods and cultures if there is a point of unity that is prior to all these differences and that defines their limits.

The history of Christology in the early Church, which Alois Grillmeier has traced expertly, teaches us today (besides much else) this one thing, that such a point of unity cannot be drawn up on the basis of any one particular philosophical system (whether ancient or modern) or, on the other hand, on that of a historical reconstruction by exegesis that claims to be able to say, thanks to its own methods, how things "really" were in the beginning. Such attempts to look for the point of unity for belief and proclamation "outside", in a philosophical or historical construct, would ultimately incapacitate the faithful and make them dependent upon specialists. Yet even the Church's Magisterium, as such, cannot in a manner of speaking "from itself" designate or dictate this point of unity. For the Magisterium, too, just like exegesis and theology in their different ways, has as its final point of reference, as its source and criterion, the rule of faith. The Magisterium checks whether certain developments in theology are in accordance with the rule of faith. It proclaims the faith in fidelity to the rule of faith, a fidelity that must constantly be renewed. Exegesis and systematic theology, for their part, can only constructively interpret Scripture and meet contemporary questions if their research and reflection grow out of a living contact with the rule of faith. Finally, the "simple" believer, who possesses neither a teaching nor a research office, has not a bit less access to the common basis of faith than bishops and theologians. For the rule of faith is not reserved for either an office or

---

[63] Ibid., pp. 4–7 and 34–36.

a level of knowledge. It is rather, as a formulated confession of faith (creed) and simultaneously as a view of faith grasped intuitively, the shared basis that, from the early Church onward, makes possible the unity in multiplicity of Christologies and theologies[64] and that even today holds together the frequently bewildering diversity of forms of expression in theology and Church and lays down their limits.

SUMMARY

The Arian problem is that of a mistaken hermeneutic of belief. The axiom is: God is one. It is on that basis that all statements about the Logos are interpreted. If God is one, and only one, then statements in Scripture attributing divinity to Christ must be so interpreted as not to call into question the fundamental axiom; such statements can therefore be true only in a figurative sense. The same hermeneutic question will be at issue at the Council of Nicaea: By what criteria, with what preconceptions, are the christological statements of the New Testament to be interpreted? In this context, the question is: Is the Logos God or creature? By Arius the question is clearly answered: The Logos is creature. Nicaea lays down as dogma the alternative solution. To this day, the Creed of Nicaea is *the* confession of faith for the Church. The question of what criteria brought about this solution is both justified and necessary.

The world of human experience is inadequate for making statements about God in his trinitarian fullness. God is in a way a community of identical nature that we can perceive only in faint images. Yet however imperfect the language may be, the concepts involved are not left to arbitrary choice; rather, God himself is in fact being addressed; our words touch on the reality of God, yet at the same time they do not comprehend him (cf. CCC 39–43). The *homoousios* is a valid and definitive statement. We can no longer go back behind the Nicene Creed. Then it was a matter of making a statement about God, who has revealed himself to men and who is also accessible to Greek thought. Nicaea is not a Hellenization of Christianity; rather, Greek thinking is extended, is changed as a result of the message of salvation. Inculturation is taking place. At Nicaea, a concept from philosophy was

---

[64] See the fine study by B. Hägglund, "Die Bedeutung der 'regula fidei' als Grundlage theologischer Aussagen", *Studia Theologica* (Lund) 12 (1958): 144.

not abruptly introduced into the language of faith; rather, the concept received a new content from its new context. Theological concepts like "image", "nature", and even "person" are not immediately clear but signify theologically a different reality from that in their original philosophical or everyday context: a reality by which they are formed anew.

There is a profound change in theology after Nicaea. From this post-Nicene restructuring arose what can be called "classical trinitarian theology". The theology of the three Cappadocians stands in this line of development and also the trinitarian theology of Augustine (d. 430), who then shaped the whole of Western theology. The Council of Chalcedon (451) was not the first great change. That is part of post-Nicene theology: the doctrine of two natures is unthinkable without the Nicene *homoousios*.

3. The Implications of the Nicene Creed

Time and again, in anti-Arian polemics, two arguments emerge with particular clarity. If the Logos were not God, then he could not reveal God. If Christ were not God, then God would not have spoken to us, would not have disclosed himself. In that case, our knowledge of God would never have reached beyond our own limitations. The second argument that the Greek Church Fathers often advance against the Arians is that the Son of God became man upon earth in order that man might be able to enter into the realm of God. If Christ were not God, then he would not have been able to bring us "divinization". To complete this chapter, we will investigate these two arguments.

a. Christ as the Perfect Image of the Father

The Arians maintained that the fact that Christ was referred to as the "image of the invisible God" (Col 1:15) demonstrated that Christ was less than God. In saying this, they assumed a Greek or Hellenistic concept of image to be self-evident, for in Greek thought the image as a matter of course meant something less in comparison with the original it copied. The Arian Logos of God is the image of God in the sense in which Greek philosophy conceived the image: it is a reflection, a faint reproduction of an unattainable original. Since it belongs to the changeable world of what is visible, it is impossible for it to capture the entire fullness of the simple and unchanging original.[65]

When Christ was created by God, "drawn out of nothingness",[66] he received from the Father—according to Arius—the gift of being "the image of God". It is thus only within the limited measure of his own creatureliness that the Son can be the image of God: "For it is clear that one who has a beginning cannot conceive or experience as he is one who has no beginning."[67] Since the Son is incapable of "searching out the Father, who exists for himself (even the Son himself has not seen his essence)",[68] so much the less can he render the Father visible, be his *perfect* image. He is thus also unable to be the perfect revelation of the Father. He can reveal no more than he is himself: a creature. The God of Arius remains enclosed within his impenetrable solitude; he is incapable of sharing his own life fully with the Son. In his concern for the transcendence of God, Arius turns the sole and most high God into a prisoner of his own greatness.

Athanasius, in contrast, maintains the paradox of a perfect image, an image in which nothing of the perfection of the original is lacking: God has an image of himself that is altogether his equal in dignity and in nature. For Athanasius, that is the quite concrete meaning of Christ's words: "I and the Father are one" (Jn 10:30), and "All that the Father has is mine" (Jn 16:15).

For the Son is really in the Father, as we can understand, since the whole being of the Son is the Father's own substance, like the rays from a light and the stream from a spring; so that anyone who sees the Son is also seeing what is the Father's own and understands that the existence of the Son, just as it is from the Father, is thus within the Father.

Yet the Father is also in the Son, because what comes from the Father and is his own is the Son, just as the sun is in its rays, the spirit in the word, and the spring in the stream. For thus whoever looks upon the Son looks upon what is the Father's own substance and understands that the Father is in the Son. For since the form and the divinity of the Father is

---

[65] On what follows, see Schönborn, *God's Human Face*, pp. 3–14, 34–43.

[66] Arius, *Letter to Eusebius of Nicomedia* (ed. Opitz 3/1:5).

[67] *The Blasphemies of Arius* 40–41, in Athanasius, *De Synodis* 15 (ed. Opitz 2/1:243); see also TzT D 4:1, text 90, p. 133.

[68] *The Blasphemies of Arius* 35–36 (ed. Opitz 2/1:243).

the being of the Son, then consequently the Son is in the Father and the Father in the Son.[69]

Between the Father and the Son exists a complete community of being. The Son is "true God from true God"; he is, as Athanasius says, "the most perfect fruit of the Father".[70] Because the Christian faith attributes divine being to the Son of God, and because it cannot accept any "gradation" of the divine being, within the context of trinitarian theology the concept of image loses any appearance of inferiority. The Son is the image of the Father and is *consubstantial* with him. This paradoxical concept of an image that is of the same being as the original does of course demand the exclusion of any aspect of sharing. The Word does not have a share of God; he *is* God. The relationship between God and the Word is not that of the Plotinic One to his first emanation. Athanasius also regards as inadequate the Arian notion of the Logos being similar to God through obedience and merit. The Word is not merely *similar* to God; he is God. While similarity concerns only a certain manner of being, in this case it is a matter of identity of nature: the Son is, as Athanasius says, "the offspring of the substance" of the Father.[71] The Catholic faith therefore confesses the paradox of an identity, without confusion, between the Father and the Son; of the Son having his origin from the Father, without this origination implying that he is in any way lesser; of an image that comes from God himself and yet possesses everything that God himself possesses: God himself has a perfect image of himself. It is in the wake of the struggle against Arianism that the first great representations of the Pantokrator appear. If the divinity of Christ is firmly lodged in believers' consciousness, then art may venture to see his divinity as the perfect image of the Father.

If the Son is begotten without being of a lesser nature than the Father, then his activity and his work will also be divine. Just as one cannot introduce into God any contradiction between the free will of the Father and the eternal begetting of the Son, there will also be no contradiction to be found between the will of the Father and that of the Son. In a marvelous passage in his work against Eunomius, Gre-

---

[69] Athanasius, *Orationes contra Arianos* 3, 3 (PG 26:328AB).
[70] Athanasius, *Contra Gentes* 46 (SC 18bis, p. 208).
[71] Athanasius, *De Synodis* 36 (ed. Opitz 2/1:263).

gory of Nyssa reflects upon the unity of the divine will. His remarks were occasioned by the Arian assertion that the Word was the passive instrument of God in the creation of the world. For that is how the Arians interpret the passage, "all things were created *through* him" (Col 1:16):

> No difference of will exists between Son and Father. For the Son is the image of the goodness [of God], in accordance with the beauty of the original. When someone sees himself in a mirror . . . , the image resembles in every way the original that produces the image in the mirror. The image in the mirror cannot move unless the movement comes from the original. And if this latter moves, then the movement of the mirror image follows necessarily.[72]

The image of the mirror, which Gregory is fond of using, combines unity and distinction: it emphasizes the complete unity of Father and Son, down to the most minute "impulse of the will", and yet preserves the existence of two hypostases. The text is an important step toward a more profound understanding of Christ's title of "image of God". For Gregory shows here that the Son is the image of the Father precisely in his will, a will that is not, of course, contrary to that of the Father: "For the image in the mirror cannot move unless the movement comes from the original." The Son's activity, as the expression of his own will, demonstrates nothing other than the will of the Father; yet not in the way of a passive instrument, but in the sense that the Son makes himself an expression of the will of the Father. There is therefore no contradiction if the Father alone is the source and origin of the divine will, and yet the Son himself and personally wills exactly the same. What was for the Arians evidence of the subordination of the Son, his obedient activity, is the very thing that now proves to be the mystery of the communion of wills of the Divine Persons, which is grounded in their unity of nature. The Arians talk about obedience and mean coercion, while precisely the obedience of the Son becomes for us an image of the Father, since the Son takes up into the whole of his existence as Son the entire will of the Father—so much so that he virtually is this will. That is why the unity of will does not exclude the distinction of persons, but brings it fully to bear, since the Son is,

---

[72] Gregory of Nyssa, *Contra Eunomium* 2, 215 (ed. Jaeger, 1:288).

particularly in his own will, in what is most "himself", most a person, the image of the will and purpose of the Father.

b. The Incarnation of the Logos and the Divinization of Man

"God made himself man, so that man might be able to become God" —these words may be taken as virtually the basic principle of soteriology in the early Church.[73] Scholasticism, the Reformation, and mysticism all held fast to this phrase. Since the beginning of the modern era, the notion of divinization has admittedly been subjected to a great variety of criticism. The exponents of the Hellenization theory see in it further, indeed, "the most striking evidence of the Hellenization of Christianity, which has been achieved at the expense of the religious morality preached by Jesus".[74] It would seem that the desire for divinization is not timely. Man, they say, should rather strive to become truly man. What is and is not meant by Christian divinization becomes clear in all its particularity, but also in its claim to validity, if we turn to the way this problem relates to Christology. If the Church talks about divinization, she can only do so with reference to the mystery of Christ.[75]

One of the great arguments against the Arian reduction of the Logos and the Pneuma to the level of creatures was that of the divinization of man. The Logos and the Pneuma could not divinize the believer if they were not themselves "of one nature with the Father". In his second oration against the Arians, Athanasius formulates this argument in its classical form:

> If the Logos had become man as a mere creature, then man would nonetheless have remained as he was—that is, not joined to God. . . . Furthermore, however, if the Son were a creature, then man would remain mortal,

---

[73] Athanasius, *De Incarnatione* 54:3 (SC 199:458). This formula is found in one form or another in all the Church Fathers, in the Middle Ages, and into modern times. For further references to it and to what follows in general, see C. Schönborn, "Über die richtige Fassung des dogmatischen Begriffs der Vergöttlichung des Menschen", *Freiburger Zeitschrift für Philosophie und Theologie* 34 (1987): 3–47; Schönborn, *From Death to Life: The Christian Journey* (San Francisco: Ignatius Press, 1995), pp. 41–63.

[74] J. Gross, *La Divinisation du chrétien d'après les Pères grecs: Contribution historique à la doctrine de la grâce* (Paris, 1938), p. 4.

[75] See J. Pelikan, *The Christian Tradition: A History of the Development of Doctrine*, 9th ed., vol. 1 (Chicago, 1984), p. 155; see also Grillmeier, *Christ in Christian Tradition* 1:371.

because not joined to God. For a creature cannot join other creatures to God. . . . And certainly a part of the creation cannot become salvation for creation, since it, too, would be in need of salvation. . . . And yet the Logos assumed the generated body so that as creator he might renew it, deify it in himself, and thus introduce us all, after his likeness, into the Kingdom of heaven. For man would not have been deified if joined to a creature, if the Son had not been true God. . . . That is why such a union [of Logos and Sarx] took place, so that he might join together the divine nature and human nature and so that the latter's salvation and divinization might be assured.[76]

Even his Arian opponents agreed with Athanasius that divinization is the ultimate aim of all God's saving activity. This presupposition appears self-evident; and thus it also frequently appears in the texts of the Fathers. Basil sums it up in a single dictum: "The highest thing of all to be desired [is] divinization."[77] For this era it seems self-evident that the acme of everything worthwhile is "becoming like God". The Gospel provides the answer to this longing, since it is nothing but the promise of divinization for everyone who accepts it in faith. Divinization is therefore the purpose of God's plan and also the object of human longing. There was agreement on that in the early Church. This explains the widespread use of the argument of divinization to demonstrate the divinity of Christ: Only someone who is God can divinize.

Yet the use of the doctrine of divinization against the Arians does not only show how profoundly, in the fourth century, the Christian concept of salvation was determined by the theme of divinization; it also led to more precise definition of this doctrine at two points. For, first: if only God can divinize, then man cannot divinize himself, and thus he is also unable to satisfy his highest longing himself, insofar as this is divinization; divinization, then, is a grace. Second: the content of divinization can be more narrowly determined: it leads, not to an identity of nature with God, but to a participation in God that is yet to be defined more closely.

It has repeatedly been said that the Christian East differs from the Christian West by, among other things, putting "divinization" where the West speaks of grace. The "very different" development of the two

---

[76] Athanasius, *Orationes contra Arianos* 2, 67–70 (ed. Tetz 1:244–47).
[77] Basil of Caesarea, *De Spiritu Sancto* 9, 23.

traditions is often emphasized.[78] Without wishing to deny such differences, we would nonetheless like to give greater emphasis to what they have in common.

The Greek Fathers' linguistic usage shows a connection between grace and divinization that seems to be taken for granted. Athanasius sets χάϱις and θεοποίεσις side-by-side as synonyms. It is constantly emphasized that θέοσις is κατὰ χάϱιν. Conversely, grace is characterized by the adjective "divinizing". Maximus the Confessor (d. 662) speaks of divinization as "supernatural grace".[79] The gracious character of divinization is made completely clear when Maximus constantly emphasizes that no creature is of itself capable of divinization, since none can comprehend God: "This can only take place by the grace of God."[80] This gracious character of divinization does not prevent its being regarded as the only goal capable of fulfilling human nature. For this, in view of this, man was created.

Divinization is an entirely undeserved grace. That in itself expresses the essential definition of the content of divinization, at least by a negative limitation. One who, through grace, is divinized and becomes god is not God according to nature, according to being. Maximus formulates the content and limitation of divinization with lapidary brevity: "Everything that God is, save an identity of being, is what one becomes who is divinized by grace."[81] Everything, apart from what it is absolutely impossible to share: being God in nature. The Eastern and the Western Churches alike hold fast to this "everything" as being the real content of salvation, the goal of creation and redemption. Time and again, from Athanasius to Gregory Palamas (d. 1359), this sharing in "everything that God is" is the yardstick by which reductions of the Christian understanding of salvation are measured.

"Everything apart from being": Does that mean that, in divinization, all the characteristics of God become characteristics of man? Does di-

---

[78] See I.-H. Dalmais, "Divinisation II: La Patristique grecque", in *Dictionnaire de Spiritualité* 3:1376–89; here, 1389; similarly, but too schematically, C. Dumont, "Katholiken und Orthodoxe am Vorabend des Konzils", in *Seit neunhundert Jahren getrennte Christenheit: Studien zur ökumenischen Begegnung mit der Orthodoxie*, ed. E. von Ivanka, pp. 111–35, here pp. 116–17 (Vienna, 1962).

[79] For references, see C. Schönborn, "Über die richtige Fassung", p. 26.

[80] Maximus the Confessor, *Quaestiones ad Thalassium* 22 (CCSerGr 7:141).

[81] Maximus the Confessor, *Ambigua ad Johannem* 41 (PG 91:1308B).

vinization not become here the annulment of creatureliness? To explain the doctrine of divinization is to consider not only the "share" of the divinizer but also that of the divinized. For the doctrine of divinization not only wishes to do justice to the claim of Christian faith that God himself is imparting himself in his salvation, but must also clarify the nature and the goal of man. The doctrine of man's being in the image of God[82] is the necessary correlative of the doctrine of divinization. Man's creatureliness is not interpreted here as radical finitude or even as "crypto-divinity", but as openness to sharing in the life of God himself in a way that is constitutive for being human.[83] Of course, there is always the danger that divinization appears to be a flight from creatureliness. However, the close solidarity between being in God's image and divinization makes it clear that divinization is essentially the realization of man's being in the image of God, in the manner of being made more like God, more in harmony with God. Only in this perspective does it become clear that divinization is not the abolition of creatureliness, and at the same time that "finitude" is inadequate as a definition of man's creatureliness.

From the first postapostolic writings onward, immortality, imperishability, indestructibility are seen as the gifts of grace by which man "shares in God".[84] Theophilus of Antioch (second/third century), for instance, speaks of the reward of immortality as a "becoming God" that is granted the one who reaches toward immortality through his obedience to God's commandments.[85] Longing for "divine eternity" is no flight from being human; rather, it corresponds to the most precise intention of the Creator, who implanted this longing within human nature.

More generally, the content of divinization is defined as sharing in God. It is the restoration and the completion of the relationship with God that is fundamental in creatureliness. It is realized as a real κοινωνία with God, as a cleaving to God, and ultimately it is described as a virtual union with God. In this way, divinization is understood as really

---

[82] The most important literature on the patristic interpretation of Genesis 1:26 is listed in Grillmeier, *Jesus der Christus* 1:92 n. 193.

[83] See on this point Gregory of Nyssa, *Oratio catechetica magna* 5:2 (ed. Jaeger 3/4, pp. 17–18).

[84] Texts in Dalmais, "Divinisation II", 1376–77.

[85] Theophilus of Antioch, *Ad Autolycum* 2:27 (PTS 44:77; OECT, pp. 68–71).

becoming God through grace. That is how the text from Psalm 82:6, "I said, you are gods", which is quoted in the Gospel of John (10:34–35), is interpreted.

"Divinization" is not a biblical concept. Its latent closeness to Neo-platonic emanationism has at all times led to a reluctance to use it. The concept of divinization probably received the most explicit clarification in being used as equivalent to the concept of adoptive sonship, υἱοθεσία, as Paul describes this: "But when the time had fully come, God sent forth his Son, born of a woman, born under the law, to redeem those who were under the law, so that we might receive adoption as sons" (Gal 4:4–5).[86] Christian θεοποίεσις is υἱοποίεσις: "In the Holy Spirit the Logos glorifies creation, in that he leads it toward the Father through divinization and through being received as sons (θεοποιῶν καὶ υιοποιῶν)."[87]

It was the anti-Arian position that helped to emphasize divinization in all clarity as the grace of adoption as sons: Athanasius steadfastly stresses that we, unlike the Son who is consubstantial with the Father, "are called sons, not by nature, but by adoption".[88] Becoming god and son of God, not φύσει, but θέσει. This may be taken virtually as shorthand for the patristic doctrine of divinization.[89]

The great Christian tradition of life and doctrine is aware of the abyss of self-worship, but it is also aware of the hope of blissful communion with God, of divinization by grace. Let us then, in conclusion, listen again to the words of Maximus:

"What no eye has seen, nor ear heard, nor the heart of man conceived, what God has prepared for those who love him" (1 Cor 2:9). For he created us for that purpose, to "become partakers of the divine nature" (2 Pet 1:4) and to gain a share in his eternity, to become like him through divinization by grace: since it is for the sake of divinization that all things are and exist and that things which did not exist were created and brought forth.[90]

---

[86] J. Scott, *Adoption as Sons of God: An Exegetical Investigation into the Background of Hyiotesia in the Pauline Corpus*, WUNT 2, 48 (Tübingen, 1992).

[87] Athanasius, *Epistula ad Serapionum* 1, 25 (PG 26:589B)

[88] Athanasius, *Orationes contra Arianos* 2, 59 (ed. Tetz 1:236).

[89] For references, see the article "θέσις", in G. Lampe, *A Patristic Greek Lexicon* (Oxford, 1961), pp. 645–46; for the medieval development, E. H. Kantorowicz, "Deus per naturam, deus per gratiam: A Note on Medieval Political Theology", *Harvard Theological Review* 45 (1952): 253–77.

[90] Maximus the Confessor, *Letter* 24 (PG 91:609C).

In the context of the Arian controversy, the doctrine of divinization received decisive clarification: once it had become a clear article of faith that the Son and the Spirit are not intermediate semi-divine beings but are "consubstantial with the Father", then the divinization that they confer can be understood, no longer as having an emanative, degraded share in the incommunicable One, but as a grace-filled share in the life of God granted through the "sonship" effected by the Spirit through, with, and in Christ.

II. The Incarnation of the Son of God

The Incarnation is the radically new element in the New Testament revelation. There are something like foreshadowings of this in the Old Testament, but of course these only emerge clearly in the light of Christmas. So in the first section the lines in the Old Testament and in Judaism that point toward the Incarnation are examined. The second section is devoted to its realization: Jesus Christ is "conceived by the Holy Spirit, born of the Virgin Mary", as we confess in faith. The third and last section is about the profession of faith in "true God and true man" at the Council of Chalcedon (451).

1. Approaches to the Incarnation of God in the Old Testament and Judaism

That God is a God who saves is among the fundamental biblical statements. He is not an "unmoved mover", a distant and transcendent God who rests in himself, not bothering about men. The biblical revelation is the history of a growing closeness between God and the people he calls his own. A growing closeness does not mean only that Israel gradually becomes aware of God's closeness. This is, rather, the history of a progressive revelation and, thereby, of a growing communion of God himself with Israel. At the climax of the prophetic preaching, in Hosea and Deutero-Isaiah, this communion is spoken of in the metaphor of the bride, of the wedding. With a bold anthropomorphism, they speak of God's repentance,[1] his anger, his sorrow, and his joy. God's joy in Israel is sung in overflowing images (cf. Zeph 3:17). This is all aimed at one central point: God's dwelling in the midst of Israel (1 Kings 6:13), his presence among the Israelites (Hos 14:5-8), which means joy for him (Is 49:18; 62:5), and also, correspondingly, that God suffers when

---

[1] J. Jeremias, *Die Reue Gottes*, 2nd ed., Biblische Studien 75 (Neukirchen and Vluyn, 1997); cf. R. Brandscheidt and Eva-Maria Faber, "Reue Gottes", *Lexikon für Theologie und Kirche*, 3rd ed. (1999), 8:1139-40.

Israel is unfaithful. The prophets' gaze is increasingly directed toward a time that is coming, in which God himself, in his love, will recreate Israel. The ever-recurring refrain in the process is: "I myself will. . . ." God himself will pasture Israel (Jer 50:19); he will heal her wounds (Is 57:18), he will indeed marry Israel, but he will also fight for Israel himself (Josh 11:6; 13:6; 1 Sam 17:46).

How can the statement that God is traveling with his people, that he is dwelling in their midst, be combined with the equally biblical statement that God is the Lord of heaven and earth, that he does not dwell in idols but is everywhere? Where is the line drawn between permissible and impermissible anthropomorphisms? Is talk about the heart of God that "recoils" in anger (Hos 11:8) not already too anthropomorphic? Christian faith has seen talk about God dwelling among men fulfilled in a strictly concrete sense in Jesus Christ: God became man (cf. Jn 1:14). From that time on, anthropomorphism in talking about God is not merely a lovely imagery but the reality of God.

Two lines of development may be discerned in the Old Testament. On the one hand, it is possible to talk about an inclination of God to humble himself and to come down to men. On the other hand, there is the tendency, especially in the prophets, to exalt man and to make him God's representative. Both these lines, the descending and the ascending, should be pursued and investigated with a view to the definitive Incarnation of God. In what follows, we will seek in both these ways to find some approach from the Old Testament-Jewish faith to the question of the Incarnation of God. In the process, the limitations of both ways will also become clear and, thus, the question may be more precisely framed.

a. God's Self-Abasement in Jewish Theology

The statement concerning the Incarnation of God is not an abstract statement about some strange metaphysical process. It refers to God's love, which goes as far as self-renunciation. Understanding the Incarnation as the kenosis, as self-emptying (cf. Phil. 2), not of God, but of the Son of God, is among the oldest christological statements. Peter Kuhn has provided a wealth of rabbinic material, the consideration of which is of value for Christology.

In reflecting upon the biblical texts, it struck rabbis that certain passages speak, in the same breath, of God's infinite grandeur and of his bending down to the lowly. "R. Johanan said: In each place (in Scripture) where you find the power of the Holy One, may he be praised, you find his self-abasement right next to it."[2] God is the wholly other. The rabbis can already see that in the fact that human behavior in general is not acquainted with this condescension but wants to assert itself and remain at the top. God, on the other hand, who is all-high, looks upon the least. Increasingly, God's greatness is praised in the very fact that he stoops down to the lowly: "Is there a greater self-abasement than that of the Holy One, praised be he?"[3] That is how the rabbinic texts begin, again and again. The whole history of God with Israel is read in this way. God's providence for Israel goes so far that the Lord humbles himself and carries out the duties of a slave for Israel, his servant. That, for instance, is how the rabbis interpret the pillar of fire in the journey through the wilderness:

"And the Lord went before them (by night in a pillar of fire to give them light . . .)" (Ex 13:21). R. José the Galilean said: If it were not written as a verse of Scripture, no one could utter this: Like a Father who carries the torch in front of his children and like a lord who carries the torch in front of his slave.[4]

For our question it is now important to see how this self-abasement is understood. It is frequently regarded as *condescension*. God does not tarry in his unapproachable transcendence, where no man can reach him. He comes down, conforms to man, makes himself small. This is often understood as God's restricting himself to what is smallest and most lowly, to the unattractive thornbush, to Sinai, the least among mountains. Rabbinic theology calls this kind of presence in self-restriction *indwelling*, "shekinah". Here, "shekinah" always refers to God himself, as he comes to man, as he can be experienced by him, turns to him at a given place. He himself is the presence among men, the dwelling among his people Israel. Wherever it says that God is doing something with his shekinah, that he lets it descend or depart, that refers to God's free action. He determines when he, as it were, humbles himself, brings himself to man.

[2] bMeg 31a = P. Kuhn, *Gottes Selbsterniedrigung in der Theologie der Rabbinen*, StANT 17 (Munich, 1968), p. 13, text 1.
[3] TB Bereshith 4 = text 4, ibid., p. 15; cf. rEx 41:4 = text 6, ibid., p. 19; JŠ 2, 161 = text 9, ibid., p. 21.
[4] MŠ 47 (on Ex 13:21) = text 11, ibid., p. 23.

God's self-abasement is interpreted as "descent". God does not remain within his transcendence, but graciously descends to men to save
them, to heal them of their sins. In that way God actually dwells among
men. In the Old Testament, there are *places* of God's presence: the
thornbush, Mount Sinai, the Tent of Meeting, the Temple. Furthermore, the shekinah also has a temporal dimension. Depending upon
the fidelity or infidelity of Israel, there is a coming and going of the
indwelling of God. Not until the eschatological age will there be a
definitive presence of God, which is the goal of the entire creation.[5]
An outstanding expression of the self-abasement of God is the Torah.
With this, God has given himself; it is, as it were, the daughter of God,
whom he has given away and yet from whom he cannot part; God has
put himself, along with the Torah, at men's disposal.[6]

The motive for this self-abasement is specified: God makes himself
like the lowliest of men, so that man can give assent to God in complete
freedom and not be overwhelmed by the greatness of his majesty. God
respects man's freedom to such an extent that he addresses the freedom
of man through his self-abasement. In addition he dares to make himself dependent upon man. He humbles himself and then relies on men
to make room for him on earth. The proud man, on the other hand,
drives him away from the world.[7] Here we are immediately struck
by how close this is to the Prologue of John: "He came to his own
home, and his own people received him not" (Jn 1:11). The midrash
never tires of praising this self-abnegation, the fact that he who fills
everything, heaven and earth, "compresses himself" into the smallest
space (such as the ark of the covenant, in the Temple).[8]

What does a comparison with the Christian understanding show?
First of all, a great similarity is striking. God comes down from heaven
to be with his people. He, the infinite One, restricts himself to the
smallest space in the world in order to live with his own people and to
assist them. Thereby he shares the fate of his people and bears everything with them, even the deepest sorrow. All of that is not only to be
found in Judaism; it is also part of what is genuinely Christian. This
distinguishes both from Greek culture, which knows nothing of God's

---

[5] Cf. ibid., pp. 69–72.
[6] Cf. ibid., p. 70.
[7] Cf. MJ Jithro, *Bachodesh* 9 = text 33, ibid. pp. 40–42, and commentary p. 71.
[8] SLv Wayiqura, *Pereq* 2:12 = text 37, ibid., p. 48.

self-abnegation; and this distinction will have a decisive effect on Christianity's encounter with the Greek world, as is shown for instance by
Celsus' polemic against the kenosis. Now, Peter Kuhn believes that the
rabbinic view of God's self-abnegation may possibly have been used
by primitive Christianity to reshape the mystery of the Incarnation
and Passion of Jesus. If that is so, then it means, however, that "a trait
that is accorded only to *God* in rabbinic Judaism" was transferred "to
Jesus".[9]

There, of course, the profound difference is shown between the Jewish view and the Christian view that all statements about abasement are
made about the Son. Where all statements about God's self-abasement
are concerned, Jewish theology is confronted by a dilemma. In mysticism, an overemphasis on this self-abnegation was such a great danger that God was, in part, seen as completely passive, at the mercy of
the world, suffering in and from the world. God's sympathetic suffering with Israel is sometimes so strongly emphasized that God ends up
seeming to need to be redeemed by man.[10]

On the other hand, rabbinic theology saw for itself the dangers of
this conception. In order not to endanger the transcendence of God,
the one personal God is never seen as being wholly and definitively
associated with one human life. God may of course acquire individual
traits of human life, yet this always remains temporary. Thus, Rabbi
Jose says: "God never came down . . . really to the earth." God and
man, however small the distance between them may become, never
completely come together. God always remains, for Rabbi Jose, still
five feet above the earth, which means: God has never wholly come
down to earth, and men have never quite climbed up to him: the distance always remains.[11] So God's self-abasement can never attain ultimate seriousness, either. Up to modern times, Jewish theology has wa-
vered between mystical overemphasis and theological qualification of
God's self-abasement, as for instance in the conflict between Hasidism
and orthodox Judaism.

The New Testament creed includes the belief that Jesus is God's shekinah. In him, God is dwelling among men. Corresponding to Jesus'

---

[9] Cf. ibid., p. 105; quotation from n. 7.
[10] Ibid., pp. 106–7.
[11] bSuk 4b + 5a; MJ Jithro, *Bachodesh* 4; MŠ 144f. = text 36, versions A, B, and C, ibid.,
pp. 45–47; cf. ibid., p. 72.

words, "Where two or three are gathered in my name, there am I in the midst of them" (Mt 18:20) is the rabbinic text where it is said that the shekinah is in the midst of those who read the Torah; God lets his shekinah dwell with them.[12] And yet nowhere is it said that the shekinah is identical with one human existence, while Christian faith professes that the concrete human life of Jesus is the self-abasement and presence of God. The time of salvation is no longer primarily the Exodus, when God was close to Israel and saved it, but the earthly existence, the life, death, and Resurrection of Jesus. These are the once-and-for-all, valid saving event and the time of salvation.

And yet God's self-abasement in Jesus, in contrast to the Jewish conception, took place in the life and death of *Christ*, and not of God (the Father). In the rabbis, the shekinah acts toward God in a purely passive way and never appears as a separate person, independent of God. Here it is "not said that there are two independent Divine Persons".[13] The Christian concept, on the other hand, is that God has divested himself by sending his Son, that the Son humbled himself and made himself the servant of all, that he suffered for Israel, and indeed as concretely as only a death by crucifixion can be. What would never have been possible in the Old Testament and in Judaism has happened here: God has "really come to earth",[14] God has really come together with men.

Yet is that not a step backward from Jewish theology? If the Son stripped himself, if it is true that, "though he was rich, yet for your sake he became poor, so that by his poverty you might become rich" (2 Cor 8:9), if all God's sympathy with men, his closeness to them and his serving them, are transferred to Christ, as occurs throughout the New Testament, then does not God himself once again become the distant and unapproachable transcendent being who sends his Son, but himself remains untouched and immovable, impassible? Such a view has nothing to do with the New Testament, even if it has turned up as a temptation in theology time and again.

The view of the New Testament is that God (the Father) himself is "involved" in the mission of the Son. Mission does not mean assigning an objectively distant task, but that God is giving himself with the Son,

---

[12] For references, see U. Luz, *Das Evangelium nach Matthäus*, vol. 3, EKK 1/3 (Zürich, 1997), p. 53.

[13] Commentary by Kuhn, *Gottes Selbsterniedrigung*, p. 68.

[14] See ibid., p. 98.

that, with him, God is giving us *everything* (cf. Rom 8:32). "In this
the love of God was made manifest among us, that God sent his only-
begotten Son into the world" (1 Jn 4:9). God *first* loved us and gave up
his Son for us. Yet these statements must be seen together with those
about Christ, especially in the hymn from Philippians, in which Christ
is discussed as the active subject, acting of his own free will. It is said of
him that "he emptied himself" (Phil 2:7). He is the presence of God,
the gift of God, the self-abasement of God, not only as the shekinah,
as a passive form of God's presence; he is rather God's nearness as one
who freely chooses thus and who brings it about himself. He is the
One sent by God, who at the same time empties himself.

By further developing the rudiments found in the Old Testament,
rabbinic theology discovered a very bold view of God's self-abasement.
The manner of this self-abasement is conceived in part as a kind of "self-
limitation" by God, as a renunciation of his power, a kenosis, as an
emptying of himself. As bold as this view was, of course, it had to
stop short of one final logical development: God never abandons the
boundaries of transcendence—something that is visually expressed in
God's never quite touching the earth, however close he may come.
This first "pass", which may be reckoned as an attempt at something
like the kenosis of the Son, remained stalled here. The limitation for
Jewish theology is that there is no Son of God as subject of the kenosis. The kenosis of the Son is in reality the self-abasement of God the
Father, who gives us everything, that of the Son, who gives himself
and lets himself be given, and that of the Spirit, who lets himself be
"poured out" and sent.

b. The Prophet as the Representative of God

Besides this descending aspect, there is an ascending one in the Old
Testament, in which the exaltation of man is emphasized. God not only
humbles himself, not merely comes down to earth himself, but he also
raises man up to himself. In the Old Testament, man is understood
as being the image of God. For man, being the image of God means
that he is "God's vizier",[15] that he is competent to act as God's deputy
in the world. This competence to act as God's substitute is evidence

---

[15] See above, chap. 1:1, "Biblical Witness to the Idea of Preexistence".

of a certain "theomorphism" in man. How far that goes in the Old
Testament can be shown in the lives that Hosea and Jeremiah lead as
prophets. In the Book of Hosea, especially in the prophet's marriage
(Hos 1; 3), the prophet is not someone who passively receives his orders. Revelation occurs in and through human experience. As mediator of this revelation, the prophet carries it within himself; his own
existence, his own "life is the place where revelation comes into existence and the medium through which it is communicated".[16] Thus, an
entire human life, with its experiences, may become the locus of the
revelation of God. That becomes particularly clear in the sufferings of
the prophets, which come to be an expression of God's suffering on
Israel's account. "The prophet is the man who not only knows about
God's pathos, so that he can communicate it, but who experiences it
in and on himself, so that his whole life is affected by it."[17] It is true
of the whole of the prophet's life that "its heart . . ." is "a sharing in
God's relationship with his people in history". The "sym-pathy" of the
prophet corresponds to the "pathos" of God. The prophet is not only
the one who proclaims the Word of God, he is "at the same time, and
first of all, a representation of God's own situation in the history with
his world". Here can be seen the "promise of the complete presence
of God in a human life", which points forward to the Incarnation.[18]

In the life of Hosea, in his sufferings, in his confrontation with his
contemporaries, we may see how God's Word appropriates a human
life to be the expression of God's situation vis-à-vis Israel. That is still
clearer in Jeremiah's case: the story of Jeremiah's sufferings is a true
"community of suffering with God".[19] Through his prophetic vocation, Jeremiah receives a plenitude of power that enables him to share,
in an unprecedented way, in God's worldwide rule. Thus, in Jeremiah,
his words and God's Word mingle in a completely new way. At the

---

[16] U. Mauser, *Gottesbild und Menschwerdung*, BHT 43 (Tübingen, 1971), p. 40; on this theme, see also H. M. Kuitert, *Gott in Menschengestalt*, BEvTh 45 (Munich, 1967); N. Füglister, "Alttestamentliche Grundlagen der neutestamentliche Christologie", in *Mysterium Salutis* 3/1:105–225, esp. 147–77; Füglister, "Prophet", in: HThG 3:367–90 (paperback ed., 1970); von Balthasar, *Glory* 6:225–304.

[17] Mauser, *Gottesbild und Menschwerdung*, p. 42.

[18] Ibid., pp. 42–43.

[19] This expression from the title of an article by H. Kremers, "Leidensgemeinschaft mit Gott im Alten Testament: Eine Untersuchung der 'biographischen' Berichte im Jeremiabuch", *Evangelische Theologie* 13 (1953): 122–40; here, p. 139.

same time, however, the prophet, as his authorized representative, along with his whole life, is "dragged into the story of God".[20] Being God's deputy occupies his whole life to such an extent that he is filled with God's sorrow and with God's anger. As Gerhard von Rad has shown, in Jeremiah the whole *humanum* is absorbed into the prophetic office.[21] Jeremiah's lamentations, amid the confident speeches of the pseudo-prophets, make him a solitary figure, misunderstood and rejected, as is God himself, whom Israel has forgotten. In his impassioned speeches about judgment, Jeremiah is torn between love and anger toward his people, and precisely in this he is a faithful representation of God. Here we have reached a climax of the biblical "image of God" anthropology, the biblical theomorphism of man.

This idea can be continued in the New Testament. Here, the Christ-event is identified with God's word and deed. Here, at the very summit of the theomorphism of man, the "anthropomorphism of God" has likewise attained a climax. It was already shown in the Old Testament that God is so disposed to human history that he takes part in the history of his people and himself suffers Israel's afflictions. Parallel to this is the history of the prophets' participation in this condition of God, genuine representatives of God. What is important here is that the prophets are not exalted into demi-gods for this purpose; rather, they represent God in their humanity.

The limitation does remain, of course, that this representation of God is never total; it remains fragmentary, and the prophet may drop out of it (as, for instance, Jeremiah in his crisis of faith). "Even with its greatest prophets in view, the Old Testament never drew the conclusion that God was as a whole entirely represented in a single human life."[22] The basic assumption of faith in Christ, by contrast, is that, in the history of the man Jesus Christ, God has acted decisively, comprehensively, and in a way that is binding in eternity.

But is this approach adequate? The prophets are not only God's spokesmen; rather, they are also his authorized representatives, an image and likeness of the Lord. Yet it is never said of any prophet that beyond this he is the "Immanuel" himself, God who is dwelling among his people. The prophet certainly is the representative of God, his

---

[20] Mauser, *Gottesbild und Menschwerdung*, p. 82.

[21] G. von Rad, "Die Konfessionen Jeremias", *Evangelische Theologie* 3 (1936): 265–76.

[22] Mauser, *Gottesbild und Menschwerdung*, p. 186.

steward, his likeness, but he is not God incarnate. God's coming in the New Testament is indeed his concrete coming in the personal history of a man. God carries out his whole work in the personal history of a man.[23] Yet even that is ultimately true only in a limited sense, since it is never, ever the history of one man, as such, in which God does all his work. What the New Testament asserts is, rather, that he does this in the human history of the Son, Jesus Christ. For that is the point of the New Testament profession of Christ, that he, who is acting on behalf of God, who is acting as "God's advocate"[24]—in whose human life, that is, God himself is acting—is in fact none other than the Son. It is, not in the life of a man, but in the human life of the Son that God is revealed; the Son reveals the Father. Only because Jesus is the Son can he reveal God as the Father. It is not because they were imperfect men that the representation of God in the prophets is fragmentary; it is not because Jesus was "the most perfect man" (or the religious genius, or the prophet) that God's representation in him was complete; rather, it is because he is the Son. The full representation of God in the human life of Jesus is based upon the fact that he alone, as the Son, can fully represent God, his Abba. "No one knows the Son except the Father, and no one knows the Father except the Son" (Mt 11:27). This qualification alone makes it possible for the God-event to take place in the human history of Jesus. This qualification is essentially more than the "theomorphism of man" in general and is not deducible from it; rather, it is only approachable from it. The New Testament suggests, on the basis equally of its implicit and of its explicit Christology, that this is not a quantitative but a qualitative difference: not a difference in the degree of human perfection, but one deriving from the fact that the prophets were called by God, while Christ is the Son; that the prophets receive the word (cf. Jer 15:16), while Christ is the Word.

Both paths of approach—the descending line of God's self-abasement in Jewish theology and the ascending path of the representation of God by the prophets in the Old Testament—come up against a boundary that cannot be overcome in this way: that between the transcendent God and the creature. Just as Jewish theology never gets as far as a true "incarnation" of God "from above", and cannot do so without

---

[23] Ibid., pp. 122–43.
[24] H. Küng, *Christsein* (Zürich, 1974), pp. 281–84. On the discussion concerning this, see H. U. von Balthasar et al., *Diskussion über Hans Küngs "Christsein"* (Mainz, 1976).

giving up God's transcendence, so also the prophets, "from below",
never get to the point where a man becomes absolutely fully and completely the representative of God. *Finiti ad infinitum nulla est proportio*—
both approaches remain stuck at this radical disproportion. However
much God, in the understanding of the Old Testament and Judaism,
"comes down" and suffers with men, he never suffers as a man. However much man is drawn into the life of God, he remains a mortal and
fragmented man.

These two approaches, "from above" and "from below", make clear
to us something that must be firmly noted here. A mere "Christology
from below" comes up against the boundary that has just become clear.
If we act on the assumption that Jesus should as a matter of course first
be regarded as a man, and it is then asked, "Is this man God's Son and
God?", then we will never ever arrive at a positive answer. A Christology that begins in this way never gets beyond the idea of a prophet.
To this Christology, Jesus can appear only as a man who is "God's advocate", but not as God who has become man. We have to presuppose
the Incarnation as the original datum of Christology: that is to say, in
practical terms, to regard the person and the life of Jesus at all times as
those of the incarnate God. The basis for this assertion will be shown
as this chapter progresses. The whole force of the Christian creed is
in fact based on the belief that this man was and is truly God's Son
(cf. Mk 15:39); not just a representative of God, but God himself, the
Son of God, who became man. And the whole weight of the Christian
faith is the fact that he who lived, hungered, and thirsted as a poor
man in Galilee is truly God.

2. *"Conceived by the Holy Spirit—Born of the Virgin Mary"*

The two lines of God's self-abasement (*descensus*) and man's exaltation
(*ascensus*) have one point of convergence: the Incarnation. How this
point took concrete shape, where and when God and man came concretely together, will be our subject in what follows.[25]

---

[25] On what follows, see C. Schönborn, "He Has Become Man", in *The Mystery of the
Incarnation* (San Francisco: Ignatius Press, 1992), pp. 47–64.

a. A Historical Question but Not Only That . . .

The conception of a human being is something that is extremely intimate. If it is spoken of, it needs the protection of reverence. The conception of Jesus, brought about by the Holy Spirit, does not belong to the marketplace of public curiosity like some novelty. If we are to try to talk about it, then our words must be appropriate to the intimacy and seclusion of this event. It is at the same time essential to take care, at this point in particular, in terms of faith and reason, not to lose sight of the wood for the exegetical trees. If the conception of Jesus by the agency of the Holy Spirit is a genuine miracle, then there are only two ways in which this could have been known: either Mary herself talked about it, or it was disclosed to others through some kind of revelation. The other possibility would be that we are dealing, not with a historical event, but with a theological construct, intended to express Jesus' special significance.

In view of the New Testament evidence, there is no doubt that it is difficult to resolve the historical question. Only Matthew and Luke mention the Virgin Birth and give details in the so-called "infancy narratives"—better called "christological prologues"—which are placed at the beginning of the two Gospels (Lk 1–2; Mt 1–2). Paul never refers to it, and neither does Mark. Whether John is aware of it is disputed. On the other hand, nowhere is it explicitly repudiated. The arguments for and against are therefore largely based on differences in the interpretation of this silence.[26] The *argumentum e silentio* must of course be used with caution.

The postapostolic tradition in the Church, on the other hand, is far from silent. There is a wealth of testimony all through the second century that professes belief in the Virgin Birth. There can be no doubt that the second-century Church (provided she did not stray into Gnosticism or other "heresies") was convinced of the *reality* of the Virgin Birth. We can offer here only the most important witnesses to this. In the early Roman Creed that every candidate for baptism had to recite, the words *natus est de Spiritu sancto et Maria Virgine*—was born of the Holy Spirit and the Virgin Mary—appear as one of the essential

---

[26] A. Vögtle, "Offene Fragen zur lukanischen Geburts- und Kindheitsgeschichte", in *Das Evangelium und die Evangelien* (Düsseldorf, 1971); cf. J. McHugh, *The Mother of Jesus in the New Testament* (London, 1975).

elements of Christian belief alongside Jesus' death and Resurrection.[27] "It is obvious that no new and strange doctrines could be incorporated in such a creed."[28] If this is true of the second half of the second century, then the evidence of the bishop and martyr Ignatius of Antioch (d. ca. 117) takes us back to the turn of the first and second centuries. In his writings also, the miraculous birth of Christ appears as one of the essential elements of the creed. Ignatius counts it among the "three mysteries of renown, which were wrought in silence": "the virginity of Mary . . . , her offspring . . . , and the death of the Lord."[29] For Ignatius, "our Lord" is "truly of the seed of David according to the flesh (cf. Rom 1:3), and the Son of God according to the will and power of God; . . . truly born of a virgin . . . , truly, under Pontius Pilate and Herod the tetrarch, nailed [to the cross] for us in His flesh."[30] Ignatius, writing around 110, offers evidence that for Antioch, his place of origin, and also for the Churches he is addressing (in Asia Minor and Rome), belief in the virginal conception of Jesus did not need to be asserted, but already formed part of the apostolic foundation of the creed. This "article of faith" is essential, furthermore, as one of the clear signs that Jesus was *really* man. It is food for thought that in the whole of the second century the Virgin Birth is never cited as an argument for the *divinity* of Jesus, but always for his true *humanity*.[31] Whence does the second-century Church derive her confession of belief in the "mystery of renown" of the virginity of Mary? Anyone who argues that the primitive Church invented this as a "theologoumenon" so as to emphasize the significance of Jesus must at the same time be

[27] DH 10; cf. W. Rordorf, ". . . qui natus est de Spiritu sancto et Maria Virgine", *Augustinianum* 20 (1980): 545–57. On the Creed, cf. J. N. D. Kelly, *Early Christian Creeds*, 3rd ed. (London, 1972); esp. for the Niceno-Constantinopolitan Creed, see F. Courth, "Historisch oder theologisch—eine falsche Alternative: Dogmatische Überlegungen zum Problem der Jungfrauengeburt", *Theologie und Glaube: Zeitschrift für den katholischen Klerus* 68 (1978): 283–96; here, pp. 287–90.

[28] J. G. Machen, *The Virgin Birth of Christ* (London, 1930), p. 4.

[29] Ignatius of Antioch, *Epistle to the Ephesians* 19:1, ed. Alexander Roberts and James Donaldson, Anti-Nicene Fathers, vol. 1 (Peabody, Mass.: Hendrickson Publishers, 1995), p. 57.

[30] Ignatius of Antioch, *Epistle to the Smyrnaeans* 1:1–2, ed. Alexander Roberts and James Donaldson, Anti-Nicene Fathers, vol. 1 (Peabody, Mass.: Hendrickson Publishers, 1995), p. 86.

[31] Machen, *Virgin Birth*, pp. 7–8; cf. D. Edwards, *The Virgin Birth in History and Faith* (London, 1943), pp. 189–96, and H. Gese, "Natus ex Virgine", in *Vom Sinai zum Zion* (Munich, 1974), pp. 130–46 (first published in: H. W. Wolf, *Probleme biblischer Theologie*, Festschrift for G. von Rad) (Munich, 1971), pp. 73–89.

in a position to explain why the Church invented something that for both the Jewish and the pagan environment could only give rise to mockery. It is illuminating to investigate the non-Christian reactions to the doctrine of the Virgin Birth. Here again, we can give only a few brief indications.

In the *Dialogue* with the rabbi Trypho written around 155 by the Christian philosopher and martyr Justin, the former says that the Jews are also waiting for the Messiah, but as "a man, from men". He accuses the Christians of telling stories that are like the myths of the Greeks, such as the myth of Perseus, to whom Danae is said to have given birth as a virgin, "after Zeus had come down in the form of gold. You should be ashamed of telling such things as the Greeks do. It would be better if you maintained that this Jesus had been born as a man from men".[32] The polemics could also become much harsher. It is possible that various stories circulated as early as the end of the first century among Jewish circles that changed the alleged virginal conception of Jesus into Mary's misconduct with a Roman soldier.

The polemics on the part of pagan writers struck the same note. Celsus, who wrote his book against Christianity in about 178, picks up the Jewish polemic and makes ironical comments on God's love affair with an insignificant Jewish girl. He says: "The mother of Jesus is said to have been repudiated by the carpenter to whom she was betrothed, because she was guilty of adultery and had given birth by a soldier named Panthera."[33] Most of the pagan criticism of this article of belief moves on much the same level.

How little the doctrine of the Virgin Birth can be explained on the basis of what was "plausible" at that period is shown by the fact that it was retained despite all these attacks. This becomes even more clear if we also take into account the disputes within the Church. In second-century Gnosticism, the Virgin Birth was sometimes denied and sometimes accepted—but if so, then it was understood in the sense of a denial of the reality of the Incarnation: the Logos is said to have passed through Mary as if through a channel.

How was it that the Church, despite severe derision, despite widespread misunderstanding, held fast to this belief so unequivocally? Perhaps a comparison with one of the other "mysteries of renown" of

---

[32] Justin, *Dialogus cum Tryphone* 49:1 (ed. Markovich, p. 150); 67:2 (Markovich, p. 185).
[33] Origen, *Contra Celsum* 1, 32 (SC 132:162).

which Ignatius of Antioch speaks will help us: Jesus' death on the Cross. His death on the Cross was something so offensive for *everyone* involved, for Jews as for pagans, but even for Christians themselves, that only the historical event itself can be the reason why people tried to understand and interpret it and then even began to proclaim it. The fact precedes the interpretation. Precisely *because* it was so difficult to comprehend, so offensive, interpretation is triggered by the fact. The Cross could never have been deduced on the basis of Jewish or Hellenistic models of interpretation. Only the fact that Jesus died that death of the accursed on the tree of shame made it possible to see in this dreadful event a meaning whose foreshadowing extends deep into the Old Testament.

It seems to us that something similar is true of the Virgin Birth. One does not "invent" something that provokes only derision and misunderstanding all around! The only interpretation that makes sense seems to us to be the following: The fact that there was a solid tradition in the primitive Church that Jesus' conception was the work of the Holy Spirit is the starting point for all attempts to understand, to interpret, and finally even to proclaim this reality that was so difficult to comprehend and, indeed, so offensive. Only this reflection unlocked the relationship to Old Testament promises and made clear the inner connection between Jesus' life and his conception through the Holy Spirit.

Does not human experience argue that this is the reasonable sequence of events? Is it not also the case that in the decisive experiences of our own lives, first of all the facts are there, events that leave their mark on our lives (such as a sudden death, a reversal, an unexpected encounter), which at first are not at all seen as ordered into a meaningful whole. Yet gradually a meaning is unlocked; what at first was so awkward, cutting right across our own plan for our life, may become the symbol of a whole new meaning in our life. What appears to others, to outsiders, only as a meaningless boulder on one's life path, may for oneself unfold profound symbolism. The fact precedes the disclosure of the meaning; the significance we have perceived, on the other hand, makes it possible to see the fact within a wider context of meaning, as one may even be able to say then: that *had* to happen, because in *that* way it made most sense; but no one would maintain that one thereby could derive and construct the fact.

As applied to our question: The Virgin Birth is too unexpected, too strange, to have been constructed as a "theologoumenon". The fact of there being a tradition about this mysterious event was the occasion for asking what it meant. Conversely, the nexus of meaning developed by the reflection of the primitive community extended the range of vision, so that this event now seemed to correspond very well to the "logic" of God's action.

When might we set the point of origin for the community's tradition about the conception of Jesus worked by the Holy Spirit? It seems to me worth considering whether the beginnings of this tradition should be seen in connection with the primitive community's experience of the Holy Spirit. Luke portrays the "birth" of the Church at Pentecost with clear parallels to the history of Jesus' birth: in both "cases", the Holy Spirit comes down and thereby brings about the miraculous birth. It seems reasonable to see a theological "construct" in this parallelism. But is it not even more reasonable to assume, conversely, that the primitive community's experience of the Spirit in Jerusalem offered first-generation Christians the opportunity of understanding "from within", on the basis of their *own* experience of the Spirit, what Jesus' conception through the Holy Spirit was all about? Is it not conceivable that the primitive Church's experience of the Holy Spirit became, for Mary herself, to some extent the "hermeneutic locus", the sphere of experience, within which it became possible for her to talk about the miracle of her own conception by the Spirit?

No doubt the primitive Church's experience of the Spirit was for them an event by which the significance of the person of Jesus became clear and comprehensible. Does it not make sense to assume that it was this experience of the Spirit, in which Mary also shared (Acts 1:14; 2:1), that first gave the primitive community the requisite background of experience and understanding to be able properly to grasp the news of Jesus' conception through the Spirit?

The idea is not so absurd if we take into consideration the fact that what was particularly characteristic of the primitive Church's experience of the Spirit was that it not only opened up their understanding of Christ, but it brought about a conformation to Christ. For Paul, the baptized person, filled with the Spirit, was "in Christ"; having died with him and risen with him, his "life is hidden with Christ in God" (Col 3:3). John goes a step farther: the baptized person is born anew, born indeed of the Spirit (cf. Jn 3:5, 8); this birth is one "not of blood nor of the will of the flesh nor of the will of man, but of God" (Jn

1:13). "One does not become the child of God through natural birth, certainly not through a process of natural development, but through a supernatural event brought about by God alone."[34] One becomes a new man, a "new creation" (2 Cor 5:17), only through a new birth. Now, at an early date many Church Fathers (Justin, Hippolytus, Irenaeus, Tertullian) and many textual witnesses read this passage from the Prologue of John in the singular: "*He* who *was* born, not of blood . . . but of God", and interpreted this text as witnessing to the conception of Jesus as the work of the Spirit. Even if this reading is probably secondary, it does at least confirm the profound consciousness of the primitive Church that a special kind of relationship existed between Christians' experience of the Spirit as rebirth through baptism and the beginning of Jesus' life brought about by the Spirit. The reality of Jesus' conception brought about by God's Spirit thus became the pledge that being "born of water and the Spirit" (Jn 3:5) really did grant a new life.[35]

Through her faith and through her undivided gift of herself to God's will, Mary is the prototype of this new life; precisely through her faith, she shares in the mystery of the Incarnation (cf. CCC 506). She is not a "surrogate mother", in the modern sense, who simply makes her body available physically. The conception of Jesus makes a demand upon her as a whole person and requires her willing acceptance in faith. Objectively, Mary could only know that she had conceived Jesus without the help of a man. The depth of what happened, however, the sheer mystery of God himself having become man here, was—even for her—only comprehensible through faith.[36]

The Christians' advocacy of the Virgin Birth, for which there is such clear testimony in the second century, was thus not a blind apologetic for some irrational oddity; rather, it was at one with the reality of God's Incarnation and the reality of the newness of this human life. The whole force of the symbols and images for this new human life is rooted in the reality of the new beginning wrought by the Spirit.

---

[34] R. Schnackenburg, *Das Johannesevangelium*, vol. 1, 7th ed., HThK 4/1 (Freiburg, 1992), p. 238.

[35] For textual witnesses, cf. Schnackenburg, *Johannesevangelium* 1:383–86.

[36] Cf. G. L. Müller, *Was heißt: Geboren von der Jungfrau Maria? Eine theologische Deutung*, QD 119 (Freiburg im Breisgau, 1989), p. 51.

b. The Symbolic Language in the Bible

Both "infancy narratives", in Luke and in Matthew, are concerned with interpreting the birth of Jesus as the appearance of the eschatological scion of David. The promised child "will be great, and will be called the Son of the Most High; and the Lord God will give to him the throne of his father David, and he will reign over the house of Jacob for ever, and of his kingdom there will be no end" (Lk 1:32–33). The scion of David who is promised is at one and the same time "Son of the Most High" and son of David. This curious "coexistence of divine birth and human genealogy"[37] had been characteristic of the Old Testament theology of the Davidic kingship. At the new king's accession to the throne, that Psalm which in the New Testament was frequently applied to Christ was sung: "You are my son, today I have begotten you" (Ps 2:7). A strange "intertwining of divine and human fatherhood".[38] Becoming king in Zion, in the "resting place" of the presence of God in his ark of the covenant, in the place belonging to God, which God had chosen for his own (cf. Ps 132), meant becoming "son of God" in a quite real sense. Thus, the king who has been "born today" can say: Yet I was created (in a marvelous way) as his king in Zion, on his holy mountain (cf. Ps 2:6).[39]

A scion of David is promised in the great prophecy from Isaiah that is familiar to us from the Christmas liturgy: "For to us a child is born, to us a son is given; and the government will be upon his shoulder" (Is 9:6). It is emphasized still more clearly that this new beginning will be "created" by God in a dark time of decline. God reigns "from this time forth and for evermore. The zeal of the LORD of hosts will do this" (Is 9:7). At the same time, the physical birth and the enthronement as a divine birth are brought very close together here. This becomes explicit in the famous prophecy to King Ahaz of the birth of Immanuel (Is 7:10–17). The true scion of David who is promised here—"Behold, a virgin shall conceive and bear a son, and shall call his name Immanuel [God with us]"—is no longer a biological son of the House of David but, rather, a new, secretly coming king who will be called "God is with us". By this promise, a judgment is virtually pronounced upon the House of David, which has become unfaithful (cf. vv. 17–20). But our

---

[37] Gese, "Natus ex Virgine", p. 134.
[38] Ibid., p. 137.
[39] Ibid., p. 139.

attention is drawn toward the *alma*, the young woman who is to bear the new and true son of David. Since the promise was not immediately carried out, hope was thenceforth increasingly directed toward a quite new, ultimate future that would surpass everything now present.

Two lines of promises increasingly converge here: the promise that God himself will come, will descend as he did at the time of the rescue from Egypt—no, in a quite new way, rather, both magnificent and definitive; and the promise that God will awaken a scion of David, who will save his people and will himself "be peace" (Mic 5:5a).

In retrospect, the primitive Church could recognize that these two lines finally converged in the birth of Jesus. In the subtle symbols and Old Testament allusions of the "infancy narratives" (especially in Luke), the message at the heart of the synoptic Gospels is made clear here: that the birth of Jesus is "itself the whole of the Gospel",[40] the good news of God's coming into this world. Luke thus gives us to understand that Mary is "the gate through which the divine salvation enters into this world",[41] pointing to her as "the daughter of Zion", on one hand, and the "ark of the covenant", on the other.

We may with some certainty see in the angel's greeting, "χαῖρε— rejoice" (Lk 1:28) an allusion to the prophecy in Zephaniah (Zeph 3:14–15): "Sing aloud, O daughter of Zion; shout, O Israel! Rejoice and exult . . . The King of Israel, the LORD, is in your midst." The angel's greeting is the proclamation of great messianic joy. In a marvelous typology, Mary is seen as the ultimate Zion, God's dwelling place among men: "Do not fear, O Zion. . . . The LORD your God is in your midst [literally, in your womb], a warrior who gives victory" (Zeph 3:16–17; cf. Lk 1:30–32).[42] Mary is thus the true Zion in person. She is the true Israel. "She is the 'people of God' bearing fruit through God's gracious power."[43]

Yet Mary also appears as the typological fulfillment of the ark of the covenant. Mary's visit to Elizabeth (Lk 1:39–56) is full of allusions to David's bringing the ark of the covenant home to Jerusalem (2 Sam

---

[40] Cf. Müller, *Was heißt: Geboren von der Jungfrau Maria?*, pp. 11 and 65; Gese, "Natus ex virgine", p. 145.

[41] Gese, "Natus ex virgine", pp. 143–44.

[42] Cf. R. Laurentin, *Struktur und Theologie der lukanischen Kindheitsgeschichte* (Stuttgart, 1976), pp. 75–82.

[43] J. Ratzinger, *Daughter Zion: Meditations on the Church's Marian Belief*, trans. John M. McDermott, S.J. (San Francisco: Ignatius Press, 1983), p. 43.

6:1–11): both things take place in the hill country of Judah; both events give rise to rejoicing (the joy of the people of Jerusalem; Elizabeth's joy and that of her child); the child's leaping within Elizabeth corresponds to David's dance of joy; finally, David's cry, "How can the ark of the LORD come to me?" and Elizabeth's exclamation, "Why is this granted me, that the mother of my Lord should come to me?" (2 Sam 6:9; Lk 1:43). Thus, Luke sees in Mary the ark of the covenant, in which and through which God definitively makes his dwelling among his people.

We may briefly refer to one final typological interpretation: the symbolism of the "indwelling of God" in Mary as Zion and as ark of the covenant is supplemented by that of the tent of meeting. The conception, brought about by the Spirit is announced by Luke in words that are clearly evocative of the cloud of God's glory that came down upon the tent of meeting (Ex 40:34–35): "The Holy Spirit will come upon you, and the power of the Most High will overshadow you; therefore the child to be born will be called holy, the Son of God" (Lk 1:35).

c. Life Wrought by the Spirit: The Root of the New Man

The symbolic language of the Bible says about the human child that Mary has conceived: He himself is the "dwelling place of God" among men. God himself is "the King of Israel . . . in your midst" (Zeph 3:15). And yet he is a human child, absolutely ordinary and undoubtedly human.

Prophets, too, were filled with the Spirit, seized by the Spirit, sometimes "even from their mother's womb", like John the Baptist (cf. Lk 1:15). The fact that the conception of Jesus is brought about by the Spirit says something more: This child is "in his origins entirely the work of God";[44] he is not only filled with the Spirit, but his inmost being and existence are determined by God's Spirit. That is the decisive assertion of the doctrine of the Virgin Birth. Let us try to break this down somewhat.

In the prophetic proclamations of the Old Testament, the coming of God is described with increasing clarity as a coming to make everything new (cf. Is 43:19). Jesus' preaching, his behavior, and his signs were experienced as something amazingly new (cf. Mk 1:22, 27; 2:12).

---

[44] H. Schürmann, *Das Lukasevangelium*, vol. 1, 4th ed., HThK 3/1 (Freiburg, 1990), p. 53.

It was above all his death and his Resurrection that were understood
by the primitive Church as the dawn of eschatological renewal (cf.
2 Cor 5:17; Rev 21:1, and so on). But what was this something new?
Was not the Preacher right to say, very skeptically, "What has been is
what will be, and what has been done is what will be done; and there
is nothing new under the sun" (Eccles 1:9)? And are not the scoffers
right who declare that nothing in the world has changed with Christ:
"Where is the promise of his coming? For ever since the Fathers fell
asleep, all things have continued as they were from the beginning of
creation" (2 Pet 3:4).

Here, the conception of Christ worked by the Spirit receives its full
importance: here is *one* man whose existence from its roots is entirely
new. In the midst of a world in which everything new merely replaces
the old in order then to become obsolete itself, there is a new kind
of human existence, a human life whose conception does not already
carry within it the seeds of death but that springs entirely from the
newness of God. The Bible knows that no man is born who does not
already stand in a history of guilt; he inherits and also begets guilt.
"Behold, I was brought forth in iniquity, and in sin did my mother
conceive me" (Ps 51:5). Even the genealogy of Jesus in the Gospel of
Matthew shows that mercilessly. Can we conceive of a human life that
was entirely free of involvement in sin from its origins? A life that was
holy and sinless from its very roots onward? This is exactly what the
conception of Jesus through the Spirit means.[45]

A sinless existence? We can often hear it said that the assertion that
Jesus was free from sin detracts from his really being human. Behind
this there is a complete misconception of sin. If sin means a No to God,
a No that also has as its consequence a break with one's neighbor, then
sin is very really and concretely the seed of death (cf. Rom 5:12). A
sinless existence, by contrast, means being human in openness to God
and neighbor. All the consequences of believing in the Virgin Birth
can be seen here: Jesus' new life results from his new conception. His
existence, being the work of the Spirit, makes possible a human life
that from its very roots is unreservedly open to God: so much so that
to him God is always Abba, Father. Yet the origin of his life, brought
about by the Spirit, is also the most profound reason for his unbeliev-
able openness in the encounter with people—here was a man the mere

---

[45] See on this K. Barth, KD 1/2:206–8.

encounter with whom brought healing. A man appeared here who left no wounded people behind him on his way. Being a man without hurting: Can human life *brought about by the Spirit* not be understood in this way? Is this not just the opposite of human life marked by sin, which always wounds, even when it devotes itself to the good?

A new kind of human life: entirely open for the Father, entirely open for men. Death, the consequence of sin, has no power over this life. And yet it is strangely vulnerable. Anyone who is thus open from the inmost source of his life outward is also "unprotected" against the cruelty of evil, of sin. If we look for the most profound reason for Jesus' openness in the fact that his existence was brought about by the Spirit, so we are also led to seek there the reason for his death. *His* path to death was not the natural consequence of his birth in the way that our birth sends us toward death. He went to his death because his life was totally unselfcentered. As he was open for everyone, everyone's guilt struck him, the completely open One: "He took our infirmities and bore our diseases", as Matthew interprets Jesus' openness in the light of the Servant of God (Mt 8:17; Is 53:4).

3. The Council of Chalcedon:
"True God—True Man"

Right from the start, both had to be firmly held in Christian theology: that Jesus is truly God and at the same time truly man. "True god and true man" is, accordingly, the formula of Chalcedon. It is already found in the writings of Irenaeus of Lyons. He observes: "This is the very same person to whom the Father makes everything subject (cf. 1 Cor 15:27). He received testimony from all that he is truly man (*vere homo*) and truly God (*vere Deus*)."[46] The formula *vere Deus, vere homo* goes back to the Pauline formula, "according to the Spirit" and "according to the flesh" (cf. Rom 1:3–4), as a criterion for judging Christ.[47] On the other hand, it must also be asked how the concrete fulfillment of Jesus' life turned out to be truly human if he is both man and God. What

---

[46] Irenaeus, *Adversus haereses* 4, 6, 7 (FChr 8/4:52–53); cf. the Council of Chalcedon, DH 301.

[47] See on this point A. Grillmeier, "Die theologische und volkssprachliche Vorbereitung der christologischen Formel von Chalcedon", in *Das Konzil von Chalkedon: Geschichte und Gegenwart*, 5th ed., ed. A. Grillmeier and H. Bacht, 1:36 (Würzburg, 1979).

does Jesus' divinity mean for his humanity? Louis Bouyer (d. 2004) emphasizes:

> At the heart of the Christological problem is our effort to understand how Christ, far from being less human because He is divine, is fully human only because He is "the fullness of divinity" [cf. Col. 1:19] incarnated in our flesh, in the body of humanity thus totally renewed.[48]

This is not a question that has only just been asked. It is posed to Christian faith as soon as it wishes to give a reflective account of that faith. A knowledge of the development of Christology is essential for this account. For in the course of its long history, various attempts at an answer have appeared, which exhibit certain typical structures. In what follows these basic patterns will be elaborated. In the process, particular emphasis will be given to Church Christology and its differentiation from other types.

a. Two "Wrong Tracks": Christologies of Separation and of Intermixture

In the discussion of Christology, there are two kinds of attempted solutions above all that repeatedly turn up. Sometimes the cleanest and most thorough possible distinction between divinity and humanity is sought; on the other hand, an approach toward an understanding is sought through a kind of mixture of the humanity and divinity.

Any schematic characterization distorts. And yet there is some justice in talking about the more *literal* exegesis of the Antiochenes and the more *allegorical* one of the Alexandrians. The same is true if we say that the Alexandrians laid more emphasis on the unity, "God in the flesh", and on the glory of the Logos in the Incarnation, while the Antiochenes emphasized rather the irrevocable distinction between divinity and humanity. The Antiochenes, we may say, were concerned above all about the true and full *humanity* of Jesus (emphasizing at the same time the immutability of God); they may be said to have had more of a sense of the psychology, the human inner life of Jesus, while the Alexandrians (with the exception of Origen) hardly spoke of that at all, but always saw the Logos—so much so, that one often has the impres-

---

[48] L. Bouyer, *The Eternal Son: A Theology of the Word of God and Christology* (Our Sunday Visitor, 1978), p. 135.

sion that the flesh (the σάρξ) was a passive instrument (ὄργανον) of the Logos, which acts alone. If Antiochene Christology carries within it the danger of dividing Christ into two subjects, then Alexandrian Christology tends to unify Logos and sarx to such an extent that they seem to be mixed together.

One speaks of the Antiochene *Logos-anthropos schema* as well as about the Alexandrian *Logos-sarx schema*, and in this way characterizes the two main directions of christological understanding. So that this presentation does not remain too schematic, in what follows two important figures will be discussed who also exercised a reciprocal influence on one another: Apollinaris of Laodicaea, a radical Alexandrian, and Nestorius, a radical Antiochene. The basic *schemas* are in harmony with the Christian faith, but both extreme positions, on the other hand, were condemned as heretical.

Before these lines are presented in detail, it should be pointed out that there was agreement on the level of the kerygma. When it emphasized the true divinity of Christ, the Council of Nicaea was trying to ensure that the proper Christian message was being preached. The common conviction of faith was and is, "Jesus Christ is true God and true man." But therein he is one and the same, the one Son of God in true humanity. The basic assertion is antecedent to the discussion: both the Alexandrian and also the Antiochene Christology are based on this. The difficulties arose because philosophical concepts were used, and indeed had to be used, for the justification and further implementation of this common faith. A terminology was sought that would be capable of testifying to both the unity of Christ and, distinct from that, the differentiation of God and man in Christ.

THE LOGOS–SARX SCHEMA IN APOLLINARIS OF LAODICAEA

The Council of Nicaea was of fundamental importance for the whole development of Christology. The confession of belief in the unqualified divinity of the Son—more precisely, the statement about the true divinity of the Son—was made within the framework of the traditional creed. It is said of Jesus Christ, quite openly, that he is not a creature but the Son of God and is thereby himself God; in order then to speak at the same time of the fact that he was born of the Virgin Mary and suffered and died under Pontius Pilate. On the basis of this statement of the obvious, the dogma of Nicaea was later able to become the

cornerstone of orthodox Christology.[49] This directness and obvious-
ness of belief with which the believer grasps his subject, becomes problematical the moment one tries to define in a formula the how of
Christ's sameness of self as the Son of God and Jesus of Nazareth.

Apollinaris of Laodicaea (d. 392)[50] was a convinced supporter of
Nicaea, a friend of Athanasius, of a speculative turn of mind, not satisfied with faith's mere assertion "that" something was so, who therefore sought an intellectual answer to the question of the Incarnation.
How can we and should we think of the unity of divine Word and
human flesh, of Logos and sarx? It is not enough for the Logos-God
simply to dwell in a man: no man is constituted thereby. In order for
the Logos to have truly become man, Logos and sarx would have to
form a unity. Yet for Apollinaris, this unity can only come into being
if the humanity is not complete. "Two complete beings cannot become one"[51] is what his students repeat back to him. For Apollinaris,
Logos and sarx are therefore parts that form one whole, just as in a human being body and soul are the parts whose combination constitutes
being human. Logically, then, in the case of Christ, the Logos takes
the place of the soul, and Logos and sarx together form the *one nature*
(μία φύσις—Apollinaris is a "Monophysite" in the strict sense of the
word, and the expression that Christ has "one nature" derives from
him). "Nature" means here a vital reality in the concrete sense. At this
point the modern, abstract concept of nature which means something
like "essence", should not be seen. Nature here, as for the Stoics, is a
free and autokinetic being (αὐτοκίνητον). In that sense, the concept is
rather closer to our modern understanding of "person". This integrated
mode of living is what Apollinaris has in mind. And that explains the
great attraction of this model: it ensures the unity of dynamic life in
Christ, as both parts form a *natural* unity.

It also follows, however, that the activity of Christ is understood
according to the same model. There is but one operation (ἐνέργεια),

---

[49] See P. Smulders, "Dogmengeschichtliche und lehramtliche Entfaltung der Christologie", in *Mysterium Salutis* 3/1:389–476, here p. 428.

[50] On what follows, see A. Grillmeier, *Christ in Christian Tradition*, vol. 1: *From the Apostolic Age to Chalcedon (451)*, trans. John Bowden, 2nd ed. (Atlanta: John Knox Press, 1975),
pp. 329–40; E. Mühlenberg, "Apollinaris von Laodicea", in *Theologische Realenzyklopädie*
3:362–71 (Berlin and New York, 1978).

[51] Ps.-Athanasius, *Contra Apollinarem* 1, 2 (PG 26:1096B).

one way Christ's life is lived, that of the Logos. Each nature and each being necessarily has its own activity, which reveals it to the outside world. Just as the soul moves the body as its instrument (ὄργανον), so the Logos alone moves its flesh. The *one* activity corresponds to the *one* nature, for each nature can possess only *one* operation of its own. In Christ, that can be only the divine activity. If, then, Apollinaris accepts only one nature in Christ, he can accept only a single mode of activity: there is no room left for genuine human operation. The unity of Christ's person is meant to be safeguarded in this way. A unified person, a concrete, living subject, comes into being only as a union of Logos and sarx.

Apollinaris thus provides a solid and plausible solution to the problem of the unity of God and man in Christ. Yet this unity has a high price. In order that Christ can be thought of as substantially, physically unified, he has to be made into a kind of intermediate being, between God and man:

> No middle being . . . contains the two extremes . . . in full measure . . .
> —they are there only in part. Now in Christ there is a middle-being . . .
> of God and man; therefore he is neither fully man nor God (alone), but
> a mixture of God and man.[52]

Alois Grillmeier has pointed out that behind this view of Christ there is an understanding of the relationship between God and the world that is still entirely Hellenistic. This is where we find the much-discussed "Hellenization of Christianity"—that is, in the notion that a "heavenly being", the Logos of God, comes down and enters into a physical symbiosis with an earthly flesh. To be able to accept such a synthesis of divine and human in a physical sense, "there needs to be an atmosphere impregnated with pagan mythologies or a world-view that is understood in a thoroughly mythical way. One must live in a completely numinous world, in order" to be "an Apollinarist".[53]

Apollinaris produced several formulations that were important for theology and were accepted or rejected only through a painstaking

---

[52] Apollinaris, *Syllog. Fragm.* 113 (ed. Lietzmann, p. 234); cf. Grillmeier, *Christ in Christian Tradition* 1:332.

[53] A. Grillmeier, "Häresie und Wahrheit: Eine häresiologische Studie als Beitrag zu einem ökumenischen Problem heute", in *Mit ihm und in ihm: Christologische Forschungen und Perspektiven* (Freiburg im Breisgau, 1975), pp. 219–44, quotation from p. 222. On the theory of Hellenization, see above, chap. 1:2c, "Beginning or End? The Hellenization Theory".

process of clarification. He spoke of the one incarnated nature of the divine Logos, which would give Monophysitism its name; but he also spoke of one person (ἕν πρόσωπον) and of one hypostasis (ὑπόστασις), terms that would then be taken over by Chalcedon. Here we have a Christology "from above", in which the element "from below" has become a passive instrument. And the fact that fidelity to the kerygma, the intuition of faith, was strong enough not to succumb to this excessive inculturation of Christianity into Hellenism is among the most astonishing phenomena in the history of Christianity.[54]

An essential part of the kerygma of the Church, firmly rooted in the biblical witness, is that Jesus was truly a man; that it was precisely through his obedience, his freedom, his suffering as a man that salvation came. Hence the reaction against the Alexandrian one-sidedness of Apollinaris was primarily motivated by soteriological considerations.

ANTIOCH, THE LOGOS–MAN *SCHEMA*, AND NESTORIUS

In the conflict with Apollinaris, Antiochene Christology formed a fundamentally different schema from that of the Logos-sarx unity, the Logos-anthropos schema: "Christ both God and man, but man in an integral humanity effective of itself in a human nature that was physically, spiritually, and intentionally autonomous."[55] This has to do with Christ's obedience. If his self-giving is to be genuinely human, so as to be the corrective for the wrong attitude of the human race in Adam, then it too must be based on a genuinely human decision. The fundamental concern of the Antiochenes is thus to emphasize, for soteriological motives, the full and unqualified humanity of Jesus. The constant governing principle in this was emphasized by Origen (d. ca. 253), Tertullian (d. ca. 220), and then later by Gregory Nazianzen (d. ca. 390): "What has not been assumed has not been redeemed" (*Quod non assumptum non sanatum*).[56] "If he [the Logos] had not assumed the whole man, then the whole man would not have been redeemed" (Origen).[57]

---

[54] Cf. Grillmeier, *Christ in Christian Tradition* 1:346–47.

[55] Grillmeier, "Häresie und Wahrheit", p. 223.

[56] A. Grillmeier, "Quod non assumptum non sanatum", in *Lexikon für Theologie und Kirche*, 2nd ed. (1963), 8:954–56. This heading is not given a place in the third edition of the *Lexikon*.

[57] Origen, *Dialogue with Heraclides* (SC 67:70)

If we now look at the "case" of Nestorius, we have to distinguish two things: on the one hand, the way in which he was understood (or misunderstood) and condemned—thus, what has gone down in the history of heresy as "Nestorianism"; on the other hand, Nestorius' own concerns, so far as they are known to us today.[58]

The *official view* of Nestorius (d. ca. 451) is easily summarized. Nestorius, Patriarch of Constantinople from 428 onward, had refused to call Mary theotokos, bearer of God. Consequences were drawn from this: If Mary is not theo-tokos, then the one she bore is not God but merely man (ψιλὸς ἄνθρωπος). But thereby, it was said, Nestorius was dividing the living unity of Christ and speaking about two, the eternal Son and Logos, on one hand, and, on the other, the temporal man Jesus, born of Mary. The connection between divinity and humanity in Jesus would then be based on the attitude of the man Jesus to the Logos. Only a moral unity would therefore exist, brought about by Jesus of Nazareth's having proved himself in obedience to God and having thus merited being united with God. That is why people also speak of "Christology of probation". In short, Nestorius taught that there were not only two natures in Christ, divinity and humanity, but also two persons.

Nestorius himself starts from a clarification of concepts. He asks in what respect we may talk about unity in Christ, and in what respect diversity. For this he refers us to the Nicene Creed. Both things are said there: that Jesus Christ is consubstantial with God and that he has a human existence. "Christ", concludes Nestorius, is "the common name of both natures".[59] If, then, we speak of the suffering of God,

[58] See on this A. Grillmeier, "Das Scandalum oecumenicum des Nestorius in kirchlich-dogmatischer und theologiegeschichtlicher Sicht", in *Mit ihm und in ihm*, pp. 245–82; Grillmeier *Christ in Christian Tradition* 1:447–63. In 1974, with the "Vienna Christological Formula", a decisive step was taken in the ecumenical discussions between the Roman Catholic and the Coptic-Orthodox Churches. H. Meyer et al., eds., *Dokumente wachsender Übereinstimmung: Sämtliche Berichte und Konsenstexte interkonfessioneller Gespräche auf Weltebene*, vol. 1: *1931–1982* (Paderborn, 1982), pp. 541–42. For documents on these discussions, see: A. Stirnemann and G. Wilfinger, eds., *Konzilien und Kircheneinheit: Zweite Wiener Altorientalenkonsultation 1973; Dokumentation des offiziellen Dialoges zwischen der Koptisch-Orthodoxen und der Römisch-Katholischen Kirche: Pro Oriente-Regionalsymposion 1991 in Wadi Natrun; Pro Oriente-Regionalsymposion 1993 in Kerala*, Pro Oriente 20 (Innsbruck, 1998); cf. E. C. Suttner, "Der christologische Konsens mit den Nicht-Chalcedonensern", *Ostkirchliche Studien* 41 (1992): 3–21.

[59] Nestorius, *Letter to Cyril 2*, in Loofs, *Die Überlieferung und Anordnung der Fragmente des*

there is a danger of describing God as "passible", changeable, in his divine existence, in his divine nature. So as to avoid this danger, Paul in the Letter to the Philippians (Phil 2), does not speak of the God-Logos as the Crucified, but of Christ.

> If you search through the whole of the New Testament, you will nowhere find death attributed to God (to the Divinity), but either to "Christ" or to the "Son" or to the "Lord". For "Christ" and "Son" and "Lord", as applied by Scripture to the Only-begotten, are expressions of the two natures and reveal sometimes the divinity, sometimes the humanity, and sometimes both.[60]

Hence, Antiochene theology has a tendency to analyze what we should regard in the life of Jesus as belonging to his divinity and what to his humanity. Lists of such attributions were drawn up: the miracles and the Transfiguration are attributed to the divinity; being hungry and thirsty and tired, to the humanity of Jesus. Attributions of this kind can easily have an artificial and forced quality; they seem to be tearing apart the unified life of Jesus. On the other hand, they can already be found in New Testament Christology, where for instance the form of God and the form of a servant are distinguished (Phil 2), or lowliness and glory (Jn 17). It is thus logical for Nestorius to remark: "Therefore the two natures belong unto Christ and not unto God the Word."[61] The subject whose suffering, Cross, and Resurrection are attested is Christ. That is why Nestorius would prefer Mary to be called *Christotokos*, but not Theotokos; because he sees in this latter term the danger of misunderstanding it to mean that Mary gave birth to God and that God (the Son) first took his beginning with his birth from Mary.

Even though his solution was not successful, Nestorius sees the central question as being the correct distinction between nature and person, between nature and the one who possesses it. For this purpose, he borrows from Gregory Nazianzen the distinction to the effect that

---

Nestorius (Halle, 1904), p. 175; German text in P. T. Camelot, *Ephesus und Chalcedon*, GÖK 2 (Mainz, 1963), pp. 228–32; = TzT D 6, no. 61 (98–103).

[60] Nestorius, *Sermon* 10 (ed. Loofs, p. 269).

[61] Nestorius, *Liber Heraclidis* (ed. P. Bedjan [Paris, 1910], p. 248). This is one of Nestorius' later writings, written after he had been condemned and shortly before his death. Cf. L. Abrahamowski, *Untersuchungen zum Liber Heraclidis des Nestorius*, CSCO 242, Subsidia 22 (Louvain, 1963); Grillmeier, *Christ in Christian Tradition* 1:501–19; here, p. 505.

the possessor of the nature is always *one*, not "one and another" (*alius et alius*), but is not *one thing*; yet he possesses "one thing and another" (*aliud et aliud*). The union of God and man in Christ does not take place in the realm of natures, of essences, but in that of the person. Despite the inadequacies of Nestorius' Christology, which were in fact the basis for its rejection by the councils, there is an intention here that remains valid. The question of the unity of Christ cannot be put on the level of essences; it must be asked on the level of person. Christological thinking will build further on this point and will clarify the question: How is it possible for one subject, one person, Jesus Christ, to have two natures, a divine and a human one? We may note this much in a negative sense: It is not possible through a kind of mixture, in which the divine and human elements would be combined as parts, as Apollinaris tried to do, since for that they would have to be two elements that could be "mixed together", like water and wine or copper and tin can be mixed. The unity of Christ cannot be a unity of natures, otherwise each of the two natures thus united would in itself be incomplete. Two complete natures can unite only when this takes place on a personal level. That is a significant step toward an understanding of person. It still remains to be seen, of course, exactly what the personal level actually is.

What stands behind Nestorius' intention is, on the one hand, the metaphysical assertion that the human and divine elements are not two competing entities and, indeed, cannot in any way be so. On the other hand, there is a soteriological assertion combined with this, that incarnation, salvation, redemption are the free, nonobligatory act of God—something that, again, can be possible only on a personal level. If, on the other hand, there were a unity of natures in Christ, then the constituent parts would have need of each other in order to form one common nature. Thus body and soul, both incomplete natures, necessarily constitute only one human being together; they depend on each other. But the unity of God and man in Christ cannot be one of this kind, otherwise the Incarnation would be a necessary fact[62] and not the free act of God, springing purely from his intention to save us, which cannot be postulated, with any degree of necessity, on the basis of nature and the order of creation.

---

[62] See A. Grillmeier, "Das Scandalum oecumenicum des Nestorius", p. 277.

Two consequences may be drawn from this for the further path of Christology. First, the two natures must be preserved in this unity, since only thus can it be shown that it is not the result of some natural necessity. Second, this unity must be a personal one, a *hypostatic union*. Nestorius is striving to penetrate this mystery through speculative thought. He is not satisfied merely to refer to the paradox; he wants to reflect on the mystery of faith. Tragically, his intellectual powers were inadequate to carry this task through to its conclusion; this was probably also because he was too impetuous as a person, and for the same reason he paid too little attention to the legitimate concerns of the Alexandrians. He did, however, point christological reflection to the right course by showing that the understanding of person is central to the question of Christology. Yet he did not succeed in freeing the concept of person from its philosophical derivation and rethinking it for the uniqueness of the problem in question, for the mystery of the person of Christ.

On the basis of this account, we can understand how it was that people could see in Nestorius' theory a kind of "archetype" of a christological blind alley, the model for the "Christology of separation". Such a Nestorian Christology of separation did in fact exist, taught by pupils of Nestorius, and may still be found even today in many popular academic presentations. This schema was formulated all the more pointedly because after Chalcedon, the "countertype", a "Christology of intermixture", existed in Monophysitism: Nestorius separates divinity and humanity and allows only a moral union while Eutyches (d. 450), the "principal witness" of the Monophysites, mingles them both by teaching that there is only one nature in Christ, so that no genuine humanity remains in Christ; the divinity, however, has been changed by the intermixture and has become capable of suffering. The temptation of constructing a kind of "dialectic of heresies" is great, especially in what concerns christological dogma, where there is a constant danger of one-sidedly overemphasizing either separation or unification.

Both types are based on a legitimate concern; each has its own truth. The Alexandrians intend above all to show that in Christ, God *really* came to men and that man has thereby *really* been accepted by God. The aim is always a real humanization of God and a real divinization of man. That is why the Alexandrians speak of "God's suffering", of "God's death"—just as Ignatius of Antioch had already spoken of the "suffering of my God"[63]—and of "God's blood".[64] To this day, these "theopaschite" formulations (which declare the suffering of God) of the Alexandrians present one of the most urgent questions of Christology, since if God himself is not engaged in Christ's work of salvation, then is it still a work of *salvation?* The Alexandrians want to hold fast to the real Incarnation, so they always emphasize: If the Logos, the Son, did not die on the Cross, then this was merely the death of a man, who—however righteous and perfect he may be—cannot be the redemption of all. That is why they constantly repeat, "God *himself* . . . became man, suffered. . . ."

One question among all theopaschite formulations remains, of course, and it is posed with some urgency again today, when there is much talk about "God's suffering", about God's changeableness and God's developing: If, in the Incarnation, God involves himself so in history, in what is finite, does he then remain the transcendent God? Does God cease to be God when he becomes man? It is precisely against this conception that Antiochene Christology is struggling, and, indeed —astonishingly—it does so for the same soteriological motive. If God becomes man, suffers, and dies, and if he no longer is and remains God in doing so, then our salvation is also empty. Both are necessary for our salvation: that Christ is God and remains God, even in his human life and work.

Talking about the suffering God always seemed unacceptable to the Antiochenes, while the Alexandrians wished precisely in that way to express the dynamic of the history of salvation: that is, that in the Christ-event God himself "became involved" in the salvation of mankind. The Antiochenes, in a more ontological perspective, see in this the danger of infringing upon God's transcendence. Time and again, they emphasize that we cannot simply speak, without differentiation, of *God's* suffering, of *God's* Incarnation; we cannot say this without qualification, but only in a certain specific respect.

---

[63] Ignatius of Antioch, *Epistle to the Romans* 6:3, ed. Loeb, trans. K. Lake (Cambridge, Mass., and London, 1977), p. 234–35.

[64] Ignatius of Antioch, *Epistle to the Ephesians* 1:1, ed. Loeb ed., trans. K. Lake (Cambridge, Mass., and London, 1977), p. 172–73.

THE DEVELOPMENT OF THE
CHRISTIAN UNDERSTANDING OF PERSON

In the arguments surrounding the theology of Nestorius and that of Apollinaris, the categories of contemporary philosophy proved to be inadequate. Lasting credit goes to the three Cappadocians, especially in connection with trinitarian theology, for having worked out the first fundamentals of a Christian concept of person. It soon became clear, of course, that when the trinitarian concept of person developed by them was applied to Christology, this necessitated a further significant stage of development. In this, the problem of Nestorius, and his use of this concept worked as a catalyst.

The question had already arisen from Nicaea regarding the confession of belief in the true divinity of Christ, and then, after the First Council of Constantinople regarding the divinity of the Holy Spirit. The subject of discussion here was precisely how Father, Son, and Holy Spirit could be truly three and yet, at the same time, the One God. The result of the theological wrestling was the gradual sense of the distinction between nature and person and, together with this, a first approach to the concept of person. That it could arrive at this only becomes comprehensible if one starts from the given data of revelation. Classical metaphysics certainly made a distinction between what is general and what is particular, in which what is general was always given precedence as being genuine, essential, true. The individual or particular was understood primarily as a limitation, as something finite. Hence the question familiar to classical metaphysics was above all that of the essence, whether in the sense of the Platonic idea or that of the Aristotelian eidos, of the "being" of things.[65] The concept of person, however, what exists-through-itself, as the ultimate particularity, as what is irreducible to any generality, was unknown to it. It was only in trinitarian theology and in Christology that the concept gradually acquired this fundamental and irrevocable sense. The process still needed a long time, of course—insofar as it is even yet completed.[66]

---

[65] See E. von Ivánka, *Plato Christianus* (Einsiedeln, 1964), pp. 44–47.

[66] This question is well summarized in G. Greshake, *Der dreieine Gott: Eine trinitarische Theologie* (Freiburg im Breisgau, 1998), esp. pp. 74–90 (bibliography); see also Greshake, "Person" 2, in *Lexikon für Theologie und Kirche*, 3rd ed. (1999), 8:46–50; M. Fuhrmann et al., "Person", in *Historisches Wörterbuch der Philosophie* (1989), 7:269–338 (see bibliography); in a wider theological perspective, see von Balthasar, TD 2:173–429; in the perspective of recent philosophy, R. Spaemann, *Personen: Versuche über den Unterschied zwischen "etwas" und*

If we ask about the history of this development, the distinction between nature and person is reduced to its simplest form by Gregory Nazianzen. Because of his writings about trinitarian theology, the Eastern Church calls him Gregory the Theologian. In his trinitarian theology, he works with the linguistic distinction between masculine and neuter:

> For the Son is not the Father—for only one is the Father, and yet he is *what* the Father is—nor is the Spirit the Son, because he comes from the Father, for only one is the Only-begotten, and yet he is *what* the Son is.[67]

There are not, then, "one thing and another" in the Trinity, yet there are "one person and another". In Christ, on the other hand, in the incarnate Son, there is not one person and another—that is, not two subjects, but just one and the same, the single subject; and yet there do exist one thing and another, divinity and humanity.[68] Gregory emphasizes time and again that this ought to be a matter, not of arguing about words, but about the subject, the reality of faith. Yet since one must also agree about linguistic usage, he and the two other great Cappadocians, Basil of Caesarea (d. 379) and Gregory of Nyssa (d. 395), tried to find as appropriate a terminology as possible. It was a brilliant and consequential "trick" by which the Cappadocians made use of two almost synonymous philosophical terms to denote this tension between nature and person, between "something else" and "someone else", the "what" (the question of being) and the "who" (the question of person): the concepts of οὐσία (being) and ὑπόστασις (hypostasis, person). In profane philosophy, οὐσία was used to describe "what is", and ὑπόστασις, "what subsists".[69] Both of them, then, mean the essence, the *what* of a thing. The Cappadocians further develop these concepts, they "Christianize" them, "baptize" them, by continuing to understand by οὐσία the *what*, but by hypostasis, the *who*, that is, the individual subject: what we call person. With these presuppositions, one can understand why, in the later discussion about the Incarnation, the *who* of Christ was called his hypostasis, while the *what*, his true divinity and his true humanity, was called οὐσία—*substantia*.

"jemand", 2nd ed. (Stuttgart, 1996); in the context of canon law and theology, L. Gerosa, *Charisma und Recht* (Einsiedeln, 1989), pp. 86–90.

[67] Gregory Nazianzen, *Oratio* 31:9 (FChr 22:290–91).

[68] Gregory Nazianzen, *Letter* 101 ad Cledonium 21 (SC 208:44–47).

[69] Cf. Theodoret of Cyr, *Eranistes*, dial. 1 (ed. Ettlinger, p. 64; PG 83:33).

What actually constitutes a "person"? What makes it possible to distinguish someone, one human being, from all others as this unmistakable and unique one? In what follows we will pursue this question as it emerged in the history of theology and try to reconstruct the development of thinking here. The assistance given by Gregory of Nyssa, the most speculative of the Cappadocians, in a famous letter "on distinguishing between nature and hypostasis"[70] is fundamental here.

Gregory takes as his starting point an observation concerning language. There are two ways of referring to reality, the general description and the personal name. If one says "a man", then a general description that applies to all men is intended. If, on the other hand, one asks: "Which man?", then the answer will be a personal name, Peter, Paul, or something similar. But how do we arrive at this personal name, at the designation of the concrete individual existence, the concrete individual man? In what does the distinctiveness of his reality consist? Thought has come up against this question since the dawn of Greek philosophy. Is the individual, the concrete reality of the individual, something we can define positively, perfect in itself, or is it just one "case" of something general, a diminishment of true being, of true reality? This question becomes most pressing when man is asking about himself, about his own existence, about his own self. Greek philosophy asks above all about being or substance. Aristotle calls the contemplation of being the first and virtually the only task of the philosopher.[71] What, then, is the being of man? Yet this question is not enough, for there is another, far more urgent, question that has been raised with increasing urgency right up to modern times, indeed, up to this day: *Who* am I? The answer to the question about substance is inadequate for this essential human question; no science, no philosophy, indeed, no other person can supply the answer here. I myself am standing here alone with this question of mine and with my mystery. "Everyone who hears that question [Who am I?] within himself knows with certainty that everyone else is destined to hear it too."[72] Here is something that is shared in common yet that leads us back again to the being of man.

---

[70] Gregory of Nyssa, *De differentia essentiae et hypostaseos* (ed. Forlin Patrucco, CorPat 11: 178–95). This text has gone down in history as letter 38 of his brother, Basil. See also Schönborn, *God's Human Face: The Christ-Icon* (San Francisco: Ignatius Press, 1994), pp. 14–33.

[71] Aristotle, *Metaphysics* 7, title and 1028b.

[72] Von Balthasar, TD 1:481–86; here, p. 486; see also A.J. Festugière, *L'Idéal religieux des Grecs et l'Évangile* (Paris, 1932), pp. 59–60.

Yet how does Gregory determine this distinction between a general denomination and a personal name? How does he make this distinction? In saying "a man", we have not yet expressed what is particular about *this* man, what is his own, but only an indeterminate general designation, the substance (οὐσία), the nature (φύσις). In order for the statement to become more definite, to acquire standing (ὑπό-στασις, German *Bestand*), it has to become more precise. Gregory calls this process of definition "characterizing", in that particular qualities and peculiarities are enumerated. These features characterize the person, the hypostasis. Peter, Paul, and James are not distinguished from one another by their being human but by their own qualities. Gregory thus arrives at this (gnoseologic) statement: The hypostasis, the person, becomes apparent and recognizable in his particular characteristics. But what are these characteristics? This means "all the inward and outward peculiarities there can be about an actual man—from his location to his moral conduct".[73] This particular man is characterized by having this color skin, this color eyes, that voice, "particular features", right up to his "character", which is sought especially in mental traits.

Descriptive sciences, too, use this method to define their subjects. But is this determination of individual qualities adequate as a way to arrive at the person? Am I "myself" only by the correct chance combination of certain characteristics? Do these in themselves make up the person? "One has the impression, on the whole, that Gregory's reflections on the hypostases are located more on the level of the individual than on that of the person", is the judgment of Ghislain Lafont.[74] Does this succeed in seeing more in the person than just one special case at a time of "being human"? Gregory does not yet seem to have succeeded in making sufficiently clear the difference between a person and an individual. What is lacking in the concept of a person with Gregory, and later with Nestorius, is the distinction between gnoseological characterization and ontological constitution. Here, of course, the danger also still remains of seeing what is real in a man as existing primarily on the level of substance. The person as name is fundamentally distinct from the characteristics the person *has*. The person as name is uniqueness and relatedness in one; it is being "thou" for God and mission.[75] Later, person will be understood as subsistence, as independence, as

---

[73] Grillmeier, "Das Scandalum oecumenicum des Nestorius", p. 266.

[74] G. Lafont, *Peut-on connaître Dieu en Jésus-Christ? Problématique* (Paris, 1969), p. 60.

[75] Cf. von Balthasar, TD 3:203–20; Greshake, *Der dreieine Gott*, pp. 175–78.

existing-from-oneself. Then "I" is more than my characteristics and also more than my self-awareness.

For the purpose of his christological analyses, Nestorius tried to go farther along the Cappadocians' path. Here, of course, the inadequacy of the existing understanding of person would be demonstrated. If we start from the proposition that Christ is true God and true man, then we assume that this implies a real human existence, a human existence with all the characteristics of being human. That leads inevitably to the notion that these characteristics form a human hypostasis, a person. If we conceive of a person as being exclusively the sum of the particular qualities of an individual, then logically we would have to reach the conclusion that in Christ there are not only two natures, but also two persons: the Divine Person, as defined by its divine characteristics, those of the eternal Son; and the human person, defined and constituted by the concrete qualities that make Jesus this particular person, that distinguish him from all other people.[76] There is no doubt as to the fact that Nestorius did indeed teach that there were two πρόσωπα in Christ. But did he understand these as being persons in the full sense? This can hardly be claimed, but his christological approach did break down in that he was unable to elaborate clearly enough how Christ is truly *one*. So it was not unjustified if, in the condemnation of Nestorius, reference was made to this point above all, that, ultimately, the unity of Christ was in some way added on subsequently, that therefore all attempts to analyze unity seem somewhat artificial. However painful the crisis provoked by Nestorius was, it caused a genuine deepening of christological reflection and the attempt to free the confession of faith in Christ more and more from the defects of the tools provided by Greek philosophy and to give it clear expression.

Apollinaris, however, speaks without distinction of the one hypostasis and the one physis (nature) of Christ, and Alexandrian theology follows his lead in this. Cyril of Alexandria (d. 444) can speak of the "one

---

[76] In a similar way, but in a different context, there is a parallel to this in twentieth-century theology, in particular in Karl Rahner's criticism of the concept of "person" in tradition and of the application made of this in the theology of the Trinity. K. Rahner, "Die Aporetik des 'Person'-Begriffs in der Trinitätslehre", in *Mysterium Salutis* 2:385–93; on the discussion concerning this, see B.J. Hilberath, *Der Personenbegriff der Trinitätslehre in Rückfrage von Karl Rahner zu Tertullians "Adversus Praxean"*, ITS 17 (Innsbruck, 1986); esp. pp. 16–66; Greshake, *Der dreieine Gott*, pp. 141–47 (bibliography).

incarnate nature of the Logos God" in the honest belief that this is an old formula from Athanasius. In doing so, he understands Christ as a concrete, individual existence. For an Antiochene, on the other hand, that would have to sound most suspicious, since the Antiochenes set a high value on clear distinctions. Jesus' being truly human is only safeguarded if the human nature is clearly distinguished from the divine. The Alexandrians are more interested in the process of incarnation. As they understand the nature as a living process, they are able to talk, with no argument, about the one physis, thus in a Monophysite way. The Antiochenes, however, look at the divine and human existence in Christ more as two conjointly given realities, hence as two natures in the metaphysical sense. Since they pay more attention to the nature of being, it is understandable that any talk of Christ's having *one* nature is for them unacceptable.

THE PERPETUATION OF THE SCHISM

There is something tragic about these two different approaches, as also about the misunderstandings to which they gave rise and which ultimately led to the unhappy schism in the Church. Political motives also played a not inconsiderable part, of course, in the conflict between Nestorius and Cyril. This led not only to the two most important christological councils, those of Ephesus (431) and Chalcedon (451), it also provided the impulse toward the first great schisms, which have still not yet been overcome today. After the Council of Ephesus came the separation from a whole group of "Nestorian" Churches; the reasons for this separation were probably as political and ethnic-national as they were dogmatic. Among these Churches is the so-called East-Syrian Church, whose region at the time of these two councils lay outside the Roman Empire, which is why this Church was not represented at Ephesus. This Church subsequently supported the position of Nestorius. Later in history it proved to be one of the most thriving of the Christian Churches. From its later patriarchal see in Babylon (Seleucia-Ctesiphon) in Persia (today, Iraq), it developed an incredible missionary activity that reached as far as China. Its influence reached over nearly the whole of Asia. At its peak, the Nestorian Church had 230 dioceses that extended across the whole of Asia, with many millions of believers. As a result of severe persecutions in the course of the centuries, it gradually dwindled away. Today the Catholikos resides in

Morton Grove (U.S.), and there are besides a few dioceses in Iran, the former heartland, in Iraq, Lebanon, India, and Australia.[77]

The Monophysite Churches, which separated from Orthodoxy after Chalcedon, still represent a considerable group today and include the Jacobite or West-Syrian Church, the Coptic Church, the Ethiopians, and the Armenians. Although here too, dogmatic grounds were not the primary cause of the separation, Ephesus and Chalcedon mark painful breaks in the history of the Church, wounds that are still open today.[78] We cannot overlook the role that the divisions among the Christian Churches played in the rise of Islam. Even though the dialogues between Orthodoxy, the so-called Ancient Eastern Churches, and the Roman Catholic Church have been very fruitful in recent years and decades, the road to unity is still a long and rocky one.[79]

b. The Council of Ephesus (431) and Cyril of Alexandria

The Third Ecumenical Council, which gathered at Ephesus in 431 at the instigation of Cyril of Alexandria, was supposed to produce an answer to the "case of Nestorius". This is not the place to go into the complex historical circumstances of this Council; social and political factors played their part.[80] It is the dogmatic result of the Council that

---

[77] Cf. *Kleine Konfessionskunde*, ed. J. A. Möhler Institute, 2nd ed. (Paderborn, 1997), pp. 102-3.

[78] On this whole subject, cf. *Kleine Konfessionskunde*, pp. 103-7; P. Neuner, *Ökumenische Theologie: Die Suche nach der Einheit der christlichen Kirchen* (Darmstadt, 1997), pp. 94-95; H.J. Schulz and P. Wiertz, "Die Altorientalischen Kirchen", in *Handbuch der Ostkirchenkunde*, ed. W. Nyssen, H.-J. Schulz, and P. Wiertz, 1:34-46 (Düsseldorf, 1984).

[79] The efforts of the PRO ORIENTE Institute, for instance, should be included here, especially the activities of the Syriac Commission and the Commission for Dialogues with the Ancient Churches of the East. See on this point the documentation from PRO ORIENTE, *Syriac Dialogue: Non-Official Consultation on Dialogue within the Syriac Tradition* (Vienna, 1994ff.); A. Stirnemann and G. Wilfinger, eds., *30 Jahre Pro Oriente: Festgabe für den Stifter Franz Kardinal König zu seinem 90. Geburtstag*, Pro Oriente 17 (Innsbruck, 1995). On the Catholics' dialogues with the Ancient Churches of the East, cf. John Paul II, encyclical *Ut unum sint*, nos. 62-63.

[80] For literature on this council: P. T. Camelot, *Ephesus und Chalcedon*, GÖK 2 (Mainz, 1963); K. Schatz, *Allgemeine Konzilien—Brennpunkte der Kirchengeschichte* (Paderborn, 1997), pp. 51-56; P. L'Huillier, *The Church of the Ancient Councils: The Disciplinary Work of the First Four Ecumenical Councils* (Crestwood, N.Y., 1996), pp. 143-54; L. Perrone, "Von Nicaea (325) nach Chalcedon (451)", in *Geschichte der Konzilien: Vom Nicaeanum bis zum Vaticanum II*, ed. G. Alberigo, pp. 21-134; here, pp. 84-100 (Düsseldorf, 1993); Grillmeier, *Christ in Christian Tradition* 1:484-87. On Cyril, cf. J. A. McGuckin, *St. Cyril of Alexandria, the Christological Controversy: Its History, Theology, and Texts*, supplements to *Vigiliae Christianae* 23 (Leiden, 1994).

is most important for our presentation. It is characteristic of the early Church's understanding of herself that the bishops of Ephesus had no desire for a new dogmatic formulation; rather, they understood every-thing they said as an interpretation and confirmation of the Creed of Nicaea. For them, the Nicene formula was the valid christological for-mulation. The Council understood itself as the legitimate interpreter of Nicaea, which was deemed to be the "epitome of the apostolic faith". Ephesus thereby offers a good example of the continuing interpretation of the apostolic faith in ever new situations and of the path that was typical of the self-concept of all the early councils.[81]

The achievement of Ephesus can be summed up in this one sen-tence, interpreting Nicaea: " 'One and the same' is first born of God and then 'on the last days' born as a man from Mary. . . . Therefore Mary may be called mother of God" (θεοτόκος).[82] In a mysterious way, the Son of God himself is the subject of the earthly life of Jesus. This declaration of belief is the great accomplishment of the Council of Ephesus. A council is not, of course, a convention of dogmatic theolo-gians. Rather, councils are dogmatic in the original sense of the word: they confess and solemnly proclaim the faith. They publicly profess the apostolic "dogmata" of the tradition. It seldom happens that councils continue theological discussions through their own "contribution to the theological discussion"; that is not their task. Ephesus declares its faith in the unity of Christ as subject. Within this confession of faith and continuing from it, theological reflection can then develop and evolve.

Cyril of Alexandria must be mentioned above all as the theologian of Ephesus. A quick look at his Christology will carry our reasoning a significant distance on the path to an understanding of person in Christology. In his numerous christologically centered writings, Cyril expounded the belief confessed by Ephesus in the wake of Nicaea.

He, who is "the image of the invisible God" (Col 1:15), . . . assumed the form of a servant (cf. Phil 2:7), not by adding a man to himself, as they [the Nestorians] say, but by giving himself this form, and indeed in

---

[81] In canon 7 the Fathers explicitly set down that no one has the right to change or replace the Nicene Creed in any way whatever. Subsequently, of course, this canon in particular was subject to repeated misunderstandings, whenever it was understood to mean that no further thinking at all about the faith was allowed. Cf. L'Huillier, *Church of the Ancient Councils*, pp. 159–63.

[82] Grillmeier, *Christ in Christian Tradition* 1:499; cf. DH 251; 253.

such a way that he thus [that is, in the form of a servant] preserved his likeness to God the Father.[83]

This quotation displays the essential features of his Christology. If we declare in faith that the Son became man, then this does mean that, even having become man, he is the Son. Cyril keeps coming back to this. He quotes, for example, from the Second Letter to the Corinthians (2 Cor 4:6), where Paul says of the glory of God that it shines in the face of Jesus Christ:

> For the only begotten Son displays in himself the glory of the Father, even when he has become man. . . . For we cannot see God in human form except in the Logos, who has become a man like us and, in doing so, has even thus [that is, as the one who became man] remained the true and "natural" Son.[84]

We can therefore perceive the glory of the Father in the incarnate Word. Believing in Jesus of Nazareth means believing in the Person of the Son of God. In this context Cyril likes to quote the episode of the man born blind. Jesus asks him, "Do you believe in the Son of God?" And he responds with a counter question: "And who is he, sir, that I may believe in him?" Jesus says, "You have seen him, and it is he who speaks to you" (Jn 9:35–37).[85] According to Cyril, this "You have seen him" presupposes that Jesus' humanity is not a kind of garment, the livery of the Logos, but that he himself is this humanity of his. Thus, Cyril can emphasize time and again that the flesh is to a certain extent the Logos; it has become a true identity.

That, then, is the decisive step brought by Cyril for the development of the understanding of person. Becoming man means that the Logos, the Son, identifies himself with the flesh, with existing as a man, and in such a way as to make it *his* existence as a man. Hence, time and again, Cyril speaks of "making his own" (ἰδιοποίεσθαι). This idea of appropriation proved extremely fruitful, especially with a view to the subsequent development of the concept of person, when it was a matter of introducing the relational element—the essential relatedness of one person to other persons, the capacity for empathy in the understanding of person—to the classic definitions of person, the person defined above all on the basis of independence and distinctive characteristics.[86]

---

[83] Cyril of Alexandria, *Quod Christus sit unus* (SC 97:450–51).

[84] Ibid. (SC 97:450–53).

[85] Cyril, *De Incarnatione* (SC 97:269).

[86] A fundamental discussion of this in von Balthasar, TD 2:189–334.

Cyril repeatedly emphasizes that the Incarnation of the Son means that the eternal Son has made existence as a man his own—so much so that it became his existence as a man, that he himself became man. To quote one example, among many:

> The Logos became man—how could that be true unless he himself (αὐτός) became flesh, that is to say, man, by making the human body his own in an indissoluble unity, so that this [body] was recognized as his own and not that of someone else.[87]

This appropriation means that the Son himself is the subject of the human life of Jesus. That is why Cyril can and must say that the Logos did not merely use a human existence as an instrument, as God spoke through the prophets, but that it is truly his human existence. Therefore, everything belonging to this human existence has been made his own by the Logos. Birth, suffering, and death can and must truly be witnessed to by the Son: otherwise, the Incarnation is a fiction. Cyril does, however, emphasize the other side of this assumption: just as the Son makes this human existence his own, so it becomes the property of this human existence to be that of the Son. In Christ, being the son becomes "the most essential property of this human existence, the characteristic trait of mankind".[88]

Cyril goes a step farther in developing a more profound Christology when he talks about the "exchange of properties", the "communication of idioms". If God becomes man, an exchange takes place between the humanity and the divinity of Christ. But what does this look like in detail? What consequences are there for Christ in this talk about the unity of God and man? This unity is not, indeed, a matter of an intermixture of what is divine and what is human; rather, it is an issue that is in the highest degree personal. Jesus' humanity is in no way distinguished from any other humanity, except in that its most particular property, in fact its most personal quality, is that of being the humanity of the Son, of being "Sonship" from the roots of its being. For Cyril, being human becomes a characteristic of the Logos, and, vice versa, being the Son a characteristic of the humanity of Christ. That may at first sound very abstract. To understand it better, we have to look closer at the soteriological perspective within which Cyril understands the communication of idioms.

---

[87] Cyril, *Quod Christus sit unus* (SC 97:336–37).
[88] Ibid. (SC 97:256–57).

"In him the whole fullness of deity dwells bodily", says Paul (Col 2:9).
And the Theologian [John the Evangelist] reveals to us the great mystery,
that the Word dwelt among us (Jn 1:14). For we are all in Christ, and
the whole, one humanity [τὸ κοινὸν πρόσωπον—literally, "the common
person of humanity"] is endowed with new life in him. . . . The Word
has dwelt among all of us in one person so that the sonship might be
transmitted from the one true Son of God to all men, through the Spirit
of holiness.[89]

Cyril, and patristic Christology with him, stands entirely within
Paul's perspective here and looks to the new beginning of humanity
and its renewal in Christ. The christological and the soteriological-
ecclesiological perspective are inseparable here. Summed up in a brief
and pregnant formula:

> Just as in Christ being the Son became a characteristic of his human exis-
> tence, through his union with the Logos, in accordance with the plan for
> salvation in [God's] economy, so it became characteristic of the Logos to
> be surrounded by a multitude of brothers and to become firstborn among
> them through his union with the flesh.[90]

The appropriation of human existence does not, therefore, mean assuming a human nature, considered abstractly, but that the Son identifies himself with the whole history of mankind, even with its whole
situation of unredemption and death. He is not ashamed to call men
his brothers (Heb 2:11). He takes on the form of a servant for the sake
of those enslaved by sin, so that they may be free, just as he in his form
of a slave is completely free.

In the Creed we profess that "one Lord Jesus Christ, the Only Begotten Son of God . . . for us men and for our salvation . . . was incarnate . . . and became man". Cyril, and the great christological tradition
of the councils and the Fathers after him, understands the Incarnation
as this taking flesh, just as the hymn in Philippians had talked about
taking the form of a servant. Before all the questions about how that
should be understood, it was known as the good news: God-with-us;
Christ is the Emmanuel (as Matthew portrays him). It is therefore with
some justice that this Christology has been called "Emmanuel Christology".[91] It is certainly a "Christology of descent", in the sense that

---

[89] Cyril, Commentary on John 1:14 (PG 73:161C).
[90] Cyril, Quod Christus sit unus (SC 97:256–57).
[91] See, for instance, H.M. Diepen, La Théologie de l'Émmanuel: Les Lignes maîtresses d'une
christologie (Paris, 1960).

the initiative and the authorship of salvation in Christ is truly God's and only God's. Yet Emmanuel does mean "God with us". Incarnation means the acceptance of human existence, the "ascent" of the whole human reality to God. Our human reality has become that of the Son. This is not merely a presence resembling that of the shekinah, similar to that of the Spirit of God in the prophets; it is no mere "indwelling", but a taking on of human existence. This central concept of taking on or acceptance, on the one hand, addresses the personal dimension of the Christ-event (only a person can accept something) and yet, on the other, also makes clear the meaning of the Christ-event for salvation history, since in the Son's accepting the form of a servant, God has accepted men and has made them sons.

Ephesus stands in the "Alexandrian" tradition. It sees the Incarnation, not as the "bundling together" of two substances (which is unthinkable on account of their incommensurability alone), but as the dramatic act of God's acceptance of humanity, no longer merely as an affirmation, but as identification in an inconceivable and incomprehensible way, as a true *becoming man* by the Son. What is said here about the person is that the characteristic trait of the person of Christ, of the Son, is that of being able to identify himself: "For by his Incarnation the Son of God has united himself in some fashion with every man" (*Gaudium et Spes*, no. 22).

c. The Council of Chalcedon (451)

Only twenty years after Ephesus, in 451, the Church again felt obliged to convene an ecumenical council, the fourth, at Chalcedon, near Constantinople, in order to attempt another step toward clarification in the christological debates that had not abated. If Ephesus, along with the Alexandrian tradition, had emphasized above all the unity of the subject—it is truly the Son of God who has become man—it was now a matter of doing justice to the concerns of the Antiochene tradition, to the fact that it did not become a mixture of God and man: to explain that he who became man remains true God and has become true man. In the liturgy for the feast of the Circumcision, it says, "He remains what he was [that is, God] and becomes what he was not [a human being]."[92]

---

[92] "Id quod fuit remansit, et quod non erit assumpsit." Book of Hours, Lauds for the Solemnity of Mary the Mother of God (January 1), antiphon to the Benedictus.

The Creed of Chalcedon does not, of course, have a good press.[93]
It is said to be too static, too essentialist, too Hellenistic, too metaphysical; and that means not sufficiently "flexible", functional, biblical, or historical. For the most part, what leads to such prejudices is
simply a quite astonishing ignorance of what Chalcedon was about.[94]
If the historical facts here were somewhat inconsequential, then this
attitude would indeed be dubious, but not tragic. But in Chalcedon
we are dealing with one of the most important ecumenical councils,
which provided the normative framework for the whole of subsequent
Christology. Chalcedon itself, in turn, fully conscious of this demand,
understood its own "formula" as a valid exposition of the apostolic
faith.

We are concerned here with an eminently ecclesiological question.
If we accept that there is a break between New Testament Christology
and the Creed of Chalcedon, a distortion of the original, then at the
same time the continuity of faith is lost; then Chalcedon together with
subsequent Christology was just a break; and then today we have to
rediscover the original New Testament witness to Christ by bypassing
this break. Yet how can this be done? Where are we to find the criteria
that will enable us to avoid what people accuse Chalcedon of doing—
dissolving Christianity in contemporary ways of thinking? That, however, is precisely what Chalcedon is not. A closer study of the Council
shows that what occupied the Council Fathers were primarily keryg-
matic concerns. They did not wish to reduce the apostolic confession
of faith in Christ to philosophical terms but, rather, to safeguard it
against any such reduction.

Precisely this concern is quite clear at Chalcedon. As already at the
Council of Ephesus, nothing new is to be defined here, but the Creed
of Nicaea is to be expounded more clearly. That is why, in the acts of
the Council, the Creed comes first and only after that the exposition
of it, which is regarded as the real formula of Chalcedon: "Following,

[93] Küng, *Christsein*, pp. 121–25; Küng, *Menschwerdung Gottes: Eine Einführung in Hegels
theologisches Denken als Prolegomena zu einer künftigen Christologie* (Zürich, 1989), pp. 611–22.

[94] For literature on the Council: Camelot, *Ephesus und Chalcedon*; Schatz, *Allgemeine Konzilien*, pp. 48–70; L'Huillier, *Church of the Ancient Councils*, pp. 181–205; Perrone, "Von
Nicaea (325) nach Chalcedon (451)", pp. 100–134; Grillmeier, *Christ in Christian Tradition*
1:520–57; on its reception, see the subsequent volumes (see above, main part, chap. 1, n.
43); A. Grillmeier and H. Bacht, eds., *Das Konzil von Chalcedon: Geschichte und Gegenwart*, 3
vols., 5th ed. (Würzburg, 1979); J. van Oort and J. Roldanus, eds., *Chalkedon: Geschichte und
Aktualität: Studien zur Rezeption der christologischen Formel von Chalkedon*, Studien der Patristis-
chen Arbeitsgemeinschaft 4 (Louvain, 1998).

then, the holy Fathers, we all with one voice teach that it should be confessed that our Lord Jesus Christ is one and the same Son."[95] This "one and the same" (ἕνα καὶ τὸν αὐτόν) appears eight times, with superabundant clarity.[96] The text of Chalcedon uses the same basic structure here as the Creed of Nicaea. The Incarnation, becoming man, is declared of the one true Son of the Father.

Nicaea proceeds on the basis of the unity of the subject. At the same time, however, it presupposes a second and essential point: that the Son is eternal and is consubstantial with the Father and that he was born in time from Mary, as a man. Yet that means—contrary to all reductions —that the truth of his humanity is professed just like the truth of his divinity. Nicaea had above all to emphasize his true divinity, against the erroneous teaching of Arianism. Chalcedon makes it clear that along with this, the Nicene Creed also declares his true humanity. The two statements are linked by the theme of the "double birth" of the Son, the eternal begetting by the Father and the human birth from Mary. That is the intuition of Chalcedon. It is none other than what defines Christology in the New Testament itself, in the Gospel of Matthew for instance, at the end of the genealogy of Jesus: "Jacob [was] the father of Joseph the husband of Mary, of whom Jesus was born, who is called Christ" (Mt 1:16). The *passivum divinum* shows that, on the one hand, Jesus was truly born as man, yet not through the usual sequence of "N begat M", but "that which is conceived in [Mary] is of the Holy Spirit" (Mt 1:20).

Chalcedon's concern is none other than that of Nicaea, and this is none other than that of the apostolic faith. The faith of a Palestinian Christian from the first century has no other reality as its object than that of a Christian of the third millennium. The question of how this faith is verbally expressed, whether in Palestine, at Nicaea, at Chalcedon, or today, is something else again. For however strongly we may hold that the formula of belief from Chalcedon is identical with the New Testament, the question still arises of why and in what way the enduring concern remains even today bound up with the words the Council used then. That confronts us with the difficult hermeneutic question of the binding authority of councils and magisterial statements. We will add only two parenthetical remarks about that:

The fact that we can talk at all today about the view of the apostolic

---

[95] Grillmeier, *Christ in Christian Tradition* 1:544; here, vv. 1–4; DH 301–2.
[96] We refer to vv. 2, 5, 6, 8, 10, 14, 16, 23.

faith, that what the Christian faith is can be discussed today, is only possible because this faith has been handed down to us today. This handing down, tradition, means first of all the apostolic tradition.[97] Since there is no access to the preaching and the testimony of Jesus except the preaching and testimony of the primitive community—more precisely, the witness, first of the Twelve and then, in the broader sense, of the disciples—tradition means quite simply the enduring relevance of the apostolic testimony. The living presence of the Risen Lord in the Church through the Spirit and the continuing commitment to the testimony of the witnesses to the Resurrection are inseparably linked together in this. Christ continues to be present in his Church "in the kerygma" (as Rudolf Bultmann rightly emphasizes), and is so in the sense that the apostolic testimony remains relevant and constitutive of unity. The Church's creeds, the councils' professions of faith and definitions, are something like windows that provide a view of this apostolic faith.

Secondly, it is necessary, in undertaking theological work, to examine the councils' formulations carefully. Just like Nicaea, Chalcedon remains an essential authority for the verification and critical examination of Christology. Any theological discourse about Jesus the Christ has to let itself be measured by this standard. Yet for that purpose one has to know the texts of Chalcedon well. That is why, in what follows, the definition will be subject to a detailed analysis.

THE CREED OF CHALCEDON

[1] Following, then, the holy Fathers, we all with one voice teach that it should be confessed that [2] our Lord Jesus Christ is [3] one and the same Son, [4/5] the Same perfect in Godhead, [6] the Same perfect in manhood, [7] truly God and truly man, [8] the Same [consisting] of a rational soul and a body, [9] *homoousios* [ὁμοούσιος, consubstantial] with the Father as to his Godhead, [10] and the Same *homoousios* [ὁμοούσιος, consubstantial] with us as to his manhood, [11] in all things like unto us, sin only excepted, [12] begotten of his Father before ages as to his Godhead, [13] and in the last days, [14] the Same, for us and for our salvation, [15] [born] of Mary the Virgin *Theotokos* [the Mother of God], as to his manhood;

---

[97] Cf. W. Knoch, *Gott sucht den Menschen: Offenbarung, Schrift, Tradition*, AMATECA 4 (Paderborn, 1997), pp. 218–307.

[16] One and the same Lord Jesus Christ, the only begotten Son, [17] made known in two natures [18] [which exist] without confusion, without change, without division, without separation; [19] the difference of the two natures having been in no wise taken away by reason of the union, [20] but rather the properties of each being preserved, [21] and [both] concurring into one Person (*prosopon*) and one *hypostasis*—[22] not parted or divided into two persons (*prosopa*), [23] but one and the same only begotten Son, [24] the divine Logos, the Lord Jesus Christ, [25] even as the prophets from of old [have spoken] concerning him, [26] and as the Lord Jesus Christ himself has taught us, [27] and as the Symbol of the Fathers has delivered to us.[98]

This text interweaves New Testament wording with that from Nicaea. Christ is perfect in his divinity (5), any notion of a "demigod" is excluded, and the *homoousios*, "consubstantial with the Father", is explicitly emphasized. He is also perfect, however, in his humanity (6). This is surely among the most important creedal statements of the Christian faith: being human is not a defect, a deficiency, but has its own essential perfection. Christ is a true man with a rational soul, a ψυχή λογική (which is said in opposition to Apollinarism, in which the human soul is replaced by the Logos), and with a body, σῶμα (which is directed against any form of Docetism). He is perfectly and completely human. The basis for this is a soteriological argument: Christ was born "for our salvation" and not in order to cancel human existence in some way. For that very reason, his human existence is the perfect, exemplary human existence, because he is "consubstantial with us", not as a superman or as some quite different being, but as a real man. That, in turn, also affects our human existence, for here is someone who is living a new human existence in our midst, "in every respect . . . as we are, yet without sinning" (Heb 4:15). Jesus' human existence is distinguished from that of all other men, not by what it is, but by how it is lived (11). It is not said how this human existence then takes concrete form, as a human existence without sin; the apostolic testimony that "no sin was found in him" (cf. 1 Pet 2:22) is merely taken up.

The "basic text" of Chalcedon views Christ as being in this twofold *communio*, with God the Father and with all men. "Consubstantial with us" signifies not only metaphysical congruence, but also a radical solidarity with the fate of man. Just as being consubstantial with the Father

---

[98] Quoted from Grillmeier, *Christ in Christian Tradition* 1:544; DH 301–2.

indicates, not merely perfect divinity, but also the fullness of community of life with the Father, so "consubstantial with us" means living together with us, the most profound community of living and suffering.

The first part of the Council's definition (1–15) is intended as a clarification of the Creed of Nicaea. For that purpose, Chalcedon returns to Nicaea's key word, to the most controversial concept of the fourth century, to the *homoousios*, and expands it: Christ is consubstantial with the Father in his divinity and consubstantial with us men in his humanity. In addition, a series of erroneous teachings are targeted: Nestorianism, Eutychianism, Monophysitism, the Docetists, the Gnostics, the Manichees, Arianism, and Apollinarism.[99] We thus do not have a complete creed. What is said clearly relates to the New Testament declaration of faith in Christ in which (apart from the Nicene *homoousios*) distinct philosophical terminology is actually lacking.

In the second part (16–27), the text begins again with "one and the same Christ, Son, Lord, Only begotten" (16), like a refrain. After that follows the famous formula of the two natures (17). What is meant by natures is clear from the context. This is a matter of the aforementioned twofold consubstantiality, Christ's unity of work, life, and being with the Father and with men. We should particularly pay attention to the formulation "*in* (ἐν) two natures" here. In the preliminary stages of the text, the talk, for the most part, was about "*from* (ἐκ) two natures", but that could be misunderstood, in the sense of Apollinarism, as a mingling. With *in*, however, it is firmly asserted that the natures continue to exist in the union (cf. 20). Chalcedon sees the unity as being safeguarded precisely in the difference.

That is how Christ is "known" (17). It is a matter of our knowing him as he really is for us, as the one living, real Christ. That is precisely the paradox of the declarations of faith in Christ in the New Testament. This Crucified One, who died on the Cross in the most human wretchedness—and what is more characteristic of human nature than the fact that it is mortal?—this man is recognized and acknowledged as "truly . . . the Son of God" (Mk 15:39). Thomas, to whom the Risen One says, "Put your finger here, and see my hands," for whom

---

[99] Cf. Grillmeier, *Christ in Christian Tradition* 1:543–44; on the origins and the structure of this text, see A. Halleux, "La Définition christologique à Chalcédoine", *Revue théologique de Louvain* 7 (1976): 3–23, 155–170.

the real human existence, even in the Risen One, becomes discernible, perceptible, replies, "My Lord and my God!" (Jn 20:28). He who is being recognized as one is genuinely true man and true God; that is his identity, which he does not hide from men. This question of recognizing his life as that of a God-man will also have to be faced by a theology of the life of Jesus.[100]

Yet how is it possible to recognize one Christ in two active natures? Is that not quite simply inconceivable? Chalcedon replies to this with one of the most astonishing formulations in the history of creedal forms, with a fourfold negation (18):

without confusion

without change   *without* separation

without division

These four adverbial constructions, carefully chosen and arranged, form in some sense a cross above all "rational argumentation"; in the words of the Apostle Paul, they take "every thought captive to obey Christ" (2 Cor 10:5). To the question of how this unity in two natures is possible, Chalcedon replies with a formula that at first appears completely paradoxical. And indeed, one can scarcely imagine a formula more enigmatic for philosophical thought: without confusion and without division—the greatest unity and a clear distinction of divinity and humanity. Two adverbial constructions emphasize the diversity, and two the unity.

Significantly, this enumeration begins with "without confusion", perhaps because Chalcedon is in the first place against the Monophysite tendency in favor of mingling. This finally makes a clean break with the temptation to see God in any way as a part, as the highest being (*summum ens*) in a comparative sense. We can probably never sufficiently reflect upon what it means that God remains the wholly transcendent One, even in becoming incarnate; that creation and Incarnation are acts of his incomprehensible freedom; and that he himself, in the very act of becoming man, is truly the One who is entirely free. Without confusion does not mean that two entities remain autonomous, side by side. In the negative sense, nothing more is being said than: no confusion. The second adverbial construction gives the first a more precise

---

[100] On this, see the following chap. 3: "The Path on Earth of the Son of God".

meaning. "Without change" means that Christ does not cease to be God when he begins to be man. This does not, of course, mean "like a block of stone" but defends against any notion of a metamorphosis of the divinity into the humanity, or vice versa. In human language, it is only with negations that we can approach the mystery. Immediately, however, "without division and without separation" is added. The negations should not simply be hastily turned into affirmations. "Without confusion" does not mean divided; that is why it has to be amplified: both without confusion and without division; a true unity, but no mixture; a true distinction, but no separation.

In what follows, the terms are further clarified. The one Christ is recognized in two natures without confusion and unchanged—that is, the distinction between the natures is not abolished by their union; rather, the qualities peculiar to each nature are preserved (19/20). The truth of Christ's being God and man can only be firmly held if both preserve their own nature and work, their own characteristics. The formula taken from Leo the Great (d. 461), "rather, what is peculiar to each of the two natures is preserved",[101] says once again that the Incarnation of God maintains and completes the human existence of Christ (20). Grillmeier sums it up thus: "Thus, the nature is the unimpaired principle of the distinction in Christ."[102]

The center of this whole section is the statement that the properties of both natures are preserved, even when they come together in one person (*hypostasis*) (21). Hypostatic union means that the unity of Christ is to be found only in his person, so that it is always a personal unity. Chalcedon simply professes this, without breaking it down further. It is implicit, however, that something decisive is being said here about person. The person of Christ unites things in itself without destroying (or confusing, or changing) what is united. Only a unity of person is able to unite without abrogating. In a brief addition here, the two other adverbial constructions are elucidated: Christ's unity of person is undivided and unseparated, "not parted or divided into two persons" (22).

---

[101] "Salva proprietate utriusque naturae." This is the only definite quotation from the *Tomus Leonis*. Cf. Halleux, "La Définition christologique", pp. 162–63; Grillmeier, *Christ in Christian Tradition* 1:547.

[102] Grillmeier, *Christ in Christian Tradition* 1:549.

The four terms are thus clarified: the defense against any mingling or transformation points in a positive sense toward the statement that the two *natures* preserve their particular characteristics; the defense against any division or separation points in a positive sense toward the statement that Christ is one as to his *person*. Thereby the structure once more becomes clear: two adverbial constructions apply to the level of the natures and emphasize the difference of the two natures; two adverbial constructions apply to the level of the person and point more toward the unity. In a quite general sense, Chalcedon could be summed up thus: the distinction unites, the unity differentiates.[103]

At the close, the creed summarizes once again and leads the argument back to the beginning: Jesus Christ is "but one and the same Son and Only-begotten, the divine Logos, the Lord" (23/24). The agreement with prophecy, with the Old Testament (25), and with Jesus' teaching in the New Testament (26), and also with Nicaea's interpretation of the apostolic faith (27), is once more underlined. The Fathers are concerned about continuity back to the origins.

THE AUTHORITY OF THE COUNCIL

For a clarification of the hermeneutic criteria for understanding what the Council said, let us briefly go into the binding force of Chalcedon.

Today we see above all the time-conditioned aspect. In a given historical situation demanding a decision, after an arduous process that for the most part shows the intricacies of ecclesiastical or secular politics, a decision was reached. The agency that made the decision, the ecumenical council, needed in the first place a *formal authority* to speak on behalf of the Church as a whole. The council is the locus at which the unity of the bishops among themselves and with the supreme head of that authority becomes manifest. Those gathered there are "teachers and judges of faith and morals for the universal Church" (*Lumen Gentium*, no. 25, 2). This authority is rooted in the infallibility of the Church, which is promised to her whenever she is rightly expounding the *depositum fidei* (*Lumen Gentium*, no. 25, 3). The desire of the Council of Chalcedon for continuity with the origins is likewise to be

---

[103] Maximus Confessor further developed this axiom. Cf. C. Schönborn, *God's Human Face*, pp. 102–24, and also Jacques Maritain's famous formula: "Distinguer pour unir": J. Maritain, *Distinguer pour unir ou Les Degrés du Savoir* (*Oeuvres complètes* 4:257–1111).

understood in this sense. An assent of faith is demanded from believers. That means concretely that they should adhere, not to the words, but to the substance, as the council intended it to be understood. It is not the *enuntiabilia* that are the focus here, but the *res*.[104]

Time-conditioned patterns of thought in the spheres of philosophy and culture meet together here. Yet—and this shows how astonishing the great documents of the Council are—the result is more than a compromise. Historically, the Creed of Chalcedon has usually been understood as an ingenious compromise between Antiochene, Alexandrian, and Roman Christology. Anyone who studies the texts of the time will ascertain that Chalcedon is not just a mixture of all that. There is something like a dimension that rises above that, which lifts Chalcedon above the prevailing circumstances and lends it an ecumenical dimension that transcends the local and political situation. This is of course no longer comprehensible simply in historical terms. An ecumenical council is "equipped" with the assistance of the Holy Spirit; it speaks with the authority of Christ—"It has seemed good to the Holy Spirit and to us" (Acts 15:28). This teaching authority is not a purely external thing; it has its own self-evidence, which is disclosed to anyone who engages with it in faith.

The *authority with regard to content* derives from the coherence of the definition of Chalcedon. This cannot, of course, be simply "proved", but it can be shown from the *nexus mysteriorum* (cf. CCC 90). If Chalcedon—in substance—is abandoned, if it is no longer the hermeneutic key to the correct understanding of the witness to Christ in the New Testament, then continuity with Christ himself is no longer being preserved. Chalcedon has no intention of replacing either the scriptural witness or the tradition of the early Church; it wishes, rather, to offer a catholic formulation of faith in Jesus Christ that is as precise and as comprehensive as possible.[105] This is not a matter of all the content of Christology—it would be wrong to expect to find everything "explained" here—for the Creed is not a christological treatise. The Council wishes, however, to indicate the necessary minimum of precision, the absolutely necessary framework within which Christology can legitimately be developed.

---

[104] Cf. Thomas Aquinas, STh II-II, q. 1, a. 2 ad 2 (DThA 15:12); CCC 170.

[105] See on this P. Knauer, "Die chalzedonische Christologie als Kriterium für jedes christliche Glaubensverständnis", *Theologie und Philosophie* 60 (1985): 1–15.

The "without confusion" and "without division" of the divinity and humanity, the "one person *in* two natures", are coordinates behind which no Christology can any longer go back. We may find other ways of talking about it, but in substance these remain constitutive for any responsible theological discourse about Jesus Christ: a real unity of divinity and humanity in Christ and an indestructible distinctiveness of what is united. A great deal in Christology was only developed later, but we must not fall back behind these terms.

CHALCEDON AS A KEY FOR THE
CHRISTIAN UNDERSTANDING OF THE WORLD

With the *safeguarding of the distinction* of the natures, Chalcedon put a stop to any reduction in the humanity of Jesus. That is why Christology, like art and religious piety, subsequently concentrated on the humanity of Jesus. But inasmuch as this humanity is at the same time "the humanity of our God" (cf. Tit 3:4), the humanity of the eternal Son, Christology has the task of reading the concrete humanity of Jesus Christ as the historical form of "translation" of his eternal Sonship.

Without confusion (truly man) and without division: Jesus is the Son of God. Behind this christological center, a further framework is molded that comprehends the whole of theology. Chalcedon is something of a "world formula", because Christ is the center, because everything has its existence in him, is created on the basis of him and directed toward him (cf. Col 1:16–17). Chalcedon is a key to anthropology.

> The truth is that only in the mystery of the incarnate Word does the mystery of man take on light. . . . He Who is "the image of the invisible God" (Col 1:15) is Himself the perfect man. . . . Since human nature as He assumed it was not annulled, by that very fact it has been raised up to a divine dignity in our respect too. (*Gaudium et Spes*, no. 22)

Here *Gaudium et Spes* is quoting Chalcedon and the Second and Third Councils of Constantinople and from that establishes the dignity of man, not only on a creation-theological basis, but also christologically. This dignity results already from man's being in the image of God, the image he is granted through creation because he is willed by God. Yet this dignity is made surpassingly clear, yet again, through the Incarnation. God has wonderfully created man and has yet more wonderfully restored him (the Christmas liturgy). Leo the Great

insists, in his Christmas homily, "Christian, recognize your dignity!"[106]
The question of the relationship of divine and human freedom is also
illuminated by Chalcedon. Both exist in Christ, without confusion and
without division; he is sovereignly free as a man—not although he is
God, but because he "incarnates" the sovereign freedom of God in a
human existence.

Yet Chalcedon also offers a key for ecclesiology. There is an analogy between the divine-human status of Christ and the Church; the
qualification "without confusion and without division" also holds true
for the reality of the Church. Sometimes—in a kind of "ecclesiological Nestorianism"—the divine and human elements are separated and
torn apart, so that a "purely profane" reality of the Church is seen, in
opposition to a purely transcendent reality of grace. On the other hand
—in rather "Monophysite" fashion—what is divine and what is human are sometimes viewed as so intermingled that everything appears
as equally holy. In contrast, Vatican II holds, in the wholly Chalcedonian tradition, that the Church is "one complex reality which coalesces
from a divine and a human element" (*Lumen Gentium*, no. 8).

The great Russian philosopher Vladimir Soloviev (d. 1900) goes
even farther in his interpretation of Chalcedon and believes that the
central christological dogma of the unconfused and undivided union of
divine and human natures can be detected even in politics. Intermin-
gling would mean caesaropapism or political messianism, when a political reality is equated with the Kingdom of God. The human element is swallowed up here. Division leads to dismissing the Incarnation
whenever too sharp a division is drawn between Church and world,
if for instance faith is no longer "incarnated" socially, politically, or
culturally, no longer maintains an institutional presence in the world
—in a word, through "the rejection of Christianity as a social force,
as an active principle of historical progress".[107]

Chalcedon's term "without confusion" guarantees the independent
reality of creation, which is not absorbed into the divine. Only this clear
distinction between what is divine and what earthly has "banished the
gods" from the world and turned it into independent nature. Yet even
here, there is a danger of Nestorianism, of the "without confusion"

---

[106] Leo the Great, *Sermo* 21:2–3 (CChr.SL 138:88); CCC 1691.
[107] V. Soloviev, *Rußland und die universale Kirche*, in Soloviev, *Werke* 3:173–74; quotation
p. 173.

being distorted into complete autonomy, which degrades the world, creation, into the material for self-realization. Vice versa, nowadays we see a trend in the opposite direction, toward divinizing the creation.

Everything said so far would remain one-sided and thus distorted unless at the same time the "without division", the unity, were emphasized. A very long tradition, from the Fathers up to mysticism, emphasizes that God became man in order that man might become God. The divinization of man corresponds to the Incarnation of God. The Incarnation is not yet the end point; God humbled himself in order to exalt us—or, as Paul says, he who is rich became poor, so as to make us rich (cf. 2 Cor 8:9). It is of the greatest importance not to forget this second aspect, since that is what gives the first its full significance. Creation is not aimed at a mere liberation of the creatures, at their "release" into their own autonomy; its goal is, rather, the exaltation of the creatures into fellowship with God. Whatever this reality is called —grace, supernatural goal, divinization—it is the principal aim of creation and Incarnation.

The desire for divinization was particularly strong in the modern period of intellectual history, but mostly in the defective form of self-idolatry, whether individual or collective. The Christian path of the divinization of man is one of an exaltation to fellowship with God that is gracious, a gift. "No longer do I call you servants, . . . but . . . friends", it says in John (15:15). Here we see the significance of Chalcedon and that of the union without confusion and without division. This exaltation of man is not the abolition of his humanity but, rather, its full realization. Here, too, Chalcedon is the key. In Christ himself, as archetype and cause for all men, the humanization of God and the divinization of man has taken place. His human existence is not swallowed up, not even in the glorification of the Resurrection and in the Exaltation. He remains man, even as the glorified Lord. God became man and eternally remains man.[108] Chalcedon wished to say nothing other than what the fundamental testimony of the New Testament is: that Jesus Christ is the origin, the center, and the goal of all.

---

[108] See above, chap. 1:3b, "The Incarnation of the Logos and the Divinization of Man".

III. The Path on Earth of the Son of God

The Council of Nicaea elucidated Jesus' claim to be God's Son. The Council of Chalcedon refers to this profession of faith when it teaches that Jesus Christ is true God and true man, that is to say, wholly God and wholly man, one person in two natures. These creedal tenets, which were elucidated through decades of struggle, form the cornerstones of the Church's understanding of the person of Christ. In the period following the first great councils, it was a matter of elucidating several more specific questions concerning his person. How do the two natures interact, in practical terms, in the life of Jesus? What does it mean for Jesus' self-awareness, that he is God and man at the same time? How do divine and human knowledge interact in him? What does this mean for his will? What significance does the earthly life of the man Jesus acquire from the fact that he is God? The third chapter is devoted to these questions.

1. Jesus' Consciousness of Himself and His Mission

There are sayings of Jesus that suggest that he expected the Kingdom of God soon: "Truly, I say to you, there are some standing here who will not taste death before they see the kingdom of God come with power" (Mk 9:1). "Truly, I say to you, you will not have gone through all the towns of Israel, before the Son of man comes" (Mt 10:23).[1] In this connection, a number of theologians at the end of the nineteenth century put the radical question of whether Jesus had been fundamentally mistaken in his expectations. In doing this, they were formulating the question of Christ's ignorance, already dealt with by the Church Fathers, in a hitherto unknown way. In the so-called question of "Jesus' imminent expectation", the issue is above all that Jesus proclaimed the Kingdom of God to be close at hand, but it then seemed not to appear.

Did in fact the Kingdom of God proclaimed by Jesus come? Did not Jesus gamble everything on one card that then failed to turn up?

---

[1] Further texts in: J. Jeremias, *New Testament Theology*, trans. John Bowden (New York: Charles Scribner's Sons, 1971), pp. 127, 134–41.

Did not time move on over him without the Kingdom of God having
come? Is not Jesus a cheated dreamer, one who dreamed of the utopia
of the Kingdom of God and took his dreams for reality? Do we not
have to admit that Jesus was mistaken? Rudolf Bultmann (d.
1976) demonstrated the inexorable consequences of this question: "In view
of the fact that the proclamation of the irruption of God's reign was
not fulfilled—that is, that Jesus' expectation of the near end of the
world turned out to be an illusion—the question arises of whether his
idea of God was not also illusory."[2]

The assertion that Jesus was mistaken thus confronts theology with
some difficult questions, for how can we believe his revelation of the
Father, his "idea of God", if he was mistaken in a point so central to
his message? And besides, is the thesis of Jesus' mistaken imminent
expectation not also contrary to Peter's question, "Lord, you know
everything" (Jn 21:17)? We therefore have to investigate the question
of Christ's knowledge thoroughly. Two attempts to avoid the question
must certainly be excluded first of all.

On the one hand, the attempt by most Church Fathers to gloss over
the ignorance of Jesus is unsatisfactory. They interpret all the texts that
suggest Jesus' ignorance pedagogically. If, for instance, Jesus asks the
sisters of Lazarus, who has just died, "Where have you laid him?" (Jn
11:34), then this is supposedly only a trick question. The statement of
Jesus that even the Son does not know the hour when the world will
end (Mk 13:32) is interpreted to the effect that Jesus did in fact know
the hour but did not wish to reveal it.

Secondly, the modern attempt to reinterpret the historical-temporal
imminent expectation in the timelessness of existential shock is inadequate. This asserts that what appears to the prophetic consciousness
as the imminent end of the world and time is to be explained by the
overpowering shock at the absoluteness of the will of God. Just as, to
every prophet, his word appears to be God's final word, so it was with
Jesus. Jesus expressed in the words of imminent apocalyptic expectation his conviction that he knew God's will and had to put it into
words.[3]

Both attempts actually avoid the question of whether Jesus was mistaken. In what follows, the question of Jesus' imminent expectation

[2] R. Bultmann, *Theology of the New Testament*, trans. Kendrick Grobel, 2nd ed. (Waco, Tex.: Baylor Univ. Press, 2007), p. 22.
[3] Ibid., p. 23.

will be used to introduce the treatment of his consciousness of himself and of his mission, with recourse to the biblical witness; this is followed by a historical survey of various attempts at an answer and, finally, an attempted theological explanation.

a. Imminent Expectation: Was Jesus Mistaken?

The so-called theory of imminent expectation has its own history. It was popularized above all by Johannes Weiss (d. 1914) and Albert Schweitzer (d. 1965). According to them, Jesus shared with his Jewish contemporaries the apocalyptic view of the world. At the time of Jesus, one supposedly lived in apocalyptic tension, expecting the early irruption of the end times in a cosmic catastrophe. This was supposedly the expectation of the Kingdom of God. Three elements are combined in this theory. First, it is assumed that people were expecting the imminent arrival of the Kingdom of God; and second, that "Kingdom of God" was an eschatological-apocalyptic concept; so as to conclude from this, thirdly, that people were therefore expecting the end of the world.

As against liberal Protestant theology (Albrecht Ritschl, d. 1889; Adolf Harnack, d. 1930), which turns Jesus into a teacher of moral behavior, these theologians emphasized Jesus' apocalyptic world view. Jesus is supposedly a radical apocalypticist who shared the feverish expectation of the end times common in his day. That was supposedly a mistake; the end of the world did not come but, instead, the Cross. And even after Easter, when Jesus' disciples were still hoping for the coming of the Kingdom, there was only disappointment: the Parousia was delayed. So one was content to make oneself at home in time. Instead of the Kingdom of God, the Church came.

The question not asked here, or not asked often enough, is: Did Jesus really have this kind of expectation? Did he understand the Kingdom of God eschatologically to such an extent that he identified it with the impending end of the world? Since then, there has been a great deal of movement here, so that Jean Carmignac (d. 1986), for instance, could speak of the illusion of "eschatology".[4]

In the first place, the texts that have been discovered in Qumran

---

[4] J. Carmignac, *Le Mirage de l'eschatologie: Royauté, Règne et Royaume de Dieu sans Eschatologie* (Paris, 1979).

in the meantime call into question the assumption that in the time of Jesus, people did generally live in eschatological tension and expectation of the end of the world.[5] Secondly, current exegesis casts doubt on whether, when Jesus talked about "the Kingdom of God", this was primarily an apocalyptic image. In fact, this appears not only as a future reality, but also as something now present, something that has already come. "If it is by the finger of God that I cast out demons, then the kingdom of God has come upon you" (Lk 11:20). It is there, like a hidden treasure that one can dig up; like a pearl that one can buy (Mt 13:44-46). It is "in your midst" (Lk 17:21). Thirdly, it is more strongly emphasized that Jesus gives no definite information about time with regard to the future. "Nowhere with Jesus is a deadline fixed."[6] The proximity of the Kingdom of God is not established as a temporal proximity, as for instance with John the Baptist, where the day of judgment is directly imminent (cf. Lk 3:9, 17).

It is thus worthwhile to raise again the question of Jesus' imminent expectation. This so often leads up a blind alley because it is put the wrong way. It is wrong to apply to Jesus a preconceived concept of the Kingdom of God, rather than vice versa, starting from the Christology and giving content to the concept in question on the basis of Jesus' actions and his preaching. Time and again, there is talk about the failure of God's Kingdom to appear and about Jesus' unfulfilled expectation. Yet nowhere in Jesus' preaching do we find any indication that Jesus himself believed his failure to be a sign that God's Kingdom had not come. No passage is to be found from which one could conclude that Jesus himself believed he had been mistaken. Certainly, the end of the world as apocalyptic had expected it did not happen. But the question still is whether Jesus himself expected this kind of end.[7]

We have to ask ourselves what Jesus' own understanding of the βασιλεία was like and whether, for him, the Kingdom of God really did not come. We have to ask ourselves what fate the Kingdom of God actually has. How does it come? Where is it? Where can it be

---

[5] J. Carmignac, "Qu'est-ce que l'Apocalyptique? Son emploi à Qumrân", *Revue de Qumran* 10 (1979): 3-35.

[6] H. Schürmann, *Gottes Reich—Jesu Geschick: Jesu ureigener Tod im Lichte seiner Basileia-Verkündigung* (Freiburg im Breisgau, 1983), p. 39.

[7] H. U. von Balthasar, *Zuerst Gottes Reich: Zwei Skizzen zur biblischen Naherwartung*, ThMed 13 (Einsiedeln, 1966); H. Merklein, *Jesu Botschaft von der Gottesherrschaft: Eine Skizze*, SBS 111, 3rd ed. (Stuttgart, 1989).

found? For obviously, the Kingdom of God fares as Jesus did: it is not recognized; it even suffers violence (Mt 11:12). We are to seek for it with all our power, make every effort to find it, to enter in through the narrow gate (Lk 13:24); we should accept it as simply as a child (Lk 18:17). All that, however, sounds quite different from an end of the world that irrupts apocalyptically.

To elucidate this question of imminent expectation (and, thereby, the relation between the proclamation of the Kingdom of God and Jesus' Passion and death), let us take the path of Jesus' message on morality. People have often all too precipitously set the time-eschatology in opposition to the moral-theological. We should in fact attempt to see both as aspects of the one Christ-event. How does Jesus declare God's will? We should not overlook the fact that Jesus, whenever he speaks of the Kingdom of God, always speaks of the Kingdom of the Father.[8] Of the coming of the Kingdom of God, it can thus only be said, "Thy Kingdom come, thy will be done" (Mt 6:10). That is how the Kingdom of God comes close. Jesus' imminent expectation is that the will of the Father be done, that his Kingdom come.

THE DECISIVE WILL OF GOD: JESUS' MORAL MESSAGE

Christ preaches that the time is fulfilled and the Kingdom of God is near. There is certainly (also) a temporal component in what is meant here (end of time, dawn of the end time, early coming of the eschaton). Yet the time is fulfilled, not because it has run its course, but because Christ himself is "the fullness of time" (cf. Gal 4:4), because the boundless fullness of the love of God has come in Jesus. The eschatological situation is not the already predetermined temporal period in which Jesus arrives; rather, his coming is itself the coming of the end time. By beginning to preach in Galilee, to heal the sick, to drive out demons, by accepting sinners into his fellowship, Jesus himself starts the ball rolling. Jesus knows that he has been sent to fulfill the eschatological gathering together of Israel. There is no doubt that Jesus intended to gather all Israel, especially the "lost sheep of . . . Israel" (Mt 15:24). Yet that can only mean—seen from the perspective of the

[8] H. Schürmann, "Das hermeneutische Hauptproblem der Verkündigung Jesu", in *Gott in Welt: Festschrift K. Rahner*, ed. H. Vorgrimler, 1:579–607 (Freiburg im Breisgau, 1964); H. Schürmann, *Das Gebet des Herrn*, 4th ed. (Freiburg im Breisgau, 1981), pp. 139–44.

whole Old Testament—that Jesus is conscious of being sent to renew God's covenant in its unconditionality, to lead all Israel to what comes forth as a constant call from the covenant that Israel should be perfect and holy as God is perfect and holy.

Just as the call of the prophets, however, brought about a separation between those who accepted it and those who rejected it, so Jesus himself has brought about the eschatological situation of separation. With reference to him, Jesus of Nazareth, eschatological salvation or doom is now being decided (cf. Mk 8:38). If he calls for recognition of the "signs of the times", this does not in the first place mean any outward, cosmic, or historical phenomena. Jesus is in his own person the "sign of the times". That is why the band of those who accept Jesus' preaching and follow him is the eschatological Israel (cf. Lk 12:32, "Fear not, little flock, for it is your Father's good pleasure to give you the kingdom"). It is unquestionably a part of the preaching of Jesus that his discourses on judgment, even though they broaden the view of the end to cosmic dimensions, see the judgment with reference to himself. This is perhaps the most impressive trait in Jesus' consciousness of his mission.[9]

Yet at least as striking is the fact that this separation, which is initiated early and soon prompts his eschatological words about the judgment (for example, Mt 11:21–22), nonetheless does not lead Jesus to carry out a separation analogous to that between the children of light and the children of darkness at Qumran. With him, rather, "weeds and wheat" are left to grow together (Mt 13:30). He refuses to have "fire come down from heaven" to consume the inhospitable Samaritans (Lk 9:54). He sends his own disciples "as sheep in the midst of wolves" (Mt 10:16), and commands them to bless those who hate them and him. The judgment is not anticipated; rather, it takes place in his self-offering on the Cross. Here we find the attitude of the Sermon on the Mount. Only on this basis can we understand what is specific to the eschatological mission of Jesus: this is how the Kingdom of God comes. Jesus knows he has been sent to save, not to judge. Yet it is precisely in his healing and saving activity, which he carries out as the fully authorized representative of the Father, that rejection, enmity, and hatred are ignited, right up to the plan to bring about his death. The

---

[9] Cf. H. U. von Balthasar, TD 5:19–54.

very fact that he is doing good (cf. Mk 3:4), that he is proclaiming the good news and bringing it to fruition, brings him enmity. But what does that signify for the coming of the Kingdom of God?

The unique feature of Jesus' mission is that this growing enmity does not alter the aim of that mission. Jesus does not excommunicate his opponents even when he most harshly threatens them with judgment. He is always concerned to save, not to judge. In this situation, from the consciousness of his mission of salvation, Jesus declares: "I say to you that hear, Love your enemies, do good to those who hate you, bless those who curse you, pray for those who abuse you" (Lk 6:27–28).

Yet how can this mission, to save and not to condemn, be sustained if enmity prevails over acceptance? What form can Jesus' mission take —and, with it, the Kingdom of God, seen in the light of the Sermon on the Mount—if those to whom Jesus knows he has been sent, with the good news of the saving love of the Father, reject him and hate him for no reason? Jesus asked himself this question. In his words to his disciples about discipleship, and likewise in the parables and the proclamation of the Kingdom of God, we find hints of an answer, two of which in particular should be mentioned: forgiving and serving.

Jesus knows he has been sent to sinners; he himself grants *forgiveness of sins* (Mk 2:1–12; Lk 7:36–50), not just in words, but most especially in acts and in images—thus, in the parable of the enormous debt that is remitted (Mt 18:27); that of the Pharisee and the tax collector (Lk 18:10–14); likewise in the three parables of the lost sheep, of the lost penny, and of the prodigal son (Lk 15), and similarly in actions, through his table fellowship with sinners. This direction of his mission, which is constant in the attitude and the preaching of Jesus, does not change, since it has its origin in Jesus' own consciousness of his mission. Thus, on the Cross he even forgives those who crucify him: "Father, forgive them; for they know not what they do" (Lk 23:34). In this attitude, Jesus knows himself to be the One who carries out and proclaims God's own will, God, who forgives through his unfathomable mercy, just like the father of the prodigal son, and knows that precisely in doing this he is bringing the Kingdom of God. Jesus reveals God's own will; in his acts of pardon it becomes manifest who the God who sent him is and what his Kingdom looks like.

Secondly, Jesus' mission finds expression in the quite unmistakable trait of *service:* "But I am among you as one who serves" (Lk 22:27). Jesus goes so far as to wash his disciples' feet (Jn 13:4–6). "When had a rabbi agreed to do such a thing?"[10] While the rabbis regard service of the pupil to the teacher as practice for learning the Torah, and hence lay great stress on hierarchical order, Jesus behaves differently. On the one hand, his demand for discipleship is more radical than that of the rabbis, yet, on the other, he is among the disciples as the one who serves. Jesus calls with authority; he makes promises; he instructs; he sends out and grants authority. The authority of Jesus should be measured by that of the rabbis. Jesus draws a clear boundary: "A disciple is not above his teacher, nor a servant above his master. It is enough for the disciple to be like his teacher, and the servant like his master" (Mt 10:24–25). Yet precisely here the other aspect appears. Precisely because Jesus, as the master, is the one who serves, the disciples must serve. That is an essential aspect of Jesus' understanding of himself. Just as the whole tenor of the Sermon on the Mount points to poverty and service, so Jesus himself understood his mission as service to the poor and the little ones. The great sermon on the final judgment raises service to the hungry, the thirsty, strangers, those who are naked, to those who are sick or in prison as the criterion. "When did we . . . not minister to you?" (Mt 25:44). "You know that those who are supposed to rule over the Gentiles lord it over them, and their great men exercise authority over them." But with the disciples it must not be like that. "Whoever would be great among you must be your servant." The basis of this is Jesus' own mission: "For the Son of man also came not to be served but to serve, and to give his life as a ransom for many" (Mk 10:42–45).

Yet what does this consistent focus of Jesus on service signify? He uses his authority, not to make people feel his power, but to heal and to save. Jesus presents himself to the disciples as a model of service. This service is not simply a moral appeal for an attitude of humility. It is an essential part of the mission of Jesus that his whole existence is such service. And that is also essentially proclamation of the Kingdom of God.

If Jesus prepares his disciples for such service and promises them hardships, persecution, and mistreatment as well, and at the same time

---

[10] E. Fascher, "Jesus der Lehrer: Ein Beitrag nach dem 'Quellort der Kirchenidee'", *Theologische Literaturzeitung* 79 (1954): 325–42, here p. 331; cf. M. Hengel, *Nachfolge und Charisma: Eine exegetisch-religionsgeschichtliche Studie zu Mt 8,21f. und Jesu Ruf in die Nachfolge* (Berlin, 1968), p. 57.

commands them to turn the other cheek (Mt 5:39), if indeed he promises them the fate of the prophets, and that means he is pointing to the possibility of death (cf. Mt 10:28), if he actually warns them against success as the sign of a false mission (cf. Lk 6:26), then we can only conclude that suffering is the hallmark of the mission.[11] That is the way Paul will see it, invoking his suffering to corroborate the authenticity of his apostolate (2 Cor 11:23–33).

Suffering is a part of Jesus' mission. His power to effect conversion stems from the fact that he is ready to endure the hatred of those he loves. He can conquer this hatred only by a love that is all the greater, a love that is stronger than death. "Having loved his own who were in the world, he loved them to the end" (Jn 13:1). Thus he opens the door for them so that they can get out of their hatred if they accept this love. Christ's death thus becomes a gesture of his love, his last word of love. Whoever, like Jesus, preaches the defenselessness of loving your enemies cannot bypass the prospect of suffering.

We have to hold both lines in view: the authority of Jesus and the lowliness of the one who serves, whose authority empowers him to serve, and to do so in an understanding of his mission as God's final mission to Israel, as the eschatological call to Israel to come back to God. The figure that emerges from all these traits, of whom Paul says that for the sake of the unsurpassable worth of knowing him, he counts all else as loss (Phil 3:8)—this figure only makes sense if it is understood as being radically "proexistence", as a "being-for" that goes as far as death.[12] It is completely along the lines of Jesus' mission that "not to be served, but to serve" is ultimately understood as being "to give his life as a ransom for many" (Mk 10:45). Not seeing that Jesus' death is a part of his mission, that his mission "to the lost sheep of the house of Israel" (Mt 10:6) ultimately includes the prospect of giving his life for Israel, indeed for "the many"—this is possible only if we overlook the whole overall shape of his preaching.

Yet does not such a path toward death stand in unresolvable conflict with Jesus' imminent expectation? How can we reconcile the fact that Jesus expects the Kingdom of God and at the same time walks toward

---

[11] Cf. Jeremias, *New Testament Theology*, p. 239–40.

[12] H. Schürmann, " 'Pro-Existenz' als christologischer Grundbegriff ", in Schürmann, *Jesus—Gestalt und Geheimnis: Gesammelte Beiträge* (Paderborn, 1994), pp. 286–315.

self-sacrifice by way of service and forgiveness of sins? Jesus did not merely preach the Kingdom of God; he risked his life for the sake of its coming. That is the heart of his proclamation of the Kingdom of God. It reveals that God himself is willing to pay much for it—indeed, everything. "Grace is expensive . . . above all because it was costly to God, because it cost God the life of his Son."[13]

The question that arose at the beginning of the twentieth century about the failure of the Kingdom of God to appear stemmed, as has been shown, from a misunderstanding of the term. The only possible way to give a correct answer is by looking at Christ himself, his activity and his preaching. Here in fact it becomes clear that the Kingdom of God has already come. Jesus was not mistaken; his eschatological hope was not disappointed. Jesus' path to Jerusalem, right up to the Cross, was the path of the Kingdom of God. It came, and it came to the Cross. That is what Mark was trying to tell us with the *climax* of his Gospel: "Truly this man was the Son of God!" (Mk 15:39). The key to the Basileia is in the Cross. In no other way did, does, or will the Kingdom of God ever come but through the Cross and Resurrection of Jesus Christ.

b. Christ's Knowledge in the History of Theology

Having first of all approached the question of Christ's knowledge and consciousness by way of a practical problem, that of Jesus' allegedly mistaken expectation of the Kingdom of God, let us now try to answer the question of what Jesus knew and whether he was aware of being God more generally; first of all, in a historical overview, followed then by theological reflection on this.[14]

It is important to be clear that the question of Jesus' omniscience and his awareness of himself as divine is above all a soteriological question. It is not irrelevant whether Jesus knew why he was dying. In what sense should we take Paul's statement, which obviously had great existential importance for him: "He loved me and gave himself for me"

---

[13] D. Bonhoeffer, *Nachfolge* (Munich, 1989), p. 31; see also H.U. von Balthasar, TD 3:237–45.

[14] See the International Theological Commission, "Jesu Selbst- und Sendungsbewußtsein", *Internationale Katholische Zeitschrift Communio* 16 (1987): 38–50; C. Schönborn, "La Conscience du Christ: Approches historico-théologiques", *Esprit et vie* 99 (1989): 81–87.

(Gal 2:20)? Paul, and the primitive Church before him, believed Jesus'
mission to be of universal significance and breadth. How far can we—
must we, may we—assume a thematic consciousness of this breadth?
What does *"pro me"* or *"pro nobis"* mean? The great figures in the
history of salvation, from Paul to Thérèse of Lisieux (d. 1897), have
understood this *"pro me"* in such a concrete sense that they lived from
a sure faith that Jesus "loved *me* and gave himself up for *me*".[15] "When
he was dying", Jesus must "have known, in a mysterious but real way
for whom he was giving up his life; otherwise it is not he who saves
us, and his death remains an external event in relation to us."[16]

This is a question for the theology of revelation. How can Christ
reveal God as the Abba if he does not know him? What is unique about
the revelation of Jesus is that he is not only one who receives revelation (like the prophets) but is himself the revealer and the revelation in
one. Jesus' incomparable intimacy with God presupposes a knowledge
and a consciousness sui generis. "No one knows the Son except the
Father, and no one knows the Father except the Son and any one to
whom the Son chooses to reveal him" (Mt 11:27).

For these two reasons, therefore, it is of the utmost significance that
Jesus knew both God and me and knows that he—as Peter says, after
being a witness of Jesus' miracles for three years—"knows everything"
(Jn 21:17). On the other hand, there are in the New Testament "awkward" testimonies that seem to witness to an ignorance on Jesus' part,
especially in the Gospel of Mark, which, on the one hand, talks in a
sovereign manner of "the Son" in an absolute sense and, on the other
hand, notes that he does not know "that day or that hour" (Mk 13:32).
In this connection, let us first take a look at the history of theology.

INTEGRATION AND PERFECTION IN PATRISTIC LITERATURE

The question of Jesus' self-awareness, as framed above, is a modern
question. The early Church was especially interested in two questions:
in the question of Jesus' being completely a man, in body, mind, and
soul; and, following from Mark 13:32, in the question of Jesus' ignorance. In the early Church, both questions were put within a so-

---

[15] See Thérèse of Lisieux, poem PN 24, stanzas 6 and 21, *The Poetry of Saint Thérèse of Lisieux*, trans. Donald Kinney, O.C.D. (Washington, D.C.: ICS Publications, 1996), pp. 124, 128.
[16] J. Guillet, "Jésus avant Pâques", *Les Quatre Fleuves* 4 (1975): 29–38, here p. 37.

teriological perspective, so that the axiom *"quod non assumptum, non sanatum"* is determinative: whatever has not been taken on by Christ in the Incarnation has not been healed, that is, redeemed.

The oldest Christology found itself obliged to fight against Docetic tendencies. It was therefore concerned in the first place with Jesus' real corporeality. Not until the Apollinarian heresy, which substituted the divine Word (λόγος) for the human mind (νοῦς), did this lead to an emphasis on the truth of Jesus' human intellectuality. As against that, Pope Damasus I (d. 384) held that the Son of man had come "as a whole, that is, in soul and body, in mind and in the entire nature of his substance" (DH 146), "to save what is lost" (Mt 18:11). Yet if we assume such a human mind in Jesus, does his human existence not inevitably acquire an autonomous subject? Does this not dissolve the Incarnation? As against this division into two subjects, the Council of Ephesus held firmly to the uniqueness of the person of the *Verbum incarnatum*. The dogma of the hypostatic union forbids us to think of the humanity of Jesus as an intelligent, spiritual human subject separate in himself. His human intelligence is not that of a man enlightened by God, but the human intelligence of the Logos of God. It follows from the hypostatic union that it is possible for Jesus' divine knowledge to be communicated to his humanity. This communication occurred, of course, with respect both for Jesus' human constitution, on the one hand, and, on the other, for the mission of salvation entrusted to the incarnate Word.

Chalcedon emphasizes that Christ is, as the same person, *perfect in divinity* and *perfect in humanity*. In accordance with the principle that the character proper to each of the two natures was preserved, it thus asserts that the reality of Jesus' humanity remains without confusion and without change (DH 301–302). According to Pope Leo's (d. 461) famous axiom that "each nature does what is proper to each in communion with the other" (DH 294), one and the same is truly God and truly man. How can we and should we think of this on the level of his consciousness? The formula *vere Deus—vere homo* has two meanings; it is declined into two principles that appear to contradict each other: the principle of integrity and that of perfection.

That Jesus increased "in wisdom and in stature, and in favor with God" (Lk 2:52), that he assumed a true human process of growth, is part of the *principle of integrity*. We may wonder whether this principle does not in some measure imply an "ignorance" on Jesus' part. If

Christ took upon himself our weaknesses, even our death, why not also ignorance? The question remains open.

The second principle, in tension with the first, is the *principle of perfection*. Christ's human existence is perfect, sinless (Heb 4:15). Can a sinless soul dwell in the darkness of ignorance? Christ has the Spirit "without measure" (cf. Jn 3:34), so that his soul, his mind, cannot be without knowledge and wisdom. After all, Paul says that in him "are hidden all the treasures of wisdom and knowledge" (Col 2:3).[17] That is why the early Church excluded practically any ignorance on the part of Christ. Mark 13:32 is thus explained, for instance, by Saint Ambrose (d. 397), in terms of the economy of salvation or pedagogically: "He himself knows the hour, but he knows it only for himself; he does not know it for me."[18] Without disputing the importance of these two principles, the perception of which represented an important step forward in the Church's understanding of the person of Christ, one would still have to note that such interpretations on the part of the Church Fathers do not do full justice to the words of the Gospels.

CHRIST'S VISION OF GOD IN THE MIDDLE AGES

The Middle Ages turned their attention to the question of how it was possible or conceivable that a human soul, a human intelligence, could contain "all the treasures of wisdom and knowledge" (Col 2:3). How is the divine knowledge communicated to the human? Gregory the Great (d. 604) said, in a wonderfully concise summary, what this was all about: "Therefore, what he knew in it [his human nature], he did not know through it."[19] His knowledge was human in application and divine in origin (since there would otherwise be no revelation).

In the thirteenth century, Scholasticism developed a very sophisticated doctrine concerning Christ's knowledge, the doctrine of Christ's *triplex scientia humana*. This differentiates between *scientia acquisita*, human knowledge that has been acquired, which Saint Thomas Aquinas (d. 1274) first taught in his *Summa*, so as to safeguard the integrity of Jesus' human existence; the *scientia infusa*, a prophetic knowledge arising from supernatural communication; and the *scientia visionis*, the

---

[17] Cf. Fulgentius of Ruspe, *Letter* 14:25–34 (CChr.SL 91:416–28).
[18] Ambrose of Milan, *Commentary on Luke* 8, 36 (SC 52:115).
[19] Gregory the Great, *Letters* 10, 21 (CChr.SL 140A: 845).

vision of God that other people will have only in eternal life. In the
Middle Ages, the immediate, divine knowledge was so much seen in
Christ that it was difficult to teach the *scientia acquisita*. Nowadays it is
the other way around: Christ has become so much a part of history
that the importance of the beatific vision of God is no longer seen. The
doctrine of the *scientia visionis* was advanced by the great teachers, such
as Saint Thomas and Saint Bonaventure (d. 1274) and by the whole
of Scholastic theology.[20] It deserves careful attention. There are three
respects in which this doctrine is usually misunderstood today.

First, as Saint Thomas emphasized, the *visio* does not mean the same
as *comprehensio*, understanding. "The soul of Christ was by no means
able to comprehend fully the nature of God."[21] The *visio* is thus certainly a contemplation, but not a comprehension, since God remains
—even for the soul of Christ—inexhaustible.

Second, the *visio* is immediate; that is, neither allegories nor concepts or images are necessary. All our objective knowledge is mediated
through *species* (sensual images, mental concepts). Without such mediation, there can be no objective knowledge. Knowledge of God cannot
be of such a kind that the Trinity would be one object of knowledge
among others. It can only be a knowledge in which God grants himself
directly to our mind, in that God himself is both what is known and the
medium through which it is known. God can be known only through
God: "In your light do we see light" (Ps 36:9).

A further misunderstanding consists, thirdly, in a mistaken interpretation of the New Testament (Johannine) "You know everything"
(Jn 21:17). Christ, so Scholastic theology says, has in his human soul a
"relative omniscience". Conceptual prejudices, however, often prevent
a correct understanding of this statement. For just as eternity is imagined to be an unending duration, so divine omniscience is imagined
as an unlimited amount of knowledge. It is more appropriate to start,

[20] J. Ernst, *Die Lehre der hochmittelalterlichen Theologen von der vollkommenen Erkenntnis Christi: Ein Versuch zur Auslegung der klassischen Dreiteilung: visio beata, scientia infusa und sci-entia acquisita* (Freiburg im Breisgau, 1971), esp. pp. 144–69 (Bonaventure) and 170–205 (Aquinas). J.-P. Torrell, *Le Christ en ses mystères: La Vie et l'oeuvre de Jésus selon saint Thomas d'Aquin*, vol. 1, Jésus et Jésus Christ 78 (Paris, 1999), pp. 135–48, arrives at a different in-terpretation of the position of Thomas; cf. Torrell, "La Vision de Dieu 'per essentiam' selon saint Thomas d'Aquin", *Micrologus* 5 (1997): 43–68.
[21] Thomas Aquinas, STh III, q. 10, a. 1 (DThA 25:258).

not from an analogy with categorical knowledge, but from the analogy with the being-with-oneself of self-awareness, which is the foundation of all objective knowledge.

So much for the misunderstandings. *Visio* means that the soul of Christ sees everything in the Father, receives everything from the Father, knows everything in the Father, not in the way of discursive knowledge, but in that of direct view, of "Inne-sein", as the German language so beautifully puts it. But back to the christological question of what the deeper meaning of the *visio*-doctrine may be. Why does the Church hold this doctrine?

The Middle Ages asked how divine knowledge and perception can be present in human knowledge and perception and be mediated by it. It is a matter of seeing whether this is at all possible. Can a finite, created capacity for perception really know God "as he is"? According to the biblical testimony, there is only one way of knowing God as he is: looking at him. In the understanding of the Bible, "looking on God" is seeing him himself, not just "his feet", not just his works, but God himself. Looking upon God is too powerful for this life. If Moses (Ex 33:20) and Elijah (1 Kings 19:11–13) see God and are still alive, that is an unusual grace. Even Moses, however, sees him only from behind, and Elijah veils his face. Thus, John can rightly say that "No one has ever seen God; the only-begotten Son, who is in the bosom of the Father, he has made him known" (Jn 1:18). "No one has seen the Father except him who is from God; he has seen the Father" (Jn 6:46; cf. 1 Jn 4:12).

According to New Testament testimony, men cannot look upon God until they do so in the perfection of the Kingdom of God: "Beloved, we are God's children now; it does not yet appear what we shall be, but we know that when he appears we shall be like him, for we shall see him as he is" (1 Jn 3:2; cf. 1 Cor 13:12; Mt 5:8). Looking upon God can only mean endless happiness, *beatitudo*, hence *visio beatifica*. Christ is able to be the one who brings complete and final revelation of God, because he is looking upon God, that is, because he has that direct relation to God without which human perception can only ever grasp what is finite.

If, then, the Middle Ages were unanimous in teaching the contemplation of God by Christ, the *scientia visionis*, it was from this soteriological motive: because only thus can Christ bring us actually, directly into touch, into contact, with God. Thomas' argument runs thus: Christ is the Way that can lead all men to the goal, to the *visio beatifica*. Yet in order to lead us there, Jesus must be not only *viator*, on the way to the goal, but also already be there himself, *comprehensor*.[22] This doctrine is therefore grounded in soteriology and the theology of revelation.

Yet the counterquestion runs thus: If Christ enjoys the *visio beatifica*, then can he still really be walking a historical path? If he already has the blessed vision of God in his earthly life, can he really suffer? The *visio* doctrine does not really contravene the *vere homo*: rather, it in fact ascribes the greatest importance to the significance for salvation of Jesus' life and its mysteries, its uniqueness (ἐφάπαξ).

The *visio* doctrine is based on a particular evaluation of the earthly life of Jesus. If, in the Middle Ages, there was perhaps less sensitivity to the historicity of Jesus' earthly life, particular attention, on the other hand, was paid to the incomparable uniqueness of the earthly history of Jesus. Here, in the actions and the suffering of Jesus, the whole of salvation came about once and for all, and here the whole revelation of the mystery of God is offered us once and for all. All this, the definitive revelation and the definitive salvation, was realized by the incarnate Word through his human will and through his human mind. It was therefore requisite that Christ should know, in his human soul, the entire revelation to be borne and the whole salvation to be effected.

The great masters of medieval theology draw a picture of Christ who "comes in the Father's name" (cf. Jn 5:43) from above, who receives everything from the Father, who knows everything from him and teaches on the basis of him. This is clearly the Christ that the Gospel of John presents to us. The medieval teachers remind us that, even if Jesus' period and his environment left their mark on him, it is still more true that he has left his mark on his, ours, and all other ages and on our whole world. This conviction was what influenced the classic view of the consciousness and knowledge of Jesus. Only a unique and incomparable consciousness can be at the source of Christ's work of revelation and redemption.

---

[22] Thomas Aquinas, STh III, q. 15, a. 10 (DThA 25:365–68).

CHRIST'S SELF-AWARENESS AS A PROBLEM IN MODERN TIMES

That brings us to the modern question about Jesus' consciousness. "The question about the self-awareness of Jesus is the central problem of the question of the historical Jesus."[23] Since the advent of historical criticism, the question of the messianic consciousness of Jesus has been raised above all. Did Jesus think he was the Messiah? Was he mistaken about the closeness of the Kingdom of God? Was it the community that first saw him that way? The answer concerning Jesus' self-awareness is of course predetermined by the way in which Jesus himself is seen. Who is he? The attempt to take an "undogmatic" Jesus of Nazareth as a starting point also determines the answer to the question of Jesus' self-awareness.

In the controversy about Modernism, the Magisterium under Pope Pius X (d. 1914) and Pope Benedict XV (d. 1922) gave an opinion on the question of the knowledge and the consciousness of Jesus.[24] In particular these documents reject the elevation of exegetical hypotheses into certainties. Thus it is said, for instance, that it is wrong to maintain that it must be taught with certainty that Jesus was mistaken in the imminent expectation question or that he was not always conscious of being the Messiah. As against the optimism of the scientism of the period, the limits of historical knowledge are pointed out. In order to understand what the Gospels say about Christ and his consciousness, one must read them in the spirit in which they were written. Historical analogy alone is inadequate, unless one wishes to reduce the mystery of Christ to a phenomenon existing strictly within history. The analogy of faith and a reading within the living tradition of the Church are necessary for an appropriate understanding of the Gospels (*Dei Verbum*, no. 12).

In a positive sense, Pius XII (d. 1958), in the encyclicals *Mystici Corporis*[25] and *Haurietis aquas*,[26] pointed out the soteriological significance of the *visio*, the loving knowledge, the *amantissima cognitio*, with which Christ comprehends everyone. The insistence of these magisterial documents on Christ's *scientia visionis* is not a persistence in opposing the

---

[23] R. Slenczka, *Geschichtlichkeit und Personsein Jesu Christi: Studien zur christologischen Problematik der historischen Jesusfrage* (Göttingen, 1967), p. 91.

[24] DH 3432-35; 3645-47.

[25] Encyclical of June 29, 1943, in: AAS 35 (1943): 200-243; extracts in: DH 3800-22.

[26] Encyclical of May 15, 1956, in: AAS 48 (1956): 316-52; extracts in: DH 3922-26.

progress of science. It is rather a question of a choice that precedes any exegetical research. The question of Christ's consciousness is posed quite differently, according to whether we take as our starting point faith in the God-man, the incarnate Word, or whether we regard Jesus from the start as an ordinary man who had a strong relationship with God. The question does not so much turn on the problem of an opposition between Magisterium and science, between dogma and exegesis; it is, rather, a matter of the presuppositions that govern the answers to our questions. One of the most valuable results of the debate over the past two centuries consists in the fact that it has become clear to how great an extent the presuppositions of the New Testament agree in essence with those of the Christology of the great councils. Wherever we meet the figure of Jesus in the Gospels, we also always touch on his mystery. All the Gospels, from Mark to John, already presuppose that Jesus is the Messiah, the Son of God (cf. Mk 1:1; 8:29); they all want to lead us to this faith (Mk 15:39; Jn 20:31); they all show that Jesus himself revealed who he was; they all presuppose that he knew this, that he was aware of it, just as he was aware of his mission to reveal the Father whom he alone knows, who has handed everything to him and whom he alone can reveal (Mt 11:27)—he, who alone can lead us to the Father (Jn 14:6). How could he know all this, except in this immediacy that the tradition calls *visio beatifica?*

c. Theological Reflection

After this brief historical survey, let us turn to two contemporary attempts.[27] Many of these are distinguished by the seriousness with which they approach the question. The almost unanimous tradition concerning Christ's knowledge does, after all, make one think. The belief that Jesus had, as a man, those three manners of knowledge cannot simply be pushed aside in a superficial way. Karl Rahner (d. 1984) attempted to take up this tradition and to develop it further. We would like briefly to present his approach, because he has influenced almost everything

---

[27] From the abundance of works on this question, we mention only a few: H. Riedlinger, *Geschichtlichkeit und Vollendung des Wissens Christi*, QD 32 (Freiburg im Breisgau, 1966); P. Kaiser, *Das Wissen Jesu Christi in der lateinischen (westlichen) Theologie*, Eichstätter Studien, n.s. 14 (Regensburg, 1982); J.-H. Nicolas, *Synthèse dogmatique: De la Trinité à la Trinité*, 3rd ed. (Freiburg, 1991), pp. 375–403; J. Maritain, *De la grâce et de l'humanité de Jésus*, in *Oeuvres complètes*, vol. 12 (Freiburg, 1992), pp. 1039–1176.

that exists today in the way of theological statements on this question. Afterward we will sketch out the position of Hans Urs von Balthasar, who carried Rahner's reflections farther.

KARL RAHNER'S BASIC DISTINCTION

Rahner starts with the assumption "that the doctrine of the hypostatic union is the basis of dogmatic statements about the self-awareness and the knowledge of Jesus".[28] He thus fixes the question in the middle, in the personal center of the incarnate Logos. He develops his thesis by elucidating, on one hand, the concepts "self-awareness and knowledge" in anthropological terms and, on the other, by delving, on the basis of this elucidation, into the implications of the hypostatic union for Christ's knowledge.

He starts by remarking that knowledge is a many-tiered structure, that at a given point in time man will consciously know some facts, for instance, but unconsciously know others. He further refers to the distinctions between reflexive conscious and borderline conscious, between conscious and explicitly perceived; he distinguishes objective conceptual consciousness and a transcendental, nonflexive knowledge that resides at the subjective pole of the consciousness. Such phenomenologically ascertainable distinctions often receive too little attention in theological reflection, even in connection with Christ's knowledge and consciousness.

It should be noted, in agreement with Rahner's remarks, that only a small part of the life of the human mind consists of reflexive consciousness. Beyond that, there is a broad area of the subconscious, to which modern psychology devotes a great deal of research. Yet there is also a dimension, too much neglected by psychology, the "superconscious", "a sphere of consciousness that is qualitatively different from the rational-objective consciousness".[29] The superconscious is simply the constantly active spiritual dimension of the human soul, the original and life-giving source of any of its intellectual activity, source of artistic "inspirations" and of the great moral choices. Without being

[28] K. Rahner, "Dogmatische Erwägungen über das Wissen und Selbstbewußtsein Christi", in *Schriften zur Theologie*, vol. 5, 3rd ed. (Zürich, 1968), pp. 222–45, here p. 227.
[29] H.-E. Hengstenberg, *Philosophische Anthropologie*, 4th ed. (Munich, 1984), p. 53; cf. J. Maritain, *L'Intuition créatrice dans l'art et dans la poésie*, in *Oeuvres complètes*, vol. 10 (Freiburg, 1985), pp. 103–601, here pp. 215–25 and 233–39.

able itself to be the subject of discussion as such, the superconscious is the hidden source of every conscious activity of man. The analogy with the superconscious allows us to form an idea of the simultaneous existence of two levels of consciousness, in which the upper level does not abolish the activity proper to the lower, but strengthens and guides it.

Rahner specifically distinguishes the form of knowledge of "an a priori nonobjective knowledge of oneself", which he calls the *Grundbefindlichkeit*, the basic mode of being, from objective knowledge. "This basic mode of being is not objective knowledge, and normally we do not deal with it; reflection never adequately catches up with this basic mode of being, even when it is explicitly directed toward it."[30]

This is Rahner's most important contribution to the analysis of the self-awareness of Christ. He is reacting against reducing perception to objective perception. He is thereby taking up a long-forgotten distinction made by Saint Augustine (d. 430) in the *De Trinitate*, to the effect that there is not only an objective "perceiving oneself", but much more fundamentally, a "knowing oneself as a whole", even if this is never completely, objectively conscious, by which the mind knows itself. Augustine calls these two kinds of knowing *nosse* and *cogitare*.[31] *Nosse* is what Rahner calls "basic mode of being", an intuitive, holistic grasp and knowledge of oneself, which is presupposed in all *cogitare*. And this knowledge is absolutely sure, without being objective.

Augustine is convinced that there is something that "every mind knows of itself and about which it is certain". One may have every possible opinion on every possible matter, yet even if he "doubts, he lives; if he doubts, he remembers why he doubts; if he doubts, he sees that he doubts; if he doubts, he wishes to be certain; if he doubts, he thinks; if he doubts, he judges that he should not assent rashly. Thus, if someone doubts anything else, he should not doubt any of this. If these processes were not, he could not doubt at all."[32] This ultimate certainty, which can never become objective knowledge, is the basis of all perception. One remark, before we come to the christological application: the distinctions in human knowledge and perception

[30] Rahner, "Dogmatische Erwägungen", p. 229.
[31] Cf. P. Agaësse, "Notes sur 'nosse' et 'cogitare'", in Augustine, *La Trinité, livres VIII–XV*, 2nd ed., BAug 16 (Paris, 1991), pp. 605–7.
[32] Augustine, *De Trinitate* 10, 10, 14 (CChr.SL 50:327–28).

asserted here would have to be applied also to the theological concept of omniscience. An elucidation that Rahner does not undertake but that is most important for our subject. Is the concept of "omniscience" a meaningful concept at all? And what might represent its corresponding finite analogy in human consciousness? Omniscience cannot be the sum of all present, past, and future propositions. One does not *become* omniscient, one cannot get from a finite to an infinite knowledge by a process of addition. Negative theology is the counterpart to this insight: the admission that any of us, as finite minds in time and space, simply cannot imagine a total knowledge.

Arising from this misunderstanding is the danger of caricaturing the idea of divine omniscience as the eye of the great watchman pursuing us. In other words, we have no access to the idea of the omniscience of God if we try it by way of "cogitare", of objective knowledge, by way of the closed series of possible and actual individual perceptions. Over against that, however, there is "nosse", as Augustine describes it. That self-knowledge and self-awareness of the finite conscious subject, the *mens* or *anima*, which never becomes a "categorial", objective knowledge, yet which is the unity that renders possible all the separate individual perceptions, "this comprehending presence that accompanies all the activities of our intelligence."[33]

Here, in this ultimate unity of the conscious subject, in which I know myself, in which I am "as it were everything",[34] is the clearest analogy to the divine omniscience, which must surely be thought of only as a unity, not as an infinite sum of perceptions. Thus Christ cannot be omniscient on the level of *cogitare*.

Rahner solves the problem of the difficult relationship between Jesus' omniscience and his limited lack of knowledge by attributing to Jesus from the beginning, on the level of nonthematic consciousness, a basic mode of being that is immediate to God, of an absolute kind; at the same time, on the level of categorial knowledge, on the other hand, a development of this original self-awareness of the absolute fact of the creaturely intellectuality having been given away to the Logos. What develops in the human life of Jesus is, accordingly, not the basis of

---

[33] L. B. Geiger, "À propos de l'omniscience divine", *Dialogue* 1 (1963): 403–5, here p. 405.

[34] Cf. Thomas Aquinas, STh I, q. 80, a. 1; q. 84, a. 2 (DThA 6:198, 261).

that basic mode of being that is immediate to God—which according to Rahner is not an objective vision—but the thematization and objectification of this basic mode of being in human concepts that are taking place. He interprets the growth of Jesus' self-consciousness as a history of the self-interpretation of Jesus' own basic mode of being. "This does not of course mean that Jesus 'came upon something' that he absolutely did not previously know but, rather, that he more and more grasps what he already always is and what he basically already knew."[35] Rahner's essay is attempting to interpret Jesus' self-awareness as at the same time the immediacy of God (*visio immediata*) and as historical knowledge, as immediate consciousness of being God's Son and as historical thematization and objectification of this consciousness.

The positive aspect of Rahner's essay is the differentiation of the question of Jesus' knowledge and consciousness through the distinction between the basic mode of being and objective, reflexive consciousness. With respect to the systematic execution, certain reservations do arise that need more detailed examination. We might mention here just the lack of a trinitarian dimension, which becomes evident particularly with a more precise definition of the object of Jesus' contemplation of God.[36] According to Rahner, in fact, Jesus' human soul directly contemplates the Logos, to a certain extent as if Jesus as a man stood over against the Son of God, the Logos, as God.[37] This tendency recurs time and again in Rahner's Christology. The question does at any rate arise whether Jesus' awareness of God truly refers primarily to his being God himself, toward divinity at all, and not rather toward an "intentional", "I-thou relationship with the Father that occurs in history".[38]

HANS URS VON BALTHASAR'S TRINITARIAN OVERVIEW

Hans Urs von Balthasar approaches the question of Jesus' self-awareness from a different direction. Following Thomas Aquinas, he sees

---

[35] Rahner, "Dogmatische Erwägungen", p. 241.

[36] For a criticism of the metaphysics, anthropology, and Christology underlying Rahner's essay, see M. Blechschmidt, *Der Leib und das Heil: Zum christlichen Verständnis der Leiblichkeit in Auseinandersetzung mit R. Bultmann und K. Rahner* (Bern, 1983).

[37] Cf. Rahner, "Dogmatische Erwägungen", p. 243.

[38] H. Riedlinger, *Geschichtlichkeit und Vollendung des Wissens Christi*, QD 32 (Freiburg im Breisgau, 1966), pp. 148–53.

the mission (thus, the entire incarnate existence of Christ as mission) in the "extension" of the eternal procession of the Son from the Father.[39] Jesus' entire earthly existence is the form of "translation", in terms of history and the economy of salvation, of his eternal existence, his manner of being God. His manner of being man is the form of translation of his manner of being God. If as God the Son he is entirely from the Father, then when he has become man he is also entirely from the Father.

The role played by Jesus is none other than that of his own person. It does not come to his person "from outside"; in him, rather, the role and the person are identical.[40] Mission and person are one. No split exists between his person and his task, as if the task were to be added; rather, Jesus is, in his entire existence, *the envoy* of the Father. Hence von Balthasar tries to reformulate Rahner's approach: Jesus' self-awareness is his awareness of his mission. We need not ask in an abstract way about any omniscience on the part of Jesus; rather, Jesus' human consciousness is—unthematically, as "basic mode of being"— the consciousness of his mission. That permits a far more concrete approach to our question, oriented toward biblical data. For it means, on the one hand, that Jesus has always been fully aware of his mission; he does not learn about it first like a prophet; but this knowing needs to be thought about, not as explicit and objective (*cogitare*), but as non-thematic, "immemorial" knowledge of the conscious subject of itself (*nosse*), which here "always" knows of its "being one" with the Father. On the other hand, however, the process of becoming conscious of this mission thematically can certainly take place in the manner of a historical process of learning.

What does the "self"-awareness of Jesus mean? Who is this person, about whose human consciousness we are asking? He is the Son of God. His "I", his "self", is that of the Son of God. This self-awareness is therefore inseparably the awareness of his unity with the One whom he calls Abba. Jesus' self-awareness is his consciousness of Abba. His human consciousness is the human translation of his eternal divine Sonship.

Jesus' knowledge, his "consciousness of majesty", is not at all from himself, but from his relationship with the Father: his consciousness of

---

[39] Cf. von Balthasar, TD 3:149–259; Thomas Aquinas, STh I, q. 43, a. 1.
[40] Cf. von Balthasar, TD 3:201.

being Son of God is not a "self-consciousness" in the sense that Jesus draws this from within himself; rather, he draws it wholly from his relationship with the Father. Jesus' self-awareness is in fact his Abba-consciousness. François Dreyfus says that "Jesus knows himself fully, in his loving gaze at the Father, since he only exists through, in, and for the Father."[41] The fact that Jesus lives on the basis of this relationship with the Father is probably most clearly expressed in Jesus' constant prayer. "When Jesus prays, then the mystery of the Son, who wholly 'lives through the Father', in intimate union with him, appears in the most personal manner."[42]

Human self-awareness is inconceivable without relationships with others. I am not aware of myself as a result of withdrawing all bridges to the outside and being with myself. There is no such thing as isolated self-awareness. Openness to and dependence on others are an essential part of human self-awareness: first of all, to the mother, the first person to whom one relates. This is not in the sense that the person is only constituted through the relationship (in an ontological sense); rather, it is essential for the person as a free conscious subject to be not only "with himself", but also "with others" and "from others".

Hence, it does not seem advisable to start on the question of Christ's knowledge from the self-awareness of Jesus. Wolfhart Pannenberg is probably right to point out that every human self-awareness is mediated and not unmediated.[43] Only in knowing other people and things, and only by this means, do we know ourselves. I get to know myself in getting to know other people/things. I do not experience myself as I am by cutting off everything outside and trying to experience myself directly; and even if I do withdraw in this way, then I am always still coming back to myself from something else.

In that sense, we may and must assume that Jesus came to know himself through others, and, like any child, especially through his mother. Yet however much the carrying out of Jesus' human existence obviously included more than a physical growth, however much human knowledge (talking, carpentry, perhaps reading and writing, and so on) was certainly also a part of it, everything seems, on the other hand, to

---

[41] F. Dreyfus, *Jésus savait-il qu'il était Dieu?* 4th ed. (Paris, 1987), p. 111.

[42] John Paul II, *Communio personarum*, vol. 5. In German: *Jesus Christus der Erlöser: Katechesen 1986-1989* (St. Ottilien, 1994), p. 155.

[43] W. Pannenberg, *Jesus, God and Man* (London and Philadelphia, 1968), pp. 344-49.

indicate that there was *one* thing Jesus did not learn: his connection with the Father. We are referring here not to the objective consciousness (*cogitare*) of that connection but, rather, to this consciousness itself (*nosse*).

Nowhere do we find any trace of Jesus having a vocation experience analogous to that of the prophets. Anton Vögtle is quite right in saying, "Anyone who does not presuppose an absolute immediacy to God on Jesus' part is right to express a feeling that there would need to have been a decisive revelation experience for Jesus, in order to explain the claims he makes as the bearer of revelation and salvation"[44]—which necessarily leads to some kind of adoptionism. The words that express Jesus' relationship with the Father sound as if Jesus knew of no beginning to it. Wherever we encounter him, Jesus always speaks and acts on the basis of this relationship. The question of whether he is thematically, reflexively conscious of this is secondary. He does it, and does it as the most obvious thing in the world. The impression is that everything Jesus does and says always comes from that, from his immemorial unity with the Father.

BASIC MODE OF BEING AND THEMATIC KNOWLEDGE

The unity between the divine and the human consciousness in Christ consists precisely in this awareness of mission. He understands himself entirely as the one who comes "from the Father" to men, as the one who "makes the Father known" (cf. Jn 1:18), "Word of the Father". This immediacy to the Father seems not only to be a basic mode of being reposing in itself, but also, in a manner difficult to grasp, to determine concretely what Jesus does, says, and knows. "Of course, the particular shape of the mission (which draws its universality from its identity with the self-consciousness of this particular 'I') can contain a wealth of content, successively revealed, but its source and measure remain the mission itself."[45] Jesus does not seem to have waited on God's word, which either came or did not come, as did the prophets (cf. Jer 15:16). We find no hesitation in his behavior, no tentative searching for what he should do, for what seems to be God's will and

---

[44] A. Vögtle, "Exegetische Erwägungen über das Wissen und Selbstbewußtsein Jesu", in *Gott in Welt: Festgabe für K. Rahner*, ed. H. Vorgrimler, 1:663 n. 157 (Freiburg im Breisgau, 1964).

[45] Von Balthasar, TD 3:166.

his assignment. Faced with the evidence of the Gospels, we can only assume that Jesus not only knows about his mission in an unthematic basic mode of being, but also knows in the concrete about his path, about his task, the word he is to speak, and the action he is to accomplish.

Jesus knows about his path. Such a mysterious saying as the one in response to Herod's threat offers some insight into Jesus' astonishing assurance: "At that very hour some Pharisees came, and said to him, 'Get away from here, for Herod wants to kill you.' And he said to them, 'Go and tell that fox, "Behold, I cast out demons and perform cures today and tomorrow, and the third day I finish my course. Nevertheless I must go on my way today and tomorrow and the day following; for it cannot be that a prophet should perish away from Jerusalem" ' '' (Lk 13:31–33). He knows what he must do. Thus he knows that he must go to the Jordan for baptism; that he must go to Jerusalem. Yet it is apparent that this does not come "from outside", as if by some power that dictates to him what he must do here and now; he knows, rather, from himself, with his own certitude, which is at the same time the certainty about the will of the Father. The experience of great saints shows that this does not mean heteronomy.

Jesus also knows the word he must speak: with what certitude his words strike home! His parables speak directly to the hearts of men. He proclaims his message with a unique authority, teaching in his own name what Moses and the prophets once proclaimed in the name of God. The hair-splitting Pharisees and scribes therefore engage him in numerous arguments yet cannot convict him of any inconsistency.

Finally, in a quite astonishing way, Jesus knows what is in men's hearts. Jesus' knowledge of men's hearts,[46] repeatedly underlined, shows that there is a direct connection between his knowledge of "what was in men" (Jn 2:25) and his immediacy to God. At the same time, a theological theme is suggested within this theme of Jesus' knowledge of hearts: "Jesus, with his knowledge of men's hearts, stands close to God, to whom the Old Testament frequently attributes an inner examination and penetration of man."[47] This theological theme (with its

---

[46] Cf. H. U. von Balthasar, *Does Jesus Know Us—Do We Know Him?* trans. Graham Harrison (San Francisco: Ignatius Press, 1983), pp. 15–23.

[47] R. Schnackenburg, *Das Johannesevangelium*, vol. 1, 7th ed., HThK 4/1 (Freiburg im Breisgau, 1992), p. 373.

implicit christological significance: Jesus stands in place of God) only makes sense if it corresponds to the historical-human reality of Jesus. All these points (knowing the path, the words, men's hearts, what has to be done) go far beyond the prophetic.

Tradition has tried to express the tension between basic mode of being and thematic knowledge by describing Christ as *simul comprehensor et viator*; as *comprehensor*, insofar as he enjoyed the immediate vision of God, as *viator* insofar as he, like every man, was *in statu viae*, on his way, gaining knowledge related to the experience of others, learning and asking, with a genuine knowledge that comes with experience and is historically determined (this is particularly expressed, for instance, in Jesus' parables, which convey the message about God's kingship in images from the everyday experience of his times).

Certainly, the *simul comprehensor et viator* saying is at first sight a paradoxical expression: How is it possible to speak of Jesus' blessed vision of God (*visio beatifica*) without dissolving his historicity? How is it possible, conversely, to assume this historicity, since Jesus as *"comprehensor"*, is in fact already "at the goal"?

Yet this paradox is, fundamentally, none other than that of the confession of faith in Christ itself: *vere Deus, vere homo*—and this, in such a way that the truth of the one (*vere Deus*) not only does not threaten the truth of the other (*vere homo*) but, rather, in fact fulfills and secures it. This basic principle, which Chalcedon presupposes for the two natures and the Third Council of Constantinople for the two wills, is equally true for the question of Jesus' knowledge.

How this *simul* of the *comprehensor* and the *viator* is to be conceived remains, of course, just as inaccessible as the *simul* of the divine and human wills or that of the very existence of Christ as both divine and human: it remains just as inconceivable as the mystery of the person of Jesus himself. Yet inconceivable does not mean unthinkable or even meaningless. There is much of which we cannot form a mental image but that can be thought about and even demonstrated.

Perhaps it will help us to visualize this *simul* if we draw on human experience for a distant analogy. There is certainly the experience that joy and pain can be present at the same time, that someone is filled with joy, for instance, in spite of intense physical pain (that may often be seen in the seriously ill). Vice versa, it is true that the deeper our joy, the greater too, in contrast, is the experience of pain. May this not provide a hint of an indication about this *simul* of immediacy to God and human experience in Jesus? Saint Thérèse of the Child Jesus said shortly before her death, "I read a beautiful passage in the Reflections of the Imitation. . . . Our Lord enjoyed all the delights of the Trinity when He was in the garden of Olives, and still his agony was none the less cruel. It's a mystery, but I assure you that I understand something about it by what I'm experiencing myself."[48]

2. Further Aspects of Jesus' Humanity

The Council of Chalcedon declared that in the unity of the person of Jesus two natures remain preserved without confusion and that each nature acts according to its proper character: "For each nature does what is proper to each in communion with the other" (DH 294). With this formula it was contradicting both Monophysitism, which denied the full humanity of Christ, and also Nestorianism, which failed to recognize the exchange of characteristics between the divine and human natures in the Divine Person of Christ. The reception of these dogmatic truths by the Church as a whole did in any case take several centuries. The three subsequent councils, the Second of Constantinople (553), the Third of Constantinople (680–681), and the Second of Nicaea (787), repeatedly took up the question anew of how to understand the relationship between the divine and human natures in Christ.[49]

Even after its condemnation by Chalcedon, Monophysitism maintained its position in Palestine, Egypt, and Syria. Concerned for the unity of the empire, in 476 Emperor Zeno of Byzantium (d. 491) issued a decree-law that prescribed a formula of unity acceptable to the Monophysites, the so-called Henotikon. Since this formula of unity ignored the definition of Chalcedon, it was rejected by Pope Felix III (d. 492). Following this, there was a schism between Rome and Byzantium that lasted until 519. Emperor Justinian (d. 565) made a fresh attempt to oblige the Monophysites (543/44) and condemned "three chapters" of the Antiochene school, which had been partially rehabilitated at Chalcedon after earlier attacks. Pope Virgilius (d. 555) at first gave his assent

---

[48] Thérèse of Lisieux, "The Yellow Notebook", July 6, in *St. Thérèse of Lisieux: Her Last Conversations*, trans. John Clarke, O.C.D. (Washington, D.C.: ICS Publications, 1977), p. 75; cf. Thomas Aquinas, STh III, q. 46, a. 8 (DThA 28:39–41).

[49] On these three councils, see G. Alberigo, ed., *Geschichte der Konzilien: Vom Nicaenum bis zum Vaticanum II* (Düsseldorf, 1993), pp. 136–69; K. Schatz, *Allgemeine Konzilien— Brennpunkte der Kirchengeschichte* (Paderborn, 1997), pp. 71–94.

to this condemnation, but he withdrew it when it was interpreted in
the West as a betrayal of Chalcedon. Justinian thereupon called a new
council at Constantinople in 553 to push through the condemnation
of the three chapters. Pope Virgilius did not take part in the council,
but after having been threatened with further violence by the emperor,
he gave a belated assent to its decisions. That is why it has gone down
in the history of the Church as the Fifth Ecumenical Council, and the
Second Council of Constantinople.[50]

Constantinople II employs the distinction between hypostasis and
nature, introduced magisterially by Chalcedon, in a sense refined by
a hundred years of discussion. While Chalcedon could still use the
term "hypostasis" to refer to the final product of the process of union
between divine and human nature, it is here specified that in Christ
this term refers to the preexistent Logos. "There is only one hypostasis
of him who is the Lord Jesus Christ, one of the Holy Trinity" (DH
424). The human nature of Christ is united with the divine Logos in
the hypostasis. This same Logos was thus the subject who worked the
miracles and who suffered the Passion (cf. DH 423). Constantinople II
also teaches that Jesus Christ is not, indeed, a human person but that
the humanity of Christ exists in a personal manner in the single person
of the Logos. The Logos adopts human nature as his own and imparts
his own subsistence to it. The hitherto simple person of the Logos
is complex after the Incarnation. In this connection, the Council says
"that the union of God the Word with the flesh animated by a rational
and intellectual soul occurred by way of synthesis, or in the hypostasis"
(DH 424). In the Incarnation, the Divine Person of the Logos thus
made itself human in authentic fashion. It lived out its personal existence in the human manner of becoming and growth. "The concept of
the 'complex person' of the Second Council of Constantinople makes
it possible for us to maintain that the incarnate Word is ultimately the
subject of the historical events of the life of Jesus, that it is this man
here, Jesus of Nazareth, a man, who is truly God's Son, a humanized
God-Son, who was truly born of the Virgin Mary and truly suffered
the Passion."[51]

[50] See A. Grillmeier, *Christ in Christian Tradition*, vol. 2/2: *The Church of Constantinople in the Sixth Century*, trans. John Cawte and Pauline Allen (Louisville, Ky., 1995), pp. 438–62; F.-X. Murphy and P. Sherwood, *Konstantinopel II und III*, GÖK 3 (Mainz, 1990), pp. 9–162.

[51] M. Bordoni, *Gesù di Nazaret: Signore e Cristo*, vol. 3 (Rome, 1986), pp. 848–49.

The profound theological significance of this new concept of the ὑπόστασις σύνθετος was first emphasized in the following century (the seventh) by Maximus the Confessor (d. 662). He was responsible for the most mature synthesis of post-Chalcedonian Christology. This was occasioned by the question of the human will of Jesus, which was elucidated dogmatically at the Third Council of Constantinople. And the subsequent controversy about the veneration of icons was ultimately concerned with the question of the true human body of Christ. This teaching was given conciliar confirmation at Nicaea II.

a. Jesus' Will and Work as God and Man

At the beginning of the seventh century, the interest in christological discussion shifted from the level of natures to the level of actions.[52] Patriarch Sergius of Constantinople (d. 638) and Emperor Heraclius (d. 641) tried to reconcile the Monophysites to the imperial Church. Sergius declared two natures in Christ, but only one operation (ἐνέργεια). He thus became the founder of Monergitism, basing his ideas in part on Severus of Antioch (d. 538), who, a hundred years earlier, had interpreted Dionysius the Pseudo-Areopagite's (fifth/sixth century) well-known expression of "divine-human" operation (Θεανδρικὴ ἐνέργεια) as being the one operation (μία ἐνέργεια) of Christ. The Patriarch Cyrus of Alexandria (d. 642) tried to create unity between the supporters and opponents of Chalcedon in his sphere of influence in 632 with the formula of one mode of activity in Christ. The monk Sophronius of Jerusalem (d. 639) wrote against his tendentious confession of faith, referring to Chalcedon.[53] In order to avoid new divisions, Patriarch Sergius issued a decree in 633, in which speaking about both a single operation and two modes of activity was forbidden. The first was said to be *suspected* by many of denying the Chalcedonian confession of two natures in Christ; the second was said to be *godless*, "since it is impossible that one and the same subject should have two wills, contradicting each other at a given

---

[52] On the question of Monothelitism and Constantinople III, see C. Schönborn, "681–1981: Ein vergessenes Konzilsjubiläum—eine versäumte ökumenische Chance", *Freiburger Zeitschrift für Philosophie und Theologie* 29 (1982): 157–74; Murphy and Sherwood, *Konstantinopel II und III*, pp. 163–211; Theresia Hainthaler, "Monothelitismus", "Monergetismus", in *Lexikon für Theologie und Kirche*, 3rd ed. (1999), 7:430–31.

[53] See C. Schönborn, *Sophrone de Jérusalem*, ThH 20 (Paris, 1972).

point".[54] In this text, generally known as the *Psephos*, the question of Christ's will arises for the first time. An edict of Emperor Heraclius in 638, the *Ekthesis*, written by Sergius, confirms, along with the ban on discussion of the question of the number of modes of operation, the declaration of faith in Christ's single will. The Monothelitism dispute begins with this document. At the urging of Saint Maximus, Monothelitism was condemned first at the Lateran Synod in 649 by Pope Martin I (d. 653) and was finally condemned at the Sixth Ecumenical Council, the Third Council of Constantinople. Because of his defense of the truth and his resistance to imperial power, Martin I had to go into exile, while Maximus even had to accept mutilation. The emperor had his tongue and his hands cut off. Saint Maximus died as a Confessor of the Faith as a result of this mutilation.[55]

THE QUESTION OF THE WILL IN THE WRITINGS OF MAXIMUS THE CONFESSOR

Maximus the Confessor opposed this distortion of the faith with substantial metaphysical analyses. He started from the fact that every living nature, in order truly to be a unique nature, must be self-moved. The movement that every living nature naturally produces is its own energy, its mode of activity, which characterizes this nature in its essence. "Since the mode of activity is natural, it is the constitutive and most typical sign of that nature."[56] It follows that nature and mode of activity belong together inseparably. If, therefore, two different natures are united in one person, then the mode of activity proper to each of the natures cannot be changed by that, otherwise the two natures themselves would be changed. The union between the two modes of activity is thus possible only on the level of person, not on that of nature. According to Maximus, the mode of activity belongs to the nature, not to the person. The person has thus no mode of activity of his own; rather, he determines the way (τρόπος) in which his own

---

[54] Sergius of Constantinople, *Psephos*, quoted in: Murphy and Sherwood, *Konstantinopel II und III*, p. 354.

[55] Documents concerning the trials of Martin I and Saint Maximus are translated and commented on in H. Rahner, *Kirche und Staat im frühen Christentum: Dokumente aus acht Jahrhunderten und ihre Deutung* (Munich, 1961), pp. 366–435; for a critical edition of the documents on the trial of Saint Maximus: *Scripta saeculi VII vitam Maximi Confessoris illustrantia* (CChr.SG 39).

[56] Maximus the Confessor, *Disputatio cum Pyrrho* (PG 91:348A).

activity, proper to his nature, takes place. This is preeminently true of the Trinity. Each Divine Person does not have his own work and will; rather, all have the same. On the other hand, each person accomplishes this one essential work and will in a way corresponding to his own "mode of existence", his own particular way of being God. The Son has no other work and will than the Father, but he works and wills what the Father wills in a different way from the Father: that is, in a way corresponding to the mode of being the Son. The same thing also happens in the complex hypostasis of the incarnate Word. Christ acts in a divine way as God and in a human way as man, and yet the particular thing about his work is that, as a man, he acts in a different human way from us, consistent with the mode of the person of the eternal Son.

The objection is repeatedly raised against the doctrine of the two wills and two modes of activity in Christ that this leads to an imperceptible doubling within Christ, to two lives being lived side-by-side within him, thus destroying the unity of Christ's life.[57] With his formal analyses, Maximus shows that it is not the natural modes of activity but the way in which these work together that is single and unified. In the one person of Christ, divine and human works and wills work together in an exchange, a mutual interpenetration (περιχώρησις), which is not on the level of the nature, but on that of the person. Only thus is it possible for the human actions of Jesus to have become the expression of his divine actions, because in Christ a human work became the work of the Divine Person of the Son of God.

> Each of us works, not insofar as he is a "who", but as a "what": that is, insofar as he is a man. Yet insofar as he is a "who", Peter for instance, or Paul, he gives a shape to the manner (τρόπος) of his work, by easing off or making an effort and by giving his work this or that shape, in accordance with his free will. That is how we recognize the distinction between persons in practice, by the way (τρόπος) they do things; in the nature (λόγος) of the work, on the other hand, we recognize the natural operation common to all men.[58]

The decisive point in the theological reflection of Maximus the Confessor with respect to the question of Jesus' human will lies in the distinction between the nature of the work (λόγος), and the manner of

---

[57] See, for instance, Pannenberg, *Jesus, God and Man*, pp. 293–95.
[58] Maximus the Confessor, *Opuscula theologica et polemica* 9 (PG 91:137A).

acting (τϱόπος). This in fact allows him to distinguish difference from contradiction. The difference between the two wills consists of the human will being, by nature, different from the divine. The contradiction or opposition between the divine will and the human, however, is not to be found in the nature of the rational will; rather, it lies in our will having a tropos distorted by sin, in the fact that the way we use our will has been distorted by sin. In Jesus Christ, the natural will is fully integrated in a direction that is freely chosen, a direction given by the person. The effect of this integration is that Jesus lives his human life entirely on the basis of his personal center, his existence as the Son. The duality of wills, natural and personal, in Jesus does not imply any discord or rebellion. According to Maximus, the unity of Jesus' will does not consist in his having only a single principle of activity, but in the fact that both his divine will and his human will express the mode of existence of his Divine Person. Jesus Christ has two wills, but their subject is always his Divine Person. There are thus two wills, but only one person who wills.

THE THIRD COUNCIL OF CONSTANTINOPLE (680/681)

The Sixth Ecumenical Council, the Third Council of Constantinople, defined this dogma in 681:

> We likewise proclaim in him [Christ], according to the teaching of the holy Fathers, two natural volitions or wills and two natural modes of activity, without division, without change, without separation, without confusion. These two natural wills are not opposed to each other, as the impious heretics say. But his human will is compliant; it does not oppose or resist. It, rather, submits to his divine and almighty will. (DH 556)

Constantinople III is concerned in this formula for the reality of the human element in the divine-human operation. It declares that it is not only when Jesus' human will is relinquished that God's will is able to assert itself and determine everything. Precisely in the decisive point of the mission of Jesus, in the sacrifice of his life "for the many", it is his free human will that reveals his oneness with the Father and achieves our salvation. Maximus the Confessor, who was the real "inspiration" for the 681 council (as he had already been before and still more directly for the 649 Lateran Synod), expressed this in a simple short formula: "Thus the Lord carried out in deed and truth (through his suffering) as man, in an obedience that never overstepped the line, what he himself had predetermined, as God, to be carried out."[59] This becomes especially clear in the scene at Gethsemane: the words of Christ's agony, "Not as I will, but as thou will" (Mt 26:39), had been advanced by the Monothelites as a biblical basis for denying any human will in Jesus. Maximus now showed that these words are in fact the expression of Jesus' human will: "In this Gospel verse, Maximus contemplates the ultimate act of the human will of Christ, and this act is 'the ultimate assent'; it is 'complete conformity' with 'the divine will, which is at the same time both his will and that of the Father'."[60] Here, a free and active human will is clearly being presumed—not, of course, in opposition to the divine will, but in the ultimate assent to it. The act of redemption lies, not in relinquishing his human will, but in his "wishing, even as a man, to fulfill the Father's will".[61]

The text of the definition made by the 681 Council in fact says only that Christ's human will "submits to his divine and almighty will" (DH 556) and avoids attributing explicitly to the human will of Christ that quality which is characteristic of the will as will: free self-determination. The Council did of course make clear, in its oration in praise of Emperor Constantine IV (d. 685), that it understood Christ's human will in this way,[62] so that its "subordination" to the divine will could be understood entirely in Maximus' sense, as "assent to" and "conformity with" the divine will, and not as just as a passive determination by the almighty divine will. These formulations certainly seem rather abstract. There is no doubt, however, that the explicit emphasis laid on the free human will in Jesus at the heart of the redemptive event does have significant consequences for our view of the human will and of human freedom in general.[63] At the 681 Council what was decisive for the relationship between divine and human freedom was stated: the self-determination of the human will is not abolished if this will entirely "submits to the divine and almighty will". We cannot therefore agree with Wolfhart Pannenberg when he says that the "determination of the human will in Christ by the almighty divine will," "taken strictly . . . excluded the independence of Jesus' human voluntary capacity, which

---

[59] Maximus the Confessor, *Ambiguorum Liber* 10:41 (PG 91:1309D).

[60] F.-M. Léthel, *Théologie de l'Agonie du Christ*, ThH 52 (Paris, 1979), p. 92.

[61] Maximus the Confessor, *Opuscula theologica et polemica ad Marinum* 6 (PG 91:68C).

[62] Mansi 11:664D.

[63] See R. Gauthier, "S. Maxime le confesseur et la psychologie de l'acte humaine", *Recherches de Théologie Ancienne et Médiévale* 21 (1954): 51–100.

constituted the real core of the will for Maximus".[64] If this were so,
then divine and human freedom would not, strictly speaking, be com-
patible.

The Third Council of Constantinople does not, of course, assert
such a compatibility in the sense of simple coexistence, which would
lose sight of the infinite distance between uncreated and created freedom. Assuming a mutual exclusion and incompatibility would however
mean committing the same mistake and would regard the two wills as
correlative, competing, and thus ultimately as being on the same level
of magnitude.[65] Monothelitism believed it had to deny the human will
because it was unable to conceive of a free human will other than as
being in competition with the divine will. The compatibility of the
divine and human wills professed by the 681 Council remains a mystery that cannot be taken in intellectually, yet whose possibility and
the reality can be seen by us, in faith, in Christ.

THE LASTING SIGNIFICANCE OF
THE THIRD COUNCIL OF CONSTANTINOPLE

The significance of the 681 conciliar creed for today is probably to be
found above all in illuminating the "level of being", the two-natures
doctrine of the Council of Chalcedon, in its implications for the "level
of action". The Council of Chalcedon's definition has always been re-
proached for considering the two natures of Christ in too static a way,
in their essence. This impression can only arise if the definition of Chalcedon is looked at in isolation. The Sixth Ecumenical Council is too
seldom consulted for an understanding of Chalcedon, even though the
Council explicitly understood its definition as a more precise interpretation of the definition of Chalcedon. If Chalcedon said of Christ that
he was "perfect in divinity, perfect in humanity", then the Council of
681 concludes from this that Christ must also have a perfect human
will.

Such a rereading of the Council of Chalcedon in the light of the 681
Council could help to find a way out of the dilemma between a more
"functional" and a more "ontological" Christology. It might show that

---

[64] Pannenberg, *Jesus, God and Man*, p. 294.

[65] On the relationship between finite and infinite freedom, see what is said by H. U. von
Balthasar, TD 2:189–316.

the ("functional") aspect, so much emphasized today, of "being for others", of the "proexistence" of Christ, attains its full force only if his human proexistence is really the human existence of the eternal Word. The reason the "for us" of the life, death, and Resurrection of Jesus is therefore more than just an ethical example because he, the eternal Son, having become man, "worked with human hands, He thought with a human mind, acted by human choice and loved with a human heart" (*Gaudium et Spes*, no. 22). Then, however, the exemplariness of Jesus also acquires its full meaning: his human actions are God's human actions.

That then implies that in Christ, acts of human freedom are not swallowed up or abolished by the divine will, and this in turn has major consequences for our understanding of human freedom. Because "our salvation was intended by the Divine Person to happen in a human manner", salvation means the restoration of human freedom. Vatican II formulated this in relation to the image of God in man: Christ is "Himself the perfect man"; "to the sons of Adam He restores the divine likeness which had been disfigured from the first sin onward" (*Gaudium et Spes*, no. 22). Just before that, the Council says: "For its part, authentic freedom is an exceptional sign of the divine image within man. For God has willed that man remain 'under the control of his own decisions,' (Ecclus 15:14) so that he can seek his Creator spontaneously, and come freely to utter and blissful perfection through loyalty to Him. Hence man's dignity demands that he act according to a knowing and free choice that is personally motivated and prompted from within, not under blind internal impulse nor by mere external pressure" (*Gaudium et Spes*, no. 17). The Council of 681 did not treat this inner connection of Christ's perfect human will with the freedom of man as made in the image of God as a specific subject. Yet even then, there could be no doubt that with the declaration of belief in Christ's free human will a declaration of belief in the freedom of man, was also pronounced just as the avowal of the full and undiluted humanity of Christ at Chalcedon included assent to the inalienable, positive individual significance of human existence.

Vladimir Soloviev (d. 1900) has impressively pointed out this connection between human dignity and the declaration of faith in Christ at the Sixth Ecumenical Council. He characterizes Monothelitism as follows:

The man-God [Christ] has no human will and does not act as a man; his humanity is purely passive and is exclusively determined by the absolute fact of his divinity. We have here before us the negation of human freedom and energy—fatalism and quietism. Humanity takes no part in the work of its redemption: God alone acts. Being passively subject to the divine fact, represented in spiritual respects by the immovable Church, in worldly respects by the sacred power of the divine Augustus—this is the Christian's sole duty. The Monothelite heresy was supported for more than fifty years by the empire and by the whole of the Eastern hierarchy, with the exception of a few monks, who were forced to seek refuge in Rome; but it was vanquished at Constantinople (in 680).[66]

Time and again Soloviev emphasizes this connection between christological orthodoxy and the Christian view of man. He sees it as the major significance of the Council of 681, that this connection "was able to pass into the general consciousness of the Church". Without a human will and without a human mode of activity, Christ's human nature would have "no real meaning: it would be a lifeless addition to the divinity."[67] Yet the result would be that "the freedom of man to bring himself into conformity with the divine will, to work freely together with it, is utterly destroyed by this higher will; in this way, the divine will appears to be something fatal for man, an absolute necessity."[68] To such an "inhuman" God, as Soloviev calls him, there is a corresponding view of man that renounces any attempt "to reshape the life of society itself in the spirit of Christ". Soloviev sees the basis for such a reshaping, and for the belief in its being possible, in the 681 Council's declaration of faith: "to complete this task, above all the free will of man, to which God allows the widest latitude, had to be at work."[69]

THE SOTERIOLOGICAL SIGNIFICANCE OF THE DOCTRINE OF THE TWO WILLS

The doctrine of Jesus' two wills also has an eminently soteriological significance. Through the way in which he wills things as a man, Christ also leads us men to be able to will as he willed. He, however

---

[66] V. Soloviev, *Rußland und die universale Kirche*, in *Deutsche Gesamtausgabe der Werke*, 3:159–60; an abridged version translated into English as *The Russian Church and the Papacy: An Abridgment of Russia and the Universal Church* (San Diego, 2001).

[67] Soloviev, *Geschichte und Zukunft der Theokratie*, in *Deutsche Gesamtausgabe* 2:449.

[68] Soloviev, *Der große Streit und die christliche Politik*, in *Deutsche Gesamtausgabe* 2:241–42).

[69] Ibid., 245–46.

—as Maximus puts it—loved us more than he loved himself, in taking our place instead of his glory and in taking upon himself death and the Passion and enmity. Because of that, the way has been opened for man to love God and neighbor more than himself. This new, eschatological mode of existence of the reign of God, has thus become possible because in Christ it became a human mode of existence, it became the way in which Christ lived out as a man his divine self-renunciation. The Christian mode of existence, of which the supreme example is the love of one's enemies, has become possible for us because in Christ it became a human mode of existence. The human will was not abolished in him but renewed.

Since the Fall, the relationship between the natural and the personal will in man has been distorted. Man actually wills what is good, because it is connatural to him and therefore pleases him. But his will is as it were, awry, so he does not do the good that he wants, but the evil that he does not want (Rom 7:19). The reason for this does not lie in the nature of the rational will but in the fact that our will has a tropos distorted by sin, in the fact that the way we use our will has been distorted by sin. By nature, man has a deep yearning for unity with his fellowmen. Egoism, however, results in the other appearing as a threat. Only love can lead to the fulfillment of this predisposition of man toward unity. The love for all men, which excludes no one, even one's enemies, seems, however, to be *contra naturam*. For what is more natural than to react against someone who does me wrong? On the other hand, there is the fact that men "tear each other apart" as a consequence of this "natural" reaction. And this tearing apart of each other is completely contrary to nature. It runs counter to the predisposition toward unity and society. It is a paradox that the most profound aspiration within man, the seeking for unity, can be put into practice only through a discontinuity in which man seems to lose himself and chooses, not himself, but the other. Yet it is precisely through this that this natural aspiration is fulfilled.[70]

Christ overcame the dialectic of enmity by forgiving his tormentors on the Cross. He thereby held true to the love of the Father who had

[70] Maximus showed this with existential clarity in the dialectic between desire and pain. See on this C. Schönborn, "Plaisir et douleur dans l'analyse de S. Maxime le Confesseur d'après les *Quaestiones ad Thalassium*", in *Maximus Confessor: Actes du Symposium sur Maxime le Confesseur*, Par. 27 (Freiburg, 1980), pp. 273–84.

sent him, right into the midst of the most extreme enmity. Thus Maximus the Confessor sees what is actually redemptive in Jesus' act of
salvation as his having broken the power of enmity.[71] Christ thereby
completed the dynamic of salvation already foreshadowed in the Old
Testament, as it emerges for instance in the reports on the relationship
between David and Saul. David twice had an opportunity to kill Saul,
who was persecuting him. Yet he does not lift his hand against him.
Twice this leads to a subsequent meeting (1 Sam 24, 26). Both times,
Saul is shaken: " 'Is this your voice, my son David?' And Saul lifted up
his voice and wept. He said to David, 'You are more righteous than I;
for you have repaid me good, whereas I have repaid you evil' " (1 Sam
24:17–18). David, the man "after God's heart" (cf. Acts 13:22), breaks
the circle of the dialectic of enmity. Both men stand naked before each
other, in their true identity, no longer as those propelled around in the
centrifuge of enmity—David as the one who is feared, Saul as the one
threatened, who therefore has to threaten and persecute in turn. David
is the "man after God's heart", because in him can be seen God's most
characteristic behavior: "You have repaid me good, whereas I have
repaid you evil" (1 Sam 24:18). That is God's behavior. God turns
the heart of Israel—not by force, for there is no conversion of that
kind. The Lord wants to speak to the heart of Israel (cf. Hos 2:16). He
wants to bring about Israel's conversion through his faithfulness, not
through his power; by his mercy, not by his justice. It is not therefore
any "physical" effective causality on God's part, to which man would
be irresistibly subjected, that brings about man's conversion, but this
other causality, which alone can have an effect on man's freedom without coercing it: the causality of love.

Thus the Son's renunciation, his love to the point of love of his enemies, becomes the path that awakens man's renunciation. Only love
can bring forth love. Loving one's enemy as the will that the other
may be (in the sense of Augustine's definition of love: *volo ut sis*, I
will that thou be) is the only way to break through the dialectic of
enmity and to reopen the sphere of a possible communion—and also
to keep it open if this openness is refused by the other, by the enemy.
It is precisely here that love of one's enemy proves to be fully and
completely natural and human, in accord with human nature, which is

---

[71] This is especially clear in his book *Liber Asceticus* (PG 90:911–57), which represents the
simplest synthesis of his spiritual teaching.

predisposed to community. Yet at the same time this can be put into practice only through constantly transcending one's own tendency to close oneself up. Of course, since this is the eschatological reshaping of human existence, it is only possible in Christ, who is the eschatologically reshaped man. This "form of existence of the Kingdom of God", whose sure criterion is love of one's enemies, is possible only on the basis of Christ, who is himself to a certain extent this form of existence.

> One cannot love the person who is tormenting him, even if he has decided to renounce the things of this world, so long as he has not in truth recognized the Lord's intention. Anyone who, by the grace of the Lord, has been able to recognize it, however, and who is trying to correspond to it can, from his heart, love even the one who hates him and torments him, just as the apostles, in this knowledge, loved.[72]

The unity of men and reconciliation with God and with men are only possible in this love, which eschatologically reshapes all the hidden, secret aspirations of man toward this unity. Love is, on the other hand, the only way in which this unity can be realized in practice without compelling the other. It brings the other to himself and touches him in his freedom, not by any compulsory measures. Love of one's enemy, in which the one who behaves in this way toward his enemy moves, defenseless, toward his heart—so that he does not become involved in the dialectic of enmity but breaks out of its diabolical circle and touches the heart of the other—lays bare the true relationship between them. Anyone who meets his enemy in this way actually sees him, not as an enemy, but—through God's eyes, so to speak—as a man, as a person, and thus makes a space for the enemy to see him himself, no longer as an enemy, but as someone who is standing defenseless and open before him.

With this question of the will, the post-Chalcedonian development of dogma points back more clearly and unambiguously to the heart of the gospel, to the form of existence of the Sermon on the Mount, to poverty, to love of one's enemy, and trust in the heavenly Father who feeds the birds and the fields. "Losing his life so as to find it" (cf. Mt 16:25), all of that has its origin and its prototype here: in the Son's new mode of existence, which makes the mode of his eternal Sonship into

---

[72] Maximus the Confessor, *Liber Asceticus* (PG 90:920A; *Drei geistliche Schriften* [Einsiedeln, 1996], pp. 62–63).

the mode of his existence as a man, in that he lives as the archetype of the Sermon on the Mount.

b. Jesus' True Body

After the resolution of the controversy about the question of whether Jesus, besides his divine will, also had a genuine human will, another christological debate very soon opened up. In 727 Emperor Leo III (d. 741) had the image of Christ on the iron gate of his palace destroyed. The Iconoclastic controversy, which lasted more than a century and led to Nicaea II, the Seventh Ecumenical Council, was beginning.[73] This controversy over icons was not about aesthetic ideas, but about theological, christological concepts. In all the contemporary literature for and against icons, there is no discussion about questions of aesthetics or of the theory of art. The question at the center of interest ran, rather: Can and may Christ be represented in an image? Saint Theodore the Studite (d. 826) emphasized that this was something of essential importance for the Christian faith when he justified the veneration of images on the basis of the faith of the ecumenical councils. Anyone who categorically condemns icons is ultimately also condemning the mystery of the Incarnation.[74] The various attitudes taken toward the veneration of icons are based on various conceptions of the relationship of the person of Christ to his human body. Is it in fact possible to glimpse the Divine Person of the Son of God in the individual traits of the body of Christ?

ENEMIES OF IMAGES

The Iconoclasts advanced a whole variety of arguments against the cult of images. Not all are of equal weight. Thus, for instance, there no doubt were abuses in the cult of images, especially in popular religion. Many miracles were reported in connection with icons, and the genuineness of these was in a good many cases rightly disputed. The questionable practice also developed of choosing an icon as a godparent, and it even supposedly happened that priests mixed powdered

---

[73] See on this C. Schönborn, *God's Human Face: The Christ-Icon* (San Francisco: Ignatius Press, 1994), pp. 135–243; G. Dumeige, *Nizäa II*, GÖK 4 (Mainz, 1985). The documents relating to the Iconoclastic controversy have been collected in H. Hennephof, *Textus byzantinos ad iconomachiam pertinentes* (Leiden, 1969).

[74] Cf. Theodore Studites, *Refutatio et subversio impiorum poematum* 30 (PG 99:472A–473A).

paint from icons into the eucharistic chalice for Communion. The most objectionable side of the veneration of icons was of course, not the ever-present possibility of abuse, but the very fact that images were venerated at all. The outward manifestations of this cult recalled in an alarming way the pagan practice of idol worship. The subtle theological distinction between veneration (προσκύνησις) of the images and worship (λατρεία) of the Lord who was portrayed was often overlooked by laypeople but even by monks. All this strengthened the opponents in their conviction that the veneration of images could not be reconciled with the purity of Christianity.

The *prohibition of images in the Old Testament* was also a powerful weapon for the Iconoclasts: "You shall not make for yourself a graven image, or any likeness of anything that is in heaven above, or that is in the earth beneath, or that is in the water under the earth" (Ex 20:4). Must not the whole debate about images appear as moot sophistry in view of this prohibition? Was it not scandalous that Jews and Muslims should have to remind Christians how serious that prohibition was? Yet however simple the prohibition of images appeared to be, the matter was nevertheless not quite so clear. The enemies of images were not all of the same mind in their interpretation of the prohibition of images. In art from the Iconoclastic period, the representation of animals was obviously tolerated alongside ornamentation. The Iconoclasts' art was differentiated from the artistic understanding of the supporters of images especially in that any veneration of images was rejected and the image was assigned a secular and decorative purpose. Yet even there, there was at least one exception. The emperors seem never to have considered disallowing the traditional veneration of the image of the emperor along with the religious veneration of images. An appeal to the biblical prohibition of images is thus obviously insufficient for understanding the theological basis of the Iconoclastic Controversy—otherwise, that prohibition would have to have been more strictly applied, with no exceptions.

The veneration of images was considered to be the *worship of dead, inanimate matter* and set in opposition to the true cult of worship "in spirit and in truth". This propensity to despise matter is one of the clearest characteristics of Iconoclasm. While other arguments changed a great deal in the course of the 120 years of the Iconoclastic controversy, this one persisted unchanged. The Iconoclastic synod of 754, for instance, says:

Let him be anathema who attempts with material colors to capture upon
inanimate and dumb icons the appearance of the saints—for such images
bring no advantage; fashioning them is a meaningless idea and an invention of the devil—instead of reproducing within themselves the virtues
of the saints, which have been handed down from them in writing, as if
in living icons, and thus being motivated to a zeal like theirs.[75]

The sharpest argument, and the one with the greatest consequences,
was directed solely against the image of Christ. In the "questions" he
presented to the Council of 754, Emperor Constantine V (d. 775)
brought a new argument into play: the veneration of images is not
merely idolatry, it is a christological heresy; even worse, it is the sum
and the summit of all christological errors. There is much to suggest
that it was Emperor Constantine himself who turned the debate about
holy images into a christological issue. He wanted to give the opposition to images a solid dogmatic foundation. Nothing could so dis-
credit the cult of images as proof that it was in contradiction to the great
christological councils. What could weigh more heavily in Byzantium
than the accusation that the supporters of images were Nestorians and
Monophysites?

The imperial theologian Nicephoros (d. 828/829) starts from the
Creed of Chalcedon and professes: "Our Lord Jesus Christ is one person (πρόσωπον) *out of* two natures, the immaterial and the material,
through the unmixed union."[76] Only that little "out of" would have
disturbed a strict Chalcedonian, who would rather have said "in two
natures". The emphasis is somewhat more problematic when Constantine says, "After this union (the resulting) reality is indivisible."[77] That
too is still the language of Chalcedon, yet Constantine is putting so
much emphasis on "indivisible" that the distinguishability of the two
natures is hardly seen any more. As for Monophysitism, for Constantine the result of the Incarnation is also an indivisible reality that has
arisen from the two natures, in which, however, for practical purposes
divinity and humanity can no longer be distinguished.

For Emperor Constantine, only the image that is essentially the same
as its original is considered a true image. He defines this yet more precisely: "If an image does not reproduce the features of the figure, how

[75] Mansi 13:345CD.
[76] Nicephoros, *Antirrhetici adversus Constantinum Copronymum* 1 (PG 100:232A).
[77] Ibid. (PG 100:248D).

the face of its model is, then that cannot possibly be an icon."[78] The icon must therefore reproduce the facial features of the person portrayed. Yet in order truly to satisfy the claim to be an icon, a true image, it has to reproduce this πρόσωπον, this "personal face", exactly *as it is*. If we draw on Constantine's definition of an image, then it follows that only something identical in all respects with the original, or, as Constantine says, "in which the whole (of the original) is preserved",[79] is an icon.

From these data Constantine now draws the following conclusion: If Christ's πρόσωπον or hypostasis cannot be separated from the two natures, and if one of the two natures, the divine, cannot be portrayed in painting, since it is uncircumscribable, then it is impossible to paint or to describe the πρόσωπον of Christ. When it is said here that the divine nature is "uncircumscribable", Constantine means by that that it is not ascertainable, it is incomprehensible, but also, in a literal sense, that it cannot be outlined by writing or drawing.

Constantine's reasoning has grim consequences for a judgment about the veneration of images. Since the one πρόσωπον of Christ cannot be separated from his two natures, the defenders of icons cannot take refuge behind the argument that they only represent Christ's human nature. For the icon always shows a "personal face". Christ's personal face, however, is of such a kind that no one can depict it, since it consists of two natures, one of which is "uncircumscribable". The supporters of images, therefore, have to choose between two heresies. If they want to hold fast to the unity of Christ, then they are also describing the eternal Word. If they want to avoid this consequence and continue to hold that Christ's divinity is uncircumscribable, then they have to say that Christ's humanity has its own personal face. The first variant implies Monophysitism; the second, Nestorianism.

The fundamental error in this line of argument lies in the false conception of the πρόσωπον of Christ. Constantine was indeed right to say that every icon represents the πρόσωπον of the one whose image it is. Yet it is a fallacy to maintain that painting an icon of Christ also "circumscribes" his "uncircumscribable" divine nature. The face of Jesus is the face of the incarnate person of the eternal Word. This human face does not 'circumscribe' the divine nature—not even the

---

[78] Ibid. (PG 100:293A).
[79] Ibid. (PG 100:228D).

human nature—but the πρόσωπον, the person of the Word. We see on the icon neither a divine nor a human nature, but the face of the divine-human person of Jesus.

The most important theologian among the early defenders of icons is without doubt John Damascene (d. 749). He was the first to present a real synthesis of the theology of icons. In reply to the accusation of the opponents of icons that the veneration of images involved too great an attachment to what was earthly, visible, and material, John emphasized, on the basis of Christology, the positive role of matter.

> In ancient times, God, who has no body and no shape, was not portrayed in images at all. Now, however, since God has become visible in the flesh and went about with men, I can portray the image of what is visible about God. I do not worship matter, but I worship the Creator of matter, who himself became matter for my sake and took it upon himself to live in matter, who by means of matter brought about my redemption.[80]

Matter was sanctified in Christ: first the body of Christ, which became holy, filled with grace, "like God", through being united with the Logos; and then, beyond that, matter in the broader sense. Here John touched a nerve for that anti-icon movement for which the materiality of the icons is a degradation of the divine archetype. Matter is not the outermost and lowermost limit of the distance from God, as in Neoplatonism, not what is most distant from spirit and, therefore, most unholy. Rather, the whole economy of salvation is always mediated through what is material. The holy image is filled with grace—indeed, in a certain sense, it is just as much a vehicle of spirit as was the one it portrays. John is more interested in the grace conveyed by the icon than with any pictorial similitude. This tendency is also seen in the way he compares icons and relics. Both have in common that they are filled with grace and with divine energy. Here, too, what is characteristic of icons, the relationship of resemblance, takes a back seat, and the icon appears above all as a shrine mediating grace.

In 787, after sixty years of persecution, the cult of images was reinstated by the council convened at Nicaea. The Council of Nicaea did not concern itself with the christological arguments of the Iconoclastic

---

[80] John Damascene, *Contra imaginum calumniatores oratio* 1, 16 (PTS 17:89).

council of 757, but confined itself to declaring the legitimacy of images
(DH 600–603; 605–609).

Veneration of images cannot be idolatry subject to the Old Testament prohibition if it is carried out in conformity to its meaning. Then
in fact it guides the hearts of those who are praying before the icon to
the living worship of him whom the icon represents. "Anyone who
venerates the icon venerates in it the person portrayed."[81] This statement sounds obvious. Yet however simple it seems, within it lies the
key to unlock the complicated christological dialectic of the Iconoclasts. In any case, it needed the great theological works of someone
like Theodore the Studite to use this key to open also the door to a
complete theology of icons.

Saint Theodore, abbot of the great Studion monastery in Constantinople, based his whole theology of images upon the paradox of
the Incarnation. "The invisible became visible."[82] The eternal Word
of the Father appeared visibly to our mortal eyes. We have therefore
seen the person of the Son of God—or, to express it theologically, the
hypostasis of the Logos. Theodore the Studite based his entire theology
of icons in this perspective. "The icon of someone represents, not his
nature, but his person",[83] he remarks. The icon is always the portrait
of a person. The icon captures only what is visible about a person: that
is, what is peculiar to him, what distinguishes him as this man from
any others. But what if this person is divine, the eternal Son of God?
Even the Iconoclasts say that each icon represents a person. Yet since
Christ is a Divine Person, we cannot portray him. If we do so, then we
are supposedly introducing into Christ a second, purely human person
who can be portrayed. To this ingenious argument Theodore replies
by briefly recalling the Church's teaching about the "complex person",
which was developed following the Fifth Ecumenical Council (553).

> If we were to assert that the flesh assumed by the Word possessed its own
> hypostasis, then the argument (of the Iconoclasts) would be valid. But we
> follow the faith of the Church and profess that the person of the eternal
> Word became the person that has two natures in common and that it has
> accorded to the (concrete) human nature, with all its characteristics that
> differentiate it from other people, an independent existence within itself.

---

[81] Mansi 13:378D–380A.
[82] Theodore Studites, *Antirrhetici adversus Iconomachos* 1 (PG 99:332A).
[83] Ibid., 3 (PG 99:405A).

That is why we are justified in saying that one and the same person of the eternal Word, "uncircumscribable" in its divine nature, is "circumscribable" in our human nature. The human nature of Christ does not exist outside of the person of the Logos, in a self-determined person existing for itself, but it receives its existence in the person of the Logos (for there is no nature that does not have its concrete existence in a hypostasis) and becomes individually visible and circumscribable in the person of the Logos.[84]

The person of the eternal Word, by taking flesh, becomes himself the vehicle and the source of a human existence in its unmistakable individuality. In other words, in those very features that distinguish Jesus as this particular individual, his Divine Person becomes visible. It is the paradox of the Incarnation that the Divine Person of the eternal Word has become "circumscribable" in the individual, personal facial features of Jesus.

Emperor Constantine was therefore right to say that the icon of Christ would "circumscribe" the eternal Word of God. But he was wrong when he then rejected the icon, since by becoming flesh, the Word "circumscribed" himself, limited, and "condensed" himself (in an expression the Church Fathers like to use)—so much so, that he was able to express himself and communicate himself within a human individuality and that, beyond that, this individual human existence became his own existence. That is the scandal of belief in the Incarnation of God. This belief says that the Divine Person of the eternal Son became visible in the individuality of Jesus of Nazareth. Thanks to his sound doctrine of the "complex person" of Christ, Theodore of Studion was able to expose with the utmost clarity the starting point for the Iconoclast theory: an inadequate, even erroneous, understanding of the person.[85]

What part does the icon play in contemplative life? Are not even the best images, after all, just images that are not in any way commensurate with the original? Are they not merely the shadows of a higher, true reality? Does not our carnal gaze at the image have a merely pedagogical significance, leading us, so far as possible, to spiritual contemplation? Theodore of Studion is decidedly opposed to such views. The icon

---

[84] Ibid., 1 (PG 99:400CD).

[85] That is also shown in the correspondence with John the Grammarian, the leading light of the second wave of Iconoclasm and of the council of 815: cf. Theodore Studites, *Letter* 2, 168 (PG 99:1532BC) = *Letter* 492 (ed. G. Fatouros, 2:726).

does have for him a function that is doubtless "anagogical". And yet the spiritual contemplation to which it leads has no other object than the icon itself, the incarnate Word. With this, Theodore is clearly distancing himself from the Platonic conception of the image. And this is the decisive point in the entire controversy with the Iconoclasts.

> If someone should say, "Since I should adore (Christ) spiritually, it is superfluous to adore him in his icon," then he should know that he is thereby renouncing the spiritual adoration of Christ. For unless with his mind he sees Christ, in human form, sitting at the right hand of the Father, then he is not adoring him at all. On the contrary: he is denying that the Word became flesh. His icon, on the other hand, is the most reliable witness that the eternal Word became identical to man.[86]

It is not enough to stop at the images. The images of themselves point beyond themselves. And yet the perspective within which the image of Christ is seen is profoundly different from that of Platonism. The visible image does not point to a purely spiritual reality but to the Risen One in his glorified body, the Lord exalted "at the right hand of the Father". The icon is, therefore, not imperfect because it belongs to the visible and material reality, since Christ himself belongs to it, even in his glorified body. It is imperfect because it is indeed only an image of Christ. Yet we feel impelled to be able to say, like the apostles, "We have seen the Lord" (Jn 20:25). We want to see him, no longer only in his picture, but himself, *in persona*. It is a matter neither of remaining attached to the icon nor of striving for a completely imageless and purely spiritual contemplation. The veneration of icons is at the same time visible and spiritual; the mystery of Christ is worshiped spiritually in his visible representation. Not until the world to come will we see Christ himself. The Incarnation of God demonstrates that the final aim of Christian contemplation cannot be a purely spiritual view. "If this were sufficient in itself, then the eternal Word would have needed to come to us only in a purely spiritual manner."[87] Yet Christ appeared "in the flesh" (cf. 1 Tim 3:16). His Incarnation is not merely a stage that will one day be outdated. Christian contemplation can therefore not bypass the way that God himself took in order to come to us.

> The painted image is for us a holy light, a healing memorial, since it shows us Christ at his birth, his baptism, working miracles, on the Cross, in

---

[86] Theodore Studites, *Letter* 2, 65 (PG 99:1288CD) = *Letter* 409 (ed. G. Fatouros, 2:569).
[87] Theodore Studites, *Antirrhetici adversus Iconomachos* 1 (PG 99:336D).

214 God Sent His Son

the tomb, rising and ascending to heaven. In all this we are not being deceived, as if none of that had happened. For what we see comes to the aid of spiritual contemplation, so that through both of these our faith in the mystery of salvation is strengthened.[88]

c. Jesus' Heart

The contemplation of the human heart of Jesus forms the crowning point after the struggles that took place during the early christological councils about the humanity of Jesus. Without a deepening of the mystery of his human heart, the contemplation of the aspects of Jesus' humanity would be incomplete.[89] The Second Vatican Council, which professes the humanity of Jesus with great emphasis, summarizes in one great arc, in *Gaudium et Spes*, which presents Christ as the true and perfect man, the stages of the Church's growing recognition of the true humanity of Jesus. Starting from the Second Council of Constantinople, with which it declares that in Christ "human nature as He assumed it was not annulled", it declares its belief in the human body, the human consciousness, and the human will of Christ. It is, however, Christ's human heart that stands as the crowning conclusion of this Council's declaration of faith. "He worked with human hands, He thought with a human mind, acted by human choice, and loved with a human heart" (*Gaudium et Spes*, no. 22).

In biblical language, the heart is the seat of the inner life, of thoughts, acts of will, and feelings. We have already spoken of Jesus' human consciousness and human will. Yet the fact that Jesus has a human heart also means that he feels as a man: "He enjoyed our 'passions'."[90] Scripture substantiates this truth in many moving instances. It tells us, for instance, about Jesus' meeting with the widow from Nain, who was taking her only son to bury him. Jesus was deeply moved with compassion and spoke to her the gentle human words of consolation, "Do not weep" (Lk 7:13). Mary's sorrow at the death of her brother Lazarus, again, had such a profound effect on him that he wept with

---

[88] Theodore Studites, *Refutatio carminum Sergii* (PG 99:456BC).

[89] Cf. M.-L. Ciappi, ed., *Le Coeur de Jésus, coeur du monde* (Paris, 1982); I. de la Potterie, *Il mistero del cuore trafitto: Fondamenti biblici della spiritualità del cuore di Gèsu* (Bologna, 1988); E. Glotin, *Le Coeur de Jésus: Approches anciennes et nouvelles* (Namur, 1997); B. Peyrous, ed., *Le Coeur du Christ pour un monde nouveau: Actes du congrès de Paray-le-Monial 13–15 octobre 1995* (Paris, 1998).

[90] Justin Martyr, *Apologia minor* 13 (PTS 38:157).

her (Jn 11:33–35). In the night before his agonizing death, from fear, he sweated blood that dripped down onto the ground (Lk 22:44).

It is already clear from the Old Testament that God feels things like men and with men. He is angry with the people who worship the golden calf (Ex 32:10); he is jealous and demands that his chosen people worship him alone (Josh 24:19–20); in his mercy, he has pity on the poor man and hears him when he cries out to him (Ex 22:27). "For the Fathers, who were brought up with the moral ideal of the Stoa, the ideal of the wise man's impassivity, where insight and will govern and master the irrational emotions, this was one of the places where it proved most difficult to achieve a synthesis of Greek inheritance and biblical faith."[91] The stumbling block of a God who suffers becomes more extreme with the Incarnation of Christ. A few Docetic heretics tried, very early on, to explain away Jesus' suffering as being merely apparent; yet the witness that Christ gives concerning his Father was thereby robbed of its core. So Irenaeus of Lyons decidedly contradicted such ideas: "If Christ had not himself suffered but had flown away from Jesus [during the suffering], how could he then have exhorted his disciples to take up the cross and follow him?"[92]

Jesus' life, however, unveils for us the heart of God's feelings: God suffers because he loves. All his feelings, whether compassion, anger, indignation, or jealousy, must always be read against the background of his personal love for us. In the humility of Bethlehem, in the unselfishness of his public ministry, in the shame of Calvary, in his death on the Cross, Jesus opens up to us his loving human heart. It is thus right that the heart of Jesus is "seen as the chief sign and symbol of that . . . love with which the divine Redeemer unceasingly loves His eternal Father and all mankind".[93] The adoration of Jesus' wounded heart, however, should not only allow us to know his love, but should also move us to a loving response. If, along with Paul, we contemplate in faith the revealed mystery and recognize that Christ "loved *me* and gave himself for *me*" (Gal 2:20), then our own heart returns this love. That is why Paul also says, "The love of Christ urges us on" (2 Cor 5:14). Saint Bonaventure expresses this truth in a unique way: "Could

---

[91] J. Ratzinger, "The Mystery of Easter: Substance and Foundation of Devotion to the Sacred Heart", in *Behold the Pierced One*, trans. Graham Harrison (San Francisco: Ignatius Press, 1986), pp. 47–69, here, p. 57.

[92] Irenaeus of Lyons, *Adversus Haereses* 3, 18, 5 (FChr 8/3:226–29).

[93] Pius XII, *Haurietis aquas* (DH 3924).

your love have been better shown than by allowing not only your body, but even your heart, to be pierced by the lance? . . . Could anyone not wish to love this Heart that was wounded for us? How could anyone not love in return someone who looks after us with such pure love?"[94]

In modern times the veneration of the heart of Jesus became especially widespread in the Latin Church particularly after the visions of Saint Margaret Mary Alacoque (d. 1690) had been recognized. As we have seen, the contemplation of the heart of Jesus was not in any case something new, but was a new deepening of a mystery that has always been the subject of contemplation. The Church Fathers, starting from John 7:37–39 and John 19:34, had already contemplated the mystery of the open heart of Jesus.[95] The pierced heart, from which flowed blood and water, they interpreted ontologically as the spring of life, as the origin of the sacraments and the Church. Of great influence in the patristic contemplation of the heart of Jesus were, for example, Augustine's typological explanations of the wounds in the heart of Jesus.

> That blood was poured out for the forgiveness of sins; that water mixes into the saving cup, it offers us both a bath and a drink. It was a model for this when Noah was ordered to make a door in the side of the ark where those animals not destined to perish might enter in, by which, the Church was prefigured. That was why the first woman was formed out of the side of the sleeping man and was called life and mother of the living. This pointed toward a great good, before the great evil of sin. Here, the second Adam fell asleep, with bowed head, upon the Cross so that a spouse might be formed for him from what flowed from the side of the one who slept.[96]

With Margaret Mary Alacoque, alongside the sacramental and ecclesial dimension in the veneration of the heart of Jesus, the idea of expiation for the indifference and ingratitude of men with regard to the zealous love of Christ, which had consumed him to the point of exhaustion, also begins to play an important role. It was always clear, from the Church's side, however, that veneration of the heart of Jesus applied to the incarnate Logos.[97] It is, especially, his human love that is

---

[94] Bonaventure, *Vitis mystica sive Tractatus de passione Domini* 3:5–6 (Opera omnia 8:164).

[95] See H. Rahner, *Symbole der Kirche* (Salzburg, 1964), pp. 177–235.

[96] Augustine, *Tractatus in Ioannis Evangelium* 120:2 (CChr.SL 36:661).

[97] Cf. L. Lies, *Gottes Herz für die Menschen: Elemente der Herz-Jesu-Frömmigkeit morgen* (Innsbruck, 1996), pp. 19–25.

being contemplated in the symbol of the heart. The heart of Jesus can then truly become the object of veneration and adoration that are due to God alone. Because it is part of the sacred humanity, it is, through the hypostatic union, always connected with the Logos. That is why we can say of the heart of Jesus what John Damascene worked out concerning the body: The heart of Jesus is certainly worthy of adoration, not of itself, but because it is inseparably united to the person of the Logos.[98]

The veneration of the heart of Jesus is thus a further example of the sacramental logic of divine revelation. God always gives himself in a concrete sign, in an image. The whole of creation is an image of God; he speaks in it. The image that definitively reveals God is Christ. In all the mysteries of revelation, however, there subsists "an indissoluble unity between the reality and its meaning".[99] Anyone who believes he can grasp the meaning without the image also loses the former. In the veneration of the human heart of Jesus, it is above all—because of the natural symbolic power of the heart—the love of God, which became human in Christ, that is being venerated.

3. On the Theology of the Life of Jesus: The Mysteries of Jesus

Hans Urs von Balthasar formulated the axiom, important for the nature and method of theology, "that theology is the doctrine of the divine meaning of the revelation of the historical events of revelation themselves—nothing above them, nothing behind them, nothing that one could take away and retain as a suprahistorical substance—and that therefore, the more the historical discloses itself in a theological sense, the more does theology develop."[100] This principle, which marks the importance, even for academic Christology, of contemplating the life of Jesus in faith, was and still is all too often overlooked by scholastic theology. The latter concentrates on illuminating the significance of his

---

[98] Cf. John Damascene, *Expositio fidei* 76:4, 3 (PTS 12:174); see also Thomas Aquinas, STh III, q. 25 a. 2 (DThA 26:189–93).

[99] John Paul II, *Fides et ratio*, no. 13.

[100] H. U. von Balthasar, *Razing the Bastions: On the Church in This Age*, trans. Brian McNeil, C.R.V. (San Francisco: Ignatius Press, 1993), p. 30.

birth, of the Incarnation of the Son of God, in its ontological respect
and that of his death in its soteriological respect. The thirty-three years
lying between the birth and the events of the Triduum seem at most
to be of significance for Christ's moral message, but not for dogmatic
reflection in relation to his person.

In resurrecting Jesus after his shameful death on the Cross, the Father
delivers his judgment on Christ's mission and work: "You are my son,
today I have begotten you" (Ps 2:7; cf. Acts 13:33). The Resurrection
is the irrevocable affirmation of and corroboration for the course of
Jesus' life on earth. Hence, Jesus' entire life as a man and his preaching are given an extraordinary significance. From it, too, springs the
Gospels' undeniable intention to give a historically accurate account
and their interest in a visualization that recalled what was characteristic
of Jesus, even if certain elements of his life, such as his lowliness and
his role as Messiah, were felt to stand in contradiction to each other. It
is these very things that are given their full and definitive meaning on
the basis of Easter. The question of what the life of Jesus was actually
like is of central importance, inasmuch as the period of the life of Jesus,
this brief span of time in the history of mankind and of Israel, represents the eschatological revelation of God and his definitive salvation.
But then the period of Jesus' lifetime, each event of his life and each
thing he said have a force that makes them distinctive. In the light of
the Resurrection the individual traits of the earthly Jesus acquire their
full christological implications, and do so precisely as historical events.
For on the basis of Easter, these occurrences, *facta et dicta*, acquire an
eschatological, eternal significance. If the Risen One is he who lived
on earth, then nothing about the earthly One is trivial. If God has,
through the Resurrection, revealed Christ to be his eschatological revelation, then we must refer to the life of Jesus, in order to read there the
individual words and features of that revelation. In the reading, getting
to know, and following the concrete figure of Jesus, it is a matter not
only of a theological task or of material for spiritual contemplation, but
of the decisive question, vital for our salvation, of whether we accept
God's revelation of himself and his saving acts, or whether we fail to
do so.[101]

---

[101] Cf. E. Schillebeeckx, *Christus: Sakrament der Gottesbegegnung*, 3rd ed. (Mainz, 1968), pp. 23–26.

a. History of the Contemplation of
the Mysteries of the Life of Jesus

The good news does not consist of "eloquent wisdom", but of Christ's life and work, of "the cross of Christ" (1 Cor 1:17). Reference to the mysteries of Christ has always been fundamental for the proclamation and worship of the Church. In the primitive Church, for instance, the faith was communicated to newly converted people, before they were received into the Church through the sacrament of baptism, with the help of the Creed, the second article of which lists the most important mysteries of Christ's life. It was in contemplating these that orthodox faith always found its fundamental support in the struggle against the various outbreaks of heretical teachings. Each heresy, just as each deepening of the awareness of faith, was connected with the neglect—or, alternatively, the deepening—of one or more of the mysteries of the life of our Lord Jesus Christ. The history of the contemplation of these mysteries is thus also of importance for the history of the Church's awareness of herself.[102]

The first heresies, such as the dualistic doctrine of the Gnostics, which were intended to keep Christianity pure and free from any stain of what is earthly, on account of a Greek preference for what was "purely spiritual", were vanquished by the early witnesses to the faith by the simple contemplation of Jesus' life. Prime examples of this are Ignatius of Antioch (d. ca. 117) and Irenaeus of Lyons. Ignatius was the first of the Church Fathers to speak of the mysteries of the life of Jesus when he produced evidence of Jesus' humanity, which the Gnostics had denied, with the "three celebrated mysteries" that took place in the stillness of God" the virginity of Mary, her childbearing, and the death of the Lord.[103] Irenaeus was especially concerned with the integrity of man's salvation, with the *salus carnis*. To that end he, too,

---

[102] On the history of the theological contemplation of the mysteries of Christ, see A. Grillmeier, "Geschichtlicher Überblick über die Mysterien Jesu im allgemeinen", in *Mysterium Salutis* 3/2:3–22; L. Scheffczyk, "Die Bedeutung der Mysterien des Lebens Jesu für Glauben und Leben des Christen", in *Die Mysterien des Lebens Jesu und die christliche Existenz*, ed. Scheffczyk, pp. 17–34 (Aschaffenburg, 1984); for the medieval period, see H.J. Sieben and W. Loeser, "Mystères de la vie du Christ", in *Dictionnaire de Spiritualité ascétique et mystique* (1980), 10:1874–86; M. Bordoni, *Gèsu di Nazaret: Signore e Cristo*, vol. 3 (Rome, 1986), pp. 361–64, 880–81; for Thomas Aquinas, cf. J.-P. Torrell, *Le Christ en ses mystères: La Vie et l'oeuvre de Jésus selon saint Thomas d'Aquin*, 2 vols., Jésus et Jésus-Christ 78–79 (Paris, 1999).

[103] Ignatius of Antioch, *Letter to the Ephesians* 19:1, ed. Loeb, trans. Kirsopp Lake (Cambridge, Mass. and London, 1977), pp. 192–93.

had to defend the true humanity of Jesus. In doing so, he emphasized the unity of the God-man Jesus Christ, referring to various mysteries: "For just as he was man in order to be tempted, so also he was Word (Logos) in order to be glorified. And in fact the Word (the Logos) was at rest during the temptation, the crucifixion, and the death. The man, however, was wholly taken up in it to conquer, to endure, to show his goodness, to rise again, and to be taken up (into heaven)."[104]

For Origen (d. ca. 253) and the Alexandrian school, the mysteries of the life of Jesus were significant above all as pedagogical revelation. The self-renunciation of the Logos in the Incarnation allows the lesser conceptual powers of man to come to some knowledge of God.[105] Origen was also the first, long before Franciscan-inspired piety, to develop his own devotion to the Child Jesus. Thus, in one of his sermons, he encourages the faithful to imitate the old man Simeon and to pray to the Child Jesus himself, since we long to talk with him and to hold him in our arms.[106]

With Saint Augustine, patristic contemplation of the life of Jesus attained a high point; he grasped the theological significance of the mysteries of Christ clearly and completely in their threefold dimension as revelation of God, redemption, and recapitulation.[107] The life of Christ proved for him the best argument against the Manichaean sect of his time, which made a radical division between spirit and matter as the principles of good and evil. By submitting to insults and ignominy, suffering injustice, being scourged and tortured, and suffering the shameful death on the Cross, Jesus showed "how easily the body submits to the soul if the latter subjects itself to God".[108]

In the fourth century, Christmas began to be celebrated in Rome. The most significant sermons on this mystery from the patristic era are by Leo the Great (d. 461), in which he proclaims the *marvelous exchange:* "He became the Son of Man, so that we might become children of God."[109] Yet Leo sees the mystery of Christmas as entirely directed toward the mystery of Easter. For Christ was born of the Virgin as true

---

[104] Irenaeus of Lyons, *Adversus Haereses* 3, 19, 3 (FChr 8/3:240–43).
[105] B. Studer, *Soteriologie: In der Schrift und Patristik*, HDG 3, 2a (Freiburg im Breisgau, 1978), pp. 91–95.
[106] Origen, *Homilien zum Lukasevangelium* 15, 5 (FChr 4/1:182).
[107] Cf. Augustine, *De vera religione* 16:30 and 16:32 (CChr.SL 32:205–206, 207).
[108] Ibid., 16:32 (CChr.SL 32:207).
[109] Leo the Great, *Sermo* 26, 2 (CChr.SL 138:126).

man and true God only in order that we might be able to die with him
to our sins in baptism and to be justified through his Resurrection.[110]

As the fine arts demonstrate, the contemplation of the mysteries of
Christ reached a climax in the Middle Ages. All the great charisms
make their specific contribution in deepening the Church's awareness.
First of all, it was particularly in the monasteries that the life of Jesus
was the subject of meditation. The Benedictines encouraged the contemplation of the mysteries, among other ways, with the widely read
Elucidarium of Honorius of Autun (d. ca. 1156), in which he passed
on the ideas of his teacher, Anselm of Canterbury (d. 1109). Thanks
to his profound meditations on the mystery of the Transfiguration,
Peter the Venerable (d. 1156), from Cluny, is seen as the spiritual father of this feast, which was late in being officially introduced in the
West and which he interpreted as an anticipation of the Resurrection
and the Ascension. The Cistercian Bernard of Clairvaux's (d. 1153)
new view of the humanity of Christ influenced subsequent medieval
contemplation of the mysteries. "Note, also, that the love of the heart
is, in a certain sense, carnal, because it stirs the heart of man for the
bodily Christ and for what Christ did and commanded in the flesh."[111]
Bernard particularly liked to meditate on the mystery of the Ascension,
on which our hope is based that "there is a dwelling prepared for us
in the Father's house" (cf. Jn 14:2).

The mendicant orders greatly influenced popular piety. Francis of
Assisi (d. 1226) deeply impressed people, both by the Christmas celebration he founded in the forest of Greccio (1223) and by his stigmata (1224). By way of Saint Bonaventure, who inspired an "affective"
piety, Francis' activity also found its way subsequently into theology.
The Dominicans, for their part, gained a great deal of influence on
medieval piety through the veneration of the Cross by Saint Catherine
of Siena (d. 1380).

In Scholastic theology, the transition from the sapiential method of
the patristic era to the analytic and synthetic methods of Scholasticism
did not at first produce any break in the contemplation of the mysteries
of the life of Christ, although the speculative problems of the hypostatic
union were less to the fore here than affective comprehension of God's

---

[110] Cf. B. Studer, *Soteriologie: In der Schrift und Patristik*, pp. 208–9.

[111] Bernard of Clairvaux, *Sermones super Cantica Canticorum* 20, 6, in *Sämtliche Werke*, vol. 5
(Innsbruck, 1994), pp. 284–85.

infinite condescension to us men. Peter Lombard (d. 1160) examines the mysteries in the third book of his *Sentences*, which were to form the basis for theological education in the Middle Ages. In doing so, he refers to Jesus' prayer, his suffering, sadness, and death particularly as evidence for his true humanity.[112] Thomas Aquinas adopted the division into speculative and concrete Christology. With (not coincidentally) 33 *quaestiones* (III, qq. 27–59), he devotes even more space in his *Summa* to the treatise on the life of Christ than he does to questions of systematic Christology. When, in the period after Thomas, speculations about the Incarnation and the hypostatic union became ever more subtle, however, his treatise on the life and suffering of Jesus was largely ignored.[113] One late exception is the presentation of the mysteries of the life of Jesus by the Jesuit theologian Francisco de Suarez (d. 1617) in his *De incarnatione*, which is probably the most extensive.[114] With its discussion of every detail, however, this work aims less at imitating them than at an almost rationalistic penetration of the events.

The *Exercises* of Ignatius Loyola (d. 1556) are based on the *Life of Jesus Christ* by the Carthusian Ludolf of Saxony (d. 1378). While Ludolf's poetic meditations are "intended to lead" people "to the mountain of heavenly glory",[115] the Ignatian meditations concentrate above all on the following of Christ as present in his Church. *The Spiritual Exercises* of Ignatius plan for the mysteries of the life of Jesus to be contemplated in the second, third, and fourth weeks. They are concerned with a theology of Christ's Kingdom as a struggle with Satan that is based on the contemplation of Jesus' earthly life and finds their all-decisive cornerstone in the Presentation in the Temple and the separation at Nazareth.[116] The importance of the Ignatian *Exercises* for the contemplation of the mysteries in the whole of the modern era can hardly be exaggerated.[117] They first of all fell on fertile soil especially in France. There, Pierre de Bérulle (d. 1629), for instance,

---

[112] Peter Lombard, *Sententiae* III, dist. 17–22 (SpicBon 5:105–40).

[113] Cf. I. Biffi, *I misteri di Cristo in Tommaso d'Aquino*, vol. 1 (Milan, 1994), pp. 61–253 and 371ff.; J.-P. Torrell, *Christ en ses mystères*.

[114] Francisco Suarez, *Opera omnia*, vol. 19 (Paris, 1877).

[115] Cf. Ludolf of Saxony, *The Life of Jesus Christ* 3, 5 (German text: S. Greiner [Einsiedeln, 1994], p. 116).

[116] Ignatius Loyola, *Exercises*, no. 135; cf. H. Rahner, *Ignatius von Loyola und das geschichtliche Werden seiner Frömmigkeit* (Graz, 1947), p. 93.

[117] This is equally true for the development of Christian art; see, for example, A. Besançon, *L'Image interdite: Une Histoire intellectuelle de l'iconoclasme* (Paris, 1994), pp. 246–47.

greatly influenced the following generation with his *Discours de l'état et des grandeurs de Jésus.* His teaching drew the spiritual consequences from contemplation of the life of Jesus: just as Christ in his humanity gave himself up wholly to his divine mission, so Christians must always remain open to the mysteries and the attitudes of Jesus, which are ever effective and ever present. "Bérullianism" lived on with Jean-Jacques Olier (d. 1657), who particularly emphasized the priesthood and the sacrifice of Christ, and John Eudes (d. 1680), who urged, by virtue of baptism, the imitation of the thoughts, feelings, and aims of Jesus.

At the beginning of the twentieth century, Abbot Columba Marmion (d. 1923) addressed some profound meditations to his monks, centered on the person of Jesus Christ, alive in us through baptism and through the grace of our adoption as sons. As a forerunner of the Liturgical Movement, he illuminates the mysteries of Christ through (among other things) our encounter with him in the liturgy.[118] Hugo Rahner (d. 1968) formulated a theology of the life of Jesus. He reads each detail and this life as a whole as revelation, as a saving event, and as the enduring archetype of our Christian life. He also points out that the whole of Christian life is founded in a sacramental isomorphism with the earthly life of Jesus.[119]

In academic theology at this period, however, the divide between speculative Christology and the contemplation of the life of Jesus was reinforced by the division of theology into exegesis and systematic theology. Dogmatics was concerned only with the speculative question of the Incarnation; exegesis, with the "historical Jesus". Dogmatics did not dare approach this area, as it was too heavily loaded with questions from the exegetical criticism of the Gospels. Various movements within the Church, however, were working to overcome historicism and individualism and were seeking a new basis for the encounter with Christ. We should mention especially the Liturgical Movement, the renewal of theology through the spirit of patristics, and a newly awakening awareness of the ecclesial life of the Christian.[120] All these movements entered into Vatican II. In the twenty-second chapter of the pastoral constitution *Gaudium et Spes,* the Council offers a

[118] Cf. C. Marmion, *Christ in His Mysteries: Spiritual and Liturgical Conferences* (London: Sands & Co.; St. Louis, Mo.: Herder, 1931).
[119] Cf. H. Rahner, *Eine Theologie der Verkündigung,* 2nd ed. (Freiburg im Breisgau, 1939); first published in *Theologie der Zeit* 3 (Vienna, 1938).
[120] See Grillmeier, *Geschichtlicher Überblick über die Mysterien Jesu im Allgemeinen,* pp. 21–22.

programmatic example for a mystery-oriented Christology. The *Catechism of the Catholic Church* also takes up this perspective and deals with the christological articles of faith in terms of the mysteries of Christ.

As yet, as Leo Scheffczyk (d. 2005), for example, remarks, theology has responded to these initiatives only in very limited ways: "In evaluating this 'anthropocentric' (in the legitimate sense) view of the Redeemer and of the redemption, recent theology rediscovered the old topos of the 'mysteries of the life of Jesus', after a long period of their neglect by strictly systematic theology . . . , but then, apparently, only momentarily."[121] After a brief appearance in the collaborative dogmatic work *Mysterium Salutis*, the theological contemplation of the life of Jesus almost completely disappeared once more from systematic textbooks.

b. The Theological Significance of the Mysteries of the Life of Jesus

From the foregoing remarks, it is already clear that talking about the "mysteries of Jesus" corresponds to a certain view of Jesus' life. It is a matter of approaching this life in the belief that Jesus is true God and true man. Only in such a contemplation, in awe and reverence, can the traces of his mysteries be found everywhere in Jesus' life. "From the swaddling clothes of his birth to the vinegar of his Passion and the shroud of his Resurrection, everything in Jesus' life was a sign of his mystery. . . . His humanity appeared as 'sacrament,' that is, the sign and instrument, of his divinity and of the salvation he brings: what was visible in his earthly life leads to the invisible mystery of his divine sonship and redemptive mission" (CCC 515).

The nature of Jesus' life as mystery clearly emerges, for instance, in the second Gospel. Mark introduces it with the central declaration that Jesus, a man who could be encountered on the roads of Palestine for thirty-three years, is the Christ, the Son of God (Mk 1:1). The subsequent accounts of individual episodes from the life of Jesus confirm this declaration through the concrete testimony of experiences, so that at the end the reader himself can say with the centurion, "Truly, this man was the Son of God" (Mk 15:39). This is supposed to dawn upon the reader and be clear to him from the life of Jesus, from what he says,

---

[121] L. Scheffczyk, "Zum theologischen Thema der Mysterien des Lebens Jesu", in *Die Mysterien des Lebens Jesu*, pp. 7–16, here p. 9.

and from his death. From the individual incidents that Mark recounts from Jesus' life, the evidence grows that he is the Christ. At the same time, the events of Jesus' life attain their meaning from this insight, which goes far beyond a merely subjective involvement. These are the words and works of the one who proved himself, through them, to be God's Son and the Messiah.

The evangelists are not interested in providing a complete report on all the events of Jesus' life. The Gospels pass over many details in which human curiosity takes a lively interest, above all, his childhood and the thirty years in Nazareth. "But there are also many other things which Jesus did; were every one of them to be written, I suppose that the world itself could not contain the books that would be written" (Jn 21:25). Thus, although every detail is infinitely valuable as a sign pointing to God, faith is concerned, not with the details, but with recognizing God in the sign. "God allowed most of the facts of his earthly life, from the objects of everyday use to the dates of his birth and his death, to be forgotten, a matter of dispute, unimportant and trivial, as it were, in the blazing light of the one fact that he came to redeem us, to complete the struggle with Satan, to rise again in newness of life."[122]

Besides Sacred Scripture, the liturgy repeatedly suggests to us the contemplation of the mysteries of Christ. Each year, from Christmas to Ascension, the Church celebrates the whole cycle of the mysteries of the earthly life of Jesus. In the commemorations, feasts, and solemnities of the Church year, she lets us live through the mysteries of the Lord in a living representation. In these feasts, we always likewise celebrate our participation in these mysteries.[123]

All the mysteries of the life of Christ have in common three basic features: they are a revelation of the Father, a mystery of redemption, and a mystery of the "recapitulation" (recapitulatio) of everything under one head. These three main features correspond to the three ways in which we share in the mysteries of Jesus: Jesus' life is the model for us; Jesus lived it for us, and he lets us live in him everything that he lived; and he lives it in us.[124]

---

[122] H. Rahner, Eine Theologie der Verkündigung, p. 98.

[123] Cf. Marmion, Christ in His Mysteries, pp. 19–22.

[124] Cf. CCC 516–521; C. Schönborn, Loving the Church: Spiritual Exercises Preached in the Presence of Pope John Paul II (San Francisco: Ignatius Press, 1998), pp. 108–16.

JESUS' LIFE—REVELATION OF THE FATHER

The mysteries of the life of Christ are a revelation of God. Augustine formulates this succinctly: "*Quia ipse Christus Verbum Dei est, etiam factum Verbi verbum nobis est*" (Because Christ is the Word of God, so also the action of the Word is for us a word).[125] No man knows God, since in his eternal perfection he transcends the ability of earthly creatures to comprehend: "God dwells in unapproachable light" (1 Tim 6:16). In his Incarnation, Christ reveals to men of simple sense, through his words from a human mouth and his works done by human hands, the inaccessible mysteries of the Creator. Each year at Christmas the Church extols this tremendous event anew in her liturgy: "In the wonder of the Incarnation your eternal Word has brought to the eyes of faith a new and radiant vision of your glory. In him we see our God made visible and so are caught up in love of the God we cannot see."[126]

The shepherds and the magi, who worship the baby lying in the manger, see God, who "chose what is weak in the world to shame the strong" (1 Cor 1:27). The inhabitants of Nazareth, who see the young carpenter at work, glimpse, in him, the Father "who is working still" (Jn 5:17). The lepers, the lame, and the blind who are healed by Jesus as he passes by experience God, who is "a God of salvation", to whom "belongs escape from death" (Ps 68:20). Jesus' life shows us the Father's face. That is why it is so important to examine Jesus' life closely, allowing the least hint, the scenes, gestures, and words of Jesus to soak in. Everything in the life of Jesus thus becomes a fulfillment of his words, "He who has seen me has seen the Father" (Jn 14:9). It becomes clear, in Jesus' life, what characteristics go to make up the perfection of his Father: his wisdom, against which no one can prevail; his power, which astounds the multitude; his unprecedented mercy toward sinners; his burning zeal for justice; his self-surrender and self-sacrificing love.

In his life, his words, and his deeds, however, Christ reveals to us not only the Father's face, but also our own: "Christ, the final Adam, by the revelation of the mystery of the Father and His love, fully reveals man to man himself and makes his supreme calling clear" (*Gaudium et Spes*, no. 22). That is why he is the model, the ideal, we should

---

[125] Augustine, *Tractatus in Ioannis Evangelium* 24, 2 (CChr.SL 36:244).
[126] Roman Missal, *Preface of Christmas I*.

follow. His birth in the manger teaches us humility; his thirty years at Nazareth teach us diligence and perseverance; the three years of his preaching teach zeal for the Kingdom of God; the three days of his Passion, obedience. That is why the concrete following of Christ is always also part of the Church's life. The Church needs saints in whom Christ becomes visible. In the *imitatio Christi*, we receive a share in his life. "I have given you an example, that you also should do as I have done to you" (Jn 13:15).

JESUS' LIFE—MYSTERY OF THE REDEMPTION

The life of Christ is a mystery of redemption. "He Who is 'the image of the invisible God' (Col 1:15), is Himself the perfect man. To the sons of Adam He restores the divine likeness which had been disfigured from the first sin onward. Since human nature as He assumed it was not annulled, by that very fact it has been raised up to a divine dignity in our respect too" (*Gaudium et Spes*, no. 22). The redemption is above all the fruit of the voluntary sacrifice of Jesus for us on the Cross, "we have redemption through his blood" (Eph 1:7). He foresaw all the humiliations, all the pains of the Cross and death, and he freely accepted all this out of his love for the Father and for us. Thus the Council of Trent teaches that "our Lord Jesus Christ, 'while we were enemies' (Rom 5:10), 'out of the great love with which he loved us' (Eph 2:4), earned justification for us through his most holy Passion on the wood of the Cross and made satisfaction for us to God the Father."[127] In their compact style, the Council Fathers at Trent emphasize two closely interconnected aspects: on one hand, through his suffering Christ has made satisfaction for us as our substitute,[128] and, on the other hand, his merit, as the quotations from Scripture show, is not conceivable apart from his infinite love for us. Paul teaches us that the most heroic and unselfish act is worthless if it does not spring from love (cf. 1 Cor 13:1–3).

The blood poured out on the Cross is not the only cause of our salvation. Even in his accepting our human nature, the Son of God is restoring in man the image of God. That is why every moment of

---

[127] Council of Trent, *Decree on Justification*, chap. 7 (DH 1529).

[128] On Christ's making satisfaction, see below, chap. 4:2, "Died for Us on the Cross: The Doctrine of Redemption".

Jesus' life is meritorious.[129] In obedience to the will of the Father, he submits to the law in every detail of his life so as to redeem men (cf. Gal 4:5). Thus, as an infant, when the rites of circumcision and presentation in the Temple were fulfilled for him in accordance with the law, he was taking the yoke of the law upon himself in order to free others from that yoke (Gal 4:4–5). At his baptism in the Jordan, it was not he, but the water that became pure, so that, purified by the sinless flesh of Christ, it might receive the power to baptize. By his obedience to his parents, he makes amends for our disobedience.[130]

In the Incarnation, in the life, suffering, and death of Jesus, salvation became tangible, audible, and visible. Some of his salvific actions live on in the Church, in sacramental form. "The mysteries of Christ's life are the foundations of what he would henceforth dispense in the sacraments, through the ministers of his Church, for 'what was visible in our Savior has passed over into his mysteries.'"[131] The sacraments are an extension in history of the redeeming gestures of Jesus, of these fundamental signs by which Christ imparts salvation—that is, imparts himself. The Church's gestures are the gestures of Christ himself, who bends over human weakness in the Church, just as he bent over the deformed body of a cripple, taking hold of it just as it is, so as to change it. The words with which he turns to the sinner Zacchaeus, for instance —"Zacchaeus, make haste and come down; for I must stay at your house today" (Lk 19:5)—are repeated at every Eucharist, when Jesus calls out to men, "I come to you!" It is also possible in the Eucharist to lean on Jesus' breast, like the disciple whom Jesus loved, for he is in us and we in him.[132]

Jesus came into the world "for us men and for our salvation" (Nicaea I, DH 125), in order to reconcile us to God by his entire earthly existence. He takes upon himself hunger, thirst, weariness, persecution, contempt, and betrayal, so that we "may have life, and have it abundantly" (Jn 10:10). "So then, Jesus lived all His mysteries for us, in order to give us to be one day where He is, by right, in the glory of His

---

[129] On the merits of Christ, see below, chap. 4:2c, "Redemption through Christ's Merit".
[130] Cf. CCC 517; Thomas Aquinas, STh III, q. 37 a. 1; q. 39 a. 1; q. 40, a. 4 (DThA 27:69, 105, 151).
[131] CCC 1115; quotation from: Leo the Great, *Tractatus* 74, 2 (CChr.SL 138A:457).
[132] Cf. L. Giussani, *Perchè la Chiesa*, vol. 2: *Il segno efficace del divino nella storia* (Milan, 1992), pp. 84–91.

Father. Yes, each of us can say, with St. Paul, . . . Christ Jesus 'loved me, and delivered Himself up for me' [Gal 2:20]."[133]

JESUS' LIFE—RECAPITULATION OF EVERYTHING

Jesus' life gathers all mankind together under one head. "For by His incarnation the Son of God has united Himself in some fashion with every man" (*Gaudium et Spes*, no. 22). By his death for love's sake, Jesus has merited salvation for us. This not to be explained simply on the basis of the "moral" effect of his act on all men. It is, rather, Christ's place as Head of believers that makes his merit effective for other people. Christ as Head and his faithful as members belong to the same body, are one "mystical person". All Christians are included in Christ. That is why Christ's meritoriousness applies to the faithful; the merit of the Head is also to the benefit of the members.[134] "The Head-body image is only a way of visualizing the fundamental fact of faith that by God's irrefragable decision, Christ is from the very beginning set at the head of men and that, hence, everything he does . . . also benefits his members."[135] This thoroughly biblical idea is important for the whole of the doctrine of redemption. God regards us as being one person in Christ, so to speak; he sees us inclusively in Christ, since "he chose us in him before the foundation of the world" (Eph 1:4).

Because Christians are members of the body of Christ, they can live in him everything that he lived. As Leo the Great says, in suffering we are crucified with Christ; we rise with him in his Resurrection; we sit with him at the right hand of the Father.[136] In the life of the Christian, therefore, everything that ever was in Jesus' life is repeated: weeping and rejoicing, being thirsty and hungry, the wedding feast and plucking the ears of corn, "*hosanna*" and "*crucifige*". For "it is no longer I who live, but Christ who lives in me" (Gal 2:20). John Eudes (d. 1680) expressed that in unsurpassable style:

> I ask you to think that our Lord Jesus Christ is your head, and you are one of his members. He is for you what the head is for the limbs. Everything

---

[133] Marmion, *Christ in His Mysteries*, p. 11.

[134] See Thomas Aquinas, STh III, q. 19, a. 4 (DThA 26:106–8); see also below, 4:2c, "Redemption through Christ's Merit".

[135] O. H. Pesch, *Theologie der Rechtfertigung bei Martin Luther und Thomas von Aquin: Versuch eines systematisch-theologischen Dialogs* (Mainz, 1967), p. 561.

[136] Cf. Leo the Great, *Tractatus* 26, 2 (CChr.SL 138:127).

that is his is also yours: mind, heart, body, soul, and all the faculties. You
must use them as if they belonged to you to serve God, to praise him, to
love, and to glorify him. You are for Christ what a limb is for the head.
That is why he urgently desires to engage all your faculties as if they were
his own to serve the Father and to glorify him.[137]

Yet not only the life of the individual Christian, but the life of the
whole Church has taken on the shape of Christ's life. In view of Christ's
poverty, it must be apparent to us "that the Church—because she is
the Mystical Body of Christ—must necessarily also be *abiectio plebis* (Ps
22:6), 'despised and rejected by men . . . as one from whom men hide
their faces' (Is 53:3), her 'appearance so marred, beyond human sem-
blance' (Is 52:14). The Church is on a journey toward the Cross."[138]
The dramatic events of Church history, which often seem all too human, can be understood only as the sharing of the whole Church in
the humiliation and the suffering of Christ.[139]

c. Contemplating Some of
the Mysteries of the Life of Jesus

Following the great spiritual masters and with particular attention to
the dimensions we have just outlined, we will now sketch out the basic features of a theology of the life of Jesus, based on a few moments
between his birth and Passion.[140] Faith in Jesus as true God and true
man makes it possible to look at his life in such a way as to discover
everywhere the traces of his inmost mystery.

THE MYSTERIES OF THE HIDDEN LIFE OF JESUS

For the most part, the mysteries of Jesus' hidden life, the events of
the first thirty years of his earthly existence, spent mostly in Nazareth,
receive little attention. Matthew tells about the flight into Egypt, the
killing of the children at Bethlehem, and the return from Egypt (Mt
2:13–23); Luke, about the finding of the twelve-year-old Jesus in the

---

[137] Jean Eudes, *Le Coeur admirable de la très sainte Mère de Dieu* 1, 5, in *Oeuvres complètes*, vol.
6 (Vanne, 1908), pp. 113–14; cf. CCC 1698.
[138] H. Rahner, *Eine Theologie der Verkündigung*, p. 114.
[139] Cf. Gertrud von le Fort, *Hymnen an die Kirche*, 22nd ed. (Munich, 1990).
[140] On the mystery of the Last Supper of Jesus, see below, chap. 5:2c, "Present in His
Eucharist".

Temple (Lk 2:41–50). The rest of the hidden life of Jesus is summed up by Luke in two verses: "And he went down with them and came to Nazareth, and was obedient to them. . . . And Jesus increased in wisdom and in stature, and in favor with God and man" (Lk 2:51–52).

From this scanty information, we may conclude that for thirty years Jesus led an inconspicuous life. In an indirect way, this is also confirmed by the questions that the inhabitants of his hometown ask when he comes back to Nazareth to teach in the synagogue: "Where did this man get all this? What is the wisdom given to him? What mighty works are wrought by his hands! Is not this the carpenter, the son of Mary and brother of James and Joses and Judas and Simon?" (Mk 6:2–3). Even if the canonical Scriptures transmit little that is definite about the first part of Jesus' life, what he did and said at that time is nonetheless part of the divine revelation. The first thirty years of Jesus' life teach us a great deal, however little the Gospels may tell about it. Jesus shows us the value of a contemplative life, of obedience, of family, and of work. Is it not a mystery beyond compare that God's Son, who took human form to save the world, to bring divine light into the darkness, first remained hidden for thirty years, known only to a few—Mary and Joseph, the shepherds, the magi, Simeon and Anna? He who possessed from his birth the fullness of grace (Jn 1:16), all the treasures of knowledge and wisdom (Col 2:3), stays for thirty years in a workshop in order to work and obey. Why did he remain "inactive" for so long when he still had to proclaim the Kingdom of God to all men?

The mystery of Jesus' hidden life teaches us, first, that man's ways are not God's ways. In God's eyes there is nothing great except what happens to his honor. The Sonship of Christ, however, his complete obedience to the Father, the expression of his infinite love, confer an infinite value upon even the least of his gestures, even if they should remain forever hidden from the eyes of men. A person's real stature is not based on the greatness of his works but on the acknowledgment that everything comes from the Father (Jn 5:19). The Kingdom of God grows in silence; it is at first above all internal, hidden in the depths of the soul. "For you have died, and your life is hidden with Christ in God" (Col 3:3).

Let us be thoroughly convinced that we shall do more work for the good of the Church, the salvation of souls, the glory of our Heavenly Father, in seeking first of all to remain united to God by a life of love and faith of which He is alone the object, than by a devouring and feverish activity which leaves us no leisure to find God again in solitude, recollection, prayer and self-detachment.[141]

Jesus was obedient to Mary and Joseph; he willingly submitted to the law, so as to overcome the disobedience of the earthly man by his obedience (Rom 5:15). He, for whom God "has put all things under his feet" (Eph 1:22), "the King of kings and Lord of lords" (1 Tim 6:15), willingly submitted to Joseph and Mary. In doing so, he was in particular fulfilling the fourth commandment, the commandment to love and obey one's parents, in a perfect way. "Help us to live as the Holy Family, united in respect and love."[142]

Jesus' subordination to his mother and his stepfather "was the temporal image of his filial obedience to his Father in heaven. The everyday obedience of Jesus to Joseph and Mary both announced and anticipated the obedience of Holy Thursday" (CCC 532). Jesus willingly submitted to his earthly parents out of love and thus by meekness and humility he won their love. "We learn in the hidden life how this 'hard-heartedness' is to be overcome; the willing submission of the Son of God in order to make Mary and Joseph share in his love is also the source of grace that we need, so that 'God's love' may be 'poured into our hearts through the Holy Spirit who has been given to us' (Rom 5:5), so that we 'become obedient from the heart' to teaching, so as to be righteous (Rom 6:17-18)."[143]

Jesus' hidden life in Nazareth is a life of work. His later teaching, his gospel, is

also "the gospel of work", because *he who proclaimed it was himself a man of work*, a craftsman like Joseph of Nazareth (cf. Mt 13:55). And if we do not find in his words a special command to work—but rather on one occasion a prohibition against too much anxiety about work and life (cf. Mt 6:25-34)—at the same time the eloquence of the life of Christ is unequivocal: he belongs to the "working world", he has appreciation and respect for human work. It can indeed be said that *he looks with love upon human work*

[141] Marmion, *Christ in His Mysteries*, p. 170.
[142] Roman Missal, collect for the Feast of the Holy Family.
[143] G. Rovira, "Der Heilssinn des verborgenen Lebens Jesu", in *Die Mysterien des Lebens Jesu*, ed. Scheffczyk, pp. 95-125, here p. 114.

and the different forms that it takes, seeing in each one of these forms a particular facet of man's likeness with God, the Creator and Father.[144]

THE MYSTERY OF JESUS' FELLOWSHIP

At the beginning of the Gospel accounts of the life of Jesus, we find the calling of the first two pairs of disciples, Simon and Andrew, James and John.[145] One feature becomes immediately apparent here that is significant for an understanding of the Kingdom of God: from the start, Jesus is in community. He is not preaching and living alone; he is always surrounded by people—even if it is only the three, Peter, James, and John, who were there at the Transfiguration and in Gethsemane. When it is said of Jesus that he was alone, then it is always to pray. We cannot imagine Jesus without fellowship—that of the circle of disciples, of God's angels, and of the Father himself. Fellowship becomes a fundamental characteristic of the coming Kingdom, of the Church *in nuce*. "The seed and beginning of the Kingdom are the 'little flock' (Lk 12:32) of those whom Jesus came to gather around him, the flock whose shepherd he is. They form Jesus' true family" (CCC 764).

Jesus gives his community a rule of life, a certain order and a task. He himself is its center. Everything is based on his word, on his directions, above all on his person. What no rabbi ever claimed for himself is in Jesus' case the starting point for his community: "Follow me" (Mk 1:17). In a rabbi's circle of pupils, the Torah stands in the center: here, it is Jesus. Students of the Torah seek out their own teachers and masters, but here, it is: "You did not choose me, but I chose you and appointed you that you should go and bear fruit and that your fruit should abide" (Jn 15:16). Jesus himself teaches his "family", his circle of disciples, a new way of living and acting (cf. Mt 5–6). He gives them a new prayer of their own, the Our Father (Lk 11:2–4).

Jesus talks about his task of gathering together the lost sheep of Israel (Mt 15:24), about his mission of seeking "the lost sheep" (Lk 15:4–7), in parables, which all contain something like an "implicit ecclesiology". He uses the image of the wedding feast (Mk 2:19), for instance, of God as the sower (Mt 13:24), and of the fisherman's net (Mt 13:47). What Jesus announces in images and parables is already beginning very

---

[144] John Paul II, encyclical *Laborem Exercens* (September 14, 1981), no. 26.
[145] Cf. Schönborn, *Loving the Church*, pp. 117–26.

concretely in the community he gathers around him.[146] "The Lord
Jesus endowed his community with a structure that will remain until
the Kingdom is fully achieved. Before all else there is the choice of
the Twelve with Peter as their head. Representing the twelve tribes
of Israel, they are the foundation stones of the new Jerusalem" (CCC
765). "[Jesus] called to him those whom he desired; and they came
to him. And he appointed twelve" (Mk 3:13–14).

What part does office play in the community Jesus has united around
himself? The ones chosen are called, not to do some neutral service,
but to be taken ever deeper into a full common destiny with Christ.
Mark says that Jesus called them, and appointed twelve "to be with
him" (Mk 3:14). This "being with him" is the first goal in the calling
of the disciples. "For their mission presupposes their being with Jesus.
And this 'being with' in no way means only a temporary affiliation
that would soon be superseded by their definitive sending out."[147] Fellowship with Christ is no passing phase in the preparation for the real
mission; rather, it is an enduring dimension of the apostolic mission.
Their apostolic ministry is supported throughout by this "being with
him". That is also what he promises at the end, in Galilee, at the start
of their worldwide mission: "And behold, I am with you always, to
the close of the age" (Mt 28:20). The fellowship of men with God
through the "love" that "never ends" (1 Cor 13:8) is the first and
most basic aim of Jesus' calling of all men. The second aspect of this
calling especially concerns those whom Jesus calls to positions of responsibility, "to be sent out to preach and have authority to cast out
demons" (Mk 3:14). To be a sacrament of Jesus Christ, to be a means
and an instrument, servants of Jesus Christ—that is the task of office
in the Church. The hierarchy, like the whole of the sacramental and
institutional order in the Church, belongs to the category of means.
Holiness, which constitutes the mystery of the Church, is, and should
be, the sole end of all the means. That is why Mary is the embodiment
of what the Church is in her nature.

---

[146] Cf. the International Theological Commission, "Jesu Selbst- und Sendungsbewußtsein", p. 46.

[147] G. Lohfink, *Braucht Gott die Kirche?* (Freiburg, 1998), p. 219.

THE SIGNS OF THE COMING KINGDOM OF GOD

From the time when he began to appear in public, Jesus accompanied his proclamation of the Kingdom of God with numerous "mighty works and wonders and signs" (Acts 2:22). Through these, Jesus was laying claim—in a language both graphic and concrete for the believing Jews of his day—to be the Messiah, as is clearly recognized in his reply to the Baptist: "Go and tell John what you hear and see: the blind receive their sight and the lame walk, lepers are cleansed and the deaf hear, and the dead are raised up, and the poor have good news preached to them. And blessed is he who takes no offense at me" (Mt 11:4–6). These saving acts witness that Jesus is the Messiah announced in the prophecies of the Old Covenant (cf. Is 26:19; 29:18; 35:5–6; 61:1).

Jesus' acts reveal first of all that he is the Anointed One who was expected, yet at the same time they prove his divinity. For the fulfillment of the Old Testament prophecies by Jesus Christ surpasses all expectations, since he accomplishes deeds that in the Old Testament are reserved to the Lord. When Jesus forgives the lame man's sins, the scribes who are present think perhaps of the Psalms, in which the Lord is praised "who forgives all your iniquity" (Ps 103:3). That is why they are offended and ask themselves, "Who can forgive sins but God alone?" (Mk 2:5–7). When Jesus, on first meeting Nathaniel, reveals to him the secrets of his heart when he was under the fig tree, the latter thinks of the Psalms that praise God as the Creator: "for you formed my inward parts, you knitted me together in my mother's womb", and hence knows the heart and the thoughts of man (Ps 139). That is why Nathaniel immediately confesses, "Rabbi, you are the Son of God! You are the King of Israel!" (Jn 1:49). When Jesus rebukes the storm and with divine omnipotence bids the waves be still, the disciples recall what the Psalms say: "Whatever the LORD pleases he does, in heaven and on earth, in the seas and all deeps. He it is who makes the clouds rise at the end of the earth, who makes lightnings for the rain and brings forth the wind from his storehouses" (Ps 135:6–7). That is why they spontaneously wonder, "Who then is this, that even wind and sea obey him?" (Mk 4:41).[148]

---

[148] See R. Glöckner, *Neutestamentliche Wundergeschichten und das Lob der Wundertaten Gottes in den Psalmen: Studien zur sprachlichen und theologischen Verwandtschaft zwischen neutestamentlichen Wundergeschichten und Psalmen* (Mainz, 1983).

What Jesus does is intended to move people to believe, since it testifies that he has been sent by the Father. The relationship between faith and signs is complex. These often occur after people have asked for them and have already put their hope in faith in Jesus, like for instance the woman who had suffered a flow of blood for twelve years, who is told, "Daughter, your faith has made you well" (Mk 5:34). In such cases, when people's hopes are realized in the way they have longed for, the miracles strengthen the faith they already have. Jesus Christ does, however, also work signs on his own initiative, so as to reveal hitherto unknown characteristics of his nature. He gives sight to the blind, because he is the light of the world (Jn 9:5). He raises Lazarus from the dead, because he is the Resurrection and the life (Jn 11:25). Often, then, the signs do not correspond to people's expectations. But that, too, is typical of Jesus' proclamation of the Kingdom of God; it is wholly new.

The signs are indeed given, but they remain signs; that is to say, they can also be misunderstood. Hence, they have to be read in such a way that one does not miss Jesus himself. He is the key to their meaning. Jesus' opponents do not repudiate the fact that signs have happened (Jn 9:16, 18), but they do refuse to believe in him. Jesus' lowly origins in Nazareth (Mk 6:3), and his attitude to the Sabbath (Mk 3:1–6) seem to them to prove that he cannot be a miracle worker accredited by God. They even accuse him of being possessed by Beelzebul (Mk 3:22). Where faith is lacking, Jesus can work no miracles (Mk 6:5). Even the greatest signs cannot force men to give their assent to Jesus in faith and obedience. Some Pharisees and scribes think about killing him, even though they have witnessed his miracles of healing since the start of his public activity (Mk 3:6). Some of the witnesses to the raising of Lazarus react in the same way (Jn 11:46–53). So although miracles, as the First Vatican Council says, are "the most certain signs (*signa certissima*) of the divine revelation" (DH 3009), no unambiguous evidence of God's intervention can be seen in them. The fear that "a miracle of this sort would compel belief, and would remove its character of free choice",[149] is accordingly unfounded. Miracles do not produce faith.[150] Yet what is at issue, where miracles are concerned, as

---

[149] W. Kasper, *Jesus the Christ*, trans. V. Green (London: Burns & Oates; New York: Paulist Press, 1977), p. 92.
[150] See the sermon "Miracles No Remedy for Unbelief", by J.H. Newman, of May 2, 1830, in *Parochial and Plain Sermons* (San Francisco: Ignatius Press, 1997), 1611–18.

Vatican I further explains, is the credibility of the Christian faith (DH
3013), not scientific evidence, but the rational and responsible moral
certainty that may be derived, within the context of life as a whole,
from sure signs that faith in Jesus Christ is not irrational.

Jesus' miracles are signs of the definitive, complete, and liberating
coming of the Kingdom of God. "By freeing some individuals from
the earthly evils of hunger, injustice, illness, and death, Jesus performed
messianic signs" (CCC 549). In his work he is bringing creation to
perfection. In Jesus' presence, concrete and even physical well-being
is granted to people. This is where the eschatological significance of
the miracles for Jesus' proclamation of the Kingdom of God becomes
apparent: "Behold, I make all things new" (Rev 21:5). The gestures
and the words of Jesus, such as his fellowship with sinners, are among
the signs of this turning point just as essentially as those signs in which
the power of the dawning Kingdom of God to make new becomes
visible. This is not a matter of a purely future salvation; rather, it is a
matter of one that is already beginning, already present: anyone who
eliminates Jesus' miracles from his activities also eliminates what is eschatological.[151]

THE MYSTERY OF JESUS' STRUGGLE WITH SATAN

Jesus is never concerned in saving acts merely with the restoration of
isolated individual cases, but always, at the same time, with the beginning of the ultimate reign of God. This is clear from Jesus' own understanding of the expulsion of demons. Contemporary Judaism was,
indeed, aware of a certain unity and organization in the power of evil,
but in the New Testament the various names for chief demons (Satan, Beelzebul, Belial, and so on) are clearly understood as powers
that belong together. In this way "evil is no longer something isolated
and fortuitous; the problem is made more radical. Behind its various
manifestations stands the ἐχθρός, the disrupter of creation."[152] Yet that
means that it is only due to Jesus Christ that we can tell what the dominion of evil truly is. From this radicalization of evil, the dimensions
of Jesus' mission become clear. It concerns the whole, the totality of
what has become the domain of injustice, the kingdom of Satan. At
no other point is the at least implicit universality of Jesus' mission so

[151] See G. Delling, *Studien zum Neuen Testament und zum hellenistischen Judentum: Gesammelte Aufsätze 1950–1968* (Göttingen, 1970), pp. 146–59.
[152] Jeremias, *New Testament Theology*, p. 94.

clearly expressed as here. Due to its whole disposition, Jesus' mission can only be aimed at universality. "The rule of God, which becomes effective in Jesus' actions, forces back the rule of Satan: that is what the banishment of demons signifies."[153]

The radicalization and universalization of the rule of evil seen in Jesus' proclamation and works also have an eschatological character. Before Jesus, no substantive connection had ever been established between the work of exorcism, the working of miracles by a charismatic figure, on the one hand, and, on the other, the end of the old world and the beginning of the new world.[154] What Jesus does for people in a real and emblematic way when he heals them and sets them free from demons is an action that is fundamental, pertaining to history and the world as a whole. Only with Jesus does driving out devils acquire an eschatological character.

For our modern mentality, few phenomena seem so closely linked to the religious and cultural context of Jesus' day as the exorcisms. Most exegetes do indeed acknowledge the exorcisms as historical fact, but they explain them from the mentality of Jesus' period. Thus, they are often interpreted as psychological, parapsychological, or psychosomatic phenomena.[155] Yet Jesus, as we have already shown, obviously saw his proclamation of the Kingdom of God, his good news to the poor, the granting of God's forgiveness to sinners together with the fact that he cast out demons, that he is the stronger one who vanquishes, binds, and plunders the strong man (Mk 3:27; Lk 11:21). That is why exorcisms form a characteristic part of his preaching and works.

In the flourishing angelology and demonology of Jewish apocalyptic, the impression is often given that the eschatological struggle between God and Belial is a struggle between titans, like an exciting wrestling match.[156] Taken in themselves, even the accounts of exorcisms in the synoptic Gospels suggest a similar view of Jesus' struggle with demons. And yet it is imperative not to stop at this picture. In reality, the struggle is being carried out on another field, at the real

---

[153] R. Schnackenburg, *Gottes Herrschaft und Reich: Eine biblisch-theologische Studie* (Freiburg im Breisgau, 1959), p. 85.

[154] G. Theissen, *Urchristliche Wundergeschichten: Ein Beitrag zur formgeschichtlichen Erforschung der synoptischen Evangelien* (Gütersloh, 1974), pp. 274–77.

[155] See O. Böcher, "Exorzismus", in *Theologische Realenzyklopädie* 10:750; a different and opposing view is taken by J. A. Sayés, *El demonio, realidad o mito?* (Madrid, 1997).

[156] D. S. Russell, *The Method and Message of Jewish Apocalyptic*, 2nd ed. (London, 1971), pp. 235–62.

heart of Jesus' mission. How Jesus conquers Satan is foreshadowed by the temptation pericope at the beginning of his public ministry, where Jesus' obedience is central. The subtle, merely suggested references to the Old Testament make it clear what is at stake.

Jesus is alone in the wilderness. The entire situation of Israel in its covenant with God is recapitulated here and lived through once again. Just as Israel, the "son of God", was forty years in the wilderness, so Jesus, the son of God, is forty days in the wilderness. This is a time for being alone with God, being alone in the terrifying nearness of God. The aim of Israel has not fulfilled, what it has failed (cf. Ps 95:10), is to be lived through again and fulfilled by Jesus. Israel, Moses, and Elijah knew this solitude, and yet the covenant as a whole remained incomplete. "The three temptations of Israel may . . . be regarded as a kind of summary of the story of its march through the wilderness."[157] Jesus recapitulates them; in the temptation of Jesus, the whole weight of the covenant God offers is placed on the scales, against which the tempter offers "all the kingdoms of the world and the glory of them" (Mt 4:8). The temptation of Jesus consists in misusing his power over the Father's heart, of tempting him, as Israel did in the wilderness, "on the day of temptation" (cf. Ps 95:8).

Jesus, however, is obedient. That is his victory over the enemy. As the letter to the Hebrews says, "Although he was a Son, he learned obedience through what he suffered" (Heb 5:8). The struggle with Satan is not carried on with a massive array of power, like a struggle of titans; rather, it begins in secret, when Jesus is completely alone with and before God. That is when the decisive victory is won, the counterimage and archetype of which is the event of the Cross, when Jesus is once more abandoned and alone before and with God.[158]

The entire question of the reign of demons is thus reduced to this one essential point. Everything else is a figurative illustration. In Jesus' solitary confrontation here with Satan, the nature of this spirit as temptation is revealed, and its nature as arrogance is exposed through the Son's steadfast obedience to the Father. The powerlessness of arrogance in the face of unwavering obedience is now disclosed.

---

[157] J. Dupont, "L'Arrière-fond biblique du récit des tentations de Jésus", *New Testament Studies* 3 (1957): 287–304, here p. 292.

[158] Cf. E. Best, *The Temptation and the Passion: The Markan Soteriology*, MSSNTS 2 (Cambridge, 1965).

With the temptation account as an introduction, the synoptic Gospels give an indication of the way in which Jesus' victory over the demons in his public ministry should be seen. "If Jesus Christ is now encountered in the Gospel, then it is the Son of God, coming from his fundamental victory over the spirit of arrogant, tempting arbitrariness, who is encountered and will now continue this victory in word and deed in his work among men and for men and will bring it to completion on the Cross."[159] God's Kingdom comes wherever the Father's will is done, not in an apocalyptic scenario, but through simple obedience. Anyone who does not see that that is Jesus' authority has invariably missed the meaning of the expulsion of demons.

It is repeatedly asked why so many cases of demonic possession turned up in Galilee right at the time of Jesus. This might be pious exaggeration by the Gospels. Yet we may take seriously the reason they themselves offer for this: "Wherever the obedient Jesus Christ makes his appearance, the essence of arrogance knows itself to be forced from concealment and called to judgment."[160] In a typical scene in Capernaum depicted by Mark (Mk 1:21–28), it is seen, for instance, that the unclean spirit "scents" the presence of the Holy One of God.[161] The demons realize what danger threatens them from Jesus and, indeed, that their time is drawing to an end. What frightens them about Jesus is not just any power, but the power of his obedience, of his sacred humanity. The fact that the devils know about precisely this is expressed in the way the demons address him, recognizing him as the obedient One ("the Holy One of God", Mk 1:24; the "Son of the most High God", Mk 5:7).[162] According to Jesus' own testimony, these can only be driven out by fasting and prayer, only by obedience (Mt 17:21; Mk 9:29). That is why Matthew can say that in Jesus' healings and casting out of demons the saying of the prophet Isaiah has been fulfilled: "He took our infirmities and bore our diseases" (Mt 8:16–17; cf. Is 53:4).

---

[159] H. Schlier, *Mächte und Gewalten im Neuen Testament*, 2nd ed., QD 3 (Freiburg im Breisgau, 1958), pp. 37–38.

[160] Ibid., p. 39.

[161] Cf. R. Pesch, *Das Markusevangelium*, 4th ed., HThK 2/1 (Freiburg im Breisgau, 1984), p. 121.

[162] See E. Broadhead, *Naming Jesus: Titular Christology in the Gospel of Mark*, JSNT.S 175 (Sheffield, 1999), pp. 97–100 and 116–23.

THE TRANSFIGURATION OF CHRIST

In her liturgy, the Church celebrates with particular emphasis four mysteries from the life of Jesus: Christmas, Epiphany, the Transfiguration, and Easter. However much these feasts may touch the feelings of God's people, they are difficult to deal with in exegesis. They are surrounded by too many miraculous elements, which make academic interpretation scent legend and myth: the angels at Christmas; the dove at the baptism; the devil in the wilderness; the cloud, the light, and the voice from heaven at the Transfiguration. There seems to be too much epiphany of the heavenly here. In the contemplation of these mysteries, however, one trait stands out that they have in common: the heavenly world always appears in scenes when Christ is especially humbled. The angels sing about Jesus' poor birth. The Father's voice reveals the Son on the occasion when he is humbled in baptism. The Father glorifies the Son when the latter takes the road to Jerusalem in order to die there. The Father always glorifies the Son at decisive turning points in his life when the latter is particularly humbling himself. It seems as if these scenes are like "rehearsals" for Easter—or as if Easter is the hidden form of the whole of Jesus' life. The glory of Easter already shines forth time and again during Jesus' lifetime.

From the day when Peter confesses that Jesus is the Christ, the Son of the living God (Mt 16:16), Jesus begins to talk about the fact that he has to go up to Jerusalem and to suffer a great deal. He speaks to the disciples about his death and his Resurrection and tells them that they, too, must deny themselves and take up their cross. Jesus' disciples do not understand, and they reject this warning. Six days later, he takes his three favorite disciples, Peter, James, and John, with him and leads them up a mountain, where he is to be transfigured.[163]

On Mount Tabor, while the disciples are sleeping and Jesus is praying, his face begins to shine like the sun, and his garments become whiter than snow. In the Transfiguration, the divinity of Jesus is shown to the three chosen apostles in unveiled clarity. During his earthly life, this has been cloaked in the weakness of human flesh. The Transfiguration does not change Jesus' nature, however, nor does it add any accidental element; rather, it allows something to appear that was already

---

[163] Cf. A. E. Ramsey, *Doxa: Gottes Herrlichkeit und Christi Verklärung* (Einsiedeln, 1969); J. Auer, "Die Bedeutung der Verklärung Christi für das Leben des Christen und für die Kirche Christi", in *Die Mysterien des Lebens Jesu*, ed. Scheffczyk, pp. 146–76.

present in the humbleness of the manger. "There was no external splendor added to the body, but an inner splendor broke forth from the divinity of the Word of God, which is hypostatically united with him in ineffable fashion."[164]

Moses and Elijah appear in order to speak with Jesus. They represent the law and the prophets of the Old Covenant. The interrelationship of all salvation history is shown here. The prophets of the Old Covenant, who announced in their prophecies the coming of the Messiah, speak with Jesus, the head of the prophets. The Old Covenant and the New do not contradict each other; rather, they confirm each other. In the Transfiguration it becomes clear that the prophets are in fact speaking of Christ and that the words of the prophets are still valid. Moses and Elijah belong to Christ forever. It also becomes clear that Jesus is the center of the Torah that Moses brought down from Mount Sinai (Mt 17:1–9 and par.).

The two prophets speak with Jesus about the "Exodus" that he is to consummate at Jerusalem (Lk 9:31). The Father, to whom he has just been speaking in prayer, answers him through the Old Testament witnesses and confides his mission to him through them. This concerns a double exodus of Jesus: on the one hand, the end of his earthly life (2 Pet 1:15), yet, on the other, he is returning to the Father, from whom he came (Jn 16:28). The words of the prophets thus frame the whole Paschal Mystery.

The disciples are drawn into the cloud and thus, in the saving event. While in the Old Testament, people were only allowed to observe from a distance (Ex 24:1, 14), at the scene of the Transfiguration, the disciples are standing in the middle of the cloud. As Thomas Aquinas remarks, only he, Jesus Christ, offers his disciples the chance to see God's glory. For first of all, they fall to the ground in fear at the voice of the Father, like Moses in the Old Covenant (Ex 34:8). "But the men are healed of this weakness by Christ, as he leads them to glory. And that is what his words mean: 'Rise, and have no fear' (Mt 17:7)."[165]

Saint Thomas also refers to the trinitarian significance of the scene of the Transfiguration: "The whole of the Trinity appeared: the Father in the voice, the Son as man, the Holy Spirit in the shining cloud."[166]

---

[164] John Damascene, *Homilia in transfigurationem salvatoris nostri Jesu Christi* 2 (PTS 29:438).

[165] Thomas Aquinas, STh III, q. 45, a. 4 (DThA 27:254).

[166] Ibid. (DThA 27:253). On this point, cf. Torrell, *Christ dans ses mystères* 1:293–97.

The love with which the Father loves the Son is also shown by the presence of the Holy Spirit. The Father's voice repeats the message already proclaimed on the occasion of the baptism: "This is my beloved Son, with whom I am well pleased" (Mt 17:5). He is thereby confirming Peter's acknowledgment of the Son of God made six days earlier: "You are the Messiah, the son of the living God", to which Jesus responded with the beatitude, "flesh and blood has not revealed this to you, but my Father who is in heaven" (Mt 16:17). Only the Father, who knows his Son, can reveal him to men. Here, the voice of the Father is confirming for the disciples what he had already led them to sense in their hearts on the basis of the words and the acts of Jesus.

The Son, however, knows the Father, and to all who believe in his name he grants the power to become children of God (Mt 11:27; Jn 1:12). That is why the Transfiguration is also a revelation of the promise to Christ's coheirs. Jesus promised his disciples that, at the end of the world, the righteous "will shine like the sun in the kingdom of their Father" (Mt 13:43). This is also the conviction of Leo the Great: "Jesus shows that he is concerned to place the hope of his Church on secure ground, so that the whole Body of Christ may know what a transformation is awaiting it, and that all its members may safely build thereon, that they may have their share in the glory that has already been revealed in advance in their Head."[167]

After this solemn proclamation, the Father adds: "Listen to him!" (Lk 9:35), at which Moses and Elijah, and even the cloud with the heavenly voice, disappear, as if to say: From now on, he is the only way that leads to the Father. "And when the voice had spoken, Jesus was found alone" (Lk 9:36). He is, for all time to come, the sole mediator; he alone fulfills the prophecies and sums up the law. For God sent his Son "to redeem those who were under the law, so that we might receive adoption as sons" (Gal 4:5).

---

[167] Leo the Great, *Tractatus* 51, 3 (CChr.SL 138A:299).

IV. The Pascha of the Son of God

The earthly path of Jesus leads to Jerusalem, leads up to Good Friday. There, his activity in the world reaches its climax. Jesus says to the disciples, "Behold, we are going up to Jerusalem; and the Son of man will be delivered to the chief priests and the scribes, and they will condemn him to death, and deliver him to the Gentiles; and they will mock him, and spit upon him, and scourge him, and kill him; and after three days he will rise" (Mk 10:33–34). The conflict concerning the claim and authority of Jesus that had been evident in Capernaum, right at the beginning of his work, now becomes acute and culminates in the trial before the high council and in the handing over of Jesus to the Roman authorities. The first section is devoted to these events. But how do these events fit into the divine plan of salvation? Jesus will ask the disciples from Emmaus, "Was it not necessary that the Christ should suffer these things and enter into his glory?" (Lk 24:26). Our reflections on who is to blame for the death of Jesus lead directly to the second section, the content of which consists of the soteriological significance of his death, the question of redemption through the Cross. A third section deals with the silence of Holy Saturday, the peace of the grave, which conceals a great mystery. Christ goes to everyone, even to the dead, in order to break the power of death.

1. Jesus Christ's Conflict with the Jewish Authorities

Interpretations of the New Testament—and not merely the early ones, but also and precisely modern and liberal commentaries—strengthen a tendency that is certainly based on the trenchant description of the Gospel. The opposition between Jesus, on one side, and the representatives of Jewish order, on the other, becomes a stereotype of contrasts. Priests, Pharisees, and scribes appear as representatives of a hardened legalism that wants to take away the freedom of any room for development. Jesus, by contrast, is the one who rises in opposition to the official powers, bringing true freedom. If we look at Jesus' relationship to Jewish authorities of his time in that way, then his struggle against authority was a failure at first, and yet this very failure laid the foundation for the progress of that revolution. The question must remain open, though, as to whether this really corresponds to Jesus' intentions and whether the priests, Pharisees, and scribes are appropriately described in that way.[1] If this representation is correct, we have to ask ourselves: Can Jesus' message, then, still be one of reconciliation? What has become of the goal of his mission to unite all mankind in himself?

If we listen carefully to the testimony of the Gospels, however, they offer a more thoroughly nuanced picture of Jesus' attitude toward the law, the Temple, and the oneness of God, which can be seen in his life, his work, and his proclamation of the Kingdom of God.[2] The Passion narratives, however, also portray a nuanced picture of Jesus' trial and of the role of the Jewish authorities in it. If this has all been taken into account, then the question of the Jews' guilt in the death of Jesus can no longer be answered in such black-and-white terms. What follows is concerned with these central themes and, thereby, also with the relationship between Judaism and Christianity as a whole. For these questions "are the volatile ones supplying the material for Jewish-Christian disputes".[3]

And the history of this division is long and painful. Although there are many in the Church, today as in the past, who always cultivate good—and even friendly—relations with Jews, and even appreciate Judaism itself, nonetheless this history is filled with many inglorious events that put a lasting strain on the relationship. Polemics, suspicions, legends of ritual murder, the medieval pogroms with their burning of the Talmud, and above all the Shoah, the most terrible occurrence, the most profound evil of the twentieth century, not indeed instigated by Christians, but nevertheless painfully anchored in their awareness and their conscience.[4] This awareness makes the following train of thought

---

[1] J. Ratzinger, *Many Religions—One Covenant: Israel, the Church, and the World*, trans. Graham Harrison (San Francisco: Ignatius Press, 1999), pp. 30-31.

[2] See above, chap. 3:3c, "Contemplating Some of the Mysteries of the Life of Jesus".

[3] Ratzinger, *Many Religions*, p. 30.

[4] See C. Schönborn, "Judentum und Christentum: Annäherungen zum Thema", *Das Jüdische Echo* 46 (1997): 15-17; Schönborn, *Die Menschen, die Kirche, das Land: Christentum als gesellschaftliche Herausforderung* (Vienna, 1998), pp. 181-204. Jean-Miguel Garrigues accurately describes the anti-Jewish ideology of National Socialism, as "a perverse neo-pagan and post-Christian imitation of an unjust religious anti-judaism" that existed both among pagans

urgent; against this background, the main theme of our reflections must be—and can only be—reconciliation, that reconciliation of Jews and pagans which is the inmost heart of Jesus' mission (Eph 2:11–22).

a. Jesus and Israel

Jesus himself was a Jew, lived in Israel, and grew up in the Jewish tradition and with Jewish worship. He understood himself as a Jew, standing in the great current of the Torah tradition. And yet, right at the start of his work, there was conflict about this. His relationship with the Pharisees and scribes, in particular, was somewhat tense from the beginning. In the eyes of many people in Israel, Jesus' actions seemed to be in contradiction with the essential customs and institutions of the chosen people: the requisite obedience to the law, to which, for the Pharisees, belonged the interpretation established by tradition; the central place of the Temple and the city of Jerusalem as the holy place, God's dwelling place; and the belief in the one God, whose glory infinitely transcends the possibilities of any man.[5]

THE LAW

The law, the Torah, is of great meaning to Jesus: he keeps it, and he attaches particular importance to its being kept: "Whoever relaxes one of the least of these commandments and teaches men so, shall be called least in the kingdom of heaven" (Mt 5:19).

The Jewish people's central task is to keep the Torah, God's instructions, which his servant Moses brought down for the people from Sinai, both in letter and in spirit; this is the true and genuine practice of their religion. At the time of Jesus, just as today, knowing this filled many Jews with faith and zeal, a zeal that can sometimes turn into extreme forms (cf. Rom 10:2). At the same time, however, a consciousness also developed of their own inadequacy, of their inability really to keep all the commandments. The feeling that no men can ever fulfill the whole law of themselves, not even if they truly want to, grew into an absolute certainty. For this reason, Israel celebrates every year the Feast of Atonement, Yom Kippur, to ask for God's forgiveness. That is why

---

and Christians. J.-M. Garrigues, ed., *L'Unique Israël de Dieu: Approches chrétiennes du Mystère d'Israël* (Limoges, 1987), p. 15.

    [5] Cf. CCC 574–76.

there is a second aspect to be considered here. God gave men the Torah also as a preparation, as something that would lead to the day on which he himself, in splendor and glory, would deal with the people of Israel through his servant, the sole Righteous One. God himself would take care of the fulfillment of the law on that day.[6]

Jesus himself is aware of his obligation to this tradition; the law has for him an incomparable importance, and he is also quite familiar with its interpretation in the rabbinic form. Matthew, who writes his Gospel for Jewish Christians in particular, portrays the beginning of the Sermon on the Mount in such a way that Jesus quite obviously appears as a Jewish teacher of the Torah. He gathers his pupils around him and sits down (Mt 5:1), a sign that what is coming now is serious and important. Even much later than this, the teacher taking his place was still a formal indication to the pupils of the beginning of instruction.[7] Jesus' proclamation is firmly connected to the law of Israel. In the words of Jacob Neusner, a rabbi of our own day:

> For his engagement with the Torah of Moses—and Matthew makes clear Jesus is profoundly engaged in Torah-learning—means that things that he will say also form a continuation, expansion, elaboration, and clarification, for instance, of the Torah. He is a teacher of the Torah, so in the framework of the Torah, he teaches the Torah and he himself adds to the Torah: so his is a labor of Torah too.[8]

This effort with respect to the Torah is taken, however, on the basis of Jesus' knowledge of his mission. Here is more than a rabbi. He himself is the Righteous One who truly brings justice (Is 42:3), who takes upon himself everything that divides men from the covenant with God, who makes the many righteous by taking their guilt upon himself (Is 53:11). The Cross is "theologically explained by its innermost solidarity with the Law and with Israel".[9] He himself takes the law farther, and he himself is the one who, with the law, leads Israel to God. His death "redeems them from the transgressions under the first covenant" (Heb 9:15).

According to the reports in the Gospels, the controversy about Jesus'

---

[6] Ratzinger, *Many Religions*, p. 33; cf. CCC 579.

[7] Cf. J. Neusner, *A Rabbi Talks with Jesus: An Intermillennial Interfaith Exchange*, rev. ed. (New York and London, 2000), p. 21.

[8] Ibid.

[9] Ratzinger, *Many Religions*, p. 32.

attitude toward the law revolved especially around two points: the
claim implied in his understanding of his proclamation and his attitude toward the Sabbath; and these two were closely interconnected.
Even from the formulations that are transmitted in the Sermon on
the Mount, *Jesus' special understanding of himself* becomes clear. When
Moses came down from Mount Sinai, he came as the voice of God.
"I am the Lord, your God"—that is how the Ten Commandments
begin (Ex 20:2); "thus says the Lord"—that is the phrase that regularly
returns in the prophets. Jesus begins in a similar way: "You have heard
that it was said to the men of old" (Mt 5:21), but then he continues,
"But *I* say to you" (Mt 5:22); at another point, Jesus praises the man
who "hears these words of *mine* and does them" (Mt 7:24; cf. Deut
11:18). For Jewish ears, there is an incredible claim here. Giving instructions on how to act, saying something about the Torah, offering
one's own interpretation—all that is possible; but to speak words that
obviously go beyond the framework of the Torah, the first five books
of Moses, would go decidedly too far. "By the criterion of the Torah,
Jesus has asked for what the Torah does not accord to anyone but
God."[10] Only God himself can speak as the source of the Torah. Jacob
Neusner describes his astonishment:

> Yes, I would have been astonished. Here is a Torah-teacher who says in
> his own name what the Torah says in God's name. It is one thing to say
> on one's own how a basic teaching of the Torah shapes the everyday:
> "Let the other's honor . . . the property . . . be as precious to you as
> your own . . ." It is quite another to say that the Torah says one thing,
> but I say . . . then to announce in one's own name what God set forth
> at Sinai. . . . I am troubled not so much by the message, though I might
> take exception to this or that, as I am by the messenger.[11]

The *Sabbath* is a part of the Jewish identity, even more than Sunday
for us Christians. Keeping the Sabbath is more than merely fulfilling a
commandment, more than merely a human or social task. The Sabbath
is observed because God himself rested on the seventh day (Gen 2:1–
4). Hence, keeping the Sabbath means imitating God himself, becoming like him. When Jesus makes the promise: "Come to me, all . . .
and I will give you rest" (Mt 11:28), then seen in the light of the law,
there is a clear connection with the Sabbath to be seen here. "How

---

[10] Neusner, *A Rabbi Talks with Jesus*, p. 49.
[11] Ibid., p. 46–47.

do I come to God? And how do I find rest?" The seventh day is the day of rest for the Lord, and now Jesus promises this rest himself (cf. Ex 20:9–10; Is 58:13–14).[12]

When the disciples pluck ears of wheat on the Sabbath to satisfy their hunger (Mt 12:1–8 and par.), then Jesus justifies their action by referring to the Temple: the priests there see to their tasks as well. Yet does not this interpretation miss the point of the Sabbath commandment? What is done in the Temple is, after all, exactly the opposite of everyday business. It is concerned precisely, not with one's own well-being, but with service to the Lord. And when Jesus puts the question, "Is it lawful on the sabbath to do good?" (Mk 3:4 and par.), is he not thereby overlooking the fact that this is not concerned with a moral question at all? The goal of the Sabbath is, after all, to be holy.[13] "The Son of man is lord of the sabbath" (Mt 12:8) carries within it the claim that what constitutes the Sabbath—finding rest in God—is given a new quality here, in Jesus. Anyone can find rest in him who will confide himself to him as Messiah in faith and trust. Jesus keeps the Torah and teaches us to keep it. And yet his horizon is different, new. To understand him, conversion is requisite; it demands that one personally entrust oneself to him.

THE TEMPLE

Jesus completely adapts himself to the rites and customs of his people,[14] and this life is closely associated with the Temple in Jerusalem.[15] He goes regularly to the sanctuary as a pilgrim, at least once a year, during his hidden life and also in the period of his public ministry.[16] Like the other Jews of his time, he understands the Temple as the privileged place for meeting with God, his Father. His indignation about the merchants and money changers in the outer court is also to be understood on the basis of this intimate relation to the Temple: "You shall not make my Father's house a house of trade!" (Jn 2:16). Even after the death and Resurrection, his disciples and the steadily growing

---

[12] Ibid., p. 76.

[13] Ibid., pp. 86–88.

[14] See above, chap. 3:3c, "Contemplating Some of the Mysteries of the Life of Jesus".

[15] On the Temple, see Y. Congar, *Le Mystère du Temple: Ou l'économie de la présence de Dieu à sa créature de la Genèse à l'Apocalypse* (Paris, 1958).

[16] See G. Lohfink, *Braucht Gott die Kirche? Zur Theologie des Volkes Gottes* (Freiburg im Breisgau, 1998), pp. 198–99.

community remained faithful to the Temple (see, for example, Acts 2:46; 3:1; 5:20–21).

Jesus' connection to the Temple in all its depth is seen in an eschatological sign. As he is standing with his disciples before the massive buildings, he says to them, "You see all these, do you not? Truly, I say to you, there will not be left here one stone upon another, that will not be thrown down" (Mt 24:2 and par.). For Jesus, the destruction of the Temple is a sign that the end times are beginning. In the long exhortation that follows in Matthew (Mt 24:3—25:46), he urges the disciples to be alert and not to let themselves be led astray. Seen against this background, the reproach alleged in the legal proceedings against Jesus, "We heard him say, 'I will destroy this temple that is made with hands, and in three days I will build another, not made with hands' " (Mk 14:58), looks distorted or at least misunderstood. Matthew is aware of a similar form of this, said in mockery of the crucified man: "You who would destroy the temple and build it in three days, save yourself! If you are the Son of God, come down from the cross" (Mt 27:40). But this saying of Jesus really cannot be judged as an attack on Israel's sanctuary.

It is John who provides us with the key to the correct understanding of this passage, when he interprets the phrase: "But he spoke of the temple of his body" (Jn 2:21). "Something greater than the temple is here" (Mt 12:6). Only someone who, in himself, surpasses the law and the instruction to build a temple can talk like this. If the Temple is a privileged place for meeting with God, then the person making this assertion must be still closer to God and must himself become for others the place where God can be met. It is perfectly understandable that such a claim should provoke uneasiness among Jews. Rabbi Neusner writes:

> When, therefore, Jesus says that something greater than the Temple is here, he can only mean that he and his disciples may do on the Sabbath what they do because they stand in the place of the priests in the Temple: the holy place has shifted, now being formed by the circle made up of the master and his disciples.[17]

JESUS AND ISRAEL'S BELIEF IN THE ONLY GOD WHO SAVES

Jesus' view of the law and the Temple arouses opposition, but the real stumbling block for his opponents is his claim to be able to forgive

---

[17] Neusner, *A Rabbi Talks with Jesus*, pp. 82–83.

sins. A different spirit is evident in Jesus' actions, especially in his attitude to tax collectors and sinners, from the one prevalent in Judaism. Every person is burdened with sin and is incapable of freeing himself of this burden by his own efforts. He will be free from sin only if God frees him and thus grants him his gracious action. In essence there is agreement here, but opinions differ about how this interrelation should be interpreted.

For Israelites, the question of sin is closely linked to the search for purity and holiness. "The belief in one God, who is Lord of *all*, must also shape the world around men."[18] But if God is the pure and holy One, then man must also be pure and holy and, likewise, everything around him. That is why it is necessary to distance oneself from everything impure and, therefore, to avoid sinners and all those in a state of impurity, so as not to "catch" it from them. This is where Jesus' message becomes a matter of contention, since he emphasizes that all men are sinners (cf. Jn 8:33–36). Everyone who does not recognize that is, in his words, overcome by blindness (Jn 9:40–41; CCC 588).

Closely connected with this idea, however, is Jesus' awareness of his mission to sinners. He comes as a doctor to the sick (Lk 5:31), to call to himself everyone who has fallen into sin. And all these are invited to the heavenly banquet, the great feast at the return of the Messiah. Jesus also visibly reinforces this for everyone with his behavior toward public sinners. He has meals with tax collectors and sinners and associates with prostitutes and outcasts. That is inconceivable for eyes and ears experienced with the law. No sinner can have a place at the Lord's table unless his sins have previously been forgiven. Yet who can forgive sins apart from God alone? Jesus' behavior expresses his special claim to be Son of God and, thereby, God himself. "If the redemption, the setting free from sins", is to be "radical and universal", then it is necessary that "Jesus' mission as Redeemer be combined here with his divine identity".[19] And indeed, Jesus makes that clear in various statements: "Something greater than Jonah is here . . . something greater than Solomon" (Mt 12:41–42), "greater than the temple" (Mt 12:6). In another place he refers it to himself when David calls the Messiah his Lord, or he asserts, "Before Abraham was, I am" (Jn 8:58), and even, "I and the Father are one" (Jn 10:30; CCC 590). Jesus' knowledge of his mission is speaking clearly in all of this.

---

[18] Lohfink, *Braucht Gott die Kirche?*, p. 113.
[19] Garrigues, *L'Unique Israël de Dieu*, p. 50.

Such a radical claim, together with Jesus' actions, also demands a radical conversion from those who follow him. It is not enough to hear and to understand his message; rather, anyone who has come to know him must align his entire life with him and his message. "He who is not with me is against me" (Mt 12:30)—that is how Jesus himself characterizes the radicality of this discipleship. Such a faith demands of man that he die to himself and thereby open himself for God's gracious action, so as to be reborn "from above" (Jn 3:7). This divine intervention is, however, still veiled at the time of Jesus' preaching; Easter day has not yet dawned, and yet it is demanded of man that he enter wholly into a relationship with Jesus. In view of this enormous demand, we can more easily appreciate the actions of the high council. Its members are acting from "ignorance" together with "hardness of heart" (Mk 3:5; Rom 11:25; CCC 591). In their situation, also, it is not at all easy to become involved with Jesus' activity and his message. That, however, is the absolute prerequisite for anyone who wants to understand Jesus; he must turn to Jesus in faith and trust.

b. The Trial of Jesus

The conflict portrayed in the Gospels culminates in the trial of Jesus, who is brought first before the high priest, next before the Sanhedrin, and finally before the Roman governor. Looked at superficially, the dispute is escalating. If we seek the more profound theological line, then the real reason for Jesus' death becomes clear, the actual discord for whose reconciliation Jesus came into the world and gave himself up to death.

The trial itself, even after the extant sources have been most carefully studied, still leaves riddles; the picture is marked by many inconsistencies. One division emerges rather clearly, by which a kind of preliminary hearing took place before the Jewish authorities, which was aimed particularly at the interrogation of witnesses and of Jesus himself, before the actual prosecution before the Roman governor, who was the only one entitled to pronounce the death sentence. The preliminary hearing before the Sanhedrin is important here. The high council, the executive committee of seventy-two leaders of the Jews in Jerusalem, consisted of three parties: the high priests, the scribes, and the elders. It was by no means all enemies of Jesus who were assembled there. The Gospels mention by name, as followers of Jesus in the leading circles of the high council, Joseph of Arimathea (Mt 27:57–60), who buried him in his own grave after his execution, and Nicodemus (Jn 3:1–13), who sought out Jesus by night because he was afraid; and they will not have been the only ones. John recounts that shortly before the Passion "many even of the authorities believed in him" (Jn 12:42). Caiaphas, again, was a skilled politician, to whom it was above all important to maintain the difficult interaction with the Roman Procurator and not to endanger his own position. This basic attitude can be heard in the sentence that has been handed down, "It is expedient for you that one man should die for the people, and that the whole nation should not perish" (Jn 11:50). To achieve these aims, he endeavored throughout his tenure in office, of about nineteen years, to nip in the bud any opposition to his policies.[20] Many of those assembled in the Sanhedrin probably thought much the same.

A precise and nuanced examination of the texts cannot and should not be undertaken here; there is enough exegetical literature on this subject.[21] A few critical moments may be emphasized. The first matter examined is the question of the Temple. The Temple is the center of Jerusalem from the religious point of view, but equally from that of politics and of economics. Any attack on the Temple is also an attack on the whole community at Jerusalem and, thus, on the high council. Only when the accusation that Jesus was opposed to the Temple and desired its destruction could not be substantiated, because the witnesses' statements were unclear or did not agree with one another— only then did the high priest change the subject and ask, "Are you the Christ, the son of the Blessed?" (Mk 14:61). Jesus' firm and assured reply expresses his self-awareness and his claim: "I am; and you will see the Son of man sitting at the right hand of Power, and coming with the clouds of heaven" (Mk 14:62).

Both the high priest, who reacts accordingly by tearing his garments, and the other members of the high council understand the claim. Yet because they are closed to faith in Jesus, they can only find him guilty, as, in their view, the Torah commands. In the eyes of the assembly this claim to reign in heaven is blasphemy and carries the death penalty—

---

[20] W. Bösen, *Der letzte Tag des Jesus von Nazaret*, new ed. (Freiburg im Breisgau, 1999), pp. 159–74.

[21] Besides the commentaries on the four Gospels, see also: Bösen, *Der letzte Tag*, pp. 156–96; R. Brown, *The Death of the Messiah: From Gethsemane to the Grave: A Commentary on the Passion Narratives in the Four Gospels*, 3 vols. (New York, 1994).

what the Torah says is quite clear on this (Lev 24:16; Num 15:30–
31; Deut 18:20; 21:22). They have the interest and the will to deal
with this matter, which is irksome for them. To that end, they look
for a legitimate opportunity, which they find. Willibald Bösen notes
that "The members of the Sanhedrin assembled for the interrogation
of Jesus cannot be absolved of guilt, but neither should one be too
hasty in accusing them of being too casual with their verdict."[22]

Even a purely historical examination shows that something greater
and more holy was at stake here than just the accusation that Jesus was
some kind of revolutionary who had come into conflict with the rul-
ing powers. This was a matter of Jesus' most personal understanding
of his mission, which he consistently followed. His path to Jerusalem
runs through the Gospels like a scarlet thread. The announcements of
his Passion, which the disciples did not at first understand (Mk 8:31–
33; 9:30–32; 10:32–34 and par.), merely express this orientation of the
whole path Jesus followed. This path is not a matter of chance or fate,
still less an unlucky accident, but it is what God wills (cf. Mk 8:33), the
path already marked out thus by God. The surrender and the violent
death appear here as an event happening "according to the definite plan
and foreknowledge of God" (Acts 2:23) that finds its completion in
the Resurrection of Jesus.

We have to take both into account, the nuanced view of the historical event and the more profound theological dimension, in asking
ourselves the difficult but, today, unavoidable question: Whose fault
is Jesus' death?

c. Christianity and Judaism—
The Question of the Guilt

In the course of a long and often dreadful history, "the Jews" were
held responsible for Jesus' death on the Cross. We would have to agree
with Jacob Neusner's assertion that it was above all a radical view on
the Christian side that provoked an "either-or" that then became the
motive for indicting the Jews as "Christ killers". "So there has been
a certain impatience with us, eternal Israel, perhaps understandably
so."[23] The idea of this guilt so influenced the relationships between

---

[22] Bösen, *Der letzte Tag*, p. 190.
[23] Neusner, *A Rabbi Talks with Jesus*, p. 23.

Christianity and Judaism for so long a time that any other way of seeing things, any attempt at rapprochement, necessarily paled in comparison.

> The history of their relations and contacts is, it must be confessed, dispiriting. The penances, persecutions and sufferings imposed upon the Jews in Christendom were usually looked upon simply as a just expression of God's punishment, and not, which would have been more Christian, as an addition to the mystery of suffering which the Church contemplates in the Cross: they point and lead on to the bottomless misunderstandings and the endless theological short-circuits that followed.[24]

What about the guilt of Jesus' contemporaries? The question of the trial and a nuanced investigation have already shown that it was in fact leading Jewish authorities who for various motives instigated and pursued the trial; it has at the same time also become clear that there were a growing number of supporters of Jesus' mission. If we follow Rabbi Neusner, then at the trial of Jesus, but also with respect to his earthly activity, in addition to acceptance in faith and direct refusal, there is also a third possible attitude, which (in modern terms) expresses both respect and inadequate understanding. Anyone adopting this point of view will not follow Jesus but neither will he fight against him. Yet how can this attitude be reconciled with Jesus' eschatological call, "He who is not with me is against me" (Mt 12:30)? Are they not already guilty by proving to be uninvolved vis-à-vis Jesus? Do we not experience, particularly nowadays, the dangerous power and the culpability of indifference? In any case, we are not going to debate this question here. This does not mean discipleship, mission, service in the Kingdom of God. It is solely a question of whether anyone who held back from Jesus through ignorance was thereby guilty of the outcome of his trial. Since this probably applies to the majority of the people of Israel at the time of Jesus, the question is relevant. We cannot allege that by

---

[24] H. U. von Balthasar, *Martin Buber and Christianity: A Dialogue between Israel and the Church*, trans. Alexander Dru (New York: Macmillan, 1961), p. 12. On this book, and on von Balthasar's position regarding Judaism, see A. Schenker, "Hans Urs von Balthasars Theologie des Judentums", *Freiburger Zeitschrift für Theologie und Philosophie* 44 (1999): 214–22. The Papal Commission for Religious Relations with the Jews notes: "In effect, the balance of these relations over two thousand years has been quite negative" (*We Remember: A Reflection on the Shoah*, March 16, 1998, no. 9 [not numbered in English]). Cf. the International Theological Commission, *Memory and Reconciliation: The Church and the Faults of the Past*, December 1999.

not being involved, they had involved themselves. It is possible not to follow Jesus and nonetheless not cry, "Crucify him!"[25]

The incited crowd who cried "Crucify him!" cannot be understood as representative of the whole of Israel. Indeed, even those who were themselves directly involved are characterized not only by obduracy, but also (above all) by ignorance. Who was directly to blame for the trial and its outcome, God alone knows. The Second Vatican Council summed it up for the Church:

> True, the Jewish authorities and those who followed their lead pressed for the death of Christ; still, what happened in His passion cannot be charged against all the Jews, without distinction, then alive, nor against the Jews of today. Although the Church is the new people of God, the Jews should not be presented as rejected or accursed by God, as if this followed from the Holy Scriptures.[26]

Yet faith cannot stop at historical questions. There is no doubt that the facts must be presented in a discriminating way, and yet the deeper meaning is essential. "Was it not necessary that the Christ should suffer these things . . . ?" (Lk 24:26), Jesus asks the two disciples on the road to Emmaus. It is a matter of seeing the death of Jesus in a more profound context as well. In this setting, the question of responsibility for Jesus' death on the Cross comes up again. Why did Jesus have to go to his death? Why did he have to take upon himself the Cross?

The Church has always known the answer to that. It is connected with knowing that man is imprisoned by sin, the slave of sin. Since all men, without distinction, are bound together in this, only God can reverse this disastrous situation by coming into the world himself, becoming man, in order to bring men out of death to life, out of darkness into light.[27] Jesus opposes sin, and it is sinners who hand him over (Heb 12:3). Sins are directed against him personally (Mt 25:45). The sins of us all hurt Christ. Ultimately, they brought him to the Cross. It is not others whom we can call to account for it, and certainly not the entire Jewish people, even if some of them were directly involved in the actual events. The *Catechismus Romanus* expresses this knowledge about guilt for the death of Jesus in this way:

---

[25] See Neusner, *A Rabbi Talks with Jesus*, pp. 23–24.

[26] Declaration on the Relation of the Church to Non-Christian Religions *Nostra Aetate*, no. 4.

[27] Cf. Garrigues, *L'Unique Israël de Dieu*, pp. 48–49.

We must regard as guilty all those who continue to relapse into their sins. Since our sins made the Lord Christ suffer the torment of the cross, those who plunge themselves into disorders and crimes crucify the Son of God anew in their hearts (for he is in them) and hold him up to contempt [Heb 6:6]. And it can be seen that our crime in this case is greater in us than in the Jews. As for them, according to the witness of the Apostle, "None of the rulers of this age understood this; for if they had, they would not have crucified the Lord of glory" [1 Cor 2:8]. We, however, profess to know him. And when we deny him by our deeds, we in some way seem to lay violent hands on him.[28]

Such a reinforced knowledge will also, however, lead us to approach the history of Judaism with some degree of sympathy. Recognizing our own guilt strengthens our solidarity with the old Israel, with the people who were "first to hear the word of God".[29] A proper relationship between the Catholic Church and Judaism will be supported by a more delicate sensibility and will also keep in view the still abiding vocation of the people of Israel. Pius XI expressed this at a time of crisis, in view of the growing threat to the Jewish people: "Anti-Semitism is indefensible. Spiritually, we [Christians] are all Semites".[30]

Knowledge of our own involvement in Jesus' suffering and death casts a different light on the question of guilt at the trial and, indeed, on the question of the significance of the historical events in Jerusalem as such, and it recedes before the far more important basic question. The realization that Jesus consciously went to his death for all sinners, to take away their sins, leads us into the middle of the doctrine on redemption.

2. Died for Us on the Cross:
The Doctrine of Redemption

At the heart of Christian faith stands the mystery of the Cross of Jesus. During the Stations of the Cross, the verse from the Good Friday liturgy is periodically prayed: "We adore you, O Christ, and we bless you, because by your holy Cross you have redeemed the world." The Christian faith is based on the fact that, on the one hand, all men need

---

[28] *Catechismus Romanus* 1, 5:1, 1; quoted in CCC 598.
[29] Sixth petition of the General Intercessions, Good Friday.
[30] Pius XI, address to a group of Belgian pilgrims on September 6, 1938. On this point, see Garrigues, *L'Unique Israël de Dieu*, pp. 13–20, and the document *We Remember*, no. 15.

salvation, redemption, and that, on the other, both of these, salvation and redemption, lie in the Cross of Christ, bought and offered to all men by Jesus' death on the Cross. Both these presuppositions are far from obvious. Can someone defend me? Redeem me? Can someone else, on my behalf, achieve liberation and salvation? And: What is redemption for?

Since antiquity, redemption has been questioned time and again in various ways. Let us cite a few variants, by way of example: redemption is said to be *unnecessary*, especially any redemption from outside ourselves—this is the point of view of Gnosis. We only have to realize for ourselves who we really are. Our true identity, our divine self, must dawn upon us; then we are redeemed, and a "redeemer" is merely the messenger who brings this knowledge. Redemption is said to be *impossible*, because everything is basically determined, is already established—thus, various forms of ancient and modern determinism and fatalism. Redemption is said *not to make sense*, because with respect to our own finitude, humility is required, and we ought not to want more than is possible.

The question of how to talk appropriately about salvation and redemption today can only receive anything approaching an answer if we ask in turn what salvation and redemption, what the Cross meant for the great witnesses of Christianity. How did they experience redemption, how did they talk about it, base their lives on it? How did they understand the Cross of Christ?

It is a fact we cannot overlook that the history of the great figures of Christianity, the saints, revolves around the *Mysterium paschale* of Christ; and at the head of them all stands Saint Paul himself. For him, the gospel is the message of the Cross. Only in the Cross does he wish to glory (Gal 6:14), only the crucified One does he wish to know (1 Cor 2:2). The Cross is a stumbling block for the Jews, foolishness for the pagans, but for those who believe, the power and the wisdom of God (1 Cor 1:18, 23–24). Dominic (d. 1221) said of himself that he learned more from the book of the Cross than from the books of theologians. The power of the Cross is experienced, for instance, by Thomas Aquinas (d. 1274) before the cross in Naples; by Saint Francis (d. 1226) in his vision when he received the stigmata on Mount Alverna, which Bonaventure (d. 1274) places in the middle of his little book *The Soul's Pilgrimage to God*; by Edith Stein (d. 1942) on her path to conversion and in her science of the Cross. These experiences are so abundant that a few words can hardly accommodate them. From the beginning, we encounter the "word of the Cross" (1 Cor 1:18) in all its power.

Yet how did Jesus himself understand his Cross? Did he attach a salvific meaning to his own death? Did he, then, understand it as a sacrifice, as a representative expiation?[31] We will return to this question at the end of this section. First, before interrogating the tradition in its qualified witnesses, we must summarize what the New Testament says about the redemption event.

OVERVIEW OF THE NEW TESTAMENT DOCTRINE OF REDEMPTION

In Jesus' own awareness of his mission, as it is transmitted to us in the New Testament, the redemption event appears to be a complex event. In the following, let us, along with Hans Urs von Balthasar, highlight five factors, which are not in competition with each other, but which each portray an essential aspect of redemption.[32]

For God to effect redemption presupposes, first, the *self-giving* of the Son "for us all", whereby he also "gives us all things" (cf. Rom 8:32). Yet Jesus does not remain completely passive in this; rather, he gives himself up willingly. He himself is the sacrifice and, at the same time, the high priest (cf. Heb 9:11–28). His blood is the expiation (Rom 5:9), the justification (Rom 5:9), the purification (1 Jn 1:7; cf. Rev 7:14) that seals the final covenant of God with men (Mt 26:28 and par.; 1 Cor 11:25).

Secondly, this self-giving for us goes so far as to become a *substitution*. He himself, "who knew no sin", is "made to be sin" for us (2 Cor 5:21), becomes "a curse" (Gal 3:13), that we may become righteous thereby. He, the wealthy one, becomes poor for our sake, that we may become rich (2 Cor 8:9). He is the Lamb of God, who takes the sin of

---

[31] For literature on this subject: H. Schürmann, *Jesu ureigener Tod* (Freiburg im Breisgau, 1975); Schürmann, *Jesus: Gestalt und Geheimnis*, ed. K. Scholtissek (Paderborn, 1994), pp. 157–265; K. Kertelege, ed., *Der Tod Jesu: Deutungen im Neuen Testament*, QD 74 (Freiburg im Breisgau, 1976); Marie-Louise Gubler, *Die frühesten Deutungen des Todes Jesu: Eine motivgeschichtliche Darstellung aufgrund der neueren exegetischen Forschung*, OBO 15 (Göttingen, 1977).

[32] Cf. von Balthasar, TD 4:240–44.

the world upon himself (Jn 1:29; cf. 1 Jn 3:5), whether this is as the sin-laden servant of God (Is 53:4) or the sacrificial lamb at the Passover festival or the scapegoat. What matters is that he carries our sins.

Thirdly, the aim of this is *setting men free*, understood first in a negative sense as "ransom" from sin (Rom 7; Jn 8:34; Rom 8:2), from the evil one (Jn 8:44; 1 Jn 3:8; Col 1:13; and so on) and from the violence of the coming judgment (1 Thess 1:10). This liberation is portrayed in the image of the payment of a high "price" (1 Cor 6:20; 7:23; 1 Pet 1:18–19), as a ransom (Mk 10:45 and par.). Following the Old Testament, expiation is seen particularly in terms of "blood" (Heb 9:12), which here stands for a violent death (Heb 9:15).

Fourthly, this liberation is, however, more than just, in the negative sense, the removal of all evil. It is at the same time the bestowal of the Holy Spirit and, thereby, an *introduction into the divine life of the Trinity*, an adoption as children, a liberation for sonship with Christ (Gal 4:6–7; Rom 5:15–17; Eph 1:5). The freedom thus bestowed is understood, not merely negatively, as freedom of choice, but positively, as freedom in the Holy Spirit, which spurs us on to good and which alone grants man his genuine opportunity for development. Only freedom of this kind can really and truly be freedom, and this is the only kind known in the New Testament (Gal 5:1, 13–26; cf. Jn 8:31–36).

And, finally, fifthly, as far as man's state of having fallen into sin is concerned, the "wrath" of God can be spoken of (Mt 3:7 and par.; Rom 1:18; Eph 2:5; Rev, passim). The event of reconciliation, on the other hand, is ascribed solely to the *love of God*. It is from love that the Son was given up for us all by the Father (Rom 8:32–39; Jn 3:16). Even if the motive of "righteousness" does play an important role, when it is a matter of the restoration and the perfection of the covenant once made with man, the source of this divine action is nonetheless, before all else, the gracious love of God.

Whoever wants to grasp the redemption event in all its complexity, as it is depicted for us in the New Testament, must take the trouble to look at these five aspects together and strive for their inner unity. The danger is that of either emphasizing one aspect as dominant and neglecting the others; or of replacing the central assertion, achieved through considering all five aspects, with an equivalent one supposedly better and more easily understood nowadays, which will be unable in any way to match the weight of the biblical statement; finally, there is the risk either of relaxing the tensions that occur between the individual aspects, of concealing them, or of not seeing them at all, and, thus, arriving at a synthesis that is merely apparent, or of letting oneself be blinded by a supposed agreement. Time and again, in the course of historical development, these dangers have been powerful and have distorted the picture of the redemption.

As focal points from the history of dogma we shall deal with three influential figures, three outstanding theologians: Anselm of Canterbury, Thomas Aquinas, and Martin Luther. They are old masters, who will no doubt still be studied in twenty or a hundred years. In order to deal creatively and without timidity with new situations, it is important to remember history. A knowledge of the great masters is a primary prerequisite for solving new problems. The three we have mentioned are particularly important for our subject, since they grappled with the question of redemption intensively and profoundly. Anselm produced the first systematic soteriology; Luther, with his dramatic view of the theology of the Cross, influenced the whole of modern soteriology. Thomas, again, undertook perhaps the most balanced synthesis. For reasons of subject matter, they will therefore be dealt with in that order in what follows.

a. Anselm of Canterbury's Doctrine of Satisfaction

Anselm of Canterbury (1033/34–1109) constructed his soteriology around a central concept, around reparation, *satisfactio*. This "theory of satisfaction" experienced much hostility, being described, for instance, as legalism. Adolf von Harnack made the accusation against Anselm that God was for him an angry, despotic private individual.[33] Yet there is also no shortage of attempts at rehabilitation, based on a more carefully nuanced view of Anselm's process of thought.[34]

---

[33] A. von Harnack, *Lehrbuch der Dogmengeschichte* vol. 3, 4th ed. (Tübingen, 1910), p. 408; F. C. Baur and A. Ritschl made similar criticisms. G. Plasger, *Die Not-Wendigkeit der Gerechtigkeit: Eine Interpretation zu "Cur Deus homo" von Anselm von Canterbury*, BGPhThMA, n.s., 38 (Münster, 1993), pp. 1–40, offers a brief survey of the history of the interpretation of Anselm.

[34] See von Balthasar, *Glory* 2:211–59; TD 4:255–61; G. Greshake, "Erlösung und Freiheit: Zur Neuinterpretation der Erlösungslehre Anselms von Canterbury", *Theologische Quartalschrift* 153 (1973): 323–45; R. Schwager, *Der wunderbare Tausch: Zur Geschichte und Deutung der Erlösungslehre Anselms von Canterbury* (Munich, 1986); R. Roques, introduction and notes to Anselm of Canterbury, *Pourquoi Dieu s'est-il fait homme*, SC 91 (Paris, 1963). Because of

Twice Anselm dealt with the question of satisfaction and Incarnation: in the book *Why God Became Man* (*Cur Deus homo*)[35] and in his *Reflections on the Redemption of Man* (*Meditatio redemptionis humanae*).[36] Both times, he proceeds according to the same principles, but these texts differ from each other in form. While *Cur Deus homo* advances systematically and speculatively, the *Meditation* is contemplative, written as a prayerful reprise of the same subject. *Cur Deus homo* talks about God, the *meditation* is directed to God.[37]

ANSELM'S METHOD

Toward the end of the book *Cur Deus homo*, Boso, Anselm's pupil and interlocutor, once again summarizes the aim of this book: "The point of the question was this: why God became man, so that he could save men by his death, since he obviously could have done it another way" (CDH 2, 18:438–39). The question with which *Cur Deus homo* is concerned is, therefore: Why in this way and not another? Anselm wants to fathom the actual history of salvation in its inner logic and necessity. Why did God choose this path of humiliation when he could, after all, have redeemed man simply by an act of will, by command?

Anselm is looking for an answer to this question that can at the same time strengthen the believer in his faith and be able to persuade the unbeliever that this faith is reasonable. The Christian's starting point is faith that is seeking understanding, *fides quaerens intellectum*. The method worked out in the *Proslogion*[38] is presupposed here: faith is the initial given, and of itself it guides us to seek understanding. For unbelievers,

---

the intensive research of recent decades, the literature on Anselm has become immense. Plasger, *Die Not-Wendigkeit der Gerechtigkeit*, and K. Kienzler, *Glauben und Denken bei Anselm von Canterbury* (Freiburg im Breisgau, 1981), as also Kienzler, *Gott ist größer: Studien zu Anselm von Canterbury*, BDS 27 (Würzburg, 1997), offer good bibliographical references.

[35] Anselm, *Cur Deus homo* (hereafter abbreviated CDH), 2, 18 (SC 91; all further quotations are taken from this edition).

[36] Anselm of Canterbury, *Meditatio* 3, redemptionis humanae (Med.) (ed. Schmitt, 3:76–91); trans. by Sr. Benedicta Ward as "Meditation on Human Redemption", in *The Prayers and Meditations of Saint Anselm*, SLG (Harmondsworth, 1973), pp. 230–37.

[37] F.-M. Léthel, *Connaître l'Amour du Christ qui surpasse toute Connaissance: La Théologie des Saints* (Venasque, 1989), p. 204.

[38] Prooemium to Anselm, *Proslogion*, in *Prayers and Meditations*, trans. B. Ward, pp. 238–39; cf. R. Theis, "Die Vernunft innerhalb der Grenzen des Glaubens: Aspekte der anselmischen Methodologie in werkgenetischer Perspektive", *Theologie und Philosophie* 72 (1997): 161–87, here esp. pp. 168–74.

however—and Anselm has Jews and Muslims concretely in mind—
it is a matter of showing that the Incarnation happened in accordance
with reason and necessity, that Christian faith itself is not contrary to
reason.[39]

Is Anselm not taking on too much here? Is it possible to show,
with compelling reasons, that things had to happen in that way and
not another? Anselm wishes to hold strictly to reason, so much so
that he wants to abstract intellectually from the factual existence of
Christ. "Demonstrate" (*probare*), "necessity" (*necessitas*), and "reason"
(*ratio*) seem to be the key words. Yet are they appropriate within the
realm of faith? Can such rational necessity be attributed to historical
events (Lessing's question!)? All that first becomes clear when a fourth
key word of Anselm's method is taken into account. After Boso has
enumerated the non-Christians' objections to Christian faith, Anselm
replies, "If they carefully considered how fittingly (*convenienter*) the
restoration of man was achieved in this way, they would not ridicule
our simplicity, but would join us in praising the wise beneficence of
God" (CDH 1, 3:220–21). Fittingness is the fourth key word. The
whole question now is: How do fittingness and necessity relate to each
other? Are they identical? Are they different?

Anselm explicitly emphasizes that these and other arguments reveal
the "ineffable beauty" of the redemption of man. In his reply, Boso
thinks that the arguments concerning fittingness are indeed beautiful
—very beautiful, in fact—but they are only pictures. Yet is all that
enough to demonstrate that the restoration is rational? Is the argument
of fittingness enough to demonstrate necessity, that God could and
had to humble himself in the Incarnation (CDH 1, 3–4:220–23)? To
modern thinking, beauty and rationality by no means belong together;
beauty is understood, rather, as a decoration, an accessory, contributing nothing to rationality. For Anselm and the medieval thinkers as a
whole, the concurrence of beauty and rationality is, on the contrary,
the best possible proof that truth prevails here.[40]

Where truth is concerned, it is not only logical deductions that are

---

[39] CDH 1, 1:211–12; 1 Pet 3:15; cf. K. Jacobi, "Begründen in der Theologie: Untersuchungen zu Anselm von Canterbury, *Philosophisches Jahrbuch der Görres-Gesellschaft* 99
(1992): 225–44, here esp. 231–34.
[40] Cf. von Balthasar, *Glory* 1:17–34.

valid; all the other dimensions must also be considered. That is why Anselm emphasizes, right at the beginning, that he is looking for a solution that will be not only generally comprehensible, but also "lovely in the beauty of its reasoning" (CDH 1, 1:212–13). For anyone praying, too, this means that he must be wholly involved with God and absorb the redemption event totally within himself: "Taste the goodness of your Redeemer, be on fire with love for your Savior. Chew the honeycomb of his words, suck their flavor, which is sweeter than honey, swallow their wholesome sweetness. Chew by thinking, suck by understanding, swallow by loving and rejoicing" (*Med.* §1).

Anselm leads his interlocutor to the point where he finally admits, "these pictures are very beautiful and reasonable" (CDH 2, 8:374–75). How do we arrive at this confession that necessity and fittingness, reason and beauty are in harmony? The tenth chapter of the book is important here, where Anselm replies to Boso's question about the argument of fittingness by showing that reason and fittingness are not mutually exclusive, not in opposition, and do not represent qualitatively differing levels of argument. With God, reason and fittingness go together; both have the same heuristic force, the same intelligibility. What is reasonable for God is likewise highly fitting; what is fitting is also highly rational. In looking for rational reasons for why God became man, it is therefore precisely a matter of ascertaining what is most appropriate to God, what is most fitting to God's being God and to his concern for salvation.[41]

THE AXIOMS OF THE INVESTIGATION

Anselm formulates three axioms, without which his entire demonstration of the rational reasons for the Incarnation cannot succeed. These axioms are presupposed, neither deduced nor "induced", and it is only within the framework of these presuppositions that the argument can demonstrate the Incarnation's inner necessity. These are presuppositions that Anselm shares with his interlocutor but also with his opponents; they mark out the common ground.

> Let it be settled between us that man is created for happiness, which cannot be attained in this life; and that no one can arrive at it without

---

[41] Cf. Roques, SC 91, pp. 80–83; Theis, "Die Vernunft innerhalb der Grenzen", pp. 179–83; Jacobi, "Begründen in der Theologie", pp. 234–38.

remission from sins; further, that no man passes through this life without sin. (CDH 1, 10:262–63)

These axioms derive from an analysis of man's situation. They offer the framework for the rational reasons and are themselves accessible to reason. Anselm prefixes this discussion with a hypothesis: "Let us therefore assume that the Incarnation of God, and what we say about that person, had never happened" (ibid.). The question to be asked, after the factual existence of Christ has been hypothetically bracketed out, is then whether it is still possible to hold by these three axioms without faith in the Redeemer. At the end of the first book, Anselm will show that the axioms can be fulfilled only in Christ. It is already apparent here, however, that the argumentation does not proceed without presuppositions; rather, it starts from a common basis that unites those taking part in the conversation. It is the very foundation that Jews, Muslims, and Christians share in common.[42] Without the previous clarification of this common basis, the conversation would be doomed to failure, and one would talk at cross-purposes.[43] The rational reasons are not, then, associated with a reason free of all presuppositions. On the other hand, the presuppositions made are not set arbitrarily, but are themselves thoroughly reasonable; they can be demonstrated with arguments, but (in this subject area, at least) we can no longer get back behind them. The fact that man is made for happiness, which in this life cannot be entirely achieved, may be demonstrated, for instance, by the transcendent nature of man. That forgiveness of sins is a prerequisite for eternal bliss is evident when a concept of immortality unconnected with any ethics whatever is adopted. That all men sin *de facto* is a reasonable assumption, provided the existence of God and man's dependence on God are admitted.

A question with respect to method arises here: Is there any point at all in trying to employ a line of reasoning about whether faith in the Incarnation makes sense without being able to presuppose these

---

[42] Cf. Jacobi, "Begründen in der Theologie", pp. 233–34, 239; Roques, SC 91, pp. 83–84.

[43] Another classic instance of this is the public appearance of Paul and Barnabas in Lystra (cf. Acts 14:7–18). Here, the common basis is so narrow that Paul only preaches God the Creator and does not speak of Christ, since that is possible only on the basis of a belief in one God. Cf. C. Schönborn, *Loving the Church: Spiritual Exercises Preached in the Presence of Pope John Paul II*, trans. John Saward (San Francisco: Ignatius Press, 1998), pp. 26–29.

or similar axioms? What this means in practice for catechetics is that preaching about Jesus without preaching about God will always be problematic.

INTERPRETATION

We are concerned with two questions, which are fundamentally one.[44] First, Anselm asks "by what necessity God became man, and why, as we believe and confess, he restored life to the world by his death" (CDH 1, 1:210–11). Could God not have effected that simply by an act of his will? Why the Incarnation of God? Why the death of Christ as redemption? Those have been essential, crucial questions for Christianity from the beginning. The scandal of God's humiliation, the scandal of the Cross, are still troublesome, and all the more troublesome since the event of the Cross is said to be God's act. Is it not a bloodthirsty God who desires his Son's death on the Cross? And yet, the New Testament kerygma speaks of the Cross of Christ as an act of God: he gave him up for us (Rom 4:25; 8:24; Acts 2:23). Here, the Incarnation is being understood on the basis of the Cross. Anselm wishes to show thereby the "ineffable beauty of our redemption, which was procured in this way" (CDH 1, 3:220–21).

Secondly, it is not a matter of coming to faith through reason but, rather, that we may "enjoy the understanding and the contemplation of what we believe", and so we may be able always to give an account of our hope. Anselm wishes to meditate on the beauty of God's plan for salvation (CDH 1, 1:210–11).

At the same time, Anselm makes an important qualification. Whatever reasons he may present for God's saving acts having happened as they did, it may be possible to discover other and more profound reasons. He does not claim to offer an exhaustive interpretation that plumbs the full depth of the mystery rationalistically.

FREEDOM AND SIN

Anselm begins his exposition of the redemption event with an analysis of the situation of sinful man before God (CDH 1, 11–24), with a

---

[44] Interpretations of CDH are found in Kienzler, *Glauben und Denken*, pp. 198–219, 345–80; Plasger, *Die Not-Wendigkeit der Gerechtigkeit*; Léthel, *Connaître l'amour du Christ*, pp. 181–203; and other, more critical interpretations in: L. Bouyer, *The Eternal Son: A Theology of the Word of God and Christology* (Our Sunday Visitor, 1978), pp. 346–48; M. Kunzler, *Porta Orientalis: Fünf Ost-West-Versuche über Theologie und Ästhetik in der Liturgie* (Paderborn, 1993), pp. 160–75.

hamartology in which he at first does not go into the Incarnation of
Christ that has actually taken place. "Every wish of a rational creature
must be subject to the will of God" (CDH 1, 11:262). Man is therefore
required to take his creatureliness seriously, what the Bible describes as
"fear of God". This concerns freedom first of all. Man is the creature
who can and should, of his own free will, accept and respond to his
origin from the Creator. That is the "uprightness of will" (*rectitudo
voluntatis*) by which we direct ourselves toward God.[45] It is thus to
God's honor that our will be subject to his will. Whoever does not
do this "takes from God what is rightly his and thus dishonors God,
and that is called 'sinning' " (ibid.). This universal order is destroyed
by sin. If men "always paid God what they owed, they would never
sin". That is why "sinning is nothing else but not paying God what
is owed him" (CDH 1, 11:262–63). But what does Anselm mean by
"what is owed" (*debitum*)? What does it mean that man owes something
to God? This is where many misunderstandings intervene. Anselm's
theory of satisfaction is often presented as though it were a matter of
appeasing God's wrath by the greatest possible sacrifice. Yet Anselm's
answer points in a quite different direction.

It is above all a matter of freedom: the freedom of God, the freedom
of Christ, and the freedom of man. Man's freedom consists in con-
ducting himself in uprightness of will and thus fitting into the divine
order. That is the *debitum* that we owe God: not just anything, but
the greatest thing we have been given by God, our freedom, our will.
Nothing else can be called honoring God but submitting our will to
him; for that corresponds to the divine order, and if we respect this,
we are honoring God. When man offends against this, then first he is
damaging himself by misusing his freedom and in this way losing it.
It will also be shown, on the other hand, that it is not unreasonable
—and thus, not inappropriate to God, not in contradiction to his love
—to understand Jesus' death as happening of his own free will and, at
the same time, as an act of obedience to the Father and, consequently,
as being the will of the Father. We will deal later with the objection
that such a way of seeing of Christ's death presupposes a cruel God.
For the moment, we may note that Anselm interprets the New Testament passages that describe Jesus' death as the will of God ("Not my
will, but thine, be done", Lk 22:42; cf. Mt 26:42) to mean that God

---

[45] Cf. Anselm of Canterbury, *De libertate arbitrii* (FChr 13:61–119).

quite simply wanted to have the reconciliation of the world take place in this way (CDH 1, 9:244–45) and, thus, the liberation that we call redemption (cf. CDH 1, 6:226–29).

SATISFACTION OR PUNISHMENT

Man has fallen from his original state through sin, and he can come to salvation only if God draws him to himself again. "And that could not occur except through forgiveness of all sins: and that occurs only by means of antecedent complete satisfaction" (*Med.*).

It has been noted, quite correctly, that the expression "God's honor" (*honor Dei*) shows the influence of courtly and knightly language and of the concepts of the feudal system. The task of interpretation is to see what is being circumscribed here by taking this knowledge into account. This concerns the honor of God, and sin is a dishonoring of God. For Anselm, sin is not (just) an individual matter. Dishonoring God is always, at the same time, dishonoring the will of God. Now, God's will is expressed in his creation. God's honor therefore extends to his works as well, to the totality of the universe. This is an ordered whole. God's honor desires and demands that the order and the beauty of the universe be respected. This ordering of the whole is supposed to guide the behavior of creatures, since it is the expression of God's will and reason. For the sake of his honor, God cannot permit the beauty of his order of creation to be damaged, even only a little. Here the theme we have already met in Athanasius appears in Anselm: God is the "shepherd" of his creation. Sin is the dishonoring of God, because it offends against the proper order.[46] In Anselm, likewise, we encounter this universalistic view, which is part of the heritage of the biblical revelation: the unity of cosmology, ontology, and ethics in a comprehensive ordering of the whole.

To dishonor God is a "theft", and anyone who does not restore what has been stolen remains in the wrong. Yet Anselm goes farther: "It is not enough merely to restore what was stolen; rather, because of the dishonor inflicted, he must give back more than he took." Some examples will illustrate that. If someone's health is impaired, then you have to pay him compensation for his suffering. Anyone whose honor has been violated must be given something that is satisfactory to him.

---

[46] See Athanasius, *De incarnatione verbi* (SC 199:384–88).

Finally, anyone who has stolen something must also give something that "could not have been demanded of him if he had not stolen what did not belong to him". That is to say, it is not enough to give something one owes in any case; it has to be something else, something special (CDH 1, 11:264–67). All that is understood by the concept "*satisfactio*". If no such satisfaction is forthcoming, however, then the only alternative is punishment. Precisely this idea offers a good starting point for modern criticism of Anselm.

The weak point in Anselm's argument seems to lie—as with Athanasius—in understanding sin as a dishonoring of God. Could not God simply forgive this? Simply overlook unrighteousness? Finally, even the Lord's Prayer requires us to forgive as God has forgiven us. Anselm counters that God's goodness cannot mean that God does something unworthy of himself. Yet it would be unworthy of him if he did something unjust or disordered. Since, however, sin is a "disorder" (*inordinatio*), it would then be unworthy of God not to punish the sinner. Anselm concludes from this that, in view of God's justice and honor, there remains only the dilemma: either satisfaction or punishment—*aut satisfactio aut poena*.

Gisbert Greshake[47] has shown, as persuasively as ever, that by listening carefully to Anselm we discover a deeper level of meaning, which leads us back to the question proved to be at the heart of the doctrine of redemption in Maximus the Confessor. It is essentially a matter of the freedom God has given man, which represents the pinnacle of the divine order. Nothing can disturb the order of creation except the misuse of human freedom, thus, sin. All other creatures are firmly tied into the laws that govern their behavior. There is no other alternative besides satisfaction or punishment for the restoration of a world disfigured by sin and falling apart.

Anselm does in fact insist that man's sin does not injure God's honor as it does that of a private individual. "It is impossible for God to lose his honor" (CDH 1, 14:276–77). God's existence as God cannot be destroyed by human sin. Therefore, God's dishonor can only mean the dishonoring of his order of creation. The need for satisfaction therefore lies entirely on man's side. "God was not obliged to redeem man in this way, but human nature needed to make satisfaction to God like

47 Greshake, "Erlösung und Freiheit", pp. 323–45.

this" (*Med.*). Anselm understands God's honor in a personal sense, and hence it is necessary to consider "how serious the sin is" (CDH 1, 21:322–23). That is why Anselm can say that God sorrows and mourns.

> Just as any man sorrows and mourns if he in any way loses what he has acquired for his needs and his advancement, so, as it were, does God sorrow and mourn too, when he sees how man, whom he created for himself, has been abducted by the devil and is to be lost to him for ever. So indeed are the damned designated lost, because they are lost to God, for whose kingdom and glorification they were created.[48]

Anselm's analysis of satisfaction starts with an analysis of interpersonal justice and reparation. That is the anthropological substratum. Adrian Schenker analyzes this situation on the basis of the Bible and with Anselm in view.[49] He shows that the principle of "satisfaction or punishment" represents a model of conflict resolution that was worked out in detail in the Old Testament. It is concerned with diminishing the use of force, with amicable agreement that should avoid any further violence. Satisfaction or "atonement" is something done as compensation, through which both parties can agree amicably and through which the injured, aggrieved party indicates his readiness to forgive, and the guilty party his readiness to ask and to accept forgiveness by an appropriate sign (the reparation). There can be only one or the other, either satisfaction or punishment, *aut satisfactio aut poena*; once satisfaction has been made, the punishment thereby becomes superfluous. Being freed from the burden of punishment goes along with the satisfaction. The social relationship has then truly been restored, and there is no need to do anything more.

It now becomes clear how close Anselm's analysis is to the biblical view. The example of compensation for suffering corresponds to the Old Testament *koper* payment, which restores the possibility of full

---

[48] From the lecture noted down by Eadmer, *De beatitudine coelestis patriae* (PL 159:601–2); as in von Balthasar, *Glory* 2:248.

[49] A. Schenker, "Honneur de Dieu et satisfaction chez saint Anselme et dans la Bible", *Sources* 11 (1985): 49–54; Schenker, "*kōper* et expiation", *Biblica* 63 (1982): 32–46. Schenker has published several studies on the meaning of reconciliation and atonement in the Old Testament, for example, *Versöhnung und Sühne: Wege gewaltfreier Konfliktlösung im Alten Testament: Mit einem Ausblick auf das Neue Testament*, BiBe, n.s., 15 (Freiburg, 1981); *Versöhnung und Widerstand: Bibeltheologische Untersuchung zum Strafen Gottes und der Menschen, besonders im Lichte von Exodus 21–22*, SBS 139 (Stuttgart, 1990); and "Das Zeichen des Blutes und die Gewißheit der Vergebung im Alten Testament", *Münchener Theologische Zeitschrift für das Gesamtgebiet der katholischen Theologie* 34 (1983): 195–213.

community. Schenker has repeatedly shown that this way of peaceful resolution of conflict by satisfaction (*koper*) replaces punishment. In this way, hatred is prevented from smoldering on because of punishment (most of all, the death penalty), and new bloodshed from coming on top of the old. There is another thing that Schenker repeatedly elaborated: that it is no alternative to say that the other person should just forgive the offender unconditionally. He shows that the act of forgiving always has to have two sides to it. It is not enough for the person who has been injured simply to forgive. This readiness to forgive is an absolute precondition for the resolution of the conflict; but the forgiveness also has to be actively accepted by gestures and signs signifying a request for forgiveness. These do not have to be enormous material actions, but they do have to involve a change of will that is made visible and that does more to ask for forgiveness than just what is "usual"; and reparation has to go beyond the damage. This is not a matter of an expensive present, but the sign does have to be such that a major reversal is visible. Only in this way can community be restored so that both parties can recover their rights and their honor. That cannot be achieved either by an unconditional forgiveness, in the sense of relinquishing what is due, nor retaliation, an act of revenge that results in new injustice.[50]

THE FREEDOM THUS REGAINED

In Anselm, satisfaction is something positive; mankind must honor God once more, in a radical way, to recognize him as Lord and freely submit to him, so that its own human freedom may once more come into its own. It is on the basis of this freedom that we must understand, as Anselm understands what is said above, that it would not be consistent with God's honor to have mercy on men without satisfaction. God does not invalidate the order of creation by his forgiveness, nor does he circumvent man's freedom. Redemption does not take place without reference to man. If God did act thus, then man would not be given back his original dignity and freedom (CDH 1, 19:310–17). Rather, redemption, if it itself is to correspond to the divine order, must "put man back in the right again, make him capable of being

---

[50] See H. Steindl, *Genugtuung: Biblisches Versöhnungsdenken—eine Quelle für Anselms Satisfaktionstheorie?* SF 71 (Freiburg, 1989).

freely responsible for redemption".[51] This concerns the "radiance of freedom".[52]

Anselm closely connects the idea of satisfaction with that of freedom. Saying that man needs to make satisfaction to God means taking him seriously as the covenant partner of God. While in Luther, and before him in Nominalism, man becomes almost a passive ball in the intradivine struggle between righteousness, in the sense of punishment, and mercy, in the sense of gratuitous absolution, Anselm quite decidedly thinks this out on the basis of the covenant. Justice, which stands in the center here, is God's covenant faithfulness to his free partner, who is respected and taken seriously in his freedom. Von Balthasar emphasizes: "To have seen the necessity of having to attain by one's own efforts the state of created freedom is one of Anselm's greatest achievements and governs his whole doctrine of freedom."[53]

Yet the final link in the chain of reasoning is still missing. If what is actually demanded is a new, total turning of human freedom toward God, so as to "heal what has been wounded", it becomes clear at the same time that such an attitude is far beyond the capacities of sinful man. The language in which Anselm expresses this should not mislead us. He speaks of the need for infinite reparation, since the injured honor is that of the infinite God. It follows from what has already been said that this does not mean a material balancing, that man would likewise never be capable of achieving. It is, rather, a matter of an infinite personal self-sacrifice, of boundless love. The satisfaction that goes beyond the injury done to God's honor must be commensurate with the divine honor itself; man has after all to achieve more, as satisfaction, than he has "stolen" through sin. Yet only God himself can "achieve" something like that. And only he can produce such freedom of change. Yet the order willed by God demands that the satisfaction, the change, be produced by a man. That is why it is necessary—and extremely appropriate—for the satisfaction to be achieved by a God-man. Man alone must but cannot make amends; God can do it, but it is not he who owes it. That is why the God-man is needed, who at the same time can and must make reparation (CDH 2, 6:362–65).

Necessity, of course, is used here in the sense of inner appropriate-

---

[51] Greshake, "Erlösung und Freiheit", p. 337; cf. von Balthasar, Glory 2:249–50.
[52] Von Balthasar, Glory 2:237.
[53] Ibid., 2:239; cf. Greshake, "Erlösung und Freiheit", p. 341.

ness, as already explained. On the basis of this idea, Anselm then develops the individual points of Christology. Why did God become man? Because only God could effect salvation, because only man was under the obligation to make reparation; that is why it was reasonable—and in that sense, necessary—that only a God-man could effect salvation. It now also becomes clear why Anselm so strongly emphasizes the fact that Jesus' death was free and willing. Only if this took place freely, in free agreement with God's will does it effect salvation (for example, CDH 2, 11:386–97). Anselm develops the whole of his Christology from this one idea, shows that the God-man has to be true God and true man and that a divine nature and a human nature must be preserved and remain in him (CDH 2, 7:364–67). Anselm lets Boso sum up:

> This debt was so great that although it had to be redeemed only by man, only God could do so, so that that man was the same as God. That is why it was necessary for God to take man into unity with his person, so that the one who by nature should have redeemed this and could not would be the person who could do so. (CDH 2, 18:438–39)

SUMMARY

For Anselm, sin means not giving to God what is owed to him—that is, not orienting one's own free will to God. The restoration of the order disturbed by sin is demanded by God's justice, which is what guarantees the divine order of the whole. Man has to effect this restoration but cannot do so on account of the weight of sin. That is why God himself became man, so that, as a man, he might give men what they need but cannot bring about: the reparation for sin. This is what Christ, the God-man, achieved by freely giving up his life, by his human will, for all men, in their place, acting on behalf of all. Such reparation is demanded by God's justice, so that his order should not be forever destroyed by sin.

At the end of *Cur Deus homo*, Anselm returns to the question of how this justice complies with the mercy of God. What seemed at times like a strictly legalistic way of thinking about justice turns out to be the highest expression of mercy.

> Yet we have found the mercy of God, which seemed to be lost to you when we were considering God's justice and man's sin, to be so great and so much in agreement with his justice that it could not be conceived as greater or more just. For what could be thought more merciful than

when God the Father says to the sinner, who has been condemned to eternal torment and has nothing by which he could free himself from it, "Take my only begotten Son and give him in your place"; and the Son says, "Take me and redeem yourself"? So they speak, more or less, when they call us and guide us to Christian faith. And what is more just than that someone is given a price that is greater than any debt should remit all debts, when this is given with appropriate love? (CDH 2, 20:454–55)

We see here quite clearly the great extent to which Anselm's doctrine of satisfaction is a doctrine of grace: God's mercy is the source of his plan of salvation. He gives us the means whereby we can reconcile ourselves with him once more. "Take me, and redeem yourself!" —both poles are being maintained, God's gracious initiative and the full play of human freedom. This is marvelously expressed in the final sentence, which represents a kind of synthesis of the whole. All the elements are summed up again here: It is just for God to remit all debts if a price is paid to him that is greater than any debt and if this price is given him with the appropriate love.

At the end of this explanation of the doctrine of satisfaction, we may say that reparation in Anselm's sense can consist only in paying the price of love, since sin, as the theft of what is due to God, is ultimately a breach of the covenant that can be healed only by the restoration of the covenant. Anselm's soteriology is really a theology of the covenant, which sets so high a price on the responsibility of human freedom because man is being taken seriously as a covenant partner.

b. Martin Luther's Theology of the Cross

Luther's doctrine of redemption represents a type that radicalizes Anselm's doctrine of satisfaction in a one-sided way that goes far beyond Anselm's intentions. It also leads directly to modern questions concerning soteriology that arose in the wake of the Reformer's teaching. That is why we are dealing with it before that of Thomas Aquinas, whose balanced synthesis comes better at the end.

PUTTING THE QUESTION

"God against God for men"—"The gracious God against the wrathful God for our benefit"—Lutheran theologians have reduced Luther's

theology of the Cross to these brief formulae.[54] Luther's view of the
effect of the event of the Cross can also be understood thus: "That
through the person and the work of Christ the change from wrath to
pardon was brought about in God himself".[55] Reconciliation is for
Luther reconciliation of the wrath of God: "Luther leaves no doubt, in
fact, that such reconciliation is necessary, in the sense of something like
a 'change of mind' in God himself that only Christ can effect."[56] The
conception of redemption is that of a "drama within God himself",
the beneficiary of which is man.

Scripture speaks of the wrath of God, of his repentance.[57] Judaism
preserved a deep sensitivity for this anthropomorphic language, but was
for the most part aware that this was speaking in parables. It is different
with Luther's understanding of the substitutional, expiatory suffering
of Christ. He interprets Jesus' death, with a full degree of harshness
and overemphasis, as meaning that God genuinely condemned Jesus,
in all seriousness, really crushed him with his wrath. Two passages are
assigned capital importance here: "For our sake [God] made him to
be sin" (2 Cor 5:21) and "Christ . . . having become a curse for us"
(Gal 3:13).

In his 1531 interpretation of the Letter to the Galatians, Luther goes
so far as to explain that Christ took upon himself not merely the consequences of sin, but the sin itself. Christ really became sin for us,
so that we might be justified. He sees Christ as being completely en-
snared in my sins and those of the world, so that in the "exchange"
man might acquire his righteousness. Indeed, Christ became a curse:
that means, quite crudely, that "he is the greatest robber, murderer,
adulterer, thief, blasphemer, and so on. There is no greater sinner than
he."[58] According to Luther, Christ's substitution means that he can

[54] Cf. Pesch, *Theologie der Rechtfertigung*, p. 126 n. 9. On the theology of the Cross, see
also H. Blaumeiser, *Martin Luthers Kreuzestheologie: Schlüssel zu seiner Deutung von Mensch
und Wirklichkeit: Eine Untersuchung anhand der Operationes in Psalmos (1519–1521)*, KKTS 60
(Paderborn, 1995) (bibliography); T. Beer, *Der fröhliche Wechsel und Streit: Grundzüge der
Theologie Martin Luthers* (Einsiedeln, 1980); C. Morerod, *Cajetan et Luther en 1518: Éd., trad.,
et commentaires des opuscules d'Augsbourg de Cajetan*, 2 vols. (Freiburg, 1994); G. Chantraine,
Érasme et Luther libre et serf arbiter: Étude historique et théologique (Paris, 1981).

[55] Cf. Pesch, *Theologie der Rechtfertigung*, pp. 132–33 n. 40.

[56] Ibid., p.127.

[57] J. Jeremias, *Die Reue Gottes*, 2nd ed., BSt 75 (Neukirchen-Vluyn, 1997).

[58] Luther, *Der große Galaterbriefkommentar* (1531/35), in WA 40/1:433.

say, "I committed the sins of all men."[59] Luther saw quite clearly that this not only broke with tradition, but also conflicted with reason; he himself called it an *absurdum*.[60] But this was supposedly precisely the foolishness of the theology of the Cross.

This was explained for Luther on the basis of the very logic of God's action; he was acting *sub contrario*. When he intends to grant grace, he shows his wrath; when he intends to set someone upright, he bows him down. In Christ's suffering on the Cross, this way of acting *sub contrario* reaches its culmination; that is why we have to read off from that how God is actually acting. Thereby Christ learns to recognize God's mercy in his trials, which works *sub contrario*. That is how Luther understands the exchange of substitution: our sin becomes Christ's sin, and his righteousness our righteousness.

At this point we must particularly examine Luther's dialectic, which is deeply rooted in his own experience, that in the time of deepest damnation, being completely turned away from God can at the same moment become a turning to God: *aversio* turns into *conversio*. Yet in justification, man remains a sinner; he remains turned away from God and lives at the same time (*simul*) turned toward God. He is *simul iustus et peccator*—at the same time righteous and a sinner. The same thing happens within Christ, in whom the greatest, the most extreme and complete sin exists together with the greatest, the supreme and complete righteousness.[61] How is it possible for two extreme opposites to come together in this one person? That is for Luther the "true logic", the coincidence of opposites.[62]

Let us start our debate with Luther's doctrine of redemption by cautiously asking whether he can rightly base himself on the Second Letter to the Corinthians (2 Cor 5:21) and the Letter to the Galatians (Gal 3:13) in order to say quite literally that Christ became sin, became a curse. The expression in the Letter to the Galatians, "become

---

[59] Ibid., pp. 442–43.

[60] Ibid., p. 434.

[61] Ibid., p. 439.

[62] Ibid., pp. 438–40; see, in agreement, K. Barth, KD 4/1:261–63; critical of this view, H. R. Schmitz, "Progrès social et changement révolutionnaire: Dialectique et révolution", *Revue Thomiste* 74 (1974): 391–451, here pp. 402–17; in the history of dogma, R. Weier and B. A. Willems, *Soteriologie: Von der Reformation bis zur Gegenwart*, HDG 3/2c (Freiburg im Breisgau, 1972), pp. 4–12; also, E. de Negri, *Offenbarung und Dialektik: Luthers Realtheologie* (Darmstadt, 1973), esp. pp. 218–23.

a curse for us" (Gal 3:13b), has a polemical context. Jewish-Christian enthusiasts were asserting that the law was a source of justification (cf. Gal 2:16; 3:2). Paul replied to them that it was the souce only of a curse, a curse from which only Christ, and not the law, can free "us" (the Jews are meant here). So as to emphasize that more sharply, Paul shows that the law affected Christ himself—for in the Book of Deuteronomy (Deut 21:23), it says "Cursed be every one who hangs on a tree" (Gal 3:13). Here Paul is probably referring to the scandal of Jesus' death, which Jews found particularly intolerable. In order to redeem us, Christ endured being condemned as a blasphemer, cursed by God's law in the eyes of Jews and of all the world. Yet Paul hardly wishes to say here that God himself cursed him—God himself wished to reconcile the world to himself through him (2 Cor 5:19). That is probably why Paul omits the words, "accursed *by God*" from the quotation from Deuteronomy, so as not to give this impression.

At this point, Paul says something that will return later: "born of a woman, born under the law" (Gal 4:4)—that Christ accepted our *conditio*, our humanity that is under the law of sin, in order to reconcile it with God in an act of perfect obedience and love. And that is how the greater part of the tradition has understood it. In the Second Letter to the Corinthians (2 Cor 5:21), Paul does not say, "God made him to be *a sinner* . . . so that in him we might become the righteousness of God." That would contradict what has just been noted: "him . . . who knew no sin". What is written, rather, is "He made him to be sin . . . so that we might become the righteousness of God". Two abstract entities are thus named here, sin and righteousness. In Paul, they are not qualities that might be ascribed to someone by a judgment about identity—neither Christ nor we are simply identical with sin. Three interpretations present themselves. First, that "For our sake God made him to be sin" means that God made him solidly united with our sinful condition, so that we might be solidly united with his condition of righteousness. He really made him one of us, but in doing so he opened up for us fellowship with him. Second, that God made him a sacrifice for sin for us (cf. 2 Cor 5:21), a *hattat*, in the double sense of that term, both sin and sacrifice for sin. According to the Book of Leviticus (Lev 6:22), the flesh of the sacrifice is eaten by the priests as something holy; yet the possibility of the sacrifice itself becoming sin is thereby excluded; rather, the sacrifice removes sin.[63] A sacrifice for sin therefore means, most nearly, a sacrifice of *expiation*. The third explanation is Luther's, according to which Jesus himself is said to have been *summus peccator et summus iustus*.

THE UNDERSTANDING OF SIN

What does it mean for Luther, in detail, that for our sake, Christ became sin and a curse? To understand how the Reformer arrived at this radical way of seeing it, which is determinative for his anthropology, Christology, and doctrine of redemption, we have to go back a bit. Luther stands particularly in the Augustinian tradition. His basic views are influenced by Augustine, but he also decisively reshaped them. Like Augustine, Luther interprets "Christ became sin and a curse" as applying to the Incarnation, to the acceptance of becoming man and of the sinful human condition. He does of course define differently from Augustine what this condition looks like.

The Augustinian monk Martin Luther takes from Augustine the distinction between *uti* and *frui*, using and enjoying. "Enjoying" (*frui*) means "adhering to something for its own sake in love", something that in the last analysis can be true only of the triune God.[64] "Using" (*uti*), on the other hand, refers to the correct attitude of man toward those things which of their nature relate to others, thus, all created things.[65] "Everything created has been created for the use of man, who makes use of it in accordance with the judgment of the reason that has been given him."[66] There is no fundamental conflict between *uti* and *frui*, between eternal and temporal life.

Where does evil come from, then? The order of things, of the world, shows man what "value" can be attributed to each thing and how he should use it. Man becomes evil when he deliberately gives up something higher and turns to something lower; not because what he is turning to is evil, but because the act of turning as such is perverse.[67] The more, therefore, that things are improperly enjoyed, over and beyond their proper use—that is to say, raised to the status of an ultimate

[63] S. Lyonnet and L. Sabourin, *Sin, Redemption and Sacrifice: A Biblical and Patristic Study*, AnBib 48 (Rome, 1970), pp. 251–53.

[64] Augustine, *De diversis quaestionibus* 83, q. 30 (CChr.SL 44A:38).

[65] Cf. Augustine, *De doctrina christiana* 1, 4 (CChr.SL 32:8).

[66] Augustine, *De diversis quaestionibus* 83, q. 30 (CChr.SL 44A:40).

[67] Augustine, *De civitate Dei* 12, 6 (CChr.SL 48:359–62).

goal—the less man is oriented toward the *frui Deo* and misses his goal, he sins.

Now, is this turnaround so radical that everything is perverted, or is it merely a deviation that can be corrected? This is clarified in Augustine's distinction between sin *in abdito* and *in aperto*, between hidden sin and outward sin. The hidden sin precedes the outward ("categorial") sin here. This inner sin is like another nature, another law, imposed on man, one of flesh, not of spirit; and if there were only it, then man would be hopelessly damned. Along with the whole tradition, however, Augustine sees that this hidden sin is not everything. Man is not totally fallen. He is less than he was, yet in his Fall he remains in some sense stuck at an intermediate stage. This, however, is the ability to "discern between the good that he has lost and the evil into which he has fallen".[68] The distinction between good and evil thus rescues a spark of the righteousness and proper orientation, and this is seen in the capacity to distinguish between *frui* and *uti*.

There is thus the possibility of a third course, between radical agreement between God's will and man's in Paradise, on the one hand, and their radical alienation in the *massa damnata*, on the other. There are particular commandments, limited commandments, and a limited transgression, which is not totally evil. "And yet transgressing a particular and limited commandment means neither mistaking the thing for God nor putting oneself in the place of God."[69] There are degrees of good and evil, then, a positive ordering. Even in his later, more radical anti-Pelagian phase, Augustine recognizes the possibility of distinguishing between lesser and more serious sins, positive ethics and positive casuistry.

The radical break in Luther is that he wants to eradicate completely this third possibility. The very fact that man thinks himself capable of relative good, distinguishes between mortal and venial sins, is precisely the deception of the man who wants to assure himself; it is the devil's trick, it is original sin. Luther reduces sin to the model of sin *in abdito* alone. At the same time, every *usus* is sinful, because in man's secret heart he is hiding the fact that he is aiming solely at replacing the *frui* of God with the *frui* of himself.

---

[68] Ibid., 14, 17 (CChr.SL 48:440).
[69] De Negri, *Offenbarung und Dialektik*, p. 12.

In his preface to the Letter to the Romans of 1515/1516, Luther had
already radically contrasted nature and grace: grace sees only God and
"leaps over (*transit*) everything that it sees between itself and God".[70]
That is the "bracketing out of the world", of everything created, a
radical either-or; it is the radicalization of the Augustinian conflict between self-love and love of God. Because Luther disconnects hidden
sin, the practical commandments, and their fulfillment, then everything
without distinction, the entire order of creation, every *usus* of creation,
is fundamentally (and equally) a grave sin. "However small the transgression may appear to be externally, however unimportant its content
and however insignificant the rule that has been broken, sin becomes
an identical, absolute action."[71]

This view means that rational ethics has basically become impossible. The idea that precisely the proper use of created things represents
a preliminary stage in the enjoyment of God, that proper joy in this
is already a reflection of blessedness, is rejected by Luther; just as he
rejects the notion that there are various degrees in the wrong use of
things—that our enjoyment of God is indeed clouded but not necessarily abolished by this.

This is shown concretely, for instance, in the concept of politics. If
the world is excluded from the confrontation between God's will and
human aversion, between grace and nature, then it is left to its own
devices. A casuistry concerning the just and unjust power is not applicable, and all authority then belongs to the things instituted by God.
Positive law, in the sense of a balanced system of norms, is rejected, and
the ruler is absolute vis-à-vis subordinates, without any intermediate
element such as law or custom. The structure that becomes apparent
here is always the same: it involves the omission of any created intermediary, in favor of a dialectic in which no third member is possible.

It is similar in the realm of individual ethics. A certain usefulness is
not, indeed, denied to good works; but they have nothing to do with
salvation; with regard to eternal life, they are excluded, for good works
are merely the wall that man erects around his own self-satisfaction and
against God.

This is still more dramatic in the view taken of Old Testament law.
What was God's intention in giving the law? God does prescribe cer-

---

[70] Luther, *Vorlesung über den Römerbrief* (1515–1516) (ed. Ficker 2:185).
[71] De Negri, *Offenbarung und Dialektik*, p. 14; cf. Pesch, *Theologie der Rechtfertigung*, p. 542.

tain works, but he has a different intention: not that man should carry them out, but that he should tremble before the law's dungeon:

> For this dungeon, this prison, signifies right and spiritual terror, by which the conscience is so confined that it can find no place in the whole, wide world where it feels safe. Indeed, so long as these terrors (*pavores*) persist, the conscience feels such great anxiety (*anxietas*) that it believes heaven and earth, were they ten times their size, are more confined (*angustiora*) than a mousehole.[72]

This trial increases to the point of hating God:

> Thereby he necessarily ends up by hating God and blaspheming. Before, without this trial, he was a great saint, served and loved God, bowed his knee and thanked him like the Pharisee (Lk 18:11). Now, however, when sin and death have been revealed, he wishes there were no God. Thus, the law gives rise to the keenest hatred of God.[73]

Christ took this trial upon himself, when, set under the law, he became for us sin and a curse.

CHRIST'S REDEEMING ACT

If Luther interprets the passages from the Letter to the Galatians and the Second Letter to the Corinthians (Gal 3:13; 2 Cor 5:21) in a radically literal sense, that springs from his own preconception. Fundamentally, Christ really did become sin and a curse in his Incarnation itself. Being human does in fact mean, de facto, existing as sin and as a curse. "The whole of man is 'flesh' for him, that is, far from God"; "*totus homo caro*" means "man, who is wholly and entirely and irremediably turned away from God, against God, by sin".[74] But for Luther that means that God himself revokes his communion with man. Indeed, according to Luther, the creature's hostility to God is in fact the result of this wrath of God. Hence, the Incarnation means primarily "joining the ranks of the sinners", and that in turn means joining sinners in their distance from God. Incarnation as such means joining the side of those with whom God has broken off relations. That is how Luther understands the Pauline "standing under the curse of the law"; Christ becomes

---

[72] WA 40/1:521; cf. De Negri, *Offenbarung und Dialektik*, p. 39.
[73] WA 40/1:487; cf. De Negri, *Offenbarung und Dialektik*, pp. 40–41.
[74] Pesch, *Theologie der Rechtfertigung*, pp. 542–43.

what we are: cursed by God.[75] "Luther explains explicitly and with provocative harshness that *everything* done by the man who is alienated from God, particularly when he is doing as much as lies in his power, is mortal sin."[76] For Luther, Christ's work makes sense only if he has taken upon himself the human condition, that is, if he himself has become "the greatest of sinners". "Our sins have to become Christ's own sins, or we perish for eternity."[77]

Yet if Christ himself becomes sin and a sinner, does this help man toward his liberation from sin? How does it help man if Christ is abandoned by God, distant from God? If, indeed, God turns from Christ, rejects him, makes him a curse? Do we not remain in our sin if Christ himself becomes a sinner? This is the point at which Luther's doctrine of justification, despite any possible convergence, differs almost insuperably from tradition. For Luther, man remains a sinner even after Christ's death, even after justification. Justification is not a state, but a legal procedure, a matter of "being constantly pronounced justified".[78] Man remains *simul iustus et peccator*. Has Christ's representative suffering and death still conquered sin and death, then, once and for all? According to Luther, justification does not consist in sin's having been eliminated once and for all, but in the fact that God, for the sake of Christ's death, no longer imputes it. Righteousness is ascribed to man, awarded to him, but it does not become "inherent" in him, does not become his attribute; it remains alien to him, external, and lies entirely on God's side. Since sin remains within man, righteousness consists merely in the constant divine action of forgiveness and of not imputing his sins.[79]

That is why, despite all the necessary refinements of understanding and real common ground, the distinction between efficient and juridical justification still remains characteristic of the difference between Lutheranism and Catholicism. Certainly, according to Luther man, after accepting grace, is at the same time both justified and a sinner. But

---

[75] Ibid., pp. 125–28. Passages in which Luther's concept of opposition is taken to extremes, such as for instance in the 1530 interpretation of Psalm 118 (117) (WA 31/1:249) must be omitted here. See on this, for example, Pesch, *Theologie der Rechtfertigung*, pp. 222–23, and H. Blaumeiser, *Martin Luthers Kreuzestheologie*.

[76] Pesch, *Theologie der Rechtfertigung*, p. 542.

[77] WA 40/1:435.

[78] Pesch, *Theologie der Rechtfertigung*, pp. 546, 212, 219.

[79] Ibid., p. 323.

the way this phrase "at the same time" is understood can scarcely be accepted on the Catholic side, because what is being rejected here is that justification is effectively a new creation of man.[80] Luther energetically rejects the idea that grace is a *qualitas animae*; it is not a reality of and in redeemed man, as it was seen by tradition before Luther. Man certainly does have "real peace of heart" (*vere pacem cordis*); but not because grace gives him a new quality of life, but because he "is sure that he has a gracious God" (*propitium deum habere se sentiat*).[81]

This understanding has far-reaching consequences.[82] Everything is set on God's side, nothing on man's. "Justification is a reality solely on God's side, that is, as God's turning toward man in forgiveness, for the sake of Christ."[83] That means however, in the final analysis, that justification is not an event by which sinners become righteous, in which man is the reality that has changed, but is ultimately a reversal within God. On the basis of an incomprehensible, never justifiable decision, God changes his decision about man. In place of the wrath man deserves, God deigns to turn and justify him. The soteriological perspective that we previously found in Paul's writings, however, is thereby altered. "It is God from whom we first learn that we have to appear before him, as it were, with security (experience of the law!). God himself provides the possibility for this in Christ. Man realizes this possibility by walking at the side of Christ. That is called believing. Together with Christ, he can face God with confidence."[84]

Luther's aim is repeatedly to note that God alone is at work. He rejects the idea of man's substantial cooperation with God and, hence, also—and above all—the idea of any possible merit on man's part.[85] Thus, the whole of the redemption event remains an event that happens on God's side, and Christ's saving act concerns God in the first place. "In his work of salvation, Christ is therefore acting first of all

---

[80] H. U. von Balthasar, *The Theology of Karl Barth: Exposition and Interpretation*, trans. Edward T. Oakes, S.J. (San Francisco: Ignatius Press, 1992), pp. 369–78, makes careful distinctions on the question of *simul iustus et peccator*. See further, Pesch: "We cannot argue away the forensic character of justification", *Theologie der Rechtfertigung*, p. 161 n. 8; pp. 182, 188, 323.

[81] Luther, *Rationis Latonisanae confutatio* (1531) (WA 8:106).

[82] These consequences take effect on the sacramental and legal plane. Cf. A. Rouco Varela and E. Corecco, *Sakrament und Recht—Antinomie in der Kirche?* ed. L. Gerosa and L. Müller, Kirchenrecht im Dialog 1 (Paderborn, 1998), pp. 11–24 and 57–62.

[83] Pesch, *Theologie der Rechtfertigung*, p. 317.

[84] Ibid., p. 549.

[85] Ibid., pp. 317–22.

toward God, and only on the strength of this and under this heading does he act toward man. Moreover, *in* Christ *God* is acting *with himself* —and only in consequence of this action with himself does he act graciously toward man."[86] Thus, a Lutheran commentator could write about Galatians 3:13: "God takes man's opposition to him into himself and allows it to spend itself there."[87] Luther himself describes the redemption as a drama within God: "The curse of God's wrath on the world battles with the blessing of grace and the eternal mercy of God in Christ. The curse wishes to condemn it and bring it to naught, but it cannot do so. The blessing is divine and everlasting, and therefore the curse must give way. If the blessing in Christ could be overcome, then God himself would also be overcome, but this is impossible."[88] God overcomes God, "God against God for us men, the gracious God against the wrathful God for our benefit".[89]

In any case, we cannot speak of a change in the strict sense here; rather, we would have to speak of a dialectic process resembling the process of *simul iustus et peccator*. Having been pronounced righteous, man remains, even in a state of justification, a sinner, and, indeed, in the radical sense of being distant from God. Yet in that he accepts in faith (*sola fide*) that God is gracious toward him, he lives in a "constant *transitus* from sin to grace".[90] Justification is not a state of being but one of continuous becoming; one that does not at some time or other cross over into being, but forever remains this "becoming".[91] Yet it is just the same and is fundamental within God; for since man remains a sinner, God's wrath remains also, but in such a way that this wrath is in *transitus* to grace. God is involved in a judicial process with himself —or, as Eberhard Jüngel says, quite consistently with Luther, "God's being is in becoming."[92]

---

[86] Ibid., p. 126.

[87] H. Asmussen, *Theologisch-kirchliche Erwägungen zum Galaterbrief,* 3rd ed. (1937); ref. Gal 3:13, cited in F. Mussner, *Der Galaterbrief,* 5th ed., HThK 9 (Freiburg im Breisgau, 1988), p. 234 n. 113.

[88] WA 40/1:440. Martin Luther, *Galatians,* Crossway Classic Commentaries (Wheaton, Ill.: Crossway, 1998), p. 154.

[89] See above, in this chapter, n. 54.

[90] Pesch, *Theologie der Rechtfertigung,* p. 120 n. 49.

[91] Cf. de Negri, *Offenbarung und Dialektik,* pp. 215–27; Schmitz, "Progrès social et changement révolutionnaire", p. 418.

[92] E. Jüngel, *Gottes Sein ist im Werden: Verantwortliche Rede vom Sein Gottes bei Karl Barth: Eine Paraphrase,* 3rd ed. (Tübingen, 1976).

It still remains to be asked, however, how this picture of what ultimately should probably be called an eternal inner dialectic within God, not to say tragedy within God, agrees with the picture of God in the New Testament. How can this view of a God who overcomes himself, whose grace prevails over his wrath, be reconciled with that in the parable of the prodigal son? The merciful father does not turn away fom his son; on the contrary, he awaits him with unchanged, unchangeable, eternal love—he is watching for him. He does not need to overcome any wrath in order to fold him in his arms; he needs, rather, to soothe the anger of the other son, the brother of the prodigal, who is just as dear and beloved to him.

Luther is formidable in matters of sin, trial, and struggle. Yet does not the redemption get too little attention from him as an act of love? He certainly did not deny this aspect, and the last thing he said was that God is "sheer grace and love",[93] that "ibi" was "nothing but the baker's oven of dilectionis".[94] "Si deus pingendus, if I were to paint, quod in the depths of his divine nature nihil aliud est quam a fire and heat, quae dicitur love for people. Econtra love est talis res, ut non humana, angelica, sed divine, indeed God himself."[95] God is love: love is God. Yet it is equally a fact for Luther that God reveals himself in hiddenness, *sub contrario*, in wrath. What is terrible remains the opposition of love and wrath behind which God is hidden and remains unpredictable, in that he chooses and blesses some people gratuitously, while others he does not choose and makes unrepentant,[96] so that, at least in *De servo arbitrio*, behind God's revealed will for all men's salvation is said to lie a hidden, unrevealed will, according to which not all men are predestined for good. At this point, Luther's own experience became decisive for his theology. Pesch rightly points out that in Luther, "the unselfconsciousness and naturalness of a loving relationship [with God] develop only slowly: gratitude, joy, peace, even love for *Christ* (who 'safeguards' men 'against God') loom large in the foreground of the religious process with Luther; the *love of God* recedes before them".[97]

The Lutheran doctrine of justification certainly has to be taken seriously as the expression of a genuine experience, an experience of

---

[93] Pesch, *Theologie der Rechtfertigung*, pp. 394–96.
[94] Sermon on 1 John 4:16 (WA 36:425).
[95] Ibid. (WA 36:424).
[96] Pesch, *Theologie der Rechtfertigung*, p. 223 n. 140.
[97] Ibid., p. 549.

faith filled with inner drama. Here, however, we come up against that boundary we mentioned at the start. Here the necessarily tripartite structure of Christian faith is reduced to a bipartite one, reduced to Scripture and experience.[98] As soon as one's own experience can no longer be questioned, criticized, and verified on the basis of a more comprehensive context of understanding and interpretation, however, it is at the mercy of all the ambivalence of mere experience. Yves Congar once observed that Luther's mistake was probably that he felt strong enough, on the basis of his experience alone, to judge, and even to some extent to disregard, 1500 years of Christian tradition. Whether one's own experience offers sufficient certainty for such an undertaking, moreover, remains questionable.

No one will deny the religious genius of Luther; his work acted as a catalyst, and a whole new tradition arose from it. Yet one may and must ask whether a particular experience has not been made into an absolute here, one that does not cover what the shared tradition of experience in the Church saw in the mystery of the Cross. Experience certainly is a quite essential theological *locus* in Christology, but not primarily and solely as the experience of a single person, but, rather, as that of the great and exemplary disciples, the saints. In the dispute over the question of indulgences, Luther more and more clearly rejected the traditional idea of the merits of the saints. Along with that, however, the invocation of the saints is inevitably also omitted,[99] which in 1519 he was still recommending but which he rejected from 1528 onward.[100] Yet thereby an important *locus* for christological verification is cancelled. In the history of the Church's christological confession of faith, the experience of the saints plays at least as great a role as dogmatic declarations of doctrine. The unity of confession and experience can be concretely grasped in Francis the poor man, in Thérèse of Lisieux,[101] in the Curé of Ars, and in *Restituta Kafka*. An important dimension was lost in the Reformation here.

Where does this view of the Cross as "penal satisfaction" come from? Anselm of Canterbury developed the idea of satisfaction. Sin has confused the order of God's works and has thereby injured God's honor. God's justice leaves only two possibilities open: *aut satisfactio*

---

[98] See above, introduction, chap. 1:2, "The Pillars Give Way".
[99] M. Lienhard, *Martin Luthers christologisches Zeugnis: Entwicklung und Grundzüge seiner Christologie* (Berlin, 1980), pp. 70, 87–88.
[100] Luther, *Vom Abendmahl Christi* (WA 26:508, no. 13).
[101] See below, the epilogue: "Jesus Is My Only Love".

aut poena—either the order that has been destroyed is repaired, or the just punishment ensues. Since, however, Christ has made reparation for sins and for the disorder they have brought about, the punishment no longer applies. Hence, for Anselm, Jesus' death is certainly not God's punishment; rather, Jesus' obedience is putting right what sin destroyed. Here Anselm is following a genuinely Pauline line of thought. Jesus' obedience is the *satisfactio* for the disobedience of sin and by that very fact renders the punishment superfluous.

In Luther, the *aut* satisfactio *aut* poena becomes an *et*—*et*, both reparation and punishment. Punishment is coming in any case, and it is only a question of who suffers it. A profound change in the image of God has taken place here. The reparation no longer avoids the punishment; rather, it means that Jesus takes the punishment upon himself. Today one will also approach this view, which is deeply disturbing, using psychological criteria.[102] In Luther, the wrath of God is to a certain extent a primary datum, and the question is how a way can lead from the justice of God—which always inflicts punishment—to his mercy. God's justice is always God's justice inflicting punishment, because man is always and necessarily a sinner.

For Luther, the doctrine of justification signifies the decisive point at which membership in the Church is determined. There are in fact, as we have seen, genuine differences on this question between the Evangelical-Lutheran conception and that of Roman Catholics. There is also, however, a shared foundation and a central concern in which there are convergences. It was in awareness of this, and after decades of dialogues, that on October 31, 1999, in Augsburg, the *Joint Declaration on the Doctrine of Justification* was signed. Although even after such a declaration unity has still not been realized and many questions remain open, nevertheless it means a great step forward on the way to healing old wounds and hope of full communion in faith.[103]

---

[102] See on this point the classic psychological studies of Luther by R. Dalbiez, *L'Angoisse de Luther* (Paris, 1974); E. Erikson, *Der junge Mann Luther: Eine psychoanalytische und historische Studie* (Frankfurt am Main, 1975).

[103] Text of the declaration: *Die gemeinsame Erklärung zur Rechtfertigungslehre: Alle offiziellen Dokumente von Lutherischem Weltbund und Vatikan*, text from VELKD 87 (Hanover, 1999). On the discussion of it, see, for instance, W. Pannenberg, "Gemeinsame Erklärung zur Rechtfertigungslehre", *Stimmen der Zeit* 217 (1999): 723–26; E. Jüngel, "Kardinale Probleme", *Stimmen der Zeit* 217 (1999): 727–35; W. Kasper, "Meilenstein auf dem Weg der Ökumene", *Stimmen der Zeit* 217 (1999): 736–39; K. Lehmann, "Was für ein Konsens wurde erreicht?" *Stimmen der Zeit* 217 (1999): 740–45.

THE AFTERMATH OF "PENAL SATISFACTION"

How great an effect Luther continued to have is shown in the further development in modern times. There are few interpretations of the death of Jesus that are so charged as talk about satisfaction, understood as punishment. A brief excursus about the difficulties associated with this concept is therefore appropriate.

The Reformers further developed the juridical view of righteousness they had inherited from the Middle Ages and laid substantially more emphasis upon it. Penal satisfaction took the place of representative satisfaction. Jesus' death was repeatedly understood as being demanded by God's punitive justice. Christ made reparation for all sins by his blood, by pacifying the wrath of God through his blood. Thus, Calvin notes in his *Institutio Religionis Christianae*:

> This was not achieved by Christ merely suffering bodily death; no, he had truly to feel the whole harshness of the divine judgment in order to turn away his wrath and to give satisfaction for his just sentence. . . . He not only gave his body as a ransom, but offered a greater and more costly sacrifice for us in that he endured in his soul the fearful torments of a damned and doomed man.[104]

The image of a wrathful father is dominant here, a God of judgment whose holy anger weighs upon us in terrifying fashion. This idea is intensified by the widespread notion that only a sinless offering can appease the judgment of God.

This view of penal satisfaction also found its way into Catholic theology, especially into books of sermons and devotional literature. There it is depicted how Christ drew down upon himself the whole force of the divine anger. Thus, his mortal agony is portrayed as being also fear before the divine judgment: "He is afraid in the face of the wrath of this justifiably angry judge, whose anger is now aflame to the point of fury; he is afraid in the face of the divine curse"—thus says a famous Catholic preacher of the nineteenth century;[105] in doing so, he refers, as Luther, Calvin, and many since them have done, to 2 Corinthians 5:21, "God made him to be sin", and to Galatians 3:13, God made him "become a curse for us". We could add as many examples as we liked from the literature of popular piety, hymns, and catechisms.[106]

---

[104] J. Calvin, *Institutio Religionis Christianae* 2, 16, 10.

[105] C. L. Gay, *Sermons de Carême*, 5th ed., vol. 2 (Tours, 1929), p. 217.

[106] See, for example, for the French region, P. Grelot, *Péché originel et rédemption* (Paris, 1973), pp. 205–18.

Even the catechism of the Council of Trent, although the Council itself did not advance the doctrine of penal satisfaction, says that the suffering of Christ "was a most pleasing sacrifice to God, which, because his Son was offered upon the altar of the Cross, completely appeased the Father's wrath and disfavor".[107] The catechism refers here to Ephesians 5:2, "Christ loved us and gave himself up for us, a fragrant offering and sacrifice to God." A different and far more comprehensive picture, by contrast, is offered by the serene synthesis of Saint Thomas Aquinas.

c. The Synthesis of Thomas Aquinas

Compared to Anselm's ascetic strictness, Saint Thomas' doctrine of redemption, in its colorful variety, seems almost baroque. Anselm has with great concentration structured everything around the central notion of satisfaction. Thomas, however, goes far back and draws on the whole variety of New Testament images of salvation. One concept cannot suffice, since all concepts are more pointers and images than exhaustive definitions.[108] First of all, therefore, the variety of themes should be presented in order then to reach the question of what the center is around which these themes can be ordered. For this, we shall present two great passages, in particular, from the *Summa Theologica:* first, from the third part, article 2 of the first question; and second, from the same part, the forty-eighth question, which takes up Anselm's *Cur Deus homo.* The two texts are complementary, the first relating to the Incarnation, and the second to the Passion. Both events are examined with a view to their significance for salvation. They show that the Incarnation and the redemption belong inextricably together. In a third section, finally, we shall examine a central theme of Thomas' soteriology, the idea of the merit of Christ.

Here, too, the presupposition of soteriology is the knowledge of sin. Man's every action has a significance for his whole life: it is either meritorious or reprehensible (STh I-II, 21, 3, 4). If man falls into sin, he veers away from the image of God in him and turns away from God. Thomas explains sin as being a break in man's relationship to God for which man alone has to answer. God never abandons man, yet the relationship also depends on man. "God never turns away from anyone any farther than that person has himself turned away from him"

---

[107] *Catechismus ex Decreto Concilii Tridentini*, pt. 1, 5th main section, §15.
[108] See on this von Balthasar, TD 4:263.

(STh II-II, 24, 10). This situation is nonetheless ominous for man, since when this orientation to God is absent, then the divine order is no longer effective for him. What that means for man is that the real goal of his life, eternal life and the beatific vision of God, is no longer attainable for him.[109]

WAS THE INCARNATION NECESSARY (STH III, Q. 1, A. 2)?

Thomas raises the same question as Anselm: Why did God become man? "Was the Incarnation of the Word of God necessary for the restoration of the human race?"[110] The whole article starts from the goodness of God, which is shown in the redemption of man. Through sin, man has fallen prey to death. If, however, it is part of God's order that man should attain to eternal life, then God has to intervene here to heal and save.[111]

First, Thomas formulates three objections. In the first place, God would have been able to bring human nature back in line even without the Incarnation. The Incarnation adds nothing to God's power in this regard. God is of himself in a position to accomplish this work; he has no need to become someone else first or to acquire new capabilities by becoming man—in addition to his being God. The Word of God could "gain no increase of power by assuming flesh" (*obi.* 1). Secondly, God cannot require any more from man than is possible. Hence, this human work of restoration would also have been possible for a man (*obi.* 2). Third, and finally, the Incarnation is unworthy of God. If God condescends to man, then what remains of his honor? Will a man still show him reverence? God does not, therefore, behave in correspondence to his divinity if he becomes man (*obi.* 3). In opposition to that, there is Holy Scripture, which unambiguously testifies that God gave up his Son for men (Jn 3:16), for our salvation (*sed contra*).

Thomas begins his reply with a clarification of concepts. There are two ways of speaking about necessity. In one instance, we mean an unconditional prerequisite for something to exist at all, thus an absolute necessity. In the other, something may be necessary in order to follow the most suitable and beneficial way to achieve something. The Incar-

---

[109] R. Cessario, *Christian Satisfaction in Aquinas: Towards a Personalist Understanding* (Washington, 1980), pp. 143–45.

[110] Thomas Aquinas, STh III, q. 1, a. 2 (DThA 25:8–14). The following quotations in parentheses were taken from this.

[111] Cessario, *Christian Satisfaction in Aquinas*, p. 158.

nation is not necessary according to the first conception, but it is, on the other hand, for the second. Many ways would have been possible for the redemption of man, but the one chosen is "better and more suitable" (*melius et convenientius*) than the others (*resp.*). In this connection, the reasons of appropriateness acquire a particular significance for Thomas, because they constitute the difference between theology and the other sciences. "He knew very well that theology is not a science of the necessary, in the way that Aristotle conceived it, but an organization of contingent data received from revelation, upon which the theologian labors to find the arrangement of God's design."[112] The way that God has shown us, then, is also the best way that the redemption could have taken place.

In what follows, Thomas explains, with two sets of five reasons of fittingness, why the path of Incarnation is the more appropriate. He begins, quite rightly, with the good, since we can "perceive first of all" the motives for the Incarnation in "how man is furthered in good" (*resp.*). In soteriology, this motive of *promotio in bono* is too often forgotten: reparation for evil is not the primary aim of the divine plan of salvation; rather, good should take the first place. The five reasons Thomas cites for the attainment of good constitute a "homage" to Augustine. First there are the three theological virtues, faith, hope, and love; they link us directly to God. The certitude we acquire through faith is strengthened, for faith is based on the Incarnation. Christ is the reason for faith. The love of God, on account of which the Incarnation happens, strengthens hope and enkindles love. The three virtues lead, fourthly, to right action, in which Christ, the incarnate Word, has given us an example and has become the standard for our ethics. Finally, the Incarnation serves the ultimate goal of man, that of full communion with God, of "full participation in the Divinity" (*resp.*), of divinization, which constitutes bliss for man.

"So also the Incarnation contributes toward breaking the power of evil" (*resp.*). Because the path toward good is barred to man by the power of sin, withdrawal from evil (*remotio mali*) is needed. For this, too, Thomas cites five reasons. First, man should not despise himself on account of his corporality. Second, the Incarnation brings man's

---

[112] J.-P. Torrell, *Saint Thomas Aquinas*, vol. 1: *The Person and His Work*, trans. Robert Royal, rev. ed. (Washington, D.C.: Catholic Univ. of America Press, 2005), p. 156; cf. G. Narcisse, *Les Raisons de Dieu: Argument de convenance et esthétique théologique selon saint Thomas d'Aquin et Hans Urs von Balthasar*, SF, n.s., 83 (Freiburg, 1997).

personal dignity before his eyes. That is to be understood purely as a promise in faith, yet at the same time it has eminently practical consequences. Anyone who is aware of his dignity is at the same time less vulnerable. At the same time, thirdly, the character of grace is emphasized. Grace is allotted us without our having merited it, and any presumption is totally inappropriate. Fourthly, human arrogance, which leads to sin, is thereby cured, and humility is encouraged. Only as the fifth and final motive does Thomas mention satisfaction, which is properly requisite for the restoration of the divine order.

If we consider the ten arguments and their order, we see how Thomas understands the redemption in its theological context. As a manifestation of God's goodness, the Incarnation finds its central reason in the mystery of the love of God for fallen man. The God-man, as an example of sinless living, lifts up fallen man to communion with God, so as to open to him the path to his final meeting with God.

It is worth noting that Thomas does not name Anselm or explicitly quote him. There are of course echoes, as for instance when Thomas notes that man could not make satisfaction for himself, yet God did not have to do it. On the whole, Thomas goes back beyond Anselm and chooses Augustine as his authority for nine of the ten arguments. By doing this, he can further develop the ideas that Anselm advanced. Two changes he makes here are significant. First, Anselm starts from man's righteousness, which he has lost through sin and which only God can restore, by freeing man from the snares of the devil, by ransoming him. Thomas latches onto this and portrays Christ as the entirely righteous man who effects this ransom with his own blood, even though he has no obligation here.

A second difference is to be found in the distinction between "being able to" and "being indebted". According to Anselm, man owes God righteousness, the uprightness of his human will. Through the corruption of sin, however, he is no longer able to furnish this *debitum*. A way out of this situation is possible only through satisfaction accomplished by Christ. Thomas makes a distinction here. God is not the only one who can cancel the debt; a sinless man could also do so. God is, however, the only one who can grant a cure for sin, which stands in the way of man's true freedom.[113] In principle, a man could make satisfaction, yet in all earthly society there is no one in the position to do so, because virtually everyone is prevented from doing so by sin.

---

[113] Cessario, *Christian Satisfaction in Aquinas*, p. 162.

God becomes man to cure man from sin and thus to make it possible for him to use his freedom in the proper manner. Thomas thus emphasizes man's empowerment for freedom as a fruit of the redemption.

THE EFFECT OF CHRIST'S PASSION (STH III, Q. 48)

While Anselm and Luther each highlight one particular theme, Thomas tries to do justice to the whole variety of themes. Hence, we will try to undertake a survey of the various dimensions of the redemption on the basis of Thomas. The question "Of the efficiency of Christ's Passion",[114] from the tractate on the life of Jesus (III, qq. 27–59) is available for this.

How was Christ's Passion effective, then? For Anselm, this means satisfaction, for Luther, substitution. Thomas describes various aspects so as to analyze the causal connection between Christ's suffering and our redemption in this way.[115] He first of all mentions four great *modi*, and devotes an article to each of them: merit, satisfaction, sacrifice, and ransom. In the fifth article, he asks whether Christ really is the Redeemer at all, or is it not the Father? That leads, finally, to the sixth question, whether Christ's Passion and death were the effective cause of our salvation. Here Thomas, in a marvelous way, surpasses everything previously said on the subject and presents a strictly theocentric view.

Thomas begins with the theme of *merit*[116] (a. 1). The objections situate the question well. First, suffering is not a free action. Since, however, only actions springing from freedom can be meritorious, then one cannot achieve any merit through suffering (*obi.* 1). Secondly, Jesus' whole life has the character of merit. Why, then, should the Passion be allotted a particular place here (*obi.* 2)? Expanding this, Thomas refers to love, thirdly, as the root of all merit. Yet this is already shown in the whole of Christ's life (*obi.* 3). The objections as a whole prove to be a reaction against a certain isolation of the Passion. As a counterargument, Thomas cites Philippians 2. God has exalted him on account of his Passion and, together with him, all who believe in him (*sed contra*).

The glorification of Christ does not take place for him as an isolated individual, but as Head of the Church and, thus, of the new humanity.

---

[114] Thomas Aquinas, STh III, q. 48 (DThA 28:82–101).

[115] Cessario, *Christian Satisfaction in Aquinas*, p. 199.

[116] For more detail on the theme of merit, see the following section, "Redemption through Christ's Merit".

This idea of the unity of Christ and Church, of the Head and the members, of the *totus Christus*, as it is called in Augustine, is fundamental for any doctrine of redemption; it is a basic biblical concept. No one lives for himself alone; no one is an island. Each action has implications for everyone. This is true in incomparably greater measure of good than it is of evil (cf. Rom 5:12–19). "Blessed are those who are persecuted for righteousness' sake"—the Sermon on the Mount has been abundantly realized in Jesus; an action of eminent righteousness has an effect on everyone.

Thomas meets the arguments in detail as follows. Suffering as such is not meritorious, but taking it upon oneself of one's own free will is (*ad 1*). Christ's entire life is meritorious, and yet there are obstacles on our side that have to be overcome by Jesus' suffering in order for us to accept salvation.[117] Jesus' Passion corresponded to what had to be achieved, in other words, the Passion was "necessary" for our sakes, in the sense of fittingness: "Was it not necessary that the Christ should suffer these things?" (*ad 3*).

On the theme of *satisfaction*, the objection is advanced that no one can make reparation for someone else (*obi.* 1). Later, Fausto Socini [Sozzini] (d. 1604) and, following him, the Socinians who were named after him, argued against the idea that it was possible to make reparation for someone else. Everyone, they said, is responsible for himself and can answer only for his own deeds, just as each can do penance only for himself.[118] Thomas replies here, presenting the idea of satisfaction once again with utmost clarity:

> *Answer:* He properly atones for an offense who offers the offended person something that person loves as much as or more than he hated the offense. Christ, however, by suffering out of love and obedience, gave more to God than was required as compensation for all the offenses of the human race. (*resp.*, DThA 28, 86)

No notion of punishment is found here; this is a matter of truly making reparation. There are three reasons why it succeeds: first, the greatness of the love, second, the dignity of his life—he himself pleads

---

[117] Cf. STh III, q. 46, a. 3, five arguments of appropriateness: showing the love of God— example of obedience and humility-meriting grace for all men—keeping oneself free from sin: see at how great a price you were ransomed—recognizing our own dignity.

[118] See on this K.-H. Menke, *Stellvertretung: Schlüsselbegriff christlichen Lebens und theologische Grundkategorie* (Einsiedeln, 1991), pp. 75–76 (with bibliography).

for us—and third, the extent of the Passion. Suffering comes only at the end, here. The first reason is thoroughly positive: the love with which God loves man. Yet nothing of the suffering is neglected: it struck him as an innocent person, undeserved, in all its force. For these three reasons, Christ's suffering makes reparation for all sins (1 Jn 2:2).

"Head and members are, as it were, one mystical person." Two people united in love can make reparation for each other. In doing so, they cannot replace personal contrition or confession, but the (external) act of satisfaction can well be achieved, just as one person may pay another's debts (*ad 1*). Satisfaction is thus not understood as deflecting wrath, but as reparation carried out instead of a punishment.

In terms of the theme of *sacrifice* (a. 3), the worst possible misunderstandings are prevalent here. "Christ loved us and gave himself up for us, a fragrant offering and sacrifice" (Eph 5:2, *sed contra*). What does this passage from Scripture mean? One misunderstanding, arising as a result of talk about penal satisfaction, is based on the notion that the destruction of something precious is always a part of any sacrifice. Yet does the idea of killing capture the central concept of sacrifice? In reaction against this, many seek to abandon the idea of sacrifice altogether. Thomas, with recourse to Augustine, points in his answer to an intermediary way. Augustine's definition is entirely biblical and wholly from the ancient world:

> A true sacrifice is every work that is done in order that we may cling to God in holy fellowship, that is to say, that has a reference to that goal of the good, through which we may be truly blessed.[119]

Sacrifice builds up fellowship. That is true likewise of the Old Testament sacrifices; they create fellowship with God and among men, that is why they almost always end with a meal, the sign of restored fellowship (cf., for example, Ex 24:11: the sacrifice to seal the covenant ends with the elders eating a meal in view of God). This connection between sacrifice and meal is seen again in the Eucharist. There, too, the sacrifice creates fellowship.[120]

---

[119] Augustine, *De civitate Dei* 10, 6 (CChr.SL 47:278); quoted in the *respondeo* (DThA 28:89).

[120] See on this point L. Bouyer, *The Eternal Son: A Theology of the Word of God and Christology* (Our Sunday Visitor, 1978), pp. 358–61; A. Schenker, *Das Abendmahl Jesu als Brennpunkt des Alten Testaments: Begegnung zwischen den beiden Testamenten—eine bibeltheologische Skizze*, BiBe 13 (Freiburg, 1977).

The theme of a *ransom* (a. 4) becomes problematical if we are not aware of the figurative nature of this description. Man has sold himself twice over: on the one hand, he is a slave to sin, and, on the other, he is in debt on account of sins already committed. Both of these mean he is unfree. Here, as in general, Thomas is thinking on the basis of man's freedom. Ransom then means liberation, enabling one to be one's own master again. In this sense, Jesus' suffering was, as it were, the price paid for ransom; he did not give gold, but gave himself up for us. This is not a matter of ransoming man from the devil, then, but ransom in relation to God and for the sake of fellowship with him.

The first four articles each present one way in which Christ was effective for our salvation in his humanity: he acquired merit, made satisfaction, offered himself as a sacrifice, and ransomed men. In the fifth article, Thomas presents the work of redemption as an act of the whole Trinity, and he develops this still further in the sixth and last article. What effects our salvation is not Christ's suffering as such, but God's gracious decision to redeem us men. At the end, Thomas sums the question up once more:

> If we relate Christ's Passion to his Godhead, then it operates as an *effective cause*; if, however, we relate it to Christ's will, it acts as merit; if, on the contrary, we consider it insofar as it takes place in Christ's body, then it acts as satisfaction, inasmuch as we are freed from the debt of punishment thereby; as *ransom*, inasmuch as we are thereby freed from the servitude of guilt as a sacrifice, inasmuch as we are thereby reconciled to God. (*ad 3*, DThA 28, p. 101)

Within these themes, which subtly circumscribe the event of redemption, one thing emerges as being especially significant. Christ redeems men because, as Head of the Church and Head of mankind, he acquires merit.

REDEMPTION THROUGH CHRIST'S MERIT

Jesus' whole life is a sacrament of salvation for us. Classical theology used the concept of merit for this. Through his entire earthly life, Christ "merited" the grace of redemption for us from the Father.[121] Each one of his earthly actions was "infinitely meritorious"; each one, however inconspicuous, is significant for our salvation. Merit is a concept that nowadays is difficult to understand and heavily loaded par-

---

[121] E. H. Schillebeeckx, *Christus: Sakrament der Gottsbegegnung* (Mainz, 1960), p. 46.

ticularly from the ecumenical point of view. And yet this category, if grasped in its original sense, is indispensable for any sense of the meaning for salvation of Jesus' life as a whole. It is no accident that Saint Thomas deals with the question of Christ's merit within the framework of the question of his human will. Only if Christ was "for us" as a man, as a God-man exercising a human will, can his life and death bring salvation for us.

While "merit" makes us think today mainly of material things, Thomas has a personal relationship in mind here. He understands merit on the basis of social interdependence:

> We have to bear in mind that each person who lives in any kind of society is, in a certain sense, a part and member of the society as a whole. Whoever does any good or evil to someone else in society—it redounds (*redundat*) on the whole of that society: just as anyone who hurts a hand in consequence hurts the (whole) man.[122]

Each action that affects someone else also affects the whole. Merit is then simply the relatedness of my actions to the other person. Thomas goes so far as to say that basically, every kind of behavior, every action, has this reference to the other—even the most "private", which pertains to myself alone. There is no such thing as an indifferent or neutral action; every act is related. Merit is then nothing but the quality of this relatedness. On the basis of this social interdependence of every action, Thomas is able to understand the quality of merit in human actions as the just claim to reward, to being reimbursed by others. Justice is always interpersonal here. It is a matter of a moral claim, not of mutual compensation. Merit signifies that there is in fact not any automatic relation between service and payment, but that it is not within our own power to receive the payment. In everyday language, we say that someone has earned our trust. That is considerably closer to an adequate concept of merit than the example of pay. Personal categories are meant here, and it is obvious that trust cannot be forced; it has to be freely given. I stand before the other person in trust and expect trust from him, which has to be given to me freely.

Can there be any merit before God, any fair claim to remuneration from him? Thomas starts from the fact that every action relates not

---

[122] Thomas Aquinas, STh I-II, q. 21, a. 3c (*Op. omn.* 2:386). Torrell understands this idea, under the concept of "Mystical Solidarity in Christ", as a gracious communion between Christ and those who belong to him. Torrell, *Le Christ en ses mystères* 2:386–92.

only to human society, but also to God, inasmuch as God is the goal of man and of all his activity, but also the origin and the goal of the entire universe. No act is indifferent in relation to God. What constitutes merit, however, is the quality of human action, insofar as it pertains to God. The idea of merit is thus, for Thomas, essentially associated with there being between God and man a real communication, a relationship built on trust. Certainly, Thomas emphasizes, just as Luther does, the fact that we cannot speak in the strict sense of any merit of man's before God, since man and God are not on the same plane; rather, man is always dependent upon God.[123] There certainly is an encounter between man and God on a personal plane, however, and it is on this plane that merit is possible. Here Thomas is aware of two kinds of merit, the *meritum de condigno* (condign merit), which presupposes a relationship between two equals, and the *meritum de congruo* (congruous merit), in which what the one in the lower position is able to achieve is credited as merit.[124]

It is against this background that we should ask about the merit of Christ. In situating the doctrine of redemption in the perspective of Christ's merit, Thomas asks concretely about Christ's human freedom, since merit presupposes a coexistence in freedom. That is why the question of merit is dealt with in connection with the two wills of Christ.[125] Only if Christ had a full human will does it make any sense to talk about merit. Accordingly, Jesus' whole life has the character of merit, because all his actions are determined by the quality of trustful loving. That is why he acquires merit, first for himself: Christ himself merited being glorified by God. That, in principle, is the same thing that is said in the Philippians hymn: Because he humbled himself, God has exalted him (Phil 2:5–11). Exaltation is granted him because he has proved himself in lowliness.[126] Gratuitousness is emphasized in the talk about resurrection and rising. The raising of Jesus is a completely gratuitous act of God, yet Scripture does bring a multitude of references to the connection between being obedient all the way to the Cross and exaltation from the grave. Christ goes trusting to his death, and this is proved right in his Resurrection.

[123] Pesch, *Theologie der Rechtfertigung*, p. 774.
[124] Thomas Aquinas, STh I-II, q. 114 (DThA 14:208–42).
[125] Ibid., III, q. 18–19 (DThA 26:62–108).
[126] Cf. ibid., III, q. 49, a. 6, *respondeo* (DThA 28:122–23).

Insofar as every human action, and, hence, especially Christ's acts on behalf of mankind as a whole, is significant, then, second, he acquires merit for all men. His activity redounds to the good of all mankind, because these are actions done from love. That is true of Jesus' whole life, but especially of his death. "Since Christ took his suffering freely upon himself, since he was offered up because he willed it (cf. Is 53:7), and since this will was motivated by love, there can be no doubt that he was meritorious in his suffering."[127]

The Passion of Christ is a source of salvation for us, not because of the awfulness of his suffering, but because of the quality of his love. But how does this affect us, how does Christ's merit reach us? Let us briefly consider a fundamental text from Saint Thomas.[128] His starting point is the Letter to the Romans: "Then as one man's trespass led to condemnation for all men, so one man's act of righteousness leads to acquittal and life for all men" (Rom 5:18). Thomas starts from the Pauline parallel between Adam and Christ. But how is Christ's effectiveness for salvation to be understood? Christ has been made Head of mankind, Head of his body, the Church, and therefore everything that he "merits" is also imputed to his members and applies to them all. Head and members constitute, as it were, one mystical person (*mystice una persona*).[129] This thoroughly biblical idea is important for the whole of the doctrine of redemption.[130]

No new automatic process is formed by that, of course, by which every man achieves redemption. In *De veritate*, Thomas goes into this question:

---

[127] Thomas Aquinas, *Comm. in Sent.* III, d. 18, q. 3, a. 5 *respondeo* (*Op. omn.* 1:325).

[128] Thomas Aquinas, STh III, q. 19, a. 4 (DThA 26:106–8).

[129] Ibid., III, q. 19, a. 4c (DThA 26:107); cf. q. 48, a. 2, ad 1 (DThA 28:86–87).

[130] The associated doctrine of the *gratia capitis*, the grace of Christ as Head of the Church and of mankind, is also the central locus for Saint Thomas' ecclesiology. Cf. M. Seckler, "Das Haupt aller Menschen: Zur Auslegung eines Thomastextes", in *Virtus Politica*, Festschrift for A. Hufnagel, ed. J. Möller and H. Kohlenberger, pp. 107–25 (Stuttgart, 1974); Y. Congar, *Die Lehre von der Kirche: Von Augustinus bis zum abendländischen Schisma*, HDG 3/3c (Freiburg im Breisgau, 1971), pp. 150–56. This concept became especially important in the Franciscan school from Alexander of Hales onward and particularly in Bonaventure. Because Christ, as Head of mankind, possesses the fullness of grace, grace can stream out from him upon all men. Alexander of Hales, *Quaestio de plenitudine gratiae Christi* (*Quaestiones disputatae "antequam esset frater"*), BFSMA 20 (pp. 731–50); Bonaventure, *Breviloquium* 4, c. 5 (*Op. omn.* 5:245–46); cf. J. Finkenzeller, "Die christologische und ekklesiologische Sicht der gratia Christi in der Hochscholastik", *Münchener Theologische Zeitschrift für das Gesamtgebiet der katholischen Theologie* 11 (1960): 169–80.

The merit of Christ is operative with sufficient efficacy as a universal cause
for men's salvation; yet this cause has to be applied to each through the
sacraments and through informed faith, which works through love. And
thus something else, beyond Christ's merit, is requisite for our salvation,
though the cause of this is the merit of Christ.[131]

Jesus' death is thus redemption from our sins and from those of all
the world. This does, however, require acceptance on the part of man:
conversion and faith are absolutely necessary. Yet this human contribution, this *aliquid aliud*, is itself, again, Christ's grace and gift and also
flows to us from his merit.

SUMMARY

Where the redemption of man is concerned, Saint Thomas, like Saint
Anselm, has man's freedom in mind. This, however, is realized in fellowship with God, who repeatedly strengthens it anew, even when
man abandons it through his own fault. Man himself has revoked his
fellowship with God by his sin; but God does not distance himself
from man.

Because man's own strength is not sufficient for him to turn to God
again, Christ intervenes on our behalf. When no human merit is possible, the power flows to us from Christ's merit, that we may once
more acquire merit ourselves. With great caution, Thomas shows us
here how divine redemption and human freedom work together. God
wants man to shine once more as the image of God and also as the
image of God to make use of his freedom. That is what the Incarnation
and Christ's Passion bring about.

The mystery of the redemption that Thomas is trying to touch fits
wonderfully into God's plan for salvation. The redemption is not only
necessary in order that God's plan might be fulfilled. Rather, God looks
for the most appropriate way to redeem man, so that what is good in
creation might be realized in the best possible way and the radiance of
divine truth might shine forth precisely in the Cross.

d. Final Reflections—Ave Crux Spes Unica

The Cross is the most succinct recapitulation of the profession of faith.
The sign of the Cross is the sign of Christian identity, the *symbolon* of

---

[131] Thomas Aquinas, *De veritate*, q. 29, a. 7, ad 8 (*Op. omn.* 3:185).

the Christian. It is a symbol precisely in its reality; and its symbolism is lost if it is dissociated from its unique, concrete, and historical reality and is "spiritualized" into a symbol in a general sense. Conversely, the historical contingency of the event should never be dissociated from the symbolic implications. The Cross is the climax of Jesus' life, the "hour" for which he is living and which signifies the fulfillment of his mission. The Cross stands at the center of God's plan for salvation. It is no arbitrary or accidental historical event, but the decision of God. And yet it is also an event that comes about through individual human actions (and omissions), which did not occur "necessarily", but was an event that was absolutely willed, caused, and carried out by men. Thus, the Cross stands at the point of intersection between historical human actions and the divine plan of salvation.

The Cross is an appalling instrument of torture, and as such it is the product of human depravity. And yet it is the sign that we celebrate in the hymn *Ave crux, spes unica* (Hail to the Cross, our only hope). The arms excruciatingly outstretched, dislocated on the Cross, are frightful to look at. And yet it is these wide-stretched arms that symbolize (in fact, actually denote) what Jesus had promised: "I, when I am lifted up from the earth, will draw all men to myself" (Jn 12:32). Thus, the Cross is a pillar of shame and a throne, tree of the curse and tree of redemption. The "exaltation" of Jesus at his crucifixion is his exaltation to the Father—"Father, glorify thy Son" (Jn 17:1).

Our contemplation of the mystery of redemption has Christ, the "symbol of himself" (Maximus the Confessor),[132] as its definitive form and its essential content. Paul can say that the whole of what is preached as the gospel is "Christ crucified" (1 Cor 1:23).

We crucified him. This shattering insight was granted to the Apostle Paul, of course, only after meeting the Resurrected One. Jesus was crucified by my sins. This knowledge was imparted to Paul at the moment when he received the overpowering insight that "Jesus died for my sins" (cf. 1 Cor 15:3; Gal 1:4). This dreadful truth, that Paul shared in the responsibility for Jesus' Cross, was something of which he first felt certain in the light of the truth that he enunciates in the Letter to the Galatians as the sum total of his conversion: "The Son of God . . . loved me and gave himself for me" (Gal 2:20).

Anselm says to his pupil Boso, "You have not yet considered how

---

[132] Maximus, *De variis difficilibus locis* (PG 91:1165D–1168A).

great the weight of sin is."[133] It is difficult for us to have the least notion
of this weight. The fact that sin, its core, is a denial of God's property
rights and thereby a renunciation of the truth about ourselves ("everything belongs to him"), and thus ultimately a rejection of God, only
becomes apparent through the Cross to which the "sin of the world"
has fastened the Son of God. And even this Cross itself is transformed
by God into an instrument of salvation.

In the parable of the wicked tenants, the logic of the account demands
that the monstrous, heinous murder of the son and heir should be repaid by a draconian punishment: "What will the owner of the vineyard
do? He will come and destroy the tenants, and give the vineyard to
others" (Mk 12:9). That would be the logical solution to the tenants'
guilt. That is the solution we deserved. Instead of which, something
unimaginable: God himself transforms the rejection of his Son by sinners into the forgiveness of their sins. Not the resolution of guilt by
the punishment deserved, but redemption from the guilt itself. Instead
of condemning the tenants to the punishment for their crime and destroying them, the owner of the vineyard does the inconceivable: he
himself delivers his son into their hands; their crime brings about his
act of benevolence. The Son dies at the hands of his murderers, yet the
Father has delivered him into their hands that he might die for them.

In his Pentecost sermon in Jerusalem, Peter says, "This Jesus, delivered up according to the definite plan and foreknowledge of God,
you crucified and killed by the hands of lawless men. But God raised
him up, having loosed the pangs of death" (Acts 2:23–24). Here, the
mystery of foreknowledge is realized to the highest degree: the very
thing that is men's crime proves—through God's good and incomprehensible decision—to be his benevolence to us. At the end of the story
of Joseph and his brothers, the former says to them, after they have
realized their guilt where he is concerned, "You meant evil against me;
but God meant it for good, to bring it about that many people should
be kept alive, as they are today" (Gen 50:20).

The Catechism adds, "From the greatest moral evil ever committed
—the rejection and murder of God's only Son, caused by the sins of
all men—God, by his grace that 'abounded all the more', brought the
greatest of goods: the glorification of Christ and our redemption. But
for all that, evil never becomes a good" (CCC 312).

---

[133] "Nondum considerasti quanti ponderis sit peccatum." CDH 1, 2:322–23.

On the Cross, Jesus overcame all human refusal of God in his one great cry of assent: "It is finished" (Jn 19:30). All the refusal of God, the sin of the world, has brought him to the Cross. On the Cross, Jesus overcame the refusal. In Gethsemane, Jesus wholly accepted the will of the Father, let himself be handed over for us, and by assenting to this with his human will ("not my will, but yours", Lk 22:42), he spoke on behalf of us all the liberating assent to the Father's will. "In him we have redemption" (Col 1:14). He is, in one person, God's assent to us and man's assent to God.

Hence, redemption means: He for me; he in my place. "He loved me and gave himself for me" (Gal 2:20). And again, in the parable of Mark 12, the wicked tenants killed the final messenger, the Son— we crucified the "Lord of glory". Yet this has not become a judgment upon us; he allowed himself to be struck by us, for us, and gave himself up for us. Beyond anything we can do, and more comprehensive than anything we can fail to do, is this "for us" of Christ.

The question of whether, with this advantage of the "for us", anything or anyone at all can still be "against us" remains of course for the time being unresolved and enigmatic: Can death be "against us", or the devil, or even we ourselves? "Who shall separate us from the love of Christ?" (Rom 8:35). Paul says he is certain that nothing can separate him from Christ. Nothing? Not even my own refusal? My saying, "I will not"? Is there no danger, then, that I might lock myself into a definite No?

Why, then, do we pray, in the Roman Canon, the first Eucharistic Prayer, "Save us from final damnation"?[134] Why do we pray in silence, before receiving Holy Communion, "By your holy body and blood free me from all my sins and from every evil. Keep me faithful to your teaching, and never let me be parted from you"?[135] At these words, the holy Curé of Ars is supposed to have wept every time.

3. Descended to the Realm of Death

The article of faith in the Creed about Jesus' death on the Cross is followed by a brief reference to his burial. Just as the corpses of the

---

[134] The Missal, Eucharistic Prayer I.
[135] The Missal, celebrant's prayer before Communion.

men among whom he lived are laid in the grave after their death, it is the same for him. In death, too, he is one of them. After that, we declare our belief that he "descended into hell" (*descendit ad inferos*). A part of man's redemption is also the fact that Jesus "tastes" death, that he really experiences the state of being dead. "It is the mystery of Holy Saturday, when Christ, lying in the tomb, reveals God's great sabbath rest after fulfillment of man's salvation, which brings peace to the whole universe."[136]

This article of faith is not easily accessible today. Here, the truth of faith is formulated in concepts drawn from a view of the world that is alien to us today. The idea of a "realm of death", an "underworld" beneath our living space, a "hell" that contains the souls of the dead, seems completely remote from our modern rational consciousness. This article of faith seems to call for " 'demythologization', a process that in this case looks devoid of danger and unlikely to provoke opposition".[137] Would it not be better, then, to do without it? That is a possibility, but is it quite honest? Since the earliest times, the Church has held to this profession of faith. Would that not be an incentive to accept it, particularly when the question seems difficult and obscure? Especially with the past century in view, a preoccupation with Holy Saturday, with the day when God is silent, seems more relevant than ever.

a. The Biblical Basis: Hell as Sheol

If we consider this article of faith in detail,[138] it seems quite clear that "realm of death", "underworld", "hell", does not mean the place of eternal damnation, but the place where the dead dwell, which in Hebrew is called *Sheol* and in Greek, *Hades* (Acts 2:31). That is the place where the souls of those who have died are held captive after death.

There are numerous examples in the New Testament to which this theological statement can be traced back. Even Peter's Pentecost sermon includes a reference. Here, a passage from Psalm 16 is presented as

---

[136] CCC 624. Cf. Jn 19:30, 42; Col 1:18–20; Heb 4:4–9.

[137] J. Ratzinger, *Introduction to Christianity*, trans. J.R. Foster, rev. ed. (San Francisco: Ignatius Press, 2004), p. 294.

[138] For interpretations of this article, see Ratzinger, *Introduction to Christianity*, pp. 293–301; T. Schneider, *Was wir glauben: Eine Auslegung des Apostolischen Glaubensbekenntnisses* (Düsseldorf, 1985), pp. 268–77; M. Bordoni, *Gèsu di Nazaret: Signore e Cristo*, vol. 3 (Rome, 1986), pp. 288–92, 521–37; W. Pannenberg, *Jesus, God and Man* (London and Philadelphia, 1968), pp. 269–74.

announcing the Resurrection: "He was not abandoned to Hades, nor did his flesh see corruption" (Acts 2:31; cf. Ps 16:10). The same sense is found in Paul's Letter to the Romans, " 'Who will descend into the abyss?' (that is, to bring Christ up from the dead)" (Rom 10:7). Two things are noted here: first, that an inseparable part of Jesus' death on the Cross is also being dead, thus, going down into the realm of death. Second, descending to the dead is associated here with ascending to the Father—thus, with the beginning of the eschatological consummation. "He who descended is he who also ascended far above all the heavens, that he might fill all things" (Eph 4:10).

The biblical witnesses confirm that Christ's descent to the dead was a genuine experience of death, the most profound expression of solidarity with men. During the three days from his death to the Resurrection, "Jesus experienced the state of death, that is, the separation of the soul from the body, in the state and in the nature of all men."[139] Jesus himself had announced this when he compared his own path to the account of the prophet Jonah: "For as Jonah was three days and three nights in the belly of the whale, so will the Son of man be three days and three nights in the heart of the earth" (Mt 12:40).

For a long time, from the earliest Fathers onward, an obscure and difficult passage from the First Letter of Peter was considered the first passage testifying to the descent into the underworld: "He went and preached to the spirits in prison" (1 Pet 3:19).[140] To find the right approach to this passage, it is necessary to take note of the context. Immediately before this verse, it says: "For Christ also died for sins once for all, the righteous for the unrighteous, that he might bring us to God, being put to death in the flesh but made alive in the spirit" (1 Pet 3:18). A duality is being addressed here: the body is dead, but the spirit is alive and contemplating God. In this condition, Christ went "to the spirits"—which means here that his authority is extended to everybody, even those who died before him. He goes to everyone, even to the dead, even to the spirits in the underworld. In death, Christ takes upon himself the whole of man's fate, even to this separation. He is dead according to the body, but according to his spirit, he goes

[139] John Paul II, *Communio personarum*, vol. 5: *Jesus Christus der Erlöser: Katechesen 1986–1989* (St. Ottilien, 1994), p. 377.
[140] Cf. A. Grillmeier, *Mit ihm und in ihm: Christologische Forschungen und Perspektiven* (Freiburg im Breisgau, 1975), pp. 76–78.

down into the underworld, although in doing so his soul is already enjoying the beatific vision of God. On the basis of this vision, he can confidently face the imprisoned spirits and also preach to them.[141]

b. The Descent into Hell as the
Victory over Death—The Anastasis Icon

This mystery of faith, which is if anything only hinted at in the testimony of Holy Scripture, was more completely developed in the theology and piety of the Fathers. This is shown especially in the Easter icons of the Eastern Church. Alongside the depiction of the women at the empty tomb, another icon soon gained acceptance, which portrays pictorially the mystery of faith of our redemption from sin and death.

The central theme of this depiction is Christ's descent to Adam in the underworld. In the earliest and clearest depictions, three people can be seen in the center: Adam, Christ, and a naked human form lying on the ground. Christ, who is surrounded by an oval halo in the manner of a mandorla, stands like a "triumphator" with one foot on the head of the man, who symbolizes Hades and who is still clinging to Adam by the leg with one hand. The gates of the underworld are broken and are lying there across one another. The Redeemer is taking Adam's hand with his right hand, and the latter has already set one foot outside the realm of death. By the side of Adam, Eve or other righteous persons from the Old Testament may appear. The picture has the title "Anastasis", Resurrection.[142]

This pictorial representation finds its literary equivalent in an old homily that is still read on Holy Saturday.

> Today a great silence reigns on earth, a great silence and a great stillness. A great silence because the King is asleep. The earth trembled and is still because God has fallen asleep in the flesh and he has raised up all who have slept ever since the world began. . . . He has gone to search for Adam, our first father, as for a lost sheep. Greatly desiring to visit those who

---

[141] John Paul II, *Communio personarum* 5:377–78.

[142] H.-J. Schulz, "Die 'Höllenfahrt' als 'Anastasis': Eine Untersuchung über Eigenart und dogmengeschichtliche Voraussetzungen byzantinischer Osterfrömmigkeit", *Zeitschrift für katholische Theologie* 81 (1959): 1–66, here p. 9; E. Lucchesi Palli, "Höllenfahrt Christi", in *Lexikon der christlichen Ikonographie* 2:322–31, here pp. 323–24; P. Plank, "Die Wiederaufrichtung des Adam und ihre Propheten: Eine neue Deutung der Anastasis-Ikone", *Ostkirchliche Studien* 41 (1992): 34–49.

live in darkness and in the shadow of death, he has gone to free from sorrow Adam in his bonds and Eve, captive with him—He who is both their God and the son of Eve. . . . "I am your God, who for your sake have become your son. . . . I order you, O sleeper, to awake. I did not create you to be a prisoner in hell. Rise from the dead, for I am the life of the dead."[143]

The silence of Holy Saturday is the whole earth's attitude of expectation. It reminds us of the silence before the creation of the world (Gen 1:2), when everything was waiting for God to act in power. So it is here, too. Christ has come into the world, and his earthly work, his life among men, and his death for sin have been achieved. To illustrate that, the preacher recalls for his listeners the connection of pain and death with the conception of the Son of God in Mary's womb.[144] But Christ's mission on earth is not yet quite completed; he has not yet gone to the dead. Not all the righteous have yet been redeemed, and the "shepherd" has not yet gathered together all of the "sheep". The righteous from the Old Testament are still not there—above all, Adam, the common ancestor. They have entangled themselves in sin through their misconduct, and on that account they are suffering "pains" in the underworld. For them, too, Christ came into the world to lead them home.

Jesus has joined the line of ancestors of the sinful race of men so as to redeem them all, as far back as Adam, the common ancestor of all men. Now, on Holy Saturday, in death, where he has become united in solidarity with them, the dead, he goes into the underworld as if in a triumphal procession, to call out all those whom death still holds in its snares: Adam, where are you? Christ now calls the dead, with whom he has declared himself united in solidarity in death, to share also in the Resurrection. Those with whom he desired to be in death, he has also chosen to live with him and to form the community of heaven. Death is unable to keep its hold upon the dead Son of God. His entry into the underworld becomes a triumphal procession. Jesus has truly died and is far from his friends on earth. "Yet Easter means at the same time Resurrection from the realm of the dead. Good Friday has not been forgotten. Only through death has Christ overcome death; only

---

[143] This ancient homily for Holy Saturday is to be found among the works of Epiphanius of Salamis (PG 43:439–64). Cf. CCC 635.

[144] Ps.-Epiphanius, *Homilia* (PG 43:443–44).

Good Friday can lead up to Easter Night." The Anastasis icon makes
that clear and visible for us. "The Resurrection is depicted against the
background of Hades. So Christ has had to descend there. There, in
the midst of the domain of death, Christ overcame death."[145]

c. The Descent into Hell in
Solidarity with the Fate of Men

While, in the East, the particular emphasis upon the divinity of Christ
and the understanding of the descent into hell as a victory over death,
which is associated with it, led to an intensification of the piety of
Easter, in Western theology this faded into the background. Interest
turned more and more to the stories of childhood and to the events of
the Passion,[146] and the *descensus*, on the other hand, was almost completely overlooked.

In the Middle Ages, the descent into the underworld was discussed
in considering the unity of Christ's person. It was noted that Christ's
body and soul had separated in death and that the soul went down into
the underworld. For medieval theologians, the essential question was
how the unity of God and man was maintained even during this descent of the soul. For Saint Thomas it is important that the correct view
of the *descensus* question not be obstructed by too dualistic a picture
of man.

> Consequently, it must be said that during the three days of Christ's death,
> the whole Christ was in the tomb, because the whole person was there,
> through the body united with him; similarly, he was wholly in hell, be-
> cause the whole person was there by reason of the soul united with him.[147]

The redemption extends to the *limbus patrum*, while the place of
damnation, the deepest level of hell, does experience Christ's victory
but has no share in it.[148]

In our own time, it is above all Hans Urs von Balthasar who concerned himself with this question. He was influenced quite particularly
here by the visions of Adrienne von Speyr, which always culminated

---

[145] Schulz, "Die 'Höllenfahrt' als 'Anastasis' ", p. 26.
[146] Ibid., pp. 1–3.
[147] Thomas Aquinas, STh III, q. 52, a. 3 (DThA 28:173).
[148] Ibid., a. 2 (DThA 28:168–69).

during the Paschal Triduum.[149] The substantial task that von Balthasar set himself was "to examine the biblical data to see in what degree the expression *descendit ad inferna* can be considered as a valid interpretation of the affirmations of the Bible".[150]

It is part of the redemptive event that Christ really and completely shared man's fate with us and thus became united in solidarity with every man. He is a man until death and was dead as a man. Just as, for von Balthasar, at death Jesus' experience of being abandoned by God—"My God, my God, why have you forsaken me?" (Ps 22:1) —stands at the center, so "he must experience, in solidarity with the sinners who have gone to the underworld, their—ultimately hopeless —separation from God", and only then has Jesus also truly suffered human death.[151]

This reflection on being abandoned by God, and on suffering the underworld as the "ultimate powerlessness of dying and being dead", provides von Balthasar with a reason to criticize the old *descensus* theology as "false triumphalism".[152] Here, it is not the power of the victorious Christ that overcomes the power of death, but the powerlessness of the one who loves, who in the encounter with death, with Adam, with hell, descends ever deeper. This love is so strong that von Balthasar can say: "This basically gives a positive answer to the dispute about whether the dead Lord descended into the farthest reaches of hell, to 'chaos', or not."[153]

In his theology, von Balthasar highlights one aspect that receives too little attention from the Fathers. Holy Saturday, the death of Christ, has

[149] The Holy Saturday visions are briefly reported by von Balthasar in: Adrienne von Speyr, "Über das Geheimnis des Karsamstags", *Internationale Katholische Zeitschrift Communio* 10 (1981): 32–39. See also von Balthasar, *First Glance at Adrienne von Speyr*, trans. Antje Lawry and Sr. Sergia Englund, O.C.D. (San Francisco: Ignatius Press, 1981).

[150] H. U. von Balthasar, *Mysterium Paschale: The Mystery of Easter*, trans. Aidan Nichols, O.P. (San Francisco: Ignatius Press, 2005), p. 149. A selection of further literature on this: von Balthasar, *Explorations in Theology*, vol. 4: *Spirit and Institution*, trans. Edward T. Oakes, S.J. (San Francisco: Ignatius Press, 1995), pp. 401–14; von Balthasar, *Kleiner Diskurs über die Hölle*, 3rd ed. (Einsiedeln, 1999); W. Maas, *Gott und die Hölle: Studien zum Descensus Christi* (Einsiedeln, 1979); Maas, "Abgestiegen zur Hölle: Aspekte eines vergessenen Glaubens-artikels", *Internationale Katholische Zeitschrift Communio* 10 (1981): 1–18; see also the entire first issue of *Internationale Katholische Zeitschrift Communio* 10 (1981).

[151] Von Balthasar, *Spirit and Institution*, p. 408.

[152] Ibid., p. 411.

[153] Ibid., p. 412.

nothing triumphal about it in the first instance. We experience that, too, with the liturgy of Holy Saturday. It is kept extremely simple; there is no celebration of the Eucharist; everything is concentrated in silent prayer and the liturgy of the daily offices, especially the readings of tenebrae. The church is bare of all ornament; the altars have been stripped. Christ's death leaves his disciples—and thus the Church— at first in bewilderment, sorrow, and fear. The believer should be still, should stop and adore. The salvation that comes about in the descent into hell is still hidden on Holy Saturday; death still has the power that is about to be taken from him.

For all our appreciation of von Balthasar's view, of course, we must also add some critical remarks. The central idea is that Christ, in "perfect self-alienation" (von Balthasar uses this concept several times), brings home the dead from the deepest abyss of hell. God himself enters into the most extreme state of distance from God and abandonment by him in order to lead into his presence even the very last people. The question von Balthasar starts with needs to be put here, too: whether this idea really does justice to the testimony found in the Bible and the Church.

Both aspects, glory and lowliness, are important. Jesus Christ really died, but in this death he was already the Blessed One, who calls into the blessed communion all the righteous who are dead with him. God condescended to lowliness, in order to snatch men from death and to lead them to the heights. "Since therefore the children share in flesh and blood, he himself likewise partook of the same nature, that through death he might destroy him who has the power of death, that is, the devil, and deliver all those who through fear of death were subject to lifelong bondage" (Heb 2:14-15). His lowliness becomes our exaltation; his servitude, our freedom; his humanization to the point of death, our divinization. "Thus the salvific power of the sacrificial death of Christ, which has achieved redemption on behalf of all mankind, is revealed and actualized."[154]

Of all the mysteries of the life of Jesus, the *descensus ad inferos* is the most enigmatic. In what does the salvific effectiveness of this moment in Jesus' life consist? Perhaps in the fact that in his death Christ meets with every man. That is more than solidarity, that is God turning di-

---

[154] John Paul II, *Communio personarum* 5:378.

rectly to the dead. Georges Bernanos envisaged the existential depth of this mystery of faith in a note in his diary:

> We truly want what he wants; without knowing it, we do in fact want our pains, our suffering, our solitude, while we imagine that we only want our pleasures. We think we are afraid of death and flee before it, while in reality we want this death, as he wanted his. Just as he sacrifices himself upon every altar at which the Mass is celebrated, so in every death he dies anew. We want everything that he wants, but we do not know that we want it; we do not know ourselves, for sin brings it about that we live on the surface of ourselves, and we only examine ourselves in order to die, and that is just where he is waiting for us.[155]

---

[155] G. Bernanos, entry in his diary for January 24, 1948.

V. The Glorification of the Son of God

Jesus' earthly life teaches us that death does not have the last word about his and our existence. It becomes manifest that existence has a meaning and that the world is not blind chaos but "cosmos"—that is, a good and ordered reality—in the last three christological mysteries of our Creed: Jesus rose again, and, having ascended into heaven, he sits at the right hand of the Father, whence he will come again to judge the living and the dead. We will now turn to these mysteries.

1. Risen from the Dead on the Third Day

There is no subject about which the early Christian writers wrote more than about the bodily Resurrection of Christ.[1] This article of faith is so scandalous that the Christian writers made every effort to make it understandable for pagans. For Judaism, insofar as it shared the Pharisees' belief in resurrection, the Resurrection of Jesus was unacceptable because it would thereby be an acknowledgment of his messianic and eschatological significance. Resurrection happens only in the last days. If Jesus, however, had risen again, then his status as Messiah would have been confirmed. For Greek culture, resurrection was an absurdity. The immortality of the soul was indeed accepted, but not a resurrection of the body. Paul had already learned that in Athens (Acts 17:31–32). The philosopher Celsus (second/third century) was filled with indignation when he wrote against this teaching around the middle of the second century: "This is a hope that is quite suitable for worms. For what human soul could still long for a decomposed body?"[2] The Neoplatonist Porphyry (d. 305) is still more clear. In his biography of Plotinus, he mentions that the latter refused to have a statue made of him—that is to say, of his body—since he had been ashamed of being in a body. "Is it not to be enough to carry the image [the body]

---

[1] For what follows, see C. Schönborn, "'Auferstehung des Fleisches' im Glauben der Kirche", *Internationale Katholische Zeitschrift Communio* 19 (1990): 13–29.

[2] Origen, *Contra Celsum* 5, 14 (SC 147:48).

with which nature enclosed us? No, you demand that I also willingly consent to leave a permanent image of the image, as if this image were something worth seeing!"[3] In his polemical work *Against the Christians*, Porphyry delivers a sharp attack against the "nonsense" of the Christian teaching about resurrection. These witnesses show not only "how much Greek culture, because of its dualism, characterized by hostility to the body, had to be philosophically opposed to the central teaching of Christianity, but also that this teaching was seen as contrary to reason and even as blasphemous".[4]

It is all the more obvious that Christian proclamation chose the hard path here and that they did little to diminish the offense of the corporality of the resurrection. The Church did not allow her faith to be "Hellenized". She has always declared, with Paul, "If Christ has not been raised, then our preaching is in vain and your faith is in vain." What Paul wrote to the Corinthians is equally true today: "If for this life only we have hoped in Christ, we are of all men most to be pitied" (1 Cor 15:14, 19). If Christ died but did not rise again, then our faith lacks any basis. If Christ remained dead, then his Cross was a senseless and horrifying death that did not redeem us. Our love would be directed toward a dead man, a corpse, and our faith would be a remembrance of a man from the past, and not of him who said, "I am with you always, to the close of the age" (Mt 28:20).

The Church Fathers saw connections of many kinds between the Resurrection and the other truths of faith. The Resurrection points first of all toward the creation. If everything that exists, spiritual as well as material, has been created and, thus, willed by God, then none of God's works is in vain. In the Resurrection of Christ, body and soul are glorified and God makes everything new.[5] And therein lies the soteriological significance of the Resurrection. Since Christ took flesh upon himself, it has become the central point of salvation. Tertullian (d. 220) reduces this to the concise formula: *Caro cardo salutis*.[6] Irenaeus of Lyons argues, on the basis of sacramental theology: when bread and wine "receive the Word of God and become the Body and Blood of Christ and when the substance of our flesh is strengthened

---

[3] Porphyry, *Vita Plotini* 1.
[4] L. Scheffczyk, *Auferstehung: Prinzip des christlichen Glaubens* (Einsiedeln, 1976), pp. 42–43.
[5] Cf. Irenaeus of Lyons, *Adversus Haereses* 5, 3–8 (FChr 8/5:38–75).
[6] Tertullian, *De resurrectione carnis* 8 (CSEL 47:36).

and supported by this, then how can they [the Gnostics] affirm that the flesh is incapable of receiving God's gift, which is eternal life? It [the flesh] is thereby nourished by the Blood and the Body of the Lord and is one of his members."[7] For the realm of eschatology there is, finally, the conviction that God cannot allow anything that he created as good to fall prey to destruction.

a. The Context of Jesus' Promises of the Resurrection

There was already a hope of resurrection among the people of the Old Testament, before the coming of Christ. It was clearly expressed for the first time in the Book of Daniel (12:2) and in the Second Book of Maccabees (7:9, 11, 13, 23, 29). The Pharisees and many of Jesus' contemporaries believed in the resurrection of the dead (cf. Acts 23:6; Jn 11:24). Jesus himself teaches it quite clearly (cf. Mk 12:18–27). The resurrection is expected "at the last day" (Jn 6:40), and it will be associated with the universal judgment (cf. Jn 5:25–29). Jesus has raised the dead (cf. Mk 5:21–42; Lk 7:11–17; Jn 11), as did the prophets before him (cf. 1 Kings 17:17–24; 2 Kings 4:8–37). These marvelous acts were probably signs of Jesus' supreme authority and also signs of the coming resurrection of the dead, but they were not that resurrection itself, since those Jesus raised returned to earthly, mortal life.

Something quite new is announced with Jesus' mysterious words about the imminent suffering and Resurrection of the Son of man. The synoptic Gospels pass on that Jesus announced his imminent suffering but also his subsequent Resurrection three times (Mk 8:31–33; 9:30–32; 10:32–34 and par.) There is no serious reason to question the genuineness of these prophecies. They are so unusual for contemporary conceptions and expectations that they cannot have been deduced from Jewish models. On the other hand, they are so consistent with everything that Jesus revealed about his mission through gestures, actions, and words that they make best sense when regarded as a faithful echo of what Jesus himself taught.[8]

---

[7] Irenaeus of Lyons, *Adversus Haereses* 5, 2 and 3 (FChr 8/5:34–35).

[8] On this, see A. Feuillet, "Les Trois Grandes Prophéties de la Passion et de la Résurrection des évangiles synoptiques. 1: Authenticité substantielle et circonstances historiques des prophéties", *Revue Thomiste* 67 (1967): 533–60.

We have to try to make clear for ourselves the enormous implications of these promises of the Passion and Resurrection. In Jesus' preaching, the gradual revelation of his identity as the Messiah, as the heavenly Son of man, and as the Son of God goes hand-in-hand with the ever clearer revelation of his imminent path of suffering and the Resurrection that is to be reached by it. The proclamation of the Kingdom of God that is coming, that is indeed already dawning, is inseparably linked with this dual revelation. Jesus proclaims the dawn of the end times, in which God will visit his people, will restore Israel, and will set up the kingdom of justice and peace. And yet the Kingdom of God comes in a different way from what was expected. Jesus himself is the heart of this Kingdom, and that is why the Kingdom of God comes only through his mission—yet that means through his dying "for many" (Mk 10:45) and through his Resurrection. Hence, it is by one's attitude to Jesus that entry into the Kingdom of God or exclusion from it is decided. The three announcements of the Passion are the immediate occasion for instructing the disciples. They are promised the same fate as Jesus: persecution and reward. The only ones to come after him are those who go with him and, in following him, take the cross upon them and thus confess him (cf. Mk 8:34–38).[9]

The Gospels give us a true-to-life sense of how dramatic the failure to understand this message of Jesus and then its realization were for the disciples. Jesus probably hinted at these connections from the very start.[10] And yet the breakthrough occurred only after Peter's confession, at Caesarea Philippi, that Jesus was the Messiah, the Son of God (Mk 8:29; Mt 16:16).[11] Now that the first of the Twelve chosen by Jesus, thanks to divine inspiration (cf. Mt 16:17), had solemnly proclaimed Jesus' identity, he started to disclose to them "that the Son of Man must suffer many things, and be rejected by the elders and the chief priests and the scribes, and be killed, and after three days rise again" (Mk 8:31). This "must" is not an external compulsion or some

---

[9] This is impressively demonstrated in H. Schürmann, *Gottes Reich—Jesu Geschick: Jesu ureigener Tod im Lichte seiner Basileia-Verkündigung* (Freiburg im Breisgau, 1983).

[10] See the second part of A. Feuillet's essay, "Signification doctrinale des prophéties", *Revue Thomiste* 68 (1968): 41–74, here p. 61.

[11] A fascinating interpretation of this passage is offered by J.-M. van Cangh and M. van Esbroeck, "La Primauté de Pierre (Mt 16:16–19) et son contexte judaïque", *Revue théologique de Louvain* 11 (1980): 310–24.

blind fate, but God's plan for salvation, which "must" be carried out in this way. The suffering, death, and Resurrection of Jesus are part of the "eschatological drama".[12] To the disciples of Jesus, this "divine necessity" is completely incomprehensible. It is all too contrary to their expectations that, instead of being the bringer of the kingdom of peace and the age of happiness, the Messiah should suffer. Jesus never, of course, said anything more sharply than when he rebuked Peter, who wanted to keep Jesus from the path of suffering: "Get behind me (ὕπαγε ὀπίσω μου), Satan! For you are not on the side of God, but of men" (Mk 8:33, literally).

b. A Historical and Transcendent Event

Jesus' announcement of his Resurrection met with incomprehension on the disciples' part. "So they kept the matter to themselves, questioning what the rising from the dead meant" (Mk 9:10). What brought them to bear witness to this inconceivable event before the world after Jesus' death? According to the joint witness of all four Gospels, the disciples reached this faith in two stages. First they found the empty tomb, and then Jesus himself appeared to them.[13]

Jewish anthropology prohibits any talk about resurrection unless the grave is empty. "How could Jesus' disciples in Jerusalem have proclaimed his Resurrection, if they could be constantly refuted merely by viewing the grave in which his body was interred?"[14] That was a necessary presupposition for the proclamation of the bodily Resurrection of Christ. The post-Easter witnesses held their ground on this concrete corporality and did so in spite of all the difficulties they encountered with the Jews, who did not expect the resurrection of the body until the Parousia, and later with the pagans, for whom the resurrection of the body was a grotesque and vulgar notion. It would have been far easier for his disciples to venerate Jesus at his grave as a martyred prophet as did the supporters of John the Baptist. The prophet Daniel

---

[12] K. H. Schelke, *Die Passion Jesu in der Verkündigung des Neuen Testamentes: Ein Beitrag zur Formgeschichte und zur Theologie des Neuen Testamentes* (Heidelberg, 1949), p. 110.

[13] H. U. von Balthasar, *Mysterium Paschale: The Mystery of Easter*, trans. Aidan Nichols, O.P. (San Francisco: Ignatius Press, 2005), pp. 232–34.

[14] W. Pannenberg, *Jesus, God and Man* (London and Philadelphia, 1968), p. 100. See also K. Schubert, "'Auferstehung Jesu' im Lichte der Religionsgeschichte des Judentums", in *Resurrexit: Actes du symposium international sur la résurrection de Jésus, Rome, 1970*, ed. E. Dhanis, pp. 207–24, here pp. 217–19 (Rome, 1974).

had promised such a certain resurrection in glory (Dan 12:2–3), and a proper martyr cult developed at their graves.[15] The lack of any indication whatever of such a cult corroborates the reports of finding an empty tomb.

The fact of the tomb being empty is in itself open to several interpretations. The high priest and elders, moreover, circulated the rumor that "his disciples came by night and stole him away while we were asleep" (Mt 28:13). Yet even the spreading of this rumor among the Jews is an important indication of the fact that the news about the empty grave was not the invention of a later generation of Christians.[16] Besides this, in all the earliest Jewish polemics against the Resurrection of Christ, there is no suggestion that the tomb had remained undisturbed.[17] The report in the Gospel of John that inside the empty tomb the linen cloths were found lying, and beside them the neatly folded napkin (Jn 20:6–7), offers indirect evidence against the rumor that the body had been stolen; for the disciples would hardly have taken the trouble to remove the shroud and leave it behind.[18] The leaving behind of the bindings shows, furthermore, that the Risen One was completely "unfettered", not leaving the tomb, as Lazarus did, with hands and feet wrapped with bindings and with a napkin hiding his face (Jn 11:44).[19] In the Resurrection, he leaves behind everything to do with death.

Gnosticism soon offered a spiritualistic reduction of the Resurrection by using the term "resurrection" to designate the ascent of the soul to God, leaving the body behind.[20] Yet between the death and the Resurrection of Jesus lies the mysterious Holy Saturday, that is to say, the time when Jesus' body lay in the tomb and the "descent into hell" of Jesus' soul. The Lord rose *from the grave*. The idea that resurrection occurs *at* death is inadequate here, as it neglects the evidence that Jesus

---

[15] P. Stuhlmacher, *Biblische Theologie des Neuen Testaments*, vol. 1: *Grundlegung: Von Jesus zu Paulus*, 2nd ed. (Göttingen, 1997), pp. 176–78; Stuhlmacher, *Was geschah auf Golgotha? Zur Heilsbedeutung von Kreuz, Tod und Auferweckung Jesu* (Stuttgart, 1998), pp. 48–50.

[16] M. Bordoni, *Gesù di Nazaret: Signore e Cristo*, vol. 2 (Rome, 1984), p. 549.

[17] H. von Campenhausen, "The Events of Easter and the Empty Tomb", in *Tradition and Life in the Church: Essays and Lectures on Church History* (London and Philadelphia, 1968), pp. 42–89, here pp. 73–77.

[18] John Chrysostom, *Homilia in Joannem* 85, 4 (PG 59:465).

[19] See what is said about the grave-cloths by J. A.T. Robinson, *The Priority of John* (London, 1985), pp. 291–94.

[20] On basic questions concerning Gnosticism, see P. Koslowski, ed., *Gnosis und Mystik in der Geschichte der Philosophie* (Zürich, 1988).

was really dead, as it is expressed in Jesus' being laid in the tomb and in the "resurrection *on the third day*".²¹ The oldest kerygma of the Church emphasizes this sequence (died—buried—rose again; cf. 1 Cor 15:3–4), which likewise corresponds to the historical course of events.

Thus, it is hard to doubt the credibility of the tradition of the empty tomb. The appearances of Jesus are the second sign of his Resurrection. "[Christ] appeared to Cephas, then to the Twelve" (1 Cor 15:5). Both signs are requisite and complement one another. For the empty grave alone still does not lead to belief in the Resurrection. Only Jesus' appearances to the disciples make it clear why his dead body is no longer in the tomb. The angels proclaim, "He is not here, but has risen" (Lk 24:5). Only the disciple whom Jesus loved sees the empty tomb, the linen wrappings, and the napkin and believes (Jn 20:8). Yet even the appearances, taken on their own, are not a certain sign of the Resurrection. These Easter appearances "could never have been taken for anything but ordinary appearances of the dead, which are everywhere, without the primitive Church's profession of the empty tomb."²²

It is repeatedly argued that the profound meaning of the Easter faith consists in the fact that Jesus' business continues. "The question of Jesus' Resurrection [is] ultimately not a question of something that happened after Good Friday, but is a question about the earthly Jesus and a question of how his cause later became an experienced reality and can be an experience of reality today."²³ The visions of Christ are thus interpreted, for instance, as the apostles working through their mourning: "At Easter, the shattered, sorrowing Peter, despite his denial of Jesus and despite the latter's death, . . . once more encountered Jesus' word of forgiveness, he 'saw' him."²⁴ The critical attitude of the first Christians to the news of Easter militates against such a denial of the factuality of the Resurrection and the associated interpretation of the Easter faith as the product of their faith. It is never said of them that they were in joyful expectation of an appearance of the risen Lord. They reacted with disbelief, rather, to the account of the empty tomb

---

²¹ Cf. J. Ratzinger, *Eschatology: Death and Eternal Life*, trans. Michael Waldstein, Dogmatic Theology 9 (Washington, D.C.: Catholic University of America Press, 1988), pp. 104–40.
²² K. Schubert, *Bibel und Geschichte* (Klosterneuburg, 1999), p. 107.
²³ W. Marxsen, *Die Auferstehung Jesu als historisches und theologisches Problem* (Gütersloh, 1964), p. 35.
²⁴ G. Lüdemann, *Die Auferstehung Jesu: Historie, Erfahrung, Theologie* (Göttingen, 1994), p. 126.

and the message of the angels delivered to them by the women. All this "seemed to them an idle tale, and they did not believe them" (Lk 24:11). On the evening of Easter Day, Jesus showed himself to the Eleven and "upbraided them for their unbelief and hardness of heart, because they had not believed those who saw him after he had risen" (Mk 16:14).

Besides that, the disciples found it not out of the question to think that Jesus' appearances were those of a ghost (Mk 6:49) or a spirit (Lk 24:37). For in Judaism—as throughout the ancient world—it was not unknown for the souls or spirits of the dead to appear. Samuel's being conjured up by the witch of En-dor, for instance (1 Sam 28:7–19), is well known. If this had been a matter of that sort of appearance of the dead man, then it would certainly have been some kind of consolation. It would have been enough for them to understand Jesus as "a prophet mighty in deed and word" (Lk 24:19), but not to believe in his Resurrection. In the accounts of his appearance in the Gospels, the initiative always lies with Christ, never with those who see him. A disciple becomes a witness to his Resurrection, not through his belief in the Resurrection, but through Christ's sovereign act in making him a witness, by showing himself to him in visible, concrete, bodily form. "The Easter appearances are not to be explained from the Easter faith of the disciples; rather, conversely, the Easter faith of the disciples is to be explained from the appearances."[25]

The identification of the person who appears takes place mainly through the identification of his body: "Why are you troubled, and why do questionings rise in your hearts? See my hands and my feet, that it is I myself" (Lk 24:38–39). The scars testify beyond all doubt who it is that the disciples are seeing (cf. Jn 20:24–29). His bodily gestures are like identifying marks (cf. Lk 24:30–31, 35). Mary Magdalen recognizes Jesus by the unmistakable tone of his voice (Jn 20:16). In the apostles' preaching, the fact of their having eaten and drunk with Jesus after his Resurrection is cited as evidence of the reality of the Resurrection (cf. Acts 10:41). Only people who already knew Jesus before Easter can be witnesses to his Resurrection. Only they can testify: It is the same person, "It is the Lord!" (Jn 21:7). Peter counts the time from Jesus' Resurrection up to the Ascension as being part of the period of his earthly life, when "the Lord Jesus went in and out

---

[25] Pannenberg, *Jesus, God and Man*, p. 96.

among us" (cf. Acts 1:21–22). The one who was crucified and the one who rose again are identical.

And yet, again, this identical body is quite different. The two disciples from Emmaus spent the better part of a day with Jesus, and yet "their eyes were kept from recognizing him" (Lk 24:16). Jesus is no longer limited by time and space. He comes through locked doors (Jn 20:19, 26), and as soon as the Emmaus disciples recognize him as the Lord, they no longer see him (Lk 24:31). With regard to Christ, Paul speaks of a "spiritual body" that supersedes the "physical body" (1 Cor 15:44). The earthly body is "animated by a soul", the resurrection body is "animated by the spirit", completely permeated by the Holy Spirit. This "inspiriting" is not to be confused with "spiritualizing" in the Gnostic sense. From this, Paul draws the conclusion that our bodies, too, will really be resurrected by the Holy Spirit and will be completely "filled" with him: "If the Spirit of him who raised Jesus from the dead dwells in you, he who raised Christ Jesus from the dead will give life to your mortal bodies also through his Spirit who dwells in you" (Rom 8:11).

The empty grave and the appearances of Christ are the historical traces of a historical event, the Resurrection of Christ. This is also a transcendent occurrence, however, which displays important differences from the other events of Jesus' life. While Lazarus, for instance, after he had been resurrected, could be seen by all those present, the risen Christ did not show himself to all people, "but to us who were chosen by God as witnesses" (Acts 10:41). There were no human witnesses to the moment of the Resurrection. The Easter liturgy, therefore, acclaims this mystery of faith in the words, "Most blessed of all nights, chosen by God to see Christ rising from the dead!"[26]

c. The Trinitarian, Ecclesiological, and Soteriological Significance of Jesus' Resurrection

Up to now we have been pursuing the question of the historicity of the Resurrection. To fathom the full importance of this mystery, we shall consider, in what follows, what this event reveals about God himself, what meeting the risen Lord meant for his disciples, and how it changes our lives even today.

---

[26] Roman Missal, Easter Vigil, *Exsultet*.

THE TRINITARIAN SIGNIFICANCE
OF JESUS' RESURRECTION

In the Resurrection event, God reveals himself as Trinity.[27] Scripture describes this event sometimes as the work of the Father, sometimes as the work of the Son, and sometimes as the work of the Holy Spirit. Although the works of the Trinity are undivided, just as the substance of the Trinity is undivided,[28] the Church is accustomed to attribute works of power to the Father, works of wisdom to the Son, and works of love to the Holy Spirit (cf. DH 3326). Thus the Father demonstrates his power by raising Christ from death to new life. *He* is the first agent of the Resurrection. As Paul writes, the Father showed "the working of his great might which he accomplished in Christ when he raised him from the dead and made him sit at his right hand in the heavenly places" (Eph 1:19–20). In the Resurrection, the Father exalts the Son to be *Kyrios* in glory (Phil 2:9–11), so that he deserves the recognition, the reverence, and the glory of the eternal name of Son of God.

Scripture, however, also speaks of a Resurrection of Jesus by his own authority, as a direct action of the Son. Thus Jesus, in his speeches before Easter, announces that the Son of man has first to suffer much and to die, but that he will then rise again (cf. Mk 8:31). In the Gospel of John, he says explicitly: "I lay down my life, that I may take it again. . . . I have power to lay it down, and I have power to take it again" (Jn 10:17–18). The Resurrection is the fullness of Christ's revelation. During Jesus' earthly life, the glory that he had with the Father, "before the world was made" (Jn 17:5), remained mysteriously hidden. In the Resurrection, however, it is revealed that in Christ "the whole fulness of deity dwells bodily" (Col 2:9). The Resurrection reveals that it is not just now that Jesus is, or will be, at one with God (Adoptionism), but that he already was for all of his earthly life.[29]

When Paul says that "Christ was raised from the dead by the glory of the Father" (Rom 6:4), he is also alluding to the role of the Holy Spirit in the Resurrection. For in the Old Testament, the glory (*kabod*) of God was closely associated with the Spirit (cf. Ex 24:17; 40:34; Ezek 10:4). The way of talking about the "power of God" also refers to the Holy Spirit. "For he was crucified in weakness, but lives by the

---

[27] Cf. H. U. von Balthasar, TL 3:167–205.

[28] Augustine, *De trinitate* 1, 4, 7 (CChr.SL 50:36).

[29] Pannenberg, *Jesus, God and Man*, p. 153.

power of God" (2 Cor 13:4).³⁰ The Holy Spirit is the "giver of life" (DH 150); he makes everything new. Raised by the power of the Holy Spirit to new life, Christ himself becomes the dispenser of the Spirit, a "life-giving Spirit" (cf. Rom 8:11; 2 Cor 4:14). On the evening of Easter Day, Jesus came to his disciples, "he breathed on them, and said to them, 'Receive the Holy Spirit' " (Jn 20:22). Just as God breathed life into Adam (Gen 2:7), so after the Resurrection Jesus breathes new life into the disciples. The breath is the Holy Spirit, who brings about the new creation. With the Resurrection, Jesus' prophecy is fulfilled, "If any one thirst, let him come to me and drink. He who believes in me"—by which he was alluding to the gift of the Spirit as living water. "For as yet the Spirit had not yet been given, because Jesus was not yet glorified" (Jn 7:37–38, 39). The outpouring of the Holy Spirit after Easter quenches man's infinite thirst for eternal life, since "this is eternal life, [to] know you the only true God, and Jesus Christ whom you have sent" (Jn 17:3).

THE ECCLESIOLOGICAL SIGNIFICANCE
OF JESUS' RESURRECTION

Many accounts of Jesus' appearances end with the commissioning of the disciples to bear witness to the risen Christ. On the evening of Easter Day, the Lord says to his disciples, "As the Father has sent me, even so I send you" (Jn 20:21). Even in the pre-Easter fellowship, the disciples received a real share in the Kingdom of God through their communion with Jesus, a share in his mission and his authority. Through his Easter appearances, the pre-Easter common destiny was incorporated into the perfection of Jesus, and they become witnesses to his glory and table companions. As his post-Easter dinner companions, they are already with him in perfection and to a certain extent come as witnesses on that basis, on the basis of what they have seen and heard, what they have touched of the word of life (1 Jn 1:1). The unique feature of the appearances of the Risen One is that they signify a unique association of the witnesses with the one to whom they are testifying—exactly what, according to Paul, makes one "an apostle".

In this perspective, the apostle appears as one whom Christ, by appearing to him, has pulled into his own eschatological perfection. The

<hr>

³⁰ Cf. F. X. Durrwell, *Die Auferstehung Jesu als Heilsmysterium* (Salzburg, 1958), pp. 106–12.

apostle comes into history out of the glory that is to come, in which he has received a share, and hence he is a witness to the Lord who will come again.[31] The identification of the Risen One with his witnesses constitutes their unique position, which Revelation brings into the picture: the twelve apostles of the Lamb are the twelve foundation stones of the messianic Jerusalem (Rev 21:14). The perfection of the disciples' pre-Easter fellowship in the communion of the witnesses with the Risen One is an event that establishes the Church. This affiliation is not, however, a privilege, but a mission. Because Jesus is the one who was sent, belonging to him means a mission. The apostles are sent out by Jesus to be his witnesses. Those "chosen by God as witnesses" (Acts 10:41) do not speak of their impressions, but—as appears quite clearly in Paul's case—are aware of being witnesses in the sense that Christ is speaking through them, through their words. Christ is present in the kerygma, in that through the appearances, what was begun in the pre-Easter mission, that Jesus did not keep to himself his mission from God but shared and transmitted it, is brought to completion. The Risen One lives in the witnesses. This identification is the basis for the normative nature of the apostolic tradition. The apostles' kerygma, as Paul argues against the Corinthians, would be vain (1 Cor 15:14) if Christ had not risen from the dead; for then this message would perhaps be a brilliant interpretation, but not the word that the apostles have experienced as a power "which is able to build you up" (Acts 20:32). "My speech and my message were not in plausible words of wisdom, but in demonstration of the Spirit and of power, that your faith might not rest in the wisdom of men but in the power of God" (1 Cor 2:4–5).

THE SOTERIOLOGICAL SIGNIFICANCE
OF JESUS' RESURRECTION

Paul confesses that Christ "was raised on the third day in accordance with the Scriptures" (1 Cor 15:4). Here time specifications place the Resurrection promises within an eschatological dimension.[32] "This is not historical, but salvation historical information. . . . The time set

---

[31] Cf. J.-M. Garrigues and M.-J. Le Guillou, "Statut eschatologique et caractère onto-logique de la succession apostolique", *Revue Thomiste* 75 (1975): 395–417.

[32] Cf. K. Lehmann, *Auferweckt am dritten Tag nach der Schrift: Früheste Christologie, Bekenntnisbildung und Schriftauslegung im Lichte von 1 Kor 15,3–5*, QD 38 (Freiburg im Breisgau, 1968).

for God's work of salvation is three days."³³ Isaiah had in fact already promised the resurrection of the Servant as part of God's plan of salvation. "It was the will of the LORD to bruise him; he has put him to grief; when he makes himself an offering for sin, he shall see his offspring, he shall prolong his days; the will of the LORD shall prosper in his hand; he shall see the fruit of the travail of his soul and be satisfied" (Is 53:10–11).³⁴ "If Jesus has risen, this for a Jew that can only mean that God himself has confirmed the pre-Easter activity of Jesus."³⁵ That means, first of all, "that God had taken Jesus' part against his murderers."³⁶ God has justified him, as the outline of the apostles' first speeches in the Acts of the Apostles asserts: "God has made him both Lord and Christ, this Jesus whom you crucified" (Acts 2:36).

The fact that according to the evidence of the New Testament, the risen Jesus is worshipped (Mt 28:9, 17; Jn 20:16), that he is invoked as Kyrie in the liturgy, shows that we have to reckon quite early on with the confession of Jesus' divinity. The proclamation of the primitive Church, from the earliest Christology onward, expressed with the title *Kyrios* the reality of the world's situation since the Resurrection. The Risen One is Kyrios. Jesus is exalted "at the right hand of God" (Rom 8:34). Hence, he is the Kyrios, he shares in God's dominion, and he is our Paraclete with the Father (Rom 8:34). "If you confess with your lips that Jesus is Lord and believe in your heart that God raised him from the dead, you will be saved" (Rom 10:9). Jesus "died and lived again, that he might be Lord both of the dead and of the living" (Rom 14:9). Since the Reformation, Protestant, but also Catholic, dogmatics have so strongly emphasized the meaning of Jesus' death for salvation that it often seems as if the Resurrection were "just a corroborative appendage to the expiatory death of Christ that justifies us".³⁷ Yet a one-sided view of Jesus' death as penal satisfaction reduces its significance for salvation to either a merely good moral example or a forensic justification in which God revokes a judicial sentence on sinful mankind and promises them his salvation. Such an interpretation cer-

---

³³ Schubert, *Bibel und Geschichte*, p. 108.
³⁴ Cf. J. Jeremias, *Der Opfertod Jesu Christi* (Stuttgart, 1963), pp. 21–22.
³⁵ Pannenberg, *Jesus, God and Man*, p. 67.
³⁶ Von Balthasar, *Mysterium Paschale*, p. 201.
³⁷ J. Kremer, *Das älteste Zeugnis der Auferstehung Christi: Eine bibeltheologische Studie zur Aussage und Bedeutung von 1 Kor 15,1–11*, SBS 17 (Stuttgart, 1966), p. 102.

tainly does not exhaust the soteriological dimension of the Resurrection.[38]

In Jesus' day, there was common and widespread belief that the resurrection of the dead would take place at the end of the ages and that it would not be an isolated resurrection of individuals, but a universal resurrection. Hope in the ultimate overcoming of death is part of the turn of the ages, the definitive coming of God's Kingdom. This hope was already making a path for itself in the Old Testament. In Isaiah, when the messianic banquet for all the peoples is promised, it says, "He will swallow up death for ever, and the Lord GOD will wipe away tears from all faces" (Is 25:8). "Resurrection as an eschatological category was familiar to Judaism only in connection with the expected turn of this age to the coming one. The idea that the eschatological event of the resurrection might be anticipated in the case of a single particular person, whoever he might be, was absolutely foreign to Judaism."[39] This is therefore something new, underivable in Christian faith.

Against the background of this expectation, what did Jesus' rising again mean, since it was obviously not a return to earthly life, but a definitive resurrection? This was not simply a living on after death, as was expected for the souls of those who died, but an actual bodily resurrection upon his return (cf. Lk 24:39), so that the tomb was really empty—yet nor was it simply a revival of the corpse, as had happened in Jesus' raising of the dead. The fact that this event was called resurrection or rising again shows that the disciples saw this event— perhaps because of Jesus' predictions, and their encounters with him as the Risen One—in connection with the universal resurrection of the last days.

Accordingly, the significance of Christ's Resurrection for the history of salvation consists above all in the fact that he did not rise from the dead alone. His Resurrection is the beginning, the cause, and in a certain sense already the realization of the universal resurrection of the dead. The universal resurrection, at the end of time, is not a different, isolated occurrence, but an inseparable part of the Resurrection of

---

[38] See above, chap. 4:2b, "The Aftermath of 'Penal Satisfaction'".

[39] Schubert, "'Auferstehung Jesu'", p. 207; cf. Schubert, "Die Entwicklung der Auferstehungslehre von der nachexilischen bis zur rabbinischen Zeit", *Biblische Zeitschrift* 6 (1962): 177–214; A.-M. Dubarle, "Die Erwartung der Unsterblichkeit im Alten Testament und im Judentum", *Concilium* (D) 6 (1970): 685–91.

Jesus. Judgment Day has already dawned. Jesus Christ's death is "the day and the hour" of the coming of God's rule as King. The Kingdom of God has dawned, and with it the end time. The new creation began on Easter morning.

The apostolic preaching expressed this in various ways. Saint Paul, for instance, says:

> But in fact Christ has been raised from the dead, the *first fruits of those who have fallen asleep*. For as by a man came death, by a man has come also the resurrection of the dead. For as in Adam all die, so also in Christ shall all be made alive. But each in his own order: *Christ the first fruits*, then at his coming those who belong to Christ. Then comes the end, when he delivers the kingdom to God the Father after destroying every rule and every authority and power. (1 Cor 15:20–24)

Christ, then, is "*the first-born from the dead*" (Col 1:18). The universal resurrection of the dead has already begun with his Resurrection. It will be realized manifestly and completely at his return. The Resurrection of Jesus was no isolated occurrence, just as his death on the Cross was not an isolated misfortune. Both events are concerned with ultimate moments of decision in history: "Already the final age of the world has come upon us (cf. 1 Cor 10:11) and the renovation of the world is irrevocably decreed" (*Lumen Gentium*, no. 48:3). Only with this view of the events of Easter do certain peculiarities of the Christian expectation of resurrection become comprehensible, and first of all the much-discussed problem of the "imminent expectation"; besides that, the idea that we have already been raised with Christ; and, finally, the other expectation—apparently in contradiction to it—that we will rise again at Christ's return.

RESURRECTION AND IMMINENT EXPECTATION

If Christ has risen, then the universal resurrection of the dead has dawned. Can it then be long before this becomes manifest? Paul—and probably the whole of the early Church with him—expected that he would himself experience on earth Christ's return. "Some have fallen asleep" (1 Cor 15:6). What will happen to them? In his earliest letter, the Apostle consoles the congregation at Thessalonica: Those who have already fallen asleep and those who remain upon earth will together be joined with Christ in his Resurrection upon his return (cf. 1 Thess 4:13–17).

Later, when the Apostle was in prison, he had to reckon with the possibility that he himself might suffer death before Christ's return. Under these circumstances, death even seemed to him desirable, since he was longing to be with Christ:

> It is my eager expectation and hope that I shall not be at all ashamed, but that with full courage now as always Christ will be honored in my body, whether by life or by death. For to me to live is Christ, and to die is gain. If it is to be life in the flesh, that means fruitful labor for me. Yet which I shall choose I cannot tell. I am hard pressed between the two. My desire is to depart and be with Christ, for that is far better. But to remain in the flesh is more necessary on your account. (Phil 1:20–24)

It is astounding that the delay in the Lord's return did not cause greater confusion in the early Church. There is only one explanation of it that makes sense: Christ was not only being expected as the One who would come back, but believed in as the One who was already present. Christ stands at the center of Christian belief and hope.[40] Before Easter, Christ had already closely united to himself the disciples whom he had himself chosen (cf. Mk 3:13), "to be with him, and to be sent out to preach" (Mk 3:14). They belong to him (cf. Lk 22:56–59), and he is with them, inseparably: "He who hears you hears me" (Lk 10:16). This belonging intimately together does not cease with the Resurrection; rather, it is given a new and universal significance and power: "And behold, I am with you always, to the close of the age" (Mt 28:20). Paul has a triumphant assurance that nothing can separate us from the love of Christ (Rom 8:35, 39).

NEW BEING IN CHRIST

The reality that illuminates everything is that of being with Christ, indeed, being in Christ, about which Saint Paul so often talks. Since we are in Christ, then: "If we live, we live to the Lord, and if we die, we die to the Lord; so then whether we live or whether we die, we are the Lord's. For to this end Christ died and lived again, that he might be Lord both of the dead and of the living" (Rom 14:8–9). This view of it makes clear why it is that our resurrection can be talked about not only as being in the future, but also in the present.

---

[40] See on this the fine work by E. Keller, *Eucharistie und Parusie: Liturgie- und theologiegeschichtliche Untersuchungen zur eschatologischen Dimension der Eucharistie anhand ausgewählter Zeugnisse aus frühchristlicher und patristischer Zeit* (Freiburg, 1989), pp. 14–17.

Saint Paul teaches that in baptism a dying with Christ takes place. So that "as Christ was raised from the dead by the glory of the Father, we too might walk in newness of life" (Rom 6:4). Those who have been baptized should regard themselves as people who are dead to sin "but alive to God in Christ Jesus" (Rom 6:11). This new life is truly a "being in Christ", in the Risen One. Hence it is that "if anyone is in Christ, he is a new creation; the old has passed away, behold, the new has come" (2 Cor 5:17). So much so that Saint Paul speaks of the baptized as having risen with Christ: "If then you have been raised with Christ, seek the things that are above, where Christ is, seated at the right hand of God" (Col 3:1). And, still more clearly, "But God, who is rich in mercy, out of the great love with which he loved us, even when we were dead through our trespasses, made us alive together with Christ (by grace you have been saved), and raised us up with him, and made us sit with him in the heavenly places" (Eph 2:4-6).[41] The new life with Christ is now, already, participation in his Resurrection. Yet this reality has not yet been completely revealed: "For you have died, and your life is hidden with Christ in God. When Christ who is our life appears, then you also will appear with him in glory" (Col 3:3-4; cf. 1 Jn 3:2).

Because being a Christian means being with Christ, the Christians' home is where Christ is: "But our commonwealth is in heaven, and from it we await a Savior, the Lord Jesus Christ" (Phil 3:20). That is why earthly existence is a time of pilgrimage,[42] "far from our home": "So we are always of good courage; we know that while we are at home in the body we are away from the Lord, for we walk by faith, not by sight. We are of good courage, and we would rather be away from the body and at home with the Lord" (2 Cor 5:6-8).

Our life is already "in Christ", yet only when "the earthly tent we live in is destroyed" (2 Cor 5:1), when we "depart" (Phil 1:23) by dying from this life "in the flesh" (Phil 1:22), will we be "at home with the Lord". Yet even then, our being with Christ will still not be

---

[41] On these assertions concerning a present resurrection, see J. Kremer, in G. Greshake and J. Kremer, *Resurrectio mortuorum: Zum theologischen Verständnis der leiblichen Auferstehung* (Darmstadt, 1986), pp. 137–57.

[42] On this, see C. Schönborn, *Existenz im Übergang: Pilgerschaft, Reinkarnation, Vergöttlichung* (Einsiedeln, 1987); Schönborn, *Die Menschen, die Kirche, das Land: Christentum als gesellschaftliche Herausforderung* (Vienna, 1998), pp. 205–44.

complete.[43] We are all in an intermediate state in the history of salvation and waiting for completion. Only when the Lord comes again
will he "change our lowly body to be like his glorious body, by the
power which enables him even to subject all things to himself" (Phil
3:21).

Thus, to sum up, we can note that being a Christian is being in Christ;
yet there is in this a threefold progression: "existence 'in Christ' in
earthly corporality; an increase in communion with Christ ('being with
Christ') in an intermediate state that is already free from earthly corporality, yet also still lacks the heavenly state; and completion through
reception of a heavenly body."[44]

BETWEEN DEATH AND RESURRECTION

The Resurrection of Christ initiates the universal resurrection, for
Christ is the "first-fruits" of those who have risen from the dead.
Since then, "the power of his resurrection" (Phil 3:10) is at work.
This power will take full effect with the return of Christ and the uni-
versal resurrection of the dead. In the meantime, it is set to work by the
Holy Spirit, who is "to complete his work on earth and bring us the
fullness of grace".[45] This intermediate time is the time of the Church's
pilgrimage.

In eschatology, the doctrine of the "last things", the intermediate
state is spoken of as the state of men between death and resurrection.
The question of this intermediate state is controversial.[46] In particular,
the doctrine of the *anima separata*, of the soul detached from the body,
often meets with incomprehension. In the name of the body-soul unity
of man, the idea of a soul from which the body has detached itself,
or which has detached itself from the body, is dismissed as "a relic of
Platonism", as "unbiblical", with repeated—inaccurate—references to

---

[43] J.-M. Garrigues, "L'Inachèvement du salut: Composante essentielle du temps de l'Église", NV 71 (1996): 13–29.

[44] C.-H. Hunzinger, "Die Hoffnung angesichts des Todes im Wandel der paulinischen
Aussagen", in *Leben angesichts des Todes: Beiträge zum theologischen Problem des Todes: Helmut
Thielicke zum 60. Geburtstag*, pp. 69–88, here p. 86 (Tübingen, 1968).

[45] Roman Missal, *Eucharistic Prayer IV*.

[46] See the account given by C. Pozo, *Teología del más allá*, 2nd ed., BAC 282 (Madrid,
(1980), pp. 463–537.

Saint Thomas Aquinas.[47] In the meantime, a "rediscovery of the soul" has begun to take place,[48] albeit uncertainly and almost with embarrassment,[49] first in philosophy[50] and then in theology, too.

Classic Catholic teaching indicates that death is the separation of body and soul. The immortal soul lingers without a body in the "intermediate state" that still separates it from reunification with its body at the universal resurrection of the dead. It took a long time before the Church's teaching about this "intermediate state" assumed a definite shape. We find it most clearly formulated in the papal constitution *Benedictus Deus* (Benedict XII, d. 1342):

> The souls of all the saints . . . have been, are, and will be in heaven and in Paradise immediately after their death, or after purification in the case of those who needed any such purification, and this is before reunification with their body and before the general judgment, after the Ascension of our Savior Jesus Christ, our Lord, into heaven.
>
> And after the Passion and death of our Lord Jesus Christ, they gazed and now gaze on the divine substance in direct contemplation and face to face. . . . In this vision they are filled with the enjoyment of the divine substance. And through this vision and through this enjoyment, the souls of those who have already died are truly happy in the possession of life and of eternal peace. . . . And this vision and this enjoyment continue without any interruption or diminishment of this vision or this enjoyment and will continue until the final judgment and from then on to all eternity. (DH 1000–1001)

The objection is occasionally made, against this traditional teaching of the Church, that the resurrection of the flesh is being reduced to a basically dispensable ornament here if, after all, the "departed souls" are already in the beatific vision of God. And indeed the question does arise as to what the resurrection of the flesh can add to this beatitude of the vision of God.

---

[47] See on this the article by M. Schulze, " 'Anima separata'—Baustein einer theologischen Lehre vom Menschen", *Internationale Katholische Zeitschrift Communio* 19 (1990): 30–36.

[48] Cf. H. Sonnemans, *Seele: Unsterblichkeit—Auferstehung: Zur griechischen und christlichen Anthropologie und Eschatologie* (Freiburg, 1984).

[49] Thus, in part, in W. Breuning, ed., *Seele: Problembegriff christlicher Eschatologie*, QD 106 (Freiburg im Breisgau, 1986).

[50] Cf. J. Seifert, *Das Leib-Seele-Problem und die gegenwärtige philosophische Diskussion: Eine systematisch-kritische Analyse*, 2nd ed. (Darmstadt, 1989).

To attempt an answer to this question, we have to go back to an old creedal statement: "I believe . . . in the resurrection of the flesh in the holy Catholic Church."[51] Georg Kretschmar comments on this formula: "resurrection of the flesh in the Church" is "a clear assertion of salvation, the hope of Christendom for the completion in the future resurrection of what is beginning now in the Church".[52] The meaning of "resurrection at the last day" is accessible to us in quite a new way if we do not consider it in an individualistic, isolated sense, but see it in connection with the mystery of the Church.

What do we all have in common, those on pilgrimage in faith and those who have fallen asleep in the Lord? Two things: we belong to the one Church, and we have all not yet risen in the body. All those who believe in Christ and have his Spirit constitute the one Church, whether they are pilgrims on earth or have departed this life and are either being purified or are already glorified and have a clear vision of the triune God.[53] The one Church in heaven and on earth has this in common, that all her members (with the exception of Mary) do not yet have the glory of bodily resurrection. The power of Christ's Resurrection is indeed already at work in all three states in ever-varying degrees. Even in this earthly, mortal life, Christ's Resurrection effects more or less distinctly a transfiguration of our body, as has been evident in many saints. Yet the frailty of bodily life reminds us that complete resurrection is still to come. In the state of purification ("the fire of purgatory"), the soul learns, now that it is no longer in the body, its powerlessness to purify itself by any act of its own. Its bodilessness, and its longing for the resurrection of the body, is that much more painful to it. The souls of those who already behold God are filled with his bliss. And yet they, too, long for the resurrection, because, being intimately united with Christ, they yearn for the final coming of his Kingdom, which will be fully realized only with the victory over the last enemy, death (cf. 1 Cor 15:27)—that is, with the resurrection of all the dead.

---

[51] Papyrus from *Dêr-Balyzeh*, quoted according to G. Kretschmar, "Auferstehung des Fleisches: Zur Frühgeschichte einer theologischen Lehrformel", in *Leben angesichts des Todes*, pp. 101–37, here p. 104.

[52] Kretschmar, "Auferstehung des Fleisches", p. 104.

[53] *Lumen Gentium*, no. 49; cf. C. Schönborn, "Die Communio der drei kirchlichen Stände", *Internationale Katholische Zeitschrift Communio* 17 (1988): 8–20.

Those souls united with Christ in bliss (the "saints in heaven") work ceaselessly with Christ to build up his body, for the salvation of men. Their longing for the resurrection of the body is not a hope for greater personal happiness. What more could they gain than the vision of the living God? They do not hope for an individual resurrection but for "the resurrection of the flesh": that is, for the completion of what has irreversibly begun with the Resurrection of Jesus. They hope for the reign of Jesus Christ, which brings salvation, to be fully realized. Only when everything has been subjected to Christ, and he has destroyed every authority and power (cf. 1 Cor 15:24), can the Resurrection of Christ prove itself definitively victorious in the resurrection of all flesh. Only then will God be "everything to every one" (1 Cor 15:28). The saints in heaven long for that, and that will be their resurrection. That is what we are asking for when we pray for the coming of his Kingdom. Origen, in his sermons on the Letter to the Romans, expressed these ideas:

> Paul speaks of "the redemption of our body". I think that points to the body of the Church as a whole. . . . The Apostle is hoping, then, for the redemption of the whole body of the Church; he thinks that perfection can be given to the individual members only when the entire body has been gathered into one.[54]

In the Creed, we declare our belief in the resurrection of the flesh. We are thereby confessing that we "wait in joyful hope for the coming of our Savior, Jesus Christ".[55] This coming, which will be our glorious resurrection—may it be to life, not to the judgment! (cf. Jn 5:29)—is that for which the whole of creation longs.

2. He is Seated at the Right Hand of God the Almighty Father

John Damascene (d. 749) who in his *Presentation of the Orthodox Faith* sums up the great tradition of the Greek Church Fathers, sets forth the meaning of the article about the Ascension as follows:

---

[54] Origen, *Commentarius in epistulam ad Romanos* 7, 5 (PG 14:1116–17).
[55] Roman Missal, embolism after the Lord's Prayer: "expectantes beatam spem et adventum Salvatoris nostri Jesu Christi".

We say that Christ sits bodily at the right hand of God the Father, but we do not teach that the right hand of the Father is a place. For how could he who is uncircumscribed have a right hand limited by place? Only beings that are circumscribed have a right hand and a left hand.—No, we understand the right hand of the Father to be the glory of honor of the Godhead, in which the Son of God existed from eternity as God and of the same substance as the Father, and in which now, having become flesh in recent times, he is seated in body, since his flesh was glorified with him. For he along with his flesh is adored in one adoration by the whole of creation.[56]

In this brief presentation are summarized the two most important statements of faith that the early Church saw as affirmed by the article in the Creed about "sitting at the Father's right hand": that Christ is God, "of the same substance as the Father", and that he did not give up being human after being glorified, but is really "bodily" seated at the right hand of the Father. Around these two fundamental christological statements are grouped a series of more ecclesiological conclusions, to which John Damascene does not refer specifically here, but which the Fathers develop abundantly. This concerns especially Christ's rule and his office as judge, the "share" of the faithful in Christ's rule, the unity of Head and body, of Christ and Church.[57]

A glance at the significance of this article of the Creed in the history of dogma shows, as if in a concave mirror, the whole of the Christian faith in summary. Let us first hear some of the witnesses to the "rule of faith" that present its meaning without polemics. We shall then cite, by way of example, some instances of christological controversy about the meaning of the "*sessio ad dexteram Patris*". Finally, we would like to raise the ecclesiological aspect of this mystery of Christ. In all three steps, it can only be a matter of brief references, a "sampling" of the treasure of the Fathers.

a. Witnesses to the "Rule of Faith"

Just as already in the New Testament, so, too, statements about Christ's being seated at the right hand of God in the early Church have to do

---

[56] John Damascene, *De fide orthodoxa* 4, 2 (PTS 12:173).

[57] On what follows, see C. Schönborn, *Existenz im Übergang*, pp. 17–33; on the biblical basis (but without agreeing with the author's conclusions), cf. M. Gourgues, *À la droite de Dieu: Résurrection de Jésus et actualisation du psaume 110,1 dans le Nouveau Testament* (Paris, 1978).

with Easter faith and with the Creed. In the Paschal homily of Bishop Melito of Sardis (second century), we find a solemn confession of faith in Christ that is completely filled with certainty of the Paschal victory of Christ and, beyond that, of his eternal reign:

> This is he
> who made the heaven and the earth,
> and in the beginning fashioned man;
> who was announced by the law and the prophets,
> who was made flesh in the Virgin,
> who was hung on the tree,
> who was buried in the earth,
> who rose from the dead,
> and ascended to the heights of heaven,
> who sits at the right hand of the Father,
> who has all authority to judge and to save,
> through whom the Father made everything
> from the beginning unto all ages.[58]

Here, far removed from any polemics, Christ is confessed as "beginning and end", as the text goes on to say, as "ineffable beginning and incomprehensible end", as King and Lord, as Alpha and Omega.[59] Irenaeus of Lyons, at the end of the second century, likewise emphasizes —against the tendency of the Gnostics to divide Christ into an earthly and a heavenly being—that the preexistent Son of God is at the same time the one who was crucified and the one who is glorified: "None other than he who was seized and who suffered and shed his blood for us, is most clearly described by Paul as Christ, the Son of God, who also rose again and was taken up into heaven, as he says himself: 'Christ Jesus, who died, yes, who is risen again, who is at the right hand of God' (Rom 8:34). . . . Jesus Christ, the Son of God, is one and the same, he who reconciled us to God through his suffering and who rose from the dead, who is at the right hand of the Father and who is perfect in everything."[60] Fulgentius of Ruspe (d. 532), in writing to Peter "about the right rule of faith", emphasizes this same identity: "One and the

---

[58] Melito of Sardis, *Peri Pascha* 104 (SC 123:124–25).
[59] Ibid.
[60] Irenaeus of Lyons, *Adversus haereses* 3, 16, 9 (SC 211:355). Just like Melito, Irenaeus interprets the New Testament's "at the right hand of God" as "at the right hand of the Father"; cf. O. Perler (SC 123:208).

same God, the Son of God . . . is, in the flesh, he who lay in the tomb and rose from the tomb; and on the fortieth day after the Resurrection, the same incarnate God ascended into heaven and sits at the right hand of God."[61] We can read in Cyril of Jerusalem (d. 387) what was said in the fourth century to the candidates for baptism in Jerusalem in the prebaptismal catechesis in the faith. The meaning of being "seated at the right hand of the Father" comes up in the same way in three places, and each time he stresses that Christ is seated at the right hand of the Father from all eternity, "for he has not been in some sense crowned by God after his suffering, as some have believed, nor has he obtained the throne on the right hand because of his patience, but ever since he exists—and he is eternally begotten—he has had royal dignity and is enthroned with the Father, since (as we said) he is God, Wisdom and Power. He reigns together with the Father and created everything for the Father's sake."[62] The emphasis here is entirely on the divinity of Christ, which is particularly highlighted by the "enthroned with": "*One* Son must be proclaimed, who before all time sits at the right hand of the Father and who did not step by step receive the privilege of sitting at his side in time only after he had suffered."[63] While Cyril hardly talks at all about Christ's humanity "sharing in glory", in the Ascension sermons of Pope Leo the Great (d. 461) this is strongly in the foreground. He invites his listeners to rejoice with the disciples that "human nature has taken its place, high above all the creatures of the heavens . . . , to attain the final goal of its exaltation on the seat of the eternal Father and to share on this throne the glory [of the Father], with whose nature it was united through the Son". Together with Christ's humanity, all men have in some sense, "inclusively", been glorified: "the Ascension of Christ signifies our own exaltation", for God's Son has "incorporated" human nature, "and has placed it at the right hand of the Father".[64]

The Syrian hymn writer Kyrillonas (fourth century) describes the event of Christ's Ascension with a most impressive, readily intelligible image, as the introduction of man into the glory of the triune God.

---

[61] Fulgentius of Ruspe, *De fide ad Petrum seu de regula fidei* 2, 11 (CChr.SL 91A:718–19).

[62] Cyril of Jerusalem, *4th Catechetical Homily* §7 (PG 33:464A).

[63] Cyril of Jerusalem, *11th Catechetical Homily* §17 (PG 33:712B); cf. also *14th Homily* §§27–30 (PG 33:861B–865A).

[64] Leo the Great, *Tractatus* 73, 4 (CChr.SL 138A:453–54).

Christ in his own person, carries his own human existence into the glory of God. Thereby he also leads Adam back to the place intended for him on the throne of the Trinity:

> My Father is waiting for me to ascend and to bring up with me body and soul, which were held prisoner by death and the devil. The angels are waiting for me to ascend and to bring up with me the lost sheep, which has been found again through my coming. Heaven is waiting for me to ascend and to bring up with me the earthly body that has by grace become God. The throne is waiting for me to ascend and be seated upon it and to seat on it with me the humbled Adam, who is now once more exalted. The cloud is waiting for me that carried me away from the mountain and now desires to serve the Virgin's Son as a carriage. Paradise and the Garden are both waiting for me to bring Adam into them and to enthrone him as ruler there.[65]

Thus, in the interpretation of the article of faith concerning Christ's Ascension, the most important questions of faith are articulated: Jesus' divinity, his being of the same substance as the Father; his human existence, which does not cease with the Resurrection but is perfected to the point of the eternal "sharing in glory" of his body; the unity of Christ's divinity and humanity, even now in his eternal rule; the identity of the one Son, Jesus Christ, through all the "stages" of salvation history.

That is what the regula fidei says, then, the rule of faith. Of course, there is no shortage of questions: Can we, along with John Damascene, seriously believe in Christ's "sitting at the right hand" in a bodily sense? Can we think of Christ's consubstantial divinity? At this point, Augustine adamantly reminds the catechumens (and us with them!) that faith is the prerequisite for understanding:

> Christ has ascended into heaven. Believe! He sits at the right hand of the Father. Believe! . . . He is there! Let not your heart say, What is he doing? Do not seek what it is not permitted to find! He is there! That is enough for you! He is blessed, and from the blessedness that is called "the right hand of the Father" comes the name of this blessedness: "the right hand of the Father."[66]

---

[65] Kyrillonas the Syrian, Second Homily on the Pascha of Christ (BKV, 2nd ed., 6:41).

[66] Augustine, De symbolo ad catechumenos 4, 11 (CChr.SL 46:195); cf. E. Dassmann, Augustinus: Heiliger und Kirchenlehrer (Stuttgart, 1993), pp. 86–100.

At the right hand means, then, being in the most supreme blessedness, where righteousness, peace, and joy are; just as the goats are assigned to the left (Mt 25:33), that is, in misery because of the labors and
torments for unrighteousness. If one speaks of God sitting, then, it is
not a bodily posture that is signified, but the judicial power that is never
absent from his rule, but always assigns to each what he deserves."[67]
Thomas Aquinas was to adopt from Augustine this metaphorical interpretation of "right" as blessedness and as judicial power.[68] Yet does
not this metaphorical view threaten the realism of the enduring corporality of Christ? Augustine does not want to dissolve it allegorically.
He also indicates, however, what is incomprehensible in this article of
faith: "Where and in what manner the body of the Lord is in heaven
is certainly an overly curious and superfluous question. It is enough
simply to believe that it is in heaven. Our frailty is not entitled to want
to penetrate the mysteries of heaven; but it is the business of our faith
to think what is elevated and reverent about the dignity of the Lord's
body."[69]

b. The Article of Faith in Controversy

Precisely this, "to think what is elevated and reverent" about Christ's
body encountered opposition early on. It is worthwhile taking a look
at the interpretation of this article of faith by the second-century
Gnostics.[70] The ever-recurring, basic conviction of Gnosticism is this:
"There is only salvation for the soul, for the body is corrupt by nature."[71] The Gnostics liked to cite Paul's words: "Flesh and blood cannot inherit the kingdom of God" (1 Cor 15:50), to support their view
that for the body, as a part of the material world, there could be no salvation and no eternal perfection.[72] Christ's Ascension, then, is for the
most part understood by Gnostics as the return of the heavenly Christ
to his original, purely spiritual state. The Gnostic Apelles (d. 185), for
instance, taught that Christ had formed a body for himself from the

---

[67] Augustine, *De fide et symbolo* 7, 14 (CSEL 41:16–17).
[68] Thomas Aquinas, STh III, q. 58, a. 1 (DThA 28:295); Thomas Aquinas, *Compendium theologiae*, c. 241 (*Op. omn.* 3:629), and so on.
[69] Augustine, *De fide et symbolo* 6, 13 (CSEL 41:16).
[70] A detailed account of this is given by A. Orbe, *Cristología Gnóstica: Introducción a la sote-riología de los siglos II y III*, vol. 2 (Madrid, 1976), pp. 535–73.
[71] Irenaeus, *Adversus haereses* 1, 24, 5 (about Basilides) (SC 264:112).
[72] Ibid., 5, 9:1–14:4 (FChr 8/5:74–123).

various cosmic materials, that this had been crucified, and that this was what he showed to his disciples after his Resurrection. But "after he had let them see his body, he gave it back to the earth from which it came; he took to himself nothing alien, but when he loosed the bond of his body, he gave back to its own everything that he made use of temporarily—what was warm to the warm, what was cold to the cold, fluid to the fluid, firm to the firm: then he went to the good Father, leaving behind in the world for believers, through his disciples, the seed of life."[73] According to a principle of Gnosticism, everything has to return again to its original place.[74] What is material must resolve itself into material, what is spirit returns—infallibly—to the spirit.

Hermogenes (d. ca. 205), not a true Gnostic, but in this point representative of the Gnostic interpretation of the Ascension, teaches that Christ "having risen after his Passion, appeared in the body to the disciples, and at his Ascension into heaven he left his body behind in the sun, but he himself came to the Father". In saying this, he refers to Psalm 18 (LXX): "In the sun he has set his tent", taking the "tent" here to mean the "earthly tent" of the body.[75] However strange this cosmology seems, the core of the statement is clear: in broad educated circles in the ancient world, a *bodily* resurrection or an eternal perfection of the body was inconceivable. Any corporeal dimension to "sitting at the right hand" is accordingly denied. In Gnosticism, "the right" is considered the word for "spiritual", "higher", "light", "manly", whereas "the left" represents the opposite of all that. In virtue of that, some Gnostics interpret Christ's being seated at the right hand of the Father in the sense that Christ is higher than God—that is, than the God who speaks to the Jews in the Old Testament and who says in the Psalm, "Sit at my right hand" (Ps 110:1). *This* God, for the Gnostics, is the evil God of the Jews, the Creator of this evil world.[76] Absurd speculation? Not necessarily, since this is essentially a matter of the conviction, which many people share today, that this world represents a confused, chaotic, and largely negative product of lower forces, from which only the knowledge (gnosis) of this nullity can lead us out.

---

[73] Hippolytus, *Refutatio omnium haeresium* 7, 38 (PTS 25:321); Orbe, *Cristología Gnóstica* 2:538.

[74] Cf. Irenaeus, *Adversus haereses* 2, 14, 4 (FChr 8/2:112).

[75] According to Hippolytus, *Refutatio omnium haeresium* 8, 17 (PTS 25:337).

[76] Cf. Orbe, *Cristología Gnóstica* 2:550–68.

While for the Gnostics "sitting at the right hand of God" is an indication that Christ leaves this God behind, for the Arians of the fourth
century, on the contrary, it is a sign that the Son is lesser than the
Father. Eusebius of Caesarea (d. 339), the great Church historian, who
was never able to overcome his conceptual proximity to Arianism,
saw Christ, the Word of God, as "the first-born of all creation" (Col
1:15), as God's first and unique creation, whom God made co-ruler
with him, who "is enthroned with him", to whom "the honor was
assigned, alone among all beings who have come into existence, to
sit at the right hand of the power and kingship of the Almighty".[77]
It seems to Eusebius unthinkable and unacceptable that this "sitting
at the right hand of God" should express the true divinity of Christ.
For him, Christ remains "a being who has come into existence", the
highest of all creatures, but not God in a substantial sense, since this
could not, for Eusebius, be reconciled with the oneness of God.

But were the defenders of Christ's true divinity, consubstantial with
the Father, right to cite Psalm 110? Is it not the case, rather, that Christ
was "exalted at the right hand of God" (Acts 2:33) only after the Resurrection? The Arians referred to the Acts of the Apostles: "God has
made him both Lord and Christ" (Acts 2:36), to support their view
that Christ was not God by nature, since he was made Lord. In contrast, Athanasius of Alexandria (d. 373) developed the view that has remained definitive for orthodox Christology: Christ is the Son of God,
and God, consubstantial with the Father. Together with the Father he
reigns eternally, which is why Psalm 110 refers to his eternal rule.[78]
That his rule is confirmed and grows, that God makes him Lord and
Messiah, Athanasius interprets as "salvation-historically":

> Christ, who is by nature Lord and eternal King, is not more Lord at the
> moment when he is sent forth, nor does he begin to be Lord and King
> only then, but he was then made also according to the flesh what he had
> always been, and with the redemption of everyone accomplished he also
> becomes Lord of the living and the dead. For from now on, everything
> serves him, and it is of this that David sings: "The Lord says to my lord,

---

[77] Eusebius of Caesarea, *Demonstratio evangelica* 5, 3 (GCS 6:219); cf. M.-J. Rondeau, "Le
'Commentaire des Psaumes' de Diodore de Tarse et l'exégèse antique du Psaume 109/110",
Revue de l'histoire des religions 88/176 (1969): 5–33, 155–88; *Revue de l'histoire des religions* 89/
177 (1970): 5–33.

[78] Athanasius of Alexandria, *Orationes contra Arianos* 2, 13 (Opitz/Tetz 1:189–90).

'Sit at my right hand, until I make your enemies your footstool'" (Ps
110:1).[79]

Eternity and salvation history, Christ's divinity and humanity, are
seen in marvelous synopsis here. He who created us has through the Incarnation becomes likewise our Redeemer, his eternal rule is extended
over all men through his glorified humanity. Concerning precisely this
last perspective there were further controversies. Does "until I make
your enemies your footstool" not mean that, when this has happened,
Christ's rule will come to an end? Does Paul not say, in this connection, "When all things are subjected to him, then the Son himself will
also be subjected to him who put all things under him, that God may
be everything to every one" (1 Cor 15:28)?

Marcellus of Ancyra (d. 374), a zealous defender of the Council
of Nicaea, a friend of Athanasius, believed that everything said about
Christ's being seated at the right hand of God meant Christ as a man
and was thus valid only for the period of the Incarnation, which had
a beginning and, so Marcellus supposed, an end. For Marcellus saw
Christ's humanity as having a temporal significance, not an eternal
one. At "the end of time", having discharged its function, it would
no longer be used. Marcellus went even farther, and that placed his orthodoxy in question: the eternal word of God, the Logos, will himself
in the end be to some extent absorbed into the Father, so that nothing
exists any more but God alone.[80] Doubt seems thereby to be cast on
the existence of the Son as a Divine Person himself.

That Christ's humanity has only a passing significance was also the
view of that powerful spiritual movement in the early Church that invoked the name of the great but controversial figure of Origen. The offense of Christ's body living forever, of his flesh forever remaining, has
prompted Christian thinkers in the sphere of Origen's influence, time
and again, to switch into allegory when this question was raised. For
Evagrius Ponticus (d. 399), the influential monastic theologian, "sitting
at the right hand of God" simply meant that the preexistent soul-spirit
of Christ was "entirely anointed with the knowledge of unity . . . ,
for right hand means, according to the interpretation of those who

---

[79] Ibid. (Opitz/Tetz 1:191).
[80] On Marcellus, see A. Grillmeier, *Christ in Christian Tradition*, vol. 1: *From the Apostolic
Age to Chalcedon (451)*, 2nd ed. (Atlanta, 1975), pp. 274–96.

have knowledge, the monad and unity".[81] What matters is this purely spiritual view, free of any image or concept, of the primordial divine unity toward which Christ is leading and to which his earthly body represents, at most, a kind of 'entry', nothing more. "Corporeality no longer has any significance for the restored world. It is merely the temporal manifestation of the *nous-Christus* for us. Only the spirit has significance, and knowledge, of all the spiritual acts."[82]

The question of whether, in such contemplation, Christ should be pictured as a man was something that very much occupied Teresa of Avila (d. 1582). Teresa recounts in her autobiography that she was very disconcerted by certain authors who were given her to read. The latter advised striving to transcend all corporal concepts, "even when referring to the humanity of Christ", since these tended to be a hindrance to contemplation. It was incomprehensible to Teresa how anyone could teach turning away from Christ's humanity as a way of spiritual life; those who teach this "quote what the Lord said to the Apostles about the coming of the Holy Spirit—I mean, at the time of His Ascension [cf. Jn 16:7]. It seems to me that if they had faith that He was both God and man as they did after the Holy Spirit came, this would not have hindered them."[83] No, the visible reality of the Lord could be no hindrance to prayer. It is fascinating how Teresa portrays her discovery of the contemplation of Christ's humanity. She spent only a short while following the wrong way of supposedly "spiritual" contemplation, which regards even God's Incarnation as too low a stage. Teresa was drawn powerfully back to Christ's humanity; visions were granted to her that strengthened her on this path: indescribable light, ineffable beauty; she was permitted to see Christ, his hands, his face, his whole person: "The Lord almost always showed Himself to me as risen, also when He appeared in the Host—except at times when He showed me His wounds in order to encourage me when I was suffering tribulation. Sometimes He appeared on the cross or in the garden, and a few times with the crown of thorns; sometimes He also

---

[81] Evagrius Ponticus, *Kephalaia gnostica* 4, 21 (PO 28:145); cf. Grillmeier, *Christ in Christian Tradition* 1:377–84.

[82] Grillmeier, *Christ in Christian Tradition* 1:383.

[83] Teresa of Avila, *Vida*, chap. 22 §1 (trans. by Kieran Kavanaugh, O.C.D., and Otilio Rodriguez, O.C.D., as *The Book of Her Life*, in *The Collected Works of St. Teresa of Avila*, vol. 1 [Washington, D.C.: ICS Publications, 1976], pp. 144, 295–96 n. 1).

appeared carrying the cross on account, as I say, of my needs and those of others. But His body was always glorified."[84] If one wishes to describe these visions as a picture, "it is a living image—not a dead man, but the living Christ. And He makes it known that he is both man and God, not as he was in the tomb, but as He was when he came out of the tomb after His resurrection. Sometimes he comes with such great majesty that no one can doubt but that is the Lord Himself. Especially after receiving Communion—for we know that He is present, since our faith tells us this."[85]

Here, the mystery of this article of the Creed is marvelously expressed, in a vivid fullness: Christ, "as he is himself", "the living Christ", man and God, the risen, glorified body, whom faith receives in the bread of life in Communion. Teresa of Avila knows that the whole sacramental dimension of the Church stands or falls with the abiding, glorified humanity of Christ. She knows that the Risen One is near us now in the Sacrament.[86]

How closely the mystery of Christ appears linked with that of the Church, particularly in this article of faith, "he is seated at the right hand of the Father", is shown by a glance at a contemporary of Teresa, who is in many ways her exact opposite. John Calvin (d. 1564) repeatedly emphasizes that Christ ascended *bodily* into heaven and that he is now there, not here; he is sitting *there* at the right hand of the Father; even if that does not suit the philosophers, the Holy Spirit teaches it. But that means, for Calvin, that he is no way bodily with us. We do indeed always have Christ with us, yet not his fleshly presence, but that of his majesty, of his Holy Spirit;[87] in body, he is *only* in heaven. Yet for Calvin, that means, further, that he cannot be *bodily* in the bread and wine of the Eucharist, that he ought not to be represented bodily on earth. "We have communion with God neither by an image nor by any other earthly object we may choose, not even by the visible elements of the Lord's Supper, but only by the Holy Spirit, who has no difficulty in uniting what is spatially separated."[88] Calvin wishes

---

[84] Ibid., 29 §4 (*Collected Works* 1:189–90).

[85] Ibid., 28 §8 (*Collected Works* 1:184).

[86] Ibid., 22 §6 (*Collected Works* 1:146–47).

[87] J. Calvin, *Institutio Religionis Christianae* 2, 16, 14.

[88] Margarete Stirm, *Die Bilderfrage in der Reformation*, QFRG 45 (Gütersloh, 1977), pp. 212–13.

to emphasize the real, corporal glorification of Jesus, and yet for him this excludes the possibility that "Jesus Christ may dwell in the bread (of the Eucharist)", for otherwise Christ would have to leave heaven. The work of the Holy Spirit, which unites us to Christ, is enough for us to have Christ present.[89] It is only consistent for Calvin to reject the image of Christ along with the bodily presence of the Lord in the Eucharist.

With the other Reformers, too, this article of the Creed is cited against the Real Presence of Christ in the Eucharist: Johannes Oecolampadius (d. 1531) and Ulrich Zwingli (d. 1531) conclude from it that Christ cannot be bodily present at the same time on the altar and in heaven. Hence, the Lord's Supper can only be a commemoration.[90] Martin Luther (d. 1546) examines the "seated at the right hand of the Father" in detail in the works he wrote in reply. He reproaches "the enthusiasts" for having a childish notion of the "right hand" of God, as if Christ were sitting there on a golden throne. In reality, this does not mean an actual place, but "the almighty power of God, which at the same time cannot be anywhere at all, and yet must be everywhere".[91] Luther does, of course, go too far in the opposite direction when he then deduces from this the ubiquity of Christ's body: "Now, wherever the right hand of God is, there must be Christ's body and blood."[92] Without going into the problem of Luther's "doctrine of ubiquity", we may note that he stands in the tradition of the rule of faith of the early Church in not seeing any contradiction between the "seated at the right hand" and Christ's presence in the Lord's Supper (as do Calvin and Zwingli), but a profound interconnection. The fact that Christ is enthroned at the Father's right hand is shown precisely in his living, bodily presence in the Eucharist.

c. The Mystery of His Present Rule

"Between the last of the mysteries of the life of Christ that have already occurred, the Ascension, and that for which we are still waiting,

[89] J. Calvin, *Institutio Religionis Christianae* 4, 17, 31.

[90] On this point, and on what follows, see M. Lienhard, *Martin Luthers christologisches Zeugnis: Entwicklung und Grundzüge seiner Christologie* (Göttingen, 1980), esp. pp. 146–84.

[91] M. Luther, WA 23, p. 133, 21–22.

[92] Ibid., p. 143, 32–33.

the Parousia, there is one mystery—and only one—that is contemporary with us: that Christ is seated at the Father's right hand."[93] This article of faith is in a sense the christological article that has the most ecclesiological relevance. Repeatedly, our brief insights into the history of the interpretation of this article have clearly shown us its ecclesiological components. That is not surprising, since it has to do precisely with the *present* relationship of Christ to his Church.

With his Resurrection and Ascension, Christ has taken possession of his Kingdom; he is the Lord, and God has exalted him "far above all rule and authority and power and dominion, and above every name that is named, not only in this age but also in that which is to come" (Eph 1:21). Jesus had indeed admitted to Pilate that his Kingdom was not of this world. Yet his final commission to his disciples runs, "All authority in heaven and on earth has been given to me. Go therefore and make disciples of all nations, baptizing them in the name of the Father and of the Son and of the Holy Spirit, teaching them to observe all that I have commanded you; and behold, I am with you always, to the close of the age" (Mt 28:18-20). The future, heavenly Kingdom of God is at the same time a present reality. However longingly the early Church called on the Lord to come again soon, "Maranatha" (1 Cor 16:22; cf. Rev 22:20), she went ahead just as decidedly to work to win men for Christ "from every nation, from all tribes and peoples and tongues" (Rev 7:9). Shortly before he returns to the Father, Jesus says to the disciples, who are asking when he is going to institute the Kingdom, "You shall receive power when the Holy Spirit has come upon you; and you shall be my witnesses" (Acts 1:8). Through the outpouring of the Holy Spirit, the Church "receives the mission to proclaim and to spread among all peoples the Kingdom of Christ and of God and to be, on earth, the initial budding forth of that kingdom. While it slowly grows, the Church strains toward the completed Kingdom and, with all its strength, hopes and desires to be united in glory with its King" (*Lumen Gentium*, no. 5).

Since the famous saying of Alfred Loisy (d. 1940) that Jesus had promised the coming of the Kingdom of God, but instead it was the Church that came,[94] we are constantly being told that we must not identify the Church with the Kingdom, since the latter is a strictly es-

---

[93] J. Daniélou, *Études d'exégèse judéo-chrétienne*, ThH 5 (Paris, 1966), p. 49.

[94] A. Loisy, *The Gospel and the Church* (Buffalo, N.Y.: Prometheus Books, 1988), p. 145.

chatological reality, whereas the Church is merely a sign of the Kingdom, pointing toward it.[95] The fundamental defect in such reductive concepts of the Church lies in their Christology: the Church is being seen too little in terms of her basis in Christ and too much in terms of her contingent historical and institutional aspect.

OUR HOME IS IN HEAVEN

The Church's proper place is where Christ is. "If then you have been raised with Christ, seek the things that are above, where Christ is, seated at the right hand of God" (Col 3:1). The Christian's yearning, therefore, as Saint Paul repeatedly expresses it, is directed toward seeing Christ face to face, in heaven. "My desire is to depart and be with Christ" (Phil 1:23). This experience, this faith, this fervent longing, spring not from a heathen egotism that seeks its own immortality, as Adolf von Harnack (d. 1930) maintained.[96] They are centered on Christ himself and his promise that "In my Father's house are many rooms . . . when I go and prepare a place for you, I will come again and will take you to myself, that where I am you may be also" (Jn 14:2–3). All the Church's expectation is based on this promise. This is where its hope is located. Thanks to Christ, the faithful already have, while here below, their "home in heaven" (Phil 3:20). They have been enrolled among the citizens of the heavenly Jerusalem (cf. Lk 10:20). Being a Christian therefore means that you have pitched your tent in heaven. Because Christ is her head, and she is his body, the Church is by nature heavenly. The wonderful *Letter to Diognetus*, from the second century, also bears witness to this when it says about the Christians, "They pass their time upon the earth, but they have their citizenship in heaven."[97] Augustine has described all this as no one else has. From the plethora of what he says about this, let us quote one paragraph:

> Your faith, dearly beloved, is clear about this, and we know that you have learned it in the instruction from the heavenly Teacher, upon whom you have set your hope: that our Lord Jesus Christ, who has already suffered

---

[95] See on this J. Carmignac, *Le Mirage de l'eschatologie: Royauté, règne et royaume de Dieu sans eschatologie* (Paris, 1979); C. Schönborn, "Das Reich Gottes und die himmlisch-irdische Kirche", in *Existenz im Übergang*, pp. 53–77.

[96] A. von Harnack, *Das Wesen des Christentums* (Leipzig, 1900; Gütersloh, 1977), p. 85.

[97] *Letter to Diognetus* 5, 9, ed. Loeb, trans. K. Lake (Cambridge, Mass. and London, 1976), pp. 360–61.

and risen again for us, is the Head of the Church, and that the Church is his Body. . . . Since, then, he is the Head of the Church, and the Church is his Body, the whole Christ is the Head and Body together, and the former has already risen. Thus we carry our Head in heaven. Our head is interceding for us. Our sinless, deathless Head is already pleading with God for our sins: so that we, too, in the end, resurrected and transformed into heavenly glory, may follow our Head. For where the Head is, the other members must also be. . . . Brothers, see the love of our Head. He is already in heaven, and yet he suffers here below as long as the Church is suffering here below. Here below, Christ hungers, here below he thirsts, is naked, is a foreigner, is ill, is in prison. For whatever his Body suffers here, that, he tells us, is what he suffers too (cf. Mt 25:42–45).[98]

He who is in heaven is nonetheless at the same time present here, present in the poor, in his word, above all in his Eucharist (cf. *Sacrosanctum Concilium*, no. 7), in which his coming reign becomes present for us.

PRESENT IN HIS EUCHARIST

At his Last Supper, Jesus gave some indication of the connection between his death and his coming reign. The messianic expectations that were attached to Jesus, intensified in Jerusalem with the hope that the Messiah would reveal himself at the Passover feast, already consist in Jesus' time of the hope that the Messiah would come in the night of the Passover: "In that night you were redeemed, and in the same night you will be redeemed in the future."[99] Not only Jesus' entry into Jerusalem, but also his Last Supper took place in this suspense of expectation. At the supper, Jesus revealed his true messianic plans. He interpreted his imminent death as the seal of the New Covenant, of the epitome of the messianic promises: "This is my blood of the covenant" (Mk 14:24; Mt 26:28). With these words he was referring to the blood of sacrifice with which Moses had sealed the covenant (Ex 24:8). Yet how could Jesus be expecting, faced with his death, that through him God would rule with a new and eternal covenant? In celebrating the Last Supper, in the instruction to repeat it in memory of him, Jesus himself gave an indication of the way in which he wishes to be the Messiah of the eschatological covenant people: by being—

---

[98] Augustine, *Sermo* 137, 1–2 (PL 38:754–55).
[99] Melkita to Ex 12:42, quoted in N. Füglister, *Die Heilsbedeutung des Pascha* (Munich, 1963), p. 223.

as the Lord and Messiah—himself the food and drink, the daily bread, of the people of the covenant. Jesus rules by giving life. The promise that death would be overcome in the messianic kingdom began to be realized in Jesus' earthly life, in his healings, in the forgiveness of sins, in his "liberating practice" of table fellowship. It becomes the ultimate reality at the Last Supper, when Jesus gives his body and blood as the source of new life. Jesus was thereby not only interpreting his death as life-giving, but he himself gave a sovereign share in his life. At the Last Supper, Jesus reveals the mystery of his messianic rule: men will live through him. As so often happens, the Johannine Christology explains in words what the synoptic Gospels show in Jesus' actions. "I come that they may have life, and have it abundantly" (Jn 10:10).

Jesus' words of renunciation show more clearly than anything else that he looks beyond death: "Truly, I say to you, I shall not drink again of the fruit of the vine until that day when I drink it new in the kingdom of God" (Mk 14:25). Joachim Jeremias interprets this mysterious passage in a twofold sense. On the one hand, Jesus himself does not take part in the Passover meal—thus, he is fasting, as intercession for Israel, which has failed to recognize God's visitation—and so he interprets his death as a representative intervention on behalf of Israel. Jesus is also looking beyond his death, however, toward the Kingdom of God. "On a transformed earth, where perfect communion with God will have become a reality through a transformation of the body, Jesus will again, as now at the Lord's Supper, act as *paterfamilias* and break the blessed bread and offer them the cup of thanksgiving—he himself being once more the giver and the server, and his own the recipients, who in eating and drinking receive the salvation gift of God: eternal life."[100]

With the instruction to "do this" again "in memory of me", Jesus bequeathed to us the celebration of his memorial as the pledge of the perfected Kingdom. Thereby, however, he was also giving the hermeneutic locus of his reign. He was already giving in advance the gift of salvation, eternal life, in memory of his death, until he comes again. This repetition of the Last Supper became an anticipation of the perfected Kingdom of God (Lk 22:16). The community then also experiences there that Jesus' eschatological rule consists in life-giving communion with him. Paul expressed this communion of the faithful with

---

[100] J. Jeremias, *The Eucharistic Words of Jesus* (London, 1966), p. 218.

Christ in graphic words. He identified the body of the Risen One with
the Eucharist and with the Church. Christ, by giving us his body in the
Eucharist, is creating a new body for himself: the Church. "We who
are many are one body, for we all partake of the one bread" (1 Cor
10:17). This identification is based on the personal encounter that Paul
had with the Risen One. In this encounter, he came to know that the
Church he was seeking to destroy was none other than Christ himself (cf. Acts 26:14-15). "From the time when he found that Christ
was looking at him in the Church he was persecuting, he could not
meet the eyes of a Christian without finding once more the gaze of
Christ." [101]

3. From Thence He Will Come to Judge the Living and the Dead

Even if Christ is the one who, in many ways, already comes to us,
nonetheless, from the beginning, Christians have been hoping for the
final coming of Christ that was promised them and for the universal
judgment. The angels announce at the Ascension, "This Jesus, who
was taken up from you into heaven, will come in the same way as you
saw him go into heaven" (Acts 1:11). "When the Son of man comes
in his glory, and all the angels with him . . ."—that is how the Lord
begins his great discourse about the judgment (Mt 25:31-46). "Come,
Lord Jesus!"—the Book of Revelation closes with this cry of longing.
It is a response to Jesus' promise, "Surely I am coming soon" (Rev
22:20). "Maranatha!" (Our Lord, come!) is how Christians prayed in
Jesus' own language (1 Cor 16:22), especially at the celebration of the
Eucharist, when they proclaimed the death of the Lord and extolled
his Resurrection until he comes again. The season of Advent turns the
believers' attention, by way of the hopeful expectation of the festival
of the Incarnation of the Savior, toward his return at the end of time.
"When he humbled himself to come among us as a man, he fulfilled
the plan you formed long ago and opened for us the way to salvation.
Now we watch for the day, hoping that the salvation promised us will
be ours when Christ our Lord will come again in his glory." [102]

---

[101] E. Mersch, *Le Corps mystique du Christ*, vol. 1 (Louvain, 1933), p. 96.
[102] Roman Missal, *Preface of Advent I*.

a. Christ Will Come Again at the End of Time

In the systematic-theological reflections of the past century, the truth of faith concerning Christ's return, so essential for the life of the Church, was often the focus of fierce debates. Countless apocalyptic images of the "Day of the Lord" seem in fact to suggest that Christ's Parousia concerns an event in history.[103] A future "end" of time is spoken of (Mt 24:14), which is depicted as the earth being "burned up" (2 Pet 3:10), as a "planetary catastrophe".[104] Albert Schweitzer (d. 1965), on the basis of such images, identified the Kingdom that Jesus had promised with the end of the world and thus reduced Christian eschatology to an event entirely within time. The "delay of the Parousia", which has now lasted two thousand years, rendered Christian eschatology untenable, in any case, in such a view. That is why some of Schweitzer's contemporaries reacted by spiritualizing Christ's eschatology, sharply separating it from the time-space dimensions of history. Karl Barth (d. 1968), in his Commentary on the Letter to the Romans, formulated the question concerning the Parousia like this: "How can the coming of that which doth not *enter in* ever be *delayed?*"[105] The eternal moment cannot be compared with other moments because it has a significance transcending all moments. In connection with the Lord's return, the question once more arises of the relation between contingent history and the absoluteness of God. Rudolf Bultmann (d. 1976) interpreted eschatology as the present experience of eternity within the vicissitudes of time. For him, therefore, "even the expectation of the end which is imminent within time" is part of mythology.[106]

For a long time now, however, there has been comprehensive criticism of these two one-sided concepts of eschatology.[107] It was seen that they were strongly influenced by the ideas of the Enlightenment and Idealism, which have very little to do with revelation. There are clear lines of development running from Johann Gottlieb Fichte's (d. 1879)

---

[103] Cf. K. H. Schelke, *Theologie des Neuen Testamentes*, vol. 4/1 (Düsseldorf, 1974), pp. 61–78.

[104] H. Schlier, *Das Ende der Zeit* (Freiburg im Breisgau, 1971), p. 67.

[105] K. Barth, *The Epistle to the Romans* (London, 1933), p. 500.

[106] R. Bultmann, *Jesus*, 8th ed. (Tübingen, 1980), p. 41; see also J. Galot, "Qu'est-ce que la parousie?" *Esprit et vie* 101 (1993): 145–54, here p. 153.

[107] See the way this conflict is depicted in J. Moltmann, *Das Kommen Gottes: Christliche Eschatologie* (Gütersloh, 1995), pp. 22–39.

position, for instance, to Bultmann and the early Barth. "Religion exalts its holy one absolutely above time as such and above transitoriness and puts him directly in possession of eternity. . . . At every moment, he has and possesses eternal life, with all its bliss, immediately and entirely."[108] Barth later distanced himself from his rejection of the "useless talk about the 'delayed' Parousia". In those days, he said, he had certainly taken seriously the otherworldliness of the coming Kingdom of God, but not its coming.[109] What the Parousia, and thus the end of the world, means ought not to be primarily approached philosophically, from the relation between "otherworldly eternity" and "contingent time", but christologically.

LIGHTNING AND THE SIGNS OF THE TIMES

The difficulty that has been only briefly suggested here is of course not just philosophical. It also has a basis in Scripture itself. Among what is said in the New Testament about Christ's Parousia, and with it about the end of time, there are two series of assertions that at first sight seem to contradict each other. There is a first series of statements in which the Parousia is something irreducible, which suddenly comes from God; and a second, in which the Parousia is seen as the end point of a development within history itself. The first shows the Parousia as something entirely transcending history, incapable of evolution; the second as the end point, within history of a development. The first series may be represented by the image of *lightning*: "For as the lightning comes from the east and shines as far as the west, so will be the coming of the Son of man" (Mt 24:27). The word *sign* may stand for the second series: "Tell us, when will this be, and what will be the sign when these things are all to be accomplished?" (Mk 13:4). How are we supposed to recognize, by the *signs of the times*, what is coming unexpectedly, suddenly, like a thief, like a flash of lightning? It is clear that if either of these two lines is taken in isolation, then two completely different eschatologies result. If the second is taken in isolation, then apocalyptic speculation begins about the time of the end of the world; if the first line is taken in isolation, then—as in the passage quoted from Fichte—history and the Parousia are completely separated. His-

---

[108] J. G. Fichte, "Grundzüge des gegenwärtigen Zeitalters", in *Gesamtausgabe*, ed. R. Lauth, vol. I/8 (Stuttgart, 1991), pp. 381–82.
[109] K. Barth, KD 2/1:716.

tory becomes a neutral matter of chronology; the Parousia becomes an ever-present experience of eternity. Both ways of looking at this are a constant temptation. Let us first look at the two lines of thought themselves more closely, so as then to be able to examine how they belong together.

The "Day of the Lord",[110] promised in the Old Testament, is in the New Testament identified with the "day of the Son of man" (cf. Lk 17:22, 24, 30), the "day of Jesus Christ" (Phil 1:6, 10; 2:16). Its coming is portrayed in various images: it comes "like a thief" (Mt 24:43; 1 Thess 5:2, 4), like a "snare" (Lk 21:34), "suddenly" (1 Thess 5:3). The sentence is constantly repeated, "You do not know on what day your Lord is coming" (Mt 24:42). The disciples' curiosity about this day is expressly forbidden: "It is not for you to know times or seasons which the Father has fixed by his own authority" (Acts 1:7). No one knows the information about that day and hour, not even the angels—indeed, not even the Son—only the Father (cf. Mk 13:32).

What is being said about the Parousia here? First, that it is completely irreducible. This is God's decision alone, gracious, redeeming, but also judging. Yet that means, secondly, that neither any special efforts on men's part nor any particular state of maturation in history or the evolution of the world can bring about the Parousia. Hence, thirdly, any calculations of the end, but also any plans for completion, are rejected. Fourth, through the identification of the Day of the Lord with the Day of Christ, the divinity of Jesus Christ is unmistakably professed.

The apocalyptic discourse in Jerusalem before the Passion (Mk 13) mentions signs by which the coming of the Parousia may be known: false Messiahs appear; the whole world is filled with wars; there are earthquakes and famines; Christians are persecuted; the holy places are laid waste. Scripture speaks mysteriously of the "man of lawlessness" who must come first (2 Thess 2:3); the Johannine Letters speak of the antichrist (1 Jn 2:18; 4:3; 2 Jn 7).[111] These are all signs that "then the end will come" (Mt 24:14). Positive signs are also mentioned. First, the Gospel must be preached throughout the whole world (Mk 13:10; Mt 24:14). Paul promises the conversion of Israel as a sign of the end

---

[110] Cf. M. Saebo, "jôm" II-IV, in *Theologisches Wörterbuch zum Alten Testament*, ed. G.J. Botterweck and H. Ringgren (Stuttgart: W. Kohlhammer, 1970) 3:566-86; W. Trilling, "ἡμέρα", in *Exegetisches Wörterbuch zum Neuen Testament* 2:296-302.

[111] Cf. J.H. Newman, "The Patristic Idea of Antichrist", in *Discussions and Arguments* (London, 1899), pp. 44-109.

(Rom 9—11). Precisely these last signs seem particularly open to a certain degree of measurability. They even seem to articulate historical conditions. As long as Israel has not been converted, Christ cannot return. As long as the Gospel has not been preached everywhere, the Parousia cannot occur.

What do the assertions in this second series mean? It seems here, first of all, that the Parousia does not come about only by God's irreducible decision, but it also has something to do with history and with what men do. Secondly, there is something like a growth, a becoming, a development of history toward the Parousia, a fulfillment and maturation of time for Christ's return. Third, this passage of time toward the Parousia is full of tensions. There are struggles, there are powers and forces that hinder the coming (1 Thess 5) but that, precisely in being unleashed, bring it about. Fourthly, these assertions, too, have a christological message: Christ is already active now in the process of this history. He gives us the Spirit; he is "with us always" (Mt 28:20), he is Lord of history.

The question of how these two series of statements may be reconciled is decisive for a Christian understanding of history. The liturgy and the Creed distinguish between a first and a second Parousia of Christ, between his coming in lowliness and his coming in glory. And a similar twofold series may be seen for the first Parousia. This is both an unexpected gift from God and also the climax of a long history of hope. If we look at Christ's first coming, it appears that two lines of Old Testament promises converge in him.[112]

LINES OF PROMISES IN THE OLD TESTAMENT

The Old Testament Scriptures promise that, at the end of time, God will come himself, with an immediacy that surpasses anything hitherto known, that he will come himself, in Israel, will dwell in Sion (cf. Is 40:3; 65:17; 4:5), and will reign over all nations. This coming of God is often portrayed as "the Day of the Lord", as the coming of God "in the last days". And yet the first coming of Christ is seen as these "last days": "in these last days [God] has spoken to us by a Son" (Heb 1:2). In New Testament Christology, this eschatological coming is seen as having been fulfilled in the coming of Christ, as is shown, for instance,

---

[112] Cf. J. Daniélou, "Christologie und Eschatologie", in *Das Konzil von Chalkedon: Geschichte und Gegenwart*, ed. A. Grillmeier and H. Bacht, 3:269–86 (Würzburg, 1954).

in the application of the prophetic exhortation to "prepare the way of the LORD" (Is 40:3) to Christ in the Gospel of Matthew (Mt 3:3). The coming of Christ is the eschatological coming of God. The Incarnation is the "Day of the Lord", the "eschaton of days" (cf. Heb 1:2). God is now dwelling among us in Christ (Jn 1:14).

Another line of Old Testament promises is fulfilled in Christ: the promise of the new man. Paul takes up the typology, familiar in Judaism, of the first Adam and last Adam. At the end of time, a new Adam is created.[113] A similar line of promise is found in the promise to Abraham of offspring in whom all nations will be blessed (Gen 12:3; cf. Gal 3:16); and again in the promise of a prophet greater than Moses (Deut 18:15, 18), and in the promise of a new shoot from David. It is well known how deeply these typologies affected the New Testament. Christ is the promised shoot of David, the prophet, the eschatological Isaac, the new Adam. This series has left its mark on messianic expectation.

These two lines, that of God's own coming and the hope of a Messiah, are not linked together in the Old Testament. Jean Daniélou (d. 1974) consequently distinguishes between two lines of eschatology in the Old Testament: the transcendental eschatology of the Day of the Lord in the apocalypses; and messianism within history, with an earthly messianic kingdom. The tremendous occurrence with Christ was that the two lines of promises come together here in his person. He is the "God with us": he is the "new man". The irreducible sudden advent of God —"the Lord whom you seek will suddenly come to his temple" (Mal 3:1)—and the hoped-for coming of the prophet, the Messiah, the new man, prepared for throughout a long history, come together in Christ. That is why Christ is the unsurpassable goal of human history and, at the same time, of God's action.

If one of these two series is taken in isolation, the mystery of Christ himself is reduced and, with it, eschatology. If the first series is treated as absolute, this leads to Docetism: Christ is not really the Son of God who has become man. The entire historical dimension of Christ loses its significance. He is only the heavenly, divine One. The rejection of the Old Testament, the guarantee of Christ's human origin, and thus of human responsibility in the history of salvation, leads to a timeless

---

[113] J. Daniélou, *Sacramentum futuri: Études sur les origines de la typologie biblique* (Paris, 1950), pp. 3–52.

and ahistorical picture of Christ, in which only his transcendent relationship with God is of interest. Gnosticism was to be one such ahistorical doctrine of salvation, and it is found again in Idealism (in the
ever-present experience of eternity). It is no accident that Bultmann
has a (one-sided) affinity with John. In the early Church, this was the
temptation of Monophysitism. The Logos who has come is (in this
view) the God-among-us who renders everything human and historical
insignificant.

If, on the contrary, the second line is viewed in isolation, then Jesus
is seen as merely a prophet, as in the Ebionite Jewish-Christian Christology. Christological adoptionism strongly emphasizes the human and
historical side and, with respect to eschatology, the historical activity
of man.[114]

Both isolations lead to christological and eschatological reductions.
It is imperative to look at both together, since both are united in the
person of Christ himself. The christological confession of faith of Chalcedon points in an unparalleled way toward the center here: Christ is
true God and true man, Son of God and son of David, at the same
time the eschaton of all of human history and the eschaton of God's
coming. There can be nothing further; neither human history nor God
himself can go any farther than this. Christ is the last man; in him,
human history has reached its goal. Hilary of Poitiers (d. 367) expresses it like this: "The Only-begotten of God was therefore born as
man from the Virgin. He willed in the fullness of time to raise man
to God in himself."[115] Even God's coming to men cannot go beyond
God's incarnation. In the person of the God-man, in the hypostatic
union, there is the highest and most perfect communion between God
and man.

Only on the basis of the divine-human mystery of Christ, who is
himself the embodiment of eschatology, is it possible to see both these
dimensions together unabbreviated. In Christ, the whole history of
mankind is not nullified, swallowed up in the eternal divine Now, but
is fulfilled as human history. In him, however, God's irreducible coming is also completed and unsurpassable. Thus Christ, the God-man,

---

[114] See above, chap. 2:1, "Approaches to the Incarnation of God in the Old Testament and
Judaism".

[115] Hilary of Poitiers, *De Trinitate* 9, 5 (PL 10:284AB).

is also the goal and completion of God's whole plan of salvation, the perfected communion between God and man.

Let us now try again, in the light of the divine-human mystery of Christ, to clarify the question of the two lines of assertions about the Parousia by returning to the signs of the Parousia and to the Parousia itself.

On the basis of the line of "signs" of the teleological meaning of history, we may note that Christ, as God-man, is the fulfillment of human history. Christ is already now the unsurpassable goal of history; he is the highest realization of the history of mankind, of God's plan for salvation. But as goal and perfection, he is also the source of the new creation. The meaning of history now consists in *anakephaleiosis* (recapitulation), in the summing up of creation in Christ, its head (Eph 1:10). History cannot surpass what has already come about in Christ, the union of God and man in Christ. Seen from Christ, there is, as the meaning of present history, only "to grow up in every way into him who is the head, into Christ" (Eph 4:15). This growth, however, is something different from the history up to Christ's first coming at the Incarnation. No new era of history comes after Christ, since with him the boundary line—though not yet the perfection—of history has arrived. The early Church therefore divided history into three eras: history *ante legem, sub lege*, and *sub gratia*. Speculations about history, such as those of Joachim of Fiore (d. 1203), who expected a progression from the age of Christ to the age of the Holy Spirit, were therefore never accepted by the Church's Magisterium.[116]

THE CHURCH IS FIGHTING
THE ENEMY WHO IS ALREADY DEFEATED

Yet is not the assertion that history has been brought to its completion with Christ pure speculation? Are not the mockers mentioned in the Second Letter of Peter right, when they say that "ever since the fathers fell asleep, all things have continued as they were from the beginning of creation" (2 Pet 3:4)? History is still continuing, and great parts of the world are really very little affected by Christ. What has the Son of God in fact achieved by his presence among men? In the time of his earthly life, he began to touch some of them so deeply, taking hold of

---

[116] Cf. H. de Lubac, *La Postérité spirituelle de Joachim de Fiore*, 2 vols. (Paris, 1979–1980).

their very being, that the same thing befell them as it did Paul, who aptly described this experience in the words, "It is no longer I who live, but Christ who lives in me" (Gal 2:20; cf. Gal 3:27). Through the gift of the Holy Spirit in baptism, they received a share in Christ's life, a share in his thinking and his striving. "The love of Christ urges us on" (2 Cor 5:14), the Apostle remarks again. This urging of Christ's love within them made time urgent for the Christians: "The appointed time has grown very short" (1 Cor 7:29).

Christ allows Christians to take part in his struggle for the salvation of the world. He has in fact already won the conclusive victory over the hostile powers and forces through his death and his Resurrection, so that the voices of heaven rejoice: "Now the salvation and the power and the kingdom of our God and the authority of his Christ have come" (Rev 12:10). Yet on earth, the Church's fight against her enemy, who has already been defeated in heaven, still rages. This fight against the devil is real and all the more bitter since his wrath is great, "because he knows that his time is short" (Rev 12:12). As is shown in the seven letters to the congregations in the Revelation of Saint John, this conflict is ultimately about the decisive struggle "within the womb of the Church . . . the Lord's wrestling as a lover with his bride, the Church".[117] "For the time has come for judgment to begin with the household of God" (1 Pet 4:17). The universal judgment is actually a judgment on the Church. That is why no kind of indifference is possible any more. What now remains as history is the history of the believer's Yes or No to the signs of Christ's presence. Christ's reign is thereby demonstrated. For those who are redeemed in Christ, it is a matter of surviving this war against an enemy who is stronger than they by remaining steadfast in Christ, by paying vigilant, sober attention to the signs of his presence.[118]

Augustine brought these ideas to light in his famous concept of the earthly city and the city of God. Human society has been divided into two groups by sin: those who live by the flesh, by sin—that is, the earthly city—and the others who live by the Spirit—the heavenly city.[119] Through the coming of Christ, the power of the devil has been

---

[117] H. U. von Balthasar, *A Theology of History* (San Francisco: Ignatius Press, 1994), pp. 149-50.

[118] On the relation between the Church's struggle and that of Mary, see H. Rahner, *Maria und die Kirche: Zehn Kapitel über das geistliche Leben*, 2nd ed. (Innsbruck, 1962), pp. 142-55.

[119] Cf. Augustine, *De civitate Dei* 14, 1 (CChr.SL 48:414).

bound on earth, until the final decision comes. Sin has not thereby been abolished yet, and the danger of going astray still remains; it has just been weakened so that the city of God, the Church, can gather her strength, so that the redeemed can grow in grace. "But then he (the devil) will be let loose, when there is only a short time remaining . . . and then those against whom he makes war will be so strengthened that with all his violence and trickery he will not be able to overcome them."[120]

The time *sub gratia* is not just harmless and insignificant for Christians: "For now, since God's time is near, since it is among us and is calling us, every time is an immediate opportunity for love. Now, because every moment challenges me, is no time for euphoric dreams about the development of the world to the omega point—the whole of evolution may be lost with *one* evil word."[121] The members of the Church do not automatically emerge as victors from this struggle. Paul announces a great "rebellion" (2 Thess 2:3), and the Revelation of John speaks of the dreadful battle at the end of time (Rev 20:7–10). Christ himself warned his disciples against premature certainty and self-satisfaction; the victory of faith has to be won by a struggle: "When the Son of man comes, will he find faith on earth?" (Lk 18:8).

CHRIST'S RETURN AS HOPE FOR ISRAEL

With the promise made to Abraham, "By you all the families of the earth shall bless themselves" (Gen 12:3), Israel received a universal mission: to be the bearer of God's promise, God's witness to all nations. For its part, Christianity, from the beginning, understood itself as sent "to all nations" (Mt 28:18–20), because all men have access to the heritage of the Father through Jesus the Messiah, the Son of God. Does the New Covenant, so we might be tempted to ask, not abolish the Old? Did not the failure to recognize Christ by a great part of the Jewish people lead to the rejection of that people? Is there any positive task at all for Israel in world history after the birth of Christ?[122]

---

[120] Ibid., 20, 8 (CChr.SL 48:713).

[121] H. Schlier, *Das Ende der Zeit*, p. 82.

[122] See on this H. U. von Balthasar, *Martin Buber and Christianity: A Dialogue between Israel and the Church*, trans. Alexander Dru (New York: Macmillan, 1961); J.-M. Garrigues, "Das messianische Israel", *Internationale Katholische Zeitschrift Communio* 24 (1995): 209–24; C. Schönborn, "Ist das Christentum eine jüdische Sekte?" in *Die Menschen, die Kirche, das Land*, pp. 183–204.

Such questions show a profound lack of self-awareness on the part of the community founded by Christ. After the destruction of the Temple in Jerusalem in A.D. 70, under reign of the Roman Emperor Vespasian, a wall of silence grew up between Jews and Christians. They ignored each other. Thus it was forgotten that there is only one Israel, only one chosen people. Jesus, for his part, did not found any community outside the people of Israel; the Church founded upon Peter is not a schismatic community like, for instance, that of Qumran. To emphasize the continuity of the Church with Israel, shortly after Jesus' announcement that he would build his Church upon the rock of Peter, both he and Peter paid the Temple tax as a sign of their belonging to the one people (Mt 17:24–27). And even if Christ's disciples were later shut out of the synagogues, they still regarded themselves as members of the people of Israel. On the other hand, God did not reject his people, despite their hardness of heart. Vatican II adopted this biblically based message as its own: "God holds the Jews most dear for the sake of their Fathers; He does not repent of the gifts He makes or of the calls He issues—such is the witness of the Apostle (cf. Rom 11:28–29). In company with the Prophets and the same Apostle, the Church awaits that day, known to God alone, on which all peoples will address the Lord in a single voice and 'serve him shoulder to shoulder' (Wis 3:9; cf. Is 66:23; Ps 65:4; Rom 11:11–32)" (*Nostra Aetate*, no. 4).

In the parable of the wicked tenants, who kill the messengers and even the owner's Son, Jesus proclaims, not that God will reject the vineyard (an Old Testament image for Israel, cf. Is 5:1), but that he will entrust the vineyard to new stewards (Mk 12:9). The chosen people will have to endure other nations sitting down at the Lord's table, even the heathens being given a share in the promise of salvation to Abraham. This had already been announced under the Old Covenant by the prophets: "My house shall be called a house of prayer for all peoples" (Is 56:7). Paul sketches what is perhaps the most cogent picture of the relation between Israel and the Church. He describes the Israel of the Old Covenant as the root of the olive tree, onto which new branches are grafted (cf. Rom 11:17). Even if God has broken off a few branches from the tree, on account of their unbelief, the tree remains Israel. And God has the power to regraft the branches that have been set aside (cf. Rom 11:23).

The destiny of the Church and that of Israel are, therefore, intrinsically, inseparably bound together in God's providence. The division of nearly two thousand years harms both of them. Without the Church, Israel falls short of its promised fullness, and without Israel the Church remains somehow rootless. The Church has in fact always been aware that without a living relationship to her roots, she cannot fulfill her destiny. What is of decisive significance here is the first excommunication pronounced by the local church in Rome, when in A.D. 144 she excluded Marcion (d. ca. 160) from her midst. He wanted to produce a "purely Christian" Bible by rejecting the Old Testament and by purifying the New from all of what he saw as Jewish elements. The Catholic Church, however, took a different path and decided in favor of the Old Testament. Nonetheless, the judgment of Hans Urs von Balthasar is probably right in saying that the Church rightly possesses Israel's Scriptures, "but books are not the whole of a living revelation: they lack Israel's heart."[123]

Like every schism, this first rent in the Church, between the Old and New Covenants, means an impoverishment of the *Christus totus*. If there is some guilt attached to the failure to recognize Christ by a great part of the Jewish people, on the other hand, we cannot fail to recognize that there is Christian guilt "which daily prevents the Church from looking as she should look according to Jesus' will."[124] The rift between Judaism and the Church has to be healed so that Christ may attain his "full stature" (cf. Eph 4:13); Christ himself, in his lament over Jerusalem, promises that he will not return until Israel recognizes him and calls to him: "Blessed is he who comes in the name of the Lord" (Mt 23:39; Ps 118:26). Only "the 'full inclusion' of the Jews (Rom 11:12) in the Messiah's salvation, in the wake of 'the full number of the Gentiles' (Rom 11:25), will enable the people of God to achieve 'the measure of the stature of the fullness of Christ' (Eph 4:13), in which 'God may be all in all' (1 Cor 15:28)" (CCC 674).

CHRIST—ALPHA AND OMEGA

Scripture testifies that not only mankind, but all creation is waiting for the Son of God to be revealed so that it, too, may attain its perfection in Christ (Rom 8:19–22). Christ's return will also bring "new heavens and a new earth" (2 Pet 3:13; Rev 21:1). This cosmic dimension to the mystery of Christ is frequently neglected. The entire creation, heaven

[123] Von Balthasar, *Einsame Zwiesprache*, p. 96.
[124] Ibid., p. 83.

and earth, things visible and invisible, "were created through him and for him" (Col 1:16). God calls everything into being in Christ and grants continued existence. Only he can say of himself, "I am the Alpha and the Omega, the first and the last, the beginning and the end" (Rev 22:13).

That is why Church Fathers like Irenaeus, Origen, Clement of Alexandria (d. ca. 216), or Gregory of Nyssa (d. 394) see the saving work of Christ not only in relation to the spiritual nature of man, but also in relation to the physical nature of the cosmos. Christ, through his Cross, embraces the whole of created reality. Thus Origen, for example, in a commentary on the Psalms, dares to praise Christ with cautious words, "whose body is all mankind and perhaps even the whole of creation".[125] He emphasizes the strength of the Cross and declares "that it was sufficient for salvation not only for the present world, but also for that of the future and even for past ages. Indeed, Christ's death means salvation not only for us, in our human state, but even for the heavenly powers."[126]

What does it mean to say that the cosmos finds its meaning and its fulfillment in Christ, that "in him all things hold together" (Col 1:17), and that all things are united in him (Eph 1:10)? Pierre Teilhard de Chardin (d. 1955), who strove more than anyone else to grasp this cosmic function of Christ, saw in such passages above all a negation of the notion, especially widespread in the Eastern world, that the All will someday dissolve into the impersonal.[127] Rather, the universe is converging upon Christ; it is being "christified". "The cosmos, since it is converging, cannot combine into a something: it must have a Someone as its goal, as is already partially, in an elementary way, the case with man."[128] The ocean into which all the spiritual streams of the universe flow has a face and a heart. If Christ, then, is the goal and thereby the inner pole of attraction for the whole history of creation, we are being given a guarantee that the tension and movement between

---

[125] Origen, *Homilia secunda in Psalmum XXXVI*, 1 (SC 411:96)

[126] Origen, *Commentarius in epistulam ad Romanos* 5, 10 (FChr 2/3:182–83). For further references to patristic literature on the theology of creation, see H. de Lubac, *Teilhard de Chardin: The Man and His Meaning*, trans. René Hague (New York: Mentor Omega Books, 1965), pp. 54–59.

[127] On the work of Teilhard de Chardin, see K. Schmitz-Moormann, *Pierre Teilhard de Chardin: Evolution, die Schöpfung Gottes* (Mainz, 1996).

[128] P. Teilhard de Chardin, *Mein Glaube*, in *Werke*, vol. 10 (Olten, 1972), p. 138.

disintegration and advance has been decided in favor of advance. In Christ "all the promises of God find their Yes" (2 Cor 1:20).

In contrast to the Eastern philosophies, which make consciousness cosmic and strive to depersonalize man and God, the Christian view of the world is based on a God who is so fundamentally personal that he personalizes the whole of creation through man. In Christ there is no contradiction between universality and personality. Thus, the structure of the universe is, indeed, not individual, but personal. This view of the world is liberating. In a world "which is open at its summit in Christ Jesus, we run no risk of suffocating! And, on the other hand, not only air comes down from these heights, but the rays of love".[129]

b. To Judge the Living and the Dead

Talk about judgment is not very popular. The *Dies irae* was banished from the liturgy; it is with horror, abhorrence, or curiosity that people see the great pictures depicting the Last Judgment, with the blessed souls and the damned, with Christ judging in majesty. How should we understand the image of Christ as judge of the world, for which there is such clear evidence in the New Testament? How can it be reconciled with what is said in John, that God did not send the Son to judge the world, but to save it (Jn 3:17; 12:47)? Can the idea of a Last Judgment be reconciled with God's grace? How can we talk about judgment, without forgetting God's mercy?[130]

We certainly cannot expect any detailed description of "how it will be" from a study of the numerous images of the judgment in the New Testament. On the other hand, it will not work to want to see here, in a demythologizing way, only statements about the present, in the sense of "we are placed before a decision".[131] It is clear that in the Scriptures the Day of Judgment is promised as the Last Judgment, as the universal judgment of the world. It is of course immediately striking that, in contrast to many apocalyptic speculations, it is not a matter of imagining future events, since a relation to the present is always implied.

---

[129] P. Teilhard de Chardin, *Le Coeur de la matière* (Paris, 1976), pp. 106–7.

[130] Cf. M. Kehl, *Und was kommt nach dem Ende? Von Weltuntergang und Vollendung, Wiedergeburt und Auferstehung* (Freiburg im Breisgau, 1999), pp. 128–33.

[131] Cf. K. Rahner, "Gericht: Letztes Gericht: Systematisch", in *Lexikon für Theologie und Kirche*, 2nd ed., 4:734–36.

The Sermon on the Mount, for instance, speaks of God's judgment
like the Old Testament does, but it intensifies it still further. Even
someone who is angry with his brother is in danger of judgment (Mt
5:21–22). Man is on his way to the judgment, that is why he should be
reconciled on the way, otherwise he will be handed over to the judge
(Mt 5:25). Here a main feature of the New Testament promise of judgment appears: Whoever does not judge, will not be judged (Mt 7:1).
In John, it says, "He who believes in him [Christ] is not condemned"
(Jn 3:18). "He who hears my word and believes him who sent me, has
eternal life; he does not come into judgment, but has passed from death
to life" (Jn 5:24). Consequently, we can then read in John, "Now is
the judgment of this world" (Jn 12:31). It thus seems to be the case
that the judgment is not undergone by everyone, but only by those
who themselves judge, do not want to forgive, close themselves up,
and are not merciful (Lk 6:20–26). This corresponds to the earliest
Christian ideas about the Parousia. In the well-known text from the
First Letter to the Thessalonians, Paul does speak of any judgment:

> For this we declare to you by the word of the Lord, that we who are alive,
> who are left until the coming of the Lord, shall not precede those who
> have fallen asleep. For the Lord himself will descend from heaven with
> a cry of command, with the archangel's call, and with the sound of the
> trumpet of God. And the dead in Christ will rise first; then we who are
> alive, who are left, shall be caught up together with them in the clouds
> to meet the Lord in the air; and so we shall always be with the Lord.
> (1 Thess 4:15–17)

Here, the "saints" do not seem to be subject to any judgment. The
idea in the Gospel of John is similar: "Do not marvel at this; for the
hour is coming when all who are in the tombs will hear his voice and
come forth, those who have done good, to the resurrection of life,
and those who have done evil, to the resurrection of judgment" (Jn
5:28–29). Here, too, there is not a judgment for everyone. It looks as
though belief in Christ sets man beyond judgment already. That also
corresponds to the idea in the early Church of baptism as a judgment.
Anyone baptized has already been judged and saved.

BEFORE CHRIST'S JUDGMENT SEAT

On the other hand, there is a clear picture of the universal judgment,
to which all men are subject. "For we must all appear before the judg-

ment seat of Christ, so that each one may receive good or evil, according to what he has done in the body" (2 Cor 5:10). The parables of judgment belong here, the judgment discourses like that in the Gospel of Matthew (Mt 25). Thus we have, on one hand, the idea that the judgment is already now, where the separation occurs on the basis of belonging to Christ; and, on the other, the great images of the universal judgment, where the separation will be carried out as in the parable of the wheat and the tares (Mt 13:24–30) or in the image of the sheep and the goats (Mt 25:33). In the one conception, the end is characterized by the Parousia; in the other, by the universal judgment.

These quite summary indications show that there are a multiplicity of not easily systematized images that speak of the judgment. This multiplicity clearly appears in the iconography. The pictures of the Last Judgment, known to us in famous examples like that by Michelangelo in the Sistine Chapel, represent only one strand of the iconographic tradition. In mosaics in the apses of ancient churches, Christ is most often depicted, not as judge, but as the one who comes again. These are images of the Parousia, as for instance in the Basilica of Saints Cosmas and Damian in Rome. It is interesting to note that the Parousia images are more liturgical than the images of judgment, which, on the other hand, are more tempting to paint. The former concentrate on the appearance of the Lord. Even the New Testament seems to speak of the Parousia more in terms of liturgy. "The New Testament conceals and reveals the unspeakable coming of Christ, using language borrowed from that sphere which is graciously enabled to express in this world the point of contact with God. The Parousia is the highest intensification and fulfilment of the Liturgy. And the Liturgy is Parousia, a Parousia-like event taking place in our midst."[132] Many of the elements of the picture of the Parousia in the New Testament, like for instance the sounding of trumpets or solemn acclamations, are liturgical in origin. Elements from the imperial liturgy and cosmic phenomena that appear in New Testament descriptions of the Parousia found their way into the liturgy.[133] They are all intended to announce the coming of Christ the Cosmokrator. In the apse mosaics, Christ appears on the clouds of heaven, and this coming is both longed for and already being celebrated in the Eucharist. This liturgical sense of

---

[132] Ratzinger, *Eschatology*, p. 203.
[133] Cf. T. Maertens, *Heidnisch-jüdische Wurzeln der christlichen Feste* (Mainz, 1965).

the Parousia is also expressed, for instance, in churches facing east. In Christian churches, prayers are directed, not, as in synagogues, toward Jerusalem, but turned toward the east, because in the liturgy Christians experience Christ's Parousia in anticipation. The typology of Christ as the rising sun (*sol oriens*) is thereby combined with the statement that Christ's return will occur "as the lightning comes from the east" (Mt 24:27). This idea also determines the portrayal of Christ in the apse, which stands for heaven.[134]

Pictures of the Last Judgment, in contrast to those of the Parousia, are motivated less by the liturgy than by moral concerns. They are concerned with men's deeds, with good or bad works. God "judges each one impartially according to his deeds" (1 Pet 1:17). "The dead were judged by what was written in the books, by what they had done" (Rev 20:12). "The fire will test what sort of work each one has done. If the work which any man has built on the foundation survives, he will receive a reward" (1 Cor 3:13–14). The pictures of the Last Judgment strongly emphasize this aspect. There, souls are weighed according to their vices and virtues, their works of mercy. Typically, these pictures of the judgment are often on the west walls of the churches, thus, in the direction of the sunset. This may also be connected with the didactic function of these pictures, which are intended to remind churchgoers once more, before they go out into the world, to be careful.

Can we draw any theological conclusions from this comparison of Parousia and judgment images? It is a question of the two aspects of eschatology we have already mentioned. The Parousia, Christ's return, is a matter of the divine, irreducible aspect of the end, coming from above. Hence, its place is in the apse, since here the coming of Christ is central. Here we are concerned, not with the works of man, but with the manifestation of Christ's rule. Thus, the gracious character of Christ's coming and its joy are to the fore. The judgment, on the contrary, is concerned with the human, historical aspect of the end,

---

[134] Cf. E. Peterson, *Frühkirche, Judentum und Gnosis* (Freiburg im Breisgau, 1959), pp. 1–35. On the direction in which the liturgy is celebrated, see also K. Gamber, *Sancta Sanctorum: Studien zur liturgischen Ausstattung der Kirche, vor allem des Altarraumes*, SPLi 10 (Regensburg, 1981); J. Ratzinger, *The Spirit of the Liturgy* (San Francisco, 2000), pp. 74–84; F. J. Dölger, *Sol salutis: Gebet und Gesang im christlichen Altertum: Mit besonderer Rücksicht auf die Ostung in Gebet und Liturgie*, 2nd ed., LF 4/5 (Münster, 1925), reprinted: LQF 16/17 (Münster, 1972), pp. 239–44; a rather critical view: O. Nussbaum, *Der Standort des Liturgen am christlichen Altar vor dem Jahre 1000: Eine archäologische und liturgiegeschichtliche Untersuchung*, 2 vols. (Bonn, 1965).

coming from below. Here, the deeds and works of each one and also human history are particularly highlighted.

These two aspects belong together. Where the judgment is the principal subject in art and preaching, there is the danger that we may be too much concerned with human achievements and too little with grace. This loss is expressed in an impoverishment of the liturgy.

THE SCARS OF THE SOUL

What does judgment mean, what standard does it use, and how can it be reconciled with God's mercy? Plato (d. ca. 348 B.C.) had already, in the *Gorgias*, recounted a myth about judgment, in which he expressed the experiences and expectations of mankind in general. "In the meadow at the crossroads where the two ways part, one leading to the Island of the Blessed, and the other to Tartarus," the souls of those who have died are judged, so Socrates tells us. "Death," he continues, "is obviously nothing but the separation of two things from each other, the soul and the body."[135] But just as the body bears traces of its life, like the scars of earlier injuries, so the same is true of the soul.

When the soul is freed from the body, then everything in it becomes visible. . . . And when it comes to the judge . . . , the latter has it brought before him and observes each person's soul without knowing whose it is. Thus he may perhaps have before him the soul of a king of Persia, or some other king or ruler, and sees nothing sound in it, but finds it thoroughly whipped and full of scars that come from perjury and injustice and that have been imprinted on his soul by each of his actions, and everything is crooked with lies and arrogance, and nothing is straight, because it has grown up without truth. And he sees how the soul is burdened with willfulness and luxury, with pride and rashness in acting with immoderation and disgracefulness. And seeing this, he sends it forth in dishonor and ignominy to the dungeon, where it will suffer the punishment it deserves. . . . Sometimes, however, he sees another soul before him that has led a pious and honorable life, the soul of an ordinary citizen, or some such person, but most probably—I would maintain, my dear Callicles— it is the soul of a philosopher, who has done what was his to do and has not chased after all kinds of useless things in his life: then he rejoices, and sends it to the Island of the Blessed.[136]

---

[135] Plato, *Gorgias* 524ab.
[136] Ibid., 525a–526c.

Worth noticing particularly, in Plato's myth, is the idea that at the judgment the dead person steps into the open. What could remain hidden in life is now manifest. Plato is depicting profound human experience here. The threat to a soul at departing this life comes not only from outside, from the hostile powers, but above all from within. For in death what is innermost is exposed. No outward appearance, no mere human favor, can help any longer. The soul stands there naked and bare. *"Quid sum miser tunc dicturus"*—"What shall I, miserable man, say then (before the judge)?", it says in that powerful hymn, the *Dies irae*. The dead person stands, in all the nakedness of its miserableness, on the threshold of the next world. What can it show for itself; how can it account for itself?

All men know that nothing can be completed in this life; everything, even the most perfect human creation, remains fragmentary. Yet must all the works that were begun and then disrupted simply pass away and decay? There is accordingly within man a cry, demanding that everything good and true and beautiful, all striving and suffering, cannot have been simply useless and meaningless. Together with this there is the question of justice, which has always stirred man. What about innocent suffering, those who missed out, who were shoved away, who had no place in the sun? Out of the painful experience that there is no justice in history arises the question of eternal justice. This longing is also expressed in Holy Scripture. God will reward those who seek him (Heb 11:6). The idea of reward and punishment is inseparable from that of the judgment. At the judgment, God will establish justice; no unrighteousness can stand before him, and anyone who has suffered injustice will be given justice. The idea of recompense is often observed in the New Testament—we may merely think, for instance, of the parable of the talents (Mt 25:14–30 and par.). Everything that happens in history has consequences. Not until all these consequences are visible is a final judgment possible. Not until the Last Judgment can history as a whole be judged. The seriousness of human freedom is at issue. All human activity is relevant; all human activity has to be accounted for before God's justice.

IN THE FACE OF CHRIST

This idea is further sharpened by Paul. Who can stand at all with his works before God (Rom 2:1—3:20)? "None is righteous, no, not one; no one understands, no one seeks for God. All have turned aside, together they have gone wrong; no one does good, not even one" (Rom 3:10–12). Does not this radical view of the nothingness of man contradict the biblical idea of reward? How can we talk about merit and reward at all, when nothing can stand before God? Is there not a contradiction between the understanding of the judgment that speaks of reward and punishment and the experience of God's holiness, before which everything is null? Only by concentrating on the mystery of Christ can both aspects be reconciled. Christ himself is the eschaton. The judgment has already been issued.

> If God is for us, who is against us? He who did not spare his own Son but gave him up for us all, will he not also give us all things with him? Who shall bring any charge against God's elect? It is God who justifies; who is to condemn? Is it Christ Jesus, who died, yes, who was raised from the dead, who is at the right hand of God, who indeed intercedes for us? Who shall separate us from the love of Christ? (Rom 8:31–35)

"In Christ God was reconciling the world to himself" (2 Cor 5:19). Thus, according to Paul, the judgment is the completion of redemption. Christ judges the world as Redeemer. At the very point at which men are subject to judgment, redemption takes place. "God has consigned all men to disobedience, that he may have mercy upon all" (Rom 11:32). This conviction that we have been saved in Christ makes understandable the certainty with which Paul says that nothing can separate us from the love of God in Christ; that it is impossible for man to save himself, to justify himself, but that God has justified us. On that basis, on the one hand, it is possible to integrate texts that do not speak of the judgment. It also becomes comprehensible why we do not need to be afraid of the judgment. Yet on the other hand, justification does not abolish human freedom. We are still free to shut ourselves up, to refuse; we still have the freedom to choose ourselves and thus become enslaved to ourselves, to our own unrighteousness. This decision, however, does not effectively occur until death, when human life reaches its ultimate limit. In death, all masks drop away, and man enters into his truth. The judgment takes place through Christ, and it is sheer mercy, undeserved salvation. It happens, however, in relation to him, in saying Yes or No to him. "Every one who acknowledges me before men, I also will acknowledge before my Father who is in heaven" (Mt 10:32). Anyone who rejects him, rejects the one who sent him (Lk 10:16). And in doing so, he rejects his life. "He who believes and is baptized will be saved; but he who does not believe will be condemned" (Mk 16:16).

Yet this does not seem to mean that those who know nothing about faith are damned. The woes and blessings seem to point farther. The standard of being human, which is Christ, can be accepted or rejected even unconsciously. Thus, for instance, those who are saved ask, "When did we see you . . . naked and clothe you?" (Mt 25:38). This—now still "anonymous"—belonging or not belonging to Christ will not be revealed before the end of the ages.

At the universal judgment, it will be made manifest what the meaning of history and of our lives is. There is a connection between the "signs of the times" and the universal judgment, in the sense that the latter is already indicated in the former. The Lord will "bring to light the things now hidden in darkness" (1 Cor 4:5). At the universal judgment, everything will step into the truth. For not until the Last Judgment will it be possible to judge the whole of history. Everything that happens in history has consequences. And not until all these consequences are visible is a just verdict possible.

There is one scene in the New Testament that gives us a symbolic hint of what the judgment will be like. After Peter has denied him three times, Jesus turns around and looks at him. What we sense in that look of Jesus is what will happen to us ourselves at the judgment. By that look we will be judged and saved. Preparing ourselves for judgment, then, means looking at the image of Christ that he has given us: his image that meets us in our neighbor; the face of *Ecce homo*, despised, mocked, and covered in scratches; yet also the shining face already transfigured. All of that is indeed only practice, yet of course decisive practice in which judgment is already taking place.

JESUS IS MY ONLY LOVE

In all ages, it has been the saints who have known Jesus best. For God can only be recognized in love, since "love is of God, and he who loves is born of God and knows God. He who does not love does not know God" (1 Jn 4:7–8). The saints are those who really love Christ, who believe in him and hope in him. Hans Urs von Balthasar grasped anew the sense of the theological role of the saints, which in the Scholastic theology of recent centuries has often not been mentioned:

> In modern times, theology and sanctity have become divorced, to the great harm of both. Except in a few cases, the saints have not been theologians, and theologians have tended to treat their opinions as a sort of by-product, classifying them as *spiritualité* or, at best, as *théologie spirituelle*. Modern hagiographers have contributed to this split by describing saints, their lives and their work almost exclusively from a historical and psychological viewpoint, as though they had no bearing upon the task of theology. This task, however, demands corresponding alterations in method: rather than consider the psychological unfolding from below, it should work out a sort of *supernatural phenomenology* of their mission from above.[1]

The saints are theologians on the basis of their lives and their mission. Hence it is of great importance for theology to be ready to listen to the saints and to learn from them. Von Balthasar speaks of the saints' dogmatics of experience. If Immanuel Kant (d. 1804) said that concepts without intuition are empty, we would have to say that theology without the existential authentication by the saints threatens to remain sterile. The otherwise somewhat audacious statement of Father François-Marie Léthel may be understood in this sense: "All saints are theologians; only the saints are theologians."[2] Thus, a few references to the teaching of Saint Thérèse of Lisieux, a doctor of the Church, whose only desire was "to love Jesus and to make him loved",[3] may help, at the end of this Christology, to deepen our reflections on the mysteries of Christ.[4]

---

[1] H. U. von Balthasar, *Two Sisters in the Spirit: Thérèse of Lisieux and Elizabeth of the Trinity*, trans. Donald Nichols et al. (San Francisco: Ignatius Press, 1992), p. 26.

[2] F.-M. Léthel, *Connaître l'amour du Christ qui surpasse toute connaissance: La Théologie des saints* (Venasque, 1989), p. 3.

[3] Thérèse of Lisieux, letter LT 220, *Letters of St. Thérèse of Lisieux*, trans. John Clarke, O.C.D., vol. 2: *1890–1897* (Washington, D.C.: Institute of Carmelite Studies, 1988), p. 1060.

[4] On what follows, see C. Schönborn, "Thérèse von Lisieux—Kirchenlehrerin", in *Die*

"IT IS NO LONGER I WHO LIVE, BUT
CHRIST WHO LIVES IN ME" (GAL 2:20)

To believe, to hope, and to love simply because God is God is the great lesson of the "little way" of Saint Thérèse. This teaching is in fact by no means new, but she had the gift and the calling to say in a new way that Christian life involves a true transformation. To live on the theological plane, we have to become poor, to love our weakness, our nothingness, to strip ourselves of everything that is not God, so that God may be God in our lives, so that he may "transform this nothingness into *fire*",[5] so that we may love him with his love:

> The weaker one is, without desires or virtues, the more suited one is for the workings of this consuming and transforming Love. . . . Ah! let us remain, then, *very far* from all that sparkles, let us love our littleness, let us love to feel nothing, then we shall be poor in spirit, and Jesus will come to look for us, and *however far* we may be, He will transform us in flames of love. . . . Oh! how I would like to be able to make you understand what I feel! . . . It is confidence and nothing but confidence that must lead us to Love.[6]

The reminder of the theological dimension of Christian life is perhaps one of the most urgent requirements for today's Church: "It is no longer I who live, but Christ who lives in me" (Gal 2:20). Thérèse discovers, with ever greater clarity, that she can find and follow this path of the theologal life, of "divinization" by grace, only if she grows more and more in childlike trust, in placing herself in Jesus' arms, in surrendering to his merciful love. The spiritual childhood of Saint Thérèse is thus a life as a child of God, animated by the spirit of God (cf. Rom 8:14).

The theology of the saints is a theology of experience. That is equally true of that of Saint Thérèse of the Child Jesus. By making her deepest feelings known, she is giving testimony for Christ; her heart is speaking to every heart. There is nothing in her life she abhors so much as lying, insincerity, and minimizing the truth of the Gospel. She would

---

Weite des Mysteriums: Christliche Identität im Dialog, Festschrift for H. Bürkle, ed. K. Krämer and A. Paus, pp. 20–44 (Freiburg im Breisgau, 2000); von Balthasar, *Two Sisters in the Spirit*; F.-M. Léthel, *L'Amour de Jésus: La Christologie de sainte Thérèse de l'Enfant-Jésus* (Paris, 1997).

[5] Thérèse of Lisieux, Ms. B, 3 verso, in *Story of a Soul: The Autobiography of Thérèse of Lisieux*, trans. John Clarke, O.C.D., 2nd ed. (Washington, D.C.: ICS Publications, 1976) p. 195.

[6] Thérèse of Lisieux, letter LT 197, *Letters of St. Thérèse of Lisieux* 2:999–1000.

never write about anything she had not tested herself or whose truth she had not verified. For her, only what has been put into practice in life can be true. Yet that does not mean that she reduces the Gospel to her own measure—it is rather that her experience takes on the shape of Jesus' experience. In her "Act of Oblation to Merciful Love", she asks, "May your *Divine Glance* cleanse my soul immediately, consuming all my imperfections, like the fire that transforms everything into itself." She thanks God for the grace that Jesus has made her "pass through the crucible of suffering". In that way he has deigned "to give me a share in this very precious Cross". That is why she hopes "in heaven to resemble You and to see shining in my glorified body the sacred stigmata of Your Passion."[7]

This reference to her own experience of Christ, to her authentic knowledge of the Christian mystery, makes it possible for her to transcend some of the reductions of the life of faith connected to her specific period. Thérèse of the Child Jesus thus had a decisive part in the "change of climate in the Church" by contributing to the improvement of the still very Jansenist-minded atmosphere at the end of the nineteenth century, when people preferred justice to love. Even the "awakening of the Church in souls"[8] owes much to her. Especially impressive are the insights she had into the other life and the state of bliss, with which she broke through all the bourgeois individualistic notions:

> I feel that I'm about to enter into my rest. But I feel especially that my mission is about to begin, my mission of making God loved as I love Him, of giving my little way to souls. If God answers my desires, my heaven will be spent on earth until the end of the world. Yes, I want to spend my heaven in doing good on earth. That isn't impossible, since from the bosom of the beatific vision, the angels watch over us. I can't make heaven a feast of rejoicing; I can't rest as long as there are souls to be saved. But when the angel will have said: "Time is no more!" [Rev 10:6], then I will take my rest; I'll be able to rejoice, because the number of the elect will be complete and because all will have entered into joy and repose. My heart beats with joy at this thought.[9]

---

[7] Thérèse of Lisieux, "Act of Oblation to Merciful Love", in *Story of a Soul*, pp. 276–77.
[8] R. Guardini, *Vom Sinn der Kirche* (Mainz, 1923), p. 1.
[9] Thérèse of Lisieux, "The Yellow Notebook", July 17, in *St. Thérèse of Lisieux: Her Last Conversations*, trans. John Clarke, O.C.D. (Washington, D.C.: ICS Publications, 1977), p. 102.

Thérèse was here expressing a favorite idea of Origen, which was further emphasized by Henri de Lubac (d. 1991) and whose theological and existential significance for a renewed eschatology have been brought to light by Cardinal Joseph Ratzinger: the idea that the saints in heaven are in active expectation and readiness to help us attain to salvation.[10]

There were certain experiences in Saint Thérèse's life that might be described as fundamental experiences, that can be regarded as decisive stages in the development of her teaching. We will single out two that seem to us particularly prominent for her Christology: the "Christmas grace", and the picture of Jesus on the Cross.

The "Christmas grace" is that of her "total conversion". Thérèse speaks of this in terms that show her profound understanding of the mystery of the Incarnation. What she experienced is completely bound up with what the Son of God is living for her; her healing, her conversion, stem from his Incarnation:

> On that luminous *night* which sheds such light on the delights of the Holy Trinity, Jesus, the gentle, *little* Child of only one hour, changed the night of my soul into rays of light. On that *night* when He made Himself subject to *weakness* and suffering for love of me, He made me *strong* and courageous, arming me with His weapons. Since that night I have never been defeated in any combat, but rather walked from victory to victory, beginning, so to speak, *"to run as a giant"*.[11]

Here, the classic doctrine of the Fathers about divinization is expressed with rare power: The Word of God "became man, that we might become divine".[12] Only Thérèse gives this doctrine an overtone that, while by no means absent from the Fathers, here, however, emphasizes with exceptional power the soteriological character both of the Incarnation and also of our divinization:

> On that night of light began the third period of my life, the most beautiful and the most filled with graces from heaven. The work I had been unable

---

[10] J. Ratzinger, *Eschatology: Death and Eternal Life*, trans. Michael Waldstein, Dogmatic Theology 9 (Washington, D.C.: Catholic University of America Press, 1988), pp. 184–86.

[11] Thérèse of Lisieux, Ms. A, 44 verso, in *Story of a Soul*, p. 97.

[12] Athanasius of Alexandria, *De incarnatione* 54:3 (SC 199:458); cf. CCC 460; see above, chap. 1:3b, "The Incarnation of the Logos and the Divinization of Man".

to do in ten years was done by Jesus in one instant, contenting himself with my *good will* which was never lacking. I could say to Him like His apostles: "Master, I fished all night and caught nothing" [Lk 5:5]. More merciful to me than He was to His disciples, Jesus *took the net Himself*, cast it, and drew it in filled with fish. He made me a fisher of *souls*. I experienced a great desire to work for the conversion of sinners, a desire I hadn't felt so intensely before. I felt *charity* enter into my soul, and the need to forget myself and to please others; since then, I've been happy![13]

The "Christmas grace" is destined for Thérèse but also, inseparably from her, for others. With Thérèse, everything is at once both entirely personal and completely apostolic. The more she absorbs divine love, the greater her desire becomes to distribute it, to increase it. And the way in which she will increasingly be a fisher of souls is already the little way, that quite simple way she will offer to all little souls: "the need to forget myself and to please others".

This little way is "theologal". The little surprise, so as not to spoil the joy of her family's Christmas with her tears and her bad mood, became a practical way to respond to the love of God, who in that night "made himself subject to weakness and suffering for love of me". At the same time, it dawned on her that it is Jesus who does everything —"Jesus took the net Himself". Thérèse felt the "desire to work for the conversion of sinners", but ascribed nothing to herself.

The account of the Christmas grace is immediately followed by that of the picture of Jesus on the Cross:

One Sunday, looking at a picture of Our Lord on the Cross, I was struck by the blood flowing from one of the divine hands. I felt a great pang of sorrow when thinking this blood was falling to the ground without anyone's hastening to gather it up. I was resolved to remain in spirit at the foot of the Cross and to receive the divine dew. I understood I was then to pour it out upon souls. The cry of Jesus on the Cross sounded continually in my heart: "I thirst!" [Jn 19:28]. These words ignited within me an unknown and very living fire. I wanted to give my Beloved to drink and I felt myself consumed with a *thirst for souls*.[14]

From the crib, Thérèse switches to the Cross. With her sure theological instinct, she unites the Incarnation and the Cross, the two pinnacles of divine self-abasement—which many theologians would like

---

[13] Thérèse of Lisieux, Ms. A, 45 verso, in *Story of a Soul*, pp. 98–99.
[14] Ibid., *Story of a Soul*, p. 99.

to set in opposition to each other—and sees them in the synoptic view of the Redeemer's love. From the day of her Clothing, she also united these two moments in her name. From the time of her "marriage" to the King of kings, which brought her the dowry of the wealth of Jesus' childhood and of his Passion, she is called Sister Thérèse of the Child Jesus of the Most Holy Face. The whole of Saint Thérèse's teaching about redemption is found summarized in the described contemplation of the picture of the Crucified, but in a quite concrete and existential way. She always sees Jesus as the God-man, with "divine hands". For her, there is no doubt that Jesus is the only Redeemer and that his blood was shed for all men in every age, without exception. Yet she also knows—with a knowledge that stirs her very depths—that this blood has to be collected and poured out "over the souls" in order to reach them, to save them.

The redeeming love of Jesus, which made him pour out his blood, kindles a fire within her, a "thirst for souls", which corresponds to Jesus' thirst on the Cross. The divine love, in its self-abasement, calls forth from Saint Thérèse a self-sacrifice that is at the same time both entirely personal and completely universal: she wants to give a drink to *her* dearly beloved, for Jesus' cry, "I thirst" (Jn 19:28), has aroused in her heart the burning desire to pour out over other souls the blood of Jesus. Thus Thérèse discovers her vocation, which is both personal and ecclesiastical: like Mary, and together with her, she has to stand at the foot of the Cross, so as to belong entirely to Jesus and, thus, to the heart of the Church. And the more her vocation becomes clear, the more she lives in "synergy" with the Church, with Mary, and with the only Redeemer. And yet there is no doubt that it is Jesus who does everything; her mediation at the Cross adds nothing to Christ's work, and yet it is essential, in order for the Redeemer's blood to reach all men.

THE MERCIFUL GOD—THEOCENTRICITY

The "little way" is abandonment to merciful love; it will always be the "way of Love".[15] Thérèse strongly accentuates her shift of emphasis from the justice of God to his merciful love. She is entirely aware of this shift and knows that she is called, by God's gracious gift, to proclaim this mission, this way. At the end of Manuscript A, she explicitly states this:

---

[15] Ibid., 84 verso, *Story of a Soul*, p. 181.

O my dear Mother! after so many graces, can I not sing with the Psalmist: *"How GOOD is the Lord, his MERCY endures forever!"* [Ps 118:1]. It seems to me that if all creatures had received the same graces I received, God would be feared by none but would be loved to the point of folly; and through *love*, not through fear, no one would ever consent to cause Him any pain. I understand, however, that all souls cannot be the same, that it is necessary there be different types in order to honor each of God's perfections in a particular way. To me He has granted His *infinite Mercy*, and *through it* I contemplate and adore the other divine perfections! All of these perfections appear to be resplendent *with love*; even His Justice (and perhaps this even more so than the others) seem to me clothed in *love*.[16]

And to show immediately how the justice of God is to be regarded "through His infinite Mercy", she adds:

What a sweet joy it is to think that God is *Just*, i.e., that He takes into account our weakness, that He is perfectly aware of our fragile nature. What should I fear then? Ah! Must not the infinitely just God, who deigns to pardon the faults of the prodigal son with so much kindness, be just also towards me who "am with Him always" [Lk 15:31]?[17]

This knowledge of God as endless mercy illumines her whole life, her prayer, and her actions, the simple convent life and the ecclesiastical mission with worldwide dimensions. Her teaching is simply song and praise for "what God did for me",[18] but she knows that she has a mission to hand on what she has received. "Saint Thérèse's view is so simplified, that everything in God and in the world now appears to her solely in this light, as if in a single mirror, that of infinite mercy."[19]

Everything in God's plan, all God's plans, find their meaning and raison d'être in his infinite mercy, his work of creation, and his plan of redemption. Is that one of the reasons—perhaps, the reason—for Saint Thérèse's universal appeal, for the astonishing and obvious fact that she is loved everywhere, in all circles and in all cultures? Thérèse revealed the graciousness of God's merciful love with irresistible power. It is because she radiates this love with her whole being that she is so attractive.

---

[16] Ibid., 83 verso, *Story of a Soul*, p. 180.

[17] Ibid., 83 verso–84 recto, *Story of a Soul*, p. 180.

[18] Ibid., 3 verso, *Story of a Soul*, p. 16; cf. Ms. C, p. 3 verso, *Story of a Soul*, pp. 208–9.

[19] Marie-Eugène de l'Enfant-Jésus, "Sainte Thérèse de l'Enfant Jésus, docteur de la vie mystique", in *Thérèse de l'Enfant Jésus Docteur de l'Amour*, Rencontre théologique et spirituelle, 1990, p. 339 (Venasque, 1991).

ONLY JESUS—CHRISTOCENTRICITY

Her synthesis has one single and precise content: *Only Jesus*. Her knowledge of God, her love for God, has one single and precise content: "He who has Jesus has everything."[20]

The name "Jesus" is omnipresent in Saint Thérèse's writings. While "Christ" is found less than twenty times in her writings, "Jesus" occurs more than sixteen hundred times. He is the sun who illumines everything. The mystery of God is given to us in Jesus. Remarkably, Thérèse never quotes the verse from the First Letter of Saint John, "God is love" (1 Jn 4:8). When she speaks of her love for Jesus, however, or of Jesus' love, she always means the Divine Person of the incarnate Word. Her christocentricity is theocentric and trinitarian. She aptly expresses that in three lines from her poem "Vivre d'amour" ("Living on Love"):

> Ah! Divine Jesus, you know I love you.
> The Spirit of Love sets me aflame with his fire!
> In loving you I attract the Father.[21]

"Loving Jesus" does not occur so much in view of Jesus' sacred humanity as was the case, following Saint Augustine and Saint Thomas Aquinas, with Saint Teresa of Avila (d. 1582), but more in the eastern perspective of *"unus ex Trinitate"*, loving the Divine Person of the Incarnate Son of God. The divine Jesus can be loved only if the fire of the Spirit of love has set the creature aflame; and through this love for Jesus, we have access to the Father—or, better said, the Father gives himself to us.

In Jesus, her only love, Thérèse finds everything: all the divine life of the blessed Trinity, the whole of creation, the Church, the last things. Let us try to sketch, in a few meager lines, what is available so much more comprehensively in Thérèse.

In her most important prayer, the "Offering of myself as a Victim of Holocaust to God's merciful love", of June 9, 1895, she turns first of all to the Trinity as a whole and then speaks above all of Jesus, though always in a trinitarian perspective:

---

[20] Thérèse of Lisieux, title of poem PN 18a, inspired by an idea of Saint John of the Cross, *The Poetry of Saint Thérèse of Lisieux*, trans. Donald Kinney, O.C.D. (Washington, D.C.: ICS Publications, 1996), p. 104.

[21] Ibid., poem PN 17, v. 2, *Poetry of Saint Thérèse*, pp. 89–90.

O My God! Most Blessed Trinity, I desire to *Love* You and make You *Loved*, to work for the glory of Holy Church by saving souls on earth and liberating those suffering in purgatory. I desire to accomplish Your will perfectly and to reach the degree of glory You have prepared for me in Your Kingdom; I desire, in a word, to be a saint, but I feel my helplessness and I beg You, O my God, to be Yourself my *Sanctity*.[22]

Further on in this prayer, Thérèse says, "I feel in my heart immense desires." The theologian to whom she submitted this text asked her to say "immeasurable desires" instead, and she agreed. Yet in reality the prayer really speaks of "immense desires": the love with which she wished to love God, and which she wanted to instill in others, was none other than the love with which God himself loved her in his Son and in which he had granted her everything (cf. Rom 8:23).

Since you loved me so much as to give me Your only Son as my Savior and Spouse, the infinite treasures of His merits are mine. I offer them to you with gladness, begging you to look upon me only in the Face of Jesus and in His heart burning with *Love*.[23]

The well-known definition of love, which Thérèse exemplified ("To love is to give everything. It's to give oneself"),[24] applies first of all to God, who has given us everything, his Son and "the infinite treasures of His merits".

THE CREATURE'S DIGNITY AND POVERTY

Like Saint Francis (d. 1226) and Saint Clare of Assisi (d. 1253), Thérèse of the Child Jesus contemplated Christ above all in the mysteries of his poverty. Along with the Incarnation and the Passion, she emphasizes Jesus' abasement in the Eucharist. In the Eucharist, in which the glorified Jesus is close to men in the most unimposing form, Thérèse sees the most extreme instance of God's humility. Here he hides himself in fact beneath a still more impenetrable veil than that of human nature.

> Hidden in the Eucharist
> I see God, the Almighty,

---

[22] Ibid., "Act of Oblation to Merciful Love", in *Story of a Soul*, p. 276.
[23] Ibid.
[24] Ibid., poem PN 54, v. 22, *Poetry of Saint Thérèse*, p. 219.

> I see the Author of life,
> Much smaller than a child![25]

Loving means becoming little. That is the "principal theme of the Incarnation": the infinite love of God gives itself by becoming little and poor. "I can't fear a God who made Himself so small for me . . . I love Him! . . . for He is only love and mercy."[26] Saint Thérèse's desire to remain little is her desire to make the one she loves, who gives himself to her in his abasement, great and beloved. We are thus approaching what constitutes the center of the message, the "little way" of Saint Thérèse: the paradox of her littleness, of her poverty, of her nothingness, on the one hand, and, on the other, the greatness of her love, the limitlessness of her desires. This is the paradox of her completely artless boldness, of the treasure of her poverty.

Thérèse, to a rare degree, lived in the knowledge of the creature's total dependence on the Creator. Yet because she knew that she had been created and that the Father looked at her "only in the Face of Jesus and in His heart burning with *Love*", she lived her dependence as a creature through the divine relationship of the Son to his Father. The whole of her teaching about spiritual childhood, about abandonment to merciful love, about spiritual poverty, has its place in the eternal Sonship of the incarnate Word. Her boldness springs from the fact that Jesus is "my beloved bridegroom" for her and that everything that is his belongs to her.

Thus, at the end of manuscript 'C', she dares to appropriate Jesus' words in his high-priestly prayer (Jn 17) to his Father; after quoting it at length as her prayer, she asks:

> Perhaps this is boldness? No, for a long time You permitted me to be bold with You. You have said to me as the father of the prodigal son said to his older son: "*EVERYTHING that is mine is yours*" (Lk 15:31). Your words, O Jesus, are mine, then, and I can make use of them to draw upon the souls united to me the favors of the heavenly Father.[27]

This boldness corresponds to her poverty. The poorer she feels herself, the more she dares to ask for everything:

---

[25] Ibid., pious recreation no. 2, 5 recto, in *Oeuvres complètes* (Paris: Éditions du Cerf and Desclée de Brouwer, 1998), p. 809.

[26] Ibid., letter LT 266, *Oeuvres complètes*, p. 624.

[27] Ibid., Ms. C, 34 verso, *Story of a Soul*, pp. 255–56.

I am only a child, powerless and weak, and yet it is my weakness that gives me the boldness of offering myself as VICTIM *of Your Love, O Jesus!* . . . In order that Love be fully satisfied, it is necessary that It lower Itself, and that It lower Itself to nothingness and transform this nothingness into *fire.*[28]

To her sister Céline (d. 1959), Thérèse writes: "The poorer you are, the more Jesus will love you. He will go far, very far in search of you."[29]

THE FIRE OF LOVE

The essential message of Saint Thérèse is this: Living the 'theologal' life, of faith, hope, and love, with an incredible realism, with a total and childlike trust, in the present, in the most insignificant details of daily life, is a way that is open to everyone and that is attractive to many "little souls".[30] Let us try to look more closely at a few of the features of this attractiveness.

What draws so many "little souls" and so many sinners to Thérèse is the fact that we never feel judged by her. On the contrary, we feel loved, accepted without the faintest reproach. In the age of the "teachers of suspicion" (*les maîtres du soupçon*), that exerts on us an astonishing and irresistible attraction.

With Thérèse, man is found to be *capax amoris*, both loved and capable of loving. There is nothing that can more effectively straighten man up, heal him, and make him happy than developing this capacity. As experience shows, an encounter with Thérèse, especially in the case of young people, often releases a blossoming of the forces within man's heart, this discovery of happiness that comes when selflessness and self-sacrifice are the response to the encounter with God's merciful love. Thérèse turns her gaze upon this capacity, which everyone has, to receive from God the love that is wholly destined for him personally:

Just as the sun shines simultaneously on the tall cedars and on each little flower as though it were alone on the earth, so Our Lord is occupied particularly with each soul as though there were no others like it. And just as in nature all the seasons are arranged in such a way as to make the

---

[28] Ibid., Ms. B, 3 verso, *Story of a Soul*, p. 195.
[29] Ibid., letter LT 211, *Letters of St. Thérèse of Lisieux* 2:1038.
[30] Ibid., Ms. B, 5 verso, *Story of a Soul*, p. 200.

humblest daisy bloom on a set day, in the same way, everything works out for the good of each soul.[31]

Thérèse reminds the Church that she is called, together with Jesus, to direct this divine gaze of love and mercy to each and every person. Thérèse uses the privilege of this unique love solely so that she may "dare to ask" Jesus "to love those whom you have given me with the love with which you loved me . . . without any merit on my part."[32] Thérèse knows that only love attracts, and that the true motive power of all missionary activity in the Church is the fire of love:

> I ask Jesus to draw me into the flames of His love, to unite me so closely to Him that He live and act in me. I feel that the more the fire of love burns within my heart, the more I shall say: "*DRAW ME*," the more also the souls who will approach me (poor little piece of iron, useless if I withdraw from the divine furnace), the more these souls *WILL RUN SWIFTLY IN THE ODOR OF THE OINTMENTS OF THEIR BELOVED*, for a soul that is burning with love cannot remain inactive.[33]

What lends such power to Saint Thérèse's message is her absolute confidence that God's mercy is all the more manifest, the lower it descends, has to show its immeasurable greatness in the most profound weakness. Every person, and above all the poor, the weak and the little ones, finds his dignity in the fact that God intends to grant him his mercy.

---

[31] Ibid., Ms. A, 3 recto, *Story of a Soul*, pp. 14–15.

[32] Ibid., Ms. C, 35 recto, *Story of a Soul*, p. 256.

[33] Ibid., Ms. C, 36 recto, *Story of a Soul*, pp. 257–58.

Abbreviations

Abbreviations for the books of the Bible follow those used by the Revised Standard Version, second Catholic edition, from which Scripture quotations have usually been taken. Texts from the Second Vatican Council are referred to by the customary abbreviated form of the opening words of the document in Latin. Abbreviations used in bibliographical references may be found in the *Internationales Abkürzungsverzeichnis für Theologie und Grenzgebiete*, by S. Schwertner, 2nd ed. (1992). Particularly important abbreviations:

CCC *Catechism of the Catholic Church.* 2nd ed. Vatican City: Libreria Editrice Vaticana, 1997.

DH Heinrich Denzinger. *Enchiridion symbolorum definitionum et declarationum de rebus fidei et morum: Kompendium der Glaubensbekenntnisse und kirchlichen Lehrentscheidungen griechisch/lateinisch— deutsch.* Edited by Peter Hünermann. 38th ed. Freiburg im Breisgau, 1999.

TzTD *Texte zur Theologie: Abteilung Dogmatik.* Edited by Wolfgang Beinert. Graz, 1989ff.

TzT F *Texte zur Theologie: Abteilung Fundamentaltheologie.* Edited by Karl-Heinz Weger. Graz, 1990ff.

Hans Urs von Balthasar

Glory *The Glory of the Lord: A Theological Aesthetics.* 7 vols. San Francisco: Ignatius Press, 1982–1989.

TD *Theo-Drama: Theological Dramatic Theory.* 5 vols. San Francisco: Ignatius Press, 1988–1998.

TL *Theo-Logic: Theological Logical Theory.* 3 vols. San Francisco: Ignatius Press, 2000–2005

Karl Barth

KD   *Kirchliche Dogmatik.* Zürich, 1932–1967.

Martin Luther

WA   *Kritische Gesamtausgabe* ("Weimar edition"). 63 vols. Weimar, 1883ff.

Thomas Aquinas

STh   *Summa Theologica*

SCG   *Summa Contra Gentiles*

Bibliography

1. Studies and Textbooks on Christology

Amato, Angelo. *Gesù il Signore: Saggia di Cristologia.* Corso di teologia sistematica 4. 5th ed. Bologna, 1999.

Antes, Peter. *Jesus zur Einführung.* Hamburg, 1998.

Auer, Johann. *Jesus Christus—Gottes und Mariä "Sohn".* KKD IV/1. Regensburg, 1986.

Baudler, Georg. *Das Kreuz: Geschichte und Bedeutung.* Düsseldorf, 1997.

Beilner, Wolfgang. *Gott als Christ erfahren.* Vol. 2: *Gott in Jesus—Jesus in Kirche.* Salzburg, 1996.

Benedict XVI, Pope. *Jesus of Nazareth: From the Baptism in the Jordan to the Transfiguration.* New York, 2007. (See also: Ratzinger, Joseph Cardinal.)

Biser, Eugen. *Das Antlitz: Eine Christologie von innen.* Düsseldorf, 1999.

Boff, Leonardo. *Jesus Christ Liberator: A Critical Christology for Our Time.* London, 1978.

Bordoni, Marcello. *Gesù di Nazaret: Signore e Cristo.* 3 vol. Rome, 1982–1986.

———. *La cristologia nell'orizzonte dello Spirito.* Brescia, 1995.

Bouyer, Louis. *The Eternal Son: A Theology of the Word of God and Christology.* Huntington, Ind., 1978.

Bujo, Benezet. *African Theology in Its Social Context.* Maryknoll, N.Y., 1992.

———. *African Theology in the Twenty-first Century: The Contribution of the Pioneers.* Nairobi, 2003.

———. *Christmas: God Becomes Man in Black Africa.* Nairobi, 1995.

Bulgakov, Sergeĭ Nikolaevich. *The Lamb of God*. Grand Rapids, Mich., 2008.

Coda, Piero. *Jesus von Nazareth: Die Geschichte einer Entdeckung*. Munich, 1993.

Courth, Franz. *Jesus Christus der Erlöser: Leitfaden zur Christologie*. Koblenz, 1993.

Dalferth, Ingo U. *Der auferweckte Gekreuzigte: Zur Grammatik der Christologie*. Tübingen, 1994.

Der schwarze Christus: Wege afrikanischer Christologie. Theologie der Dritten Welt 12. Freiburg, 1989.

Dini, Averardo. *Gesù nostro contemporanea*. Brescia, 1997.

Doré, Joseph, ed. Jésus et Jésus-Christ series. Paris, Desclée.

Dupuis, Jacques. *Jésus-Christ à la rencontre des religions*. Paris, 1989.

Duquoc, Christian. *Christologie*. 2 vols. Paris, 1968–1972.

Ernst, Josef, ed. *Jesus Christus—Gottes Sohn: Herausforderung 2000*. Paderborn, 1998.

Evdokimov, Michel. *Le Christ dans la tradition et la littérature russe*. Paris, 1996.

Evdokimov, Paul. *Le Christ dans la pensée russe*. Paris, 1970.

Fernández, Bonifacio. *El Cristo del Seguimiento*. Madrid, 1995.

Forte, Bruno. *Gesù di Nazaret: Storia di Dio, Dio della storia*. Rome, 1981.

Giussani, Luigi. *At the Origin of the Christian Claim*. Montreal and Buffalo, 1998.

Gonzalez, Faus J. I. *Cristo es misterio de Dios: Cristología e soteriología*. 2 vols. Madrid, 1976.

Hünermann, Peter. *Jesus Christus: Gottes Wort in der Zeit: Eine systematische Christologie*. 2nd ed. Münster, 1997.

Iammarone, Giovanni. *Gesù di Nazaret: Messia del Regno e Figlio di Dio: Lineamenti di cristologia*. Padua, 1995.

Kasper, Walter. *Jesus the Christ*. New York, 1986.

Kessler, Hans. "Jesus Christus—Weg des Lebens". In *Handbuch der Dogmatik*, edited by Theodor Schneider, 1:241–442. Düsseldorf, 1992.

Kuschel, Karl-Josef. *Im Spiegel der Dichter: Mensch, Gott und Jesus in der Literatur des 20. Jahrhunderts*. Düsseldorf, 1997.

———. *Jesus im Spiegel der Weltliteratur*. Düsseldorf, 1999.

Manemann, Jürgen, and Johann Baptist Metz, eds. *Christologie nach Auschwitz: Stellungnahmen im Anschluß an Thesen von Tiemo Rainers Peters*. Münster, 1998.

Marquardt, Friedrich-Wilhelm. *Das christliche Bekenntnis zu Jesus dem Juden: Eine Christologie*. 2 vols. Gütersloh, 1990–1993.

Menke, Karl-Heinz. *Die Einzigkeit Jesu Christi im Horizont der Sinnfrage*. Einsiedeln, 1995.

Meyendorff, Jean. *Le Christ dans la théologie byzantine*. Paris, 1969.

Moioli, Giovanni. *La Parola della Croce*. Milan, 1994.

Moltmann, Jürgen. *The Way of Jesus Christ: Christology in Messianic Dimensions*. Minneapolis, 1993.

Müller, Gerhard Ludwig. "Christologie—Die Lehre von Jesus dem Christus". In *Glaubenszugänge: Lehrbuch der Katholischen Dogmatik*, edited by Beinert Wolfgang, 2:1–297. Paderborn, 1995.

———. *Katholische Dogmatik: Für Studium und Praxis der Theologie*. 3rd ed. Freiburg im Breisgau, 1998. 254–387 (Christologie/Soteriologie).

Niekamp, Gabriele. *Christologie 'nach Auschwitz': Kritische Bilanz für die Religionsdidaktik aus dem christlich-jüdischen Dialog*. Freiburg, 1994.

O'Collins, Gerald. *Christology: A Biblical, Historical and Systematic Study of Jesus Christ*. Oxford, 1998.

Ocariz, Fernando, Lucas F. Mateo Seco, and José A. Riestra. *El Misterio de Jesucristo: Lecciones de cristologia y soteriologia*. Pamplona, 1991.

Pannenberg, Wolfhart. *Grundzüge der Christologie*. Gütersloh, 1964.

————. *Systematic Theology.* Vol. 2. 3rd ed. Grand Rapids, Mich., 2001. (Chap. on Christology and Soteriology).

Pavlou, Telesphora. *Saggio di cristologia neo-ortodossa.* Rome, 1995.

Pelikan, Jaroslav. *Jesus Christus: Erscheinungsbild und Wirkung in 2000 Jahren Kulturgeschichte.* Zürich, 1986.

Philippe, Marie-Dominique. *Le Mystère du Christ crucifié et glorifié.* Paris, 1996.

Piolanti, Antonio. *Dio Uomo.* 2nd ed. Vatican City, 1995.

Pröpper, Thomas. *Erlösungsglaube und Freiheitsgeschichte: Eine Skizze zur Soteriologie.* 3rd ed. Munich, 1991.

Ratzinger, Joseph Cardinal. *A New Song for the Lord: Faith in Christ and Liturgy Today.* New York, 1996. (See also: Benedict XVI, Pope.)

Richter, Klemens, ed. *Christologie der Liturgie: Der Gottesdienst der Kirche —Christusbekenntnis und Sinaibund.* Freiburg, 1995.

Sayes, Jose Antonio. *Señor y Cristo.* Pamplona, 1995.

Schwager, Raymund, ed. *Relativierung der Wahrheit? Kontextuelle Christologie auf dem Prüfstand.* QD 170. Freiburg im Breisgau, 1998.

Sesboüé, Bernard. *Jésus-Christ dans la tradition de l'Eglise: Pour une actualisation de la christologie de Chalcédonie.* Paris, 1982.

————. *Jésus-Christ l'Unique Médiateur: Essai sur la rédemption et le salut.* Vol. 1: *Problématique et relecture doctrinal.* Paris, 1988; vol. 2: *Les Récits du salut: Proposition de sotériologie narrative.* Paris, 1991.

Slater, Thomas B. *Christ and Community: A Socio-Historical Study of the Christology of Relevation.* Sheffield, 1999.

Sobrino, Jon. *Christ the Liberator: A View from the Victims.* Maryknoll, N.Y., 2001.

————. *Jesus the Liberator: A Historical-Theological Reading of Jesus of Nazareth.* Maryknoll, N.Y., 1993.

Sölle, Dorothee. *Christ the Representative: An Essay in Theology after the Death of God.* Philadelphia, 1967.

Staniloae, Dumitru. *Orthodoxe Dogmatik.* Vol. 2. Zürich, 1990.

Stettler, Hanna. *Philosophische Christologie: Eine Hinführung*. Einsiedeln, 1998.

Stock, Alex. *Poetische Dogmatik*. Paderborn, 1995ff.

Tilliette, Xavier. *Philosophische Christologie: Eine Hinführung*. Einsiedeln, 1998.

Trembelas, Panagiotes N. *Dogmatique de l'Église Orthodoxe catholique*. 3 vols. Chevetogne, 1966–1970.

Werbick, Jürgen. *Soteriologie*. Düsseldorf, 1990.

Wiederkehr, Dietrich. "Entwurf einer systematischen Christologie". In *Mysterium Salutis* III/1, pp. 477–648. Einsiedeln, 1970.

Wilfred, Felix. *From the Dusty Soil: Contextual Reinterpretation of Christianity*. Madras, 1995.

Ziegenaus, Anton. *Jesus Christus: Die Fülle des Heils*, Katholische Dogmatik 4. Aachen, 2000.

2. History of Christology

a. Collected Texts

Baumotte, Manfred, ed. *Die Frage nach dem historischen Jesus: Texte aus drei Jahrhunderten*. Gütersloh, 1984.

Il Cristo: Scrittori greci e latini. Edited by the Fondazione Lorenzo Valla. 5 vols. Vol. 1: *Testi teologici e spirituali dal I al IV secolo*; vol. 2: *Testi teologici e spirituali in lingua greca dal IV al VII secolo*; vol. 3: *Testi teologici e spirituali in lingua latina da Agostino ad Anselmo di Canterbury*; vol. 4: *Testi teologici e spirituali in lingua latina da Abelardo a San Bernardo*; vol. 5: *Testi teologici e spirituali da Riccardo di San Vittore a Caterina da Siena*. Milan, 1984–1992.

Karpp, Heinrich. *Textbuch zur altkirchlichen Christologie: Theologie und Oikonomia*. Neukirchen-Vluyn, 1972.

Niemann, Franz-Josef. *Jesus der Offenbarer*. TzT F 5. Graz, 1990.

Ohlig, Karl-Heinz. *Christologie*. TzT D 4. Vol. 1: *Von den Anfängen bis zur Spätantike*. Vol. 2: *Vom Mittelalter bis zur Gegenwart*. Graz, 1989.

b. Biblical Christology

Anderson, Paul N. *The Christology of the Fourth Gospel: Its Unity and Disunity in the Light of John 6.* Tübingen, 1996.

Blank, Josef. *Jesus von Nazareth: Geschichte und Relevanz.* 4th ed. Freiburg im Breisgau, 1975.

Boismard, Marie-Émile. *Jésus, un homme de Nazareth, raconté par Marc l'evangeliste.* Paris, 1996.

Broadhead, Edwin K. *Naming Jesus: Titular Christology in the Gospel of Mark.* Sheffield, 1999.

Buckwalter, Douglas H. *The Character and Purpose of Luke's Christology.* Cambridge, 1996.

Carell, Peter R. *Jesus and the Angels: Angelology and the Christology of the Apocalypse of John.* Cambridge, 1997.

Cullmann, Oscar. *The Christology of the New Testament.* Philadelphia, 1959.

Dautzenberg, Gerhard. *Studien zur Theologie der Jesustradition.* Stuttgart, 1995.

Dreyfus, François. *Did Jesus Know He was God?* Chicago, 1989.

Essen, Georg. *Historische Vernunft und Auferweckung Jesu: Theologie und Historik im Streit um den Begriff geschichtlicher Wirklichkeit.* Mainz, 1995.

Gnilka, Joachim. *Jesus von Nazaret: Botschaft und Geschichte.* 3rd ed. Freiburg im Breisgau, 1994.

Hahn, Ferdinand. *Christologische Hoheitstitel: Ihre Geschichte im frühen Christentum.* FRLANT 83. 5th ed. Göttingen, 1995.

Hengel, Martin. *The Son of God: The Origin of Christology and the History of Jewish-Hellenistic Religion.* Philadelphia, 1976.

Hofius, Ottfried, and Hans-Christian Kammler. *Johannesstudien: Untersuchungen zur Theologie des vierten Evangeliums.* Tübingen, 1996.

Jonge, Marinus de. *Christology in Context: The Earliest Christian Response to Jesus.* Philadelphia, 1988.

Karrer, Martin. *Jesus Christus im Neuen Testament*. Göttingen, 1998.

Kügler Joachim. *Der andere König: Religionsgeschichtliche Perspektiven auf die Christologie des Johannesevangeliums*. Stuttgart, 1999.

Landmesser, Christof, ed. *Jesus Christus als Mitte der Schrift: Studien zur Hermeneutik des Evangeliums*. Berlin, 1997.

Lang, Hartmut G. *Christologie und Ostern: Untersuchungen im Grenzgebiet von Exegese und Systematik*. Tübingen, 1999.

Miler, Jean. *Les Citations d'accomplissement dans l'Évangile de Matthieu: Quand Dieu se rend present en toute humanité*. Rome, 1999.

Mussner, Franz. *Jesus von Nazareth im Umfeld Israels und der Urkirche*. In *Gesammelte Aufsätze*, edited by Theobald Michael. Tübingen, 1999.

Orchard, Helen C. *Courting Betrayal: Jesus as Victim in the Gospel of John*. Sheffield, 1998.

Rahner, Johanna. *"Er aber sprach vom Tempel seines Leibes": Jesus von Nazareth als Ort der Offenbarung Gottes im vierten Evangelium*. Bodenheim, 1998.

Schnackenburg, Rudolf. *Jesus Christus: Im Spiegel der vier Evangelien*. Freiburg, 1998.

Schürmann, Heinz. *Jesus: Gestalt und Geheimnis*. Edited by Klaus Scholtissek. Paderborn, 1994.

Zwiep, Arie W. *The Ascension of the Messiah in Lukan Christology*. Leiden, 1997.

c. History of Theology

Grillmeier, Alois. *Christ in Christian Tradition*. Vol. 1: *From the Apostolic Age to Chalcedon*, 2nd ed. (London, 1975); vol. 2: *From the Council of Chalcedon (451) to Gregory the Great (590–604)*: part 1: *Reception and Contradiction: The Development of the Discussion about Chalcedon from 451 to the Beginning of the Reign of Justinian* (London, 1987); vol. 2, part 2: *The Church of Constantinople in the Sixth Century*, in collaboration with Theresia Hainthaler (London, 1995); vol. 2, part 4: *The Church of Alexandria with Nubia and Ethiopia after 451*, in collaboration with Theresia Hainthaler (London, 1996). In preparation: vol. 2, part 3: *The Churches of Jerusalem and Antiochia from 451 to 600*; vol. 2, part 5: *The Western Latin Church in the Sixth Century.*

Grillmeier, Alois, and Heinrich Bacht. *Das Konzil von Chalkedon: Geschichte und Gegenwart.* 3 vols. 5th ed. Würzburg, 1979.

Harnack, Adolf von. *Lehrbuch der Dogmengeschichte.* 3 vols. 4th ed. Tübingen, 1909 (Nachdruck Darmstadt, 1964).

Pelikan, Jaroslav. *The Christian Tradition: A History of the Development of Doctrine.* 5 vols. Chicago, 1971–1989.

Schmaus, Michael, Alois Grillmeier, Leo Scheffczyk, and Michael Seybold. *Handbuch der Dogmengeschichte.* Freiburg im Breisgau, 1951ff.; esp. III/1, a–c (Christology); III/2, a–c (Soteriology).

Sesboüé, Bernard, ed. *Histoire des Dogmes.* Vol. 1: *Le Dieu du salut.* Paris, 1994.

Scripture Index

Index

Last Judgment, 361–68
Last Supper, 346–47
law, Jesus' view of, 246–49
Lazarus, 57, 317, 320
Leo III, 206
Leo the Great, 160, 163–64, 177,
220–21, 229, 243, 335
Lessing, Gotthold Ephraim, 38, 39
Léthel, François-Marie, 24, 371
Der letzte der Gerechten (Nach-
manides), 42
Levi, Solomon, 42
Lévinas, Emmanuel, 21–22
liberation aspect of redemption,
260–61
lightning image, 350–51, 364
liturgy, as celebrations, 223, 225,
241, 363–64
Logos. *See specific topics, e.g.,* earthly
Jesus, mysteries of; Incarnation;
preexistence of Jesus
Lohfink, Gerhard, 23
Loisy, Alfred, 344
Lombard, Peter, 222
love: and baptism, 328; enemies,
59–60, 171–72, 174, 203–5; in
God's self-abasement, 111–16;
in Jesus' suffering, 215–17, 227,
228–29; in Luther's redemption
theology, 285; as redemption
aspect, 260–61; and science crisis,
39; teaching of saints, 371, 372–
74; in theology of Thérèse of
Lisieux, 375–82; in Thomas
Aquinas' redemption theology,
291, 294–95, 298–300
Ludolf of Saxony, 222
Luther, Martin, 35, 274–89, 343

Marcellus of Ancyra, 340
Marcion, 359
Margaret Mary Alacoque, 216
Mark the Apostle, 74
Marmion, Columba, 223
Martin I, 196

Mary, 121–26, 127–29, 137, 138,
149, 155, 232, 234
Mary Magdalen, 319
Maximus the Confessor, 14, 106,
108–9, 196–99, 204
Mediatio redemptionis humanae
(Anselm), 262
mediator role, 75–76, 79–81
Melito of Sardis, 66–67, 334
merit theme, in Thomas Aquinas'
redemption theology, 293–94,
296–300
Milan, Edict of, 81, 94–95
mirror image, Gregory's, 103
mission of Jesus: and apostles, 322–
23, 344; as foundation of Christology, 65–69; self-awareness of,
170–75, 188, 251–52, 315–16;
and struggle with Satan, 237–39;
in Transfiguration message, 241–
43; and trial of Jesus, 252–54. *See
also* Incarnation; Redemption *en-
tries*; will of Jesus, understandings
Monergitism, 195
Monophysitism, 134–36, 140, 148,
193–94, 208
Monothelitism, 196, 199, 201–2
Moses, 242, 248
Mussner, Franz, 20
mysteries of Jesus. *See* earthly Jesus,
mysteries of
Mystici Corporis, 182–83

Nachmanides, Moses, 42
Nathaniel, 235
natural science crisis, 37–39
neo-Arianism, 41
Nestorian Church, 147–48
Nestorius, 137–41, 146
Neusner, Jacob, 247, 248, 254
Nicaea, Council of, 78, 81–83,
133–35, 210–11. *See also* Nicene
Creed
Nicaea II, Council of, 193
Nicene Creed: and Chalcedon coun-

* xtology of Chalcedon corresponds with the experience of Xian life p 14